1001
FUNDRAISING IDEAS & STRATEGIES

FOR CHARITY AND OTHER NOT-FOR-PROFIT GROUPS IN CANADA

JIM HAWKINS
WITH FILES FROM
TONY JUNOR & CAROLINE WALKER

Fitzhenry & Whiteside

1001 Fundraising Ideas and Strategies
for Charity and Other Not-for-Profit Groups in Canada

© 1998 Fitzhenry & Whiteside

Canadian Cataloguing in Publication Data

Hawkins, D. James (Derek James), 1947-
   1001 Fundraising Ideas and Strategies
   for Charity and Other Not-for-Profit Groups in Canada

ISBN 1-55041-280-9

1. Fund raising – Canada. 2. Nonprofit organizations – Finance. I Title
II. Title: 1001 Fundraising Ideas and Strategies
for Charity and Other Not-for-Profit Groups in Canada

HV41.9.C3H38 1997   658.15'224   C97-932434-3

Printed and bound in Canada

Fitzhenry & Whiteside
195 Allstate Parkway
Markham, Ontario
L3R 4T8

web site: www.fitzhenry.ca   e mail: godwit@fitzhenry.ca

Design: Darrell McCalla
Cover photo: Tony Stone Images/John Lund

For
Amanda, Ian and Emmeline

If every good intent
became a good deed,
no one would need
a charity fundraiser.

Life's greatest rewards stem from love and money,
though few men have a surfeit of either.
But, the more you give of one,
the more you'll deserve the other.

CONTENTS

THE EVENT GUIDE

How to use the following guide to plan your events:

Each idea in this book has been annotated in various ways to make it easy to find suitable events and to enable you to put together a complete fundraising program.

Each event or idea is classified in a number of differing ways:

- The specific nature of the fundraising organization
- The size of the organization
- The time required to organize the event or to permit it to come to fruition
- The season of the year when the event would be most effective

To choose a suitable event, start by determining the general TYPE of fundraising entity to which your group belongs.

The classifications used in the guide are:

- ARTS AND THEATRE
- CHILDREN & YOUTH
- ENVIRONMENTAL
- FITNESS, SPORTS & SOCIAL
- HEALTH RELATED
- RELIGIOUS
- SERVICE CLUBS
- WOMEN'S GROUPS
- GENERAL: Ideas suitable for use by most or all fundraising groups

Now determine the SIZE of your group:

- SMALL: One Chapter with less than 100 members

- MEDIUM: Up to 10 Chapters, or a regional organization with less than 500 members
- LARGE: National or International organization

Note: Individual Chapters of medium or large organizations will be able to use ideas designated as suitable for small organizations but an organization with a single chapter would probably be unable to operate events designated for medium or large organizations.

Now decide how much time you have to plan and implement the event. The guide categorizes events in the following four time frames:

- LESS THAN FOUR WEEKS
- UP TO SIX MONTHS
- UP TO ONE YEAR
- MORE THAN ONE YEAR

Finally, decide on the time of the year when you wish to hold the event. Each event is categorized into SPRING, SUMMER, FALL and WINTER.

Once you have decided on any particular event refer to Chapter 4 pg. 59 (Advertising & Publicity) and Chapter 2 pg. 17 (Tips and Advice), which will give you tips and ideas on how to organize the event and how to make the most from it.

INTRODUCTION

This book is intended to be useful to every professional and volunteer fundraiser, whether the need is for ten or ten million dollars.

I have selected over a thousand of my most successful events and fundraising ideas from around the world. Some have been used as fundraising vehicles for many years, in many different cultures, while others are to the best of my knowledge totally innovative. Fundraising events are similar to fashions. It is very difficult to design something absolutely new, and even when you believe that you have, chances are that someone will claim original ownership to the scheme.

I have included events and advice applicable to all types and sizes of Canadian organization and have tried to choose those events which I think are most effective. Successful fundraising depends just as much on the ability of the fundraiser as it does on the choice of event. Successful fundraising also relies on the ability to predict which event will be popular in the right location at the right time. You and your group must decide what events are appropriate, what will be popular with your membership and supporters, and what will raise money. Use this book as a guide, but at the end of the day only you and your team can make your fundraising effort work.

Every organization needs funds. Without ample funding, no organization can exist, yet many organizations procrastinate about fundraising events. This fact was made very clear to me in 1991, when I invited one particular organization to appear on my television show to publicize an upcoming event, a golf tournament taking place the following month. (My program, "All in a Good Cause," was a non-confrontational showcase intended to enhance fundraising and public awareness of charity and N.F.P. groups in Ontario.)

The organization in question decided that its executive committee would decide which individual spokesperson should appear on my program. They told me I would be contacted with a name as soon as a decision had been made. Two plus years later, I received a letter thanking me for my kind invitation, and notifying me of the name of the person scheduled to appear on my show!

You never raise money unless you DO something. The longer the delay the more difficult the task becomes. It is always easier to raise money when you have money, but many organizations wait until they have almost run out of funds before putting serious effort into raising more.

Most executive committees worry about fundraising, discuss it, worry some more, read books, worry even more, talk to others, hold more committee meetings, worry even more, and find it very difficult to come to a consensus about what should be done. The primary cause of this moribund attitude is fear of failure. What if no one buys a ticket, no one shows up and no one donates? Well, that's life.

Life is a series of gruelling journeys between brief stops at places of success. Sometimes the journey ends in failure.

Failure on occasions is inevitable, but failure is only failure if you choose to see it that way. In an ideal world, every charitable fundraising event would be a huge success. In an ideal world, charitable fundraising events would not be necessary. Learning and growing is as much a part of fundraising as it is of life itself. The biggest mistake most volunteer and some professional organizations can make, is to change fundraisers every year, or to dispense with the services of a fundraiser who has failed to make money from a specific event. People learn from their mistakes, not from their successes.

Make sure your organization has people who are willing and able to make a fundraising event work, and accept that failure may be part of the process.

Before launching into a mega-fundraising campaign, evaluate your needs carefully. Fundraising is hard work, and is becoming increasingly harder. Fiscal responsibility is the watchword of this era, so be clear about your objectives. There is usually a world of difference between what you should do and what you would really like to do. Raise money for those things you really need. Use your resources wisely.

HUMAN RESOURCES

Volunteer and charitable organizations provide millions of people with a sense of community belonging, enabling them to gain peer approval and recognition while establishing an individual feeling of worth and self-esteem, leading to self-fulfilment. For this reason, many organizations become self-preserving entities and, in some instances, continue to exist long after the original objectives have been achieved.

More people who volunteer time to an organization are likely to give up and leave when they feel their services are not being properly utilized, than when they feel they are being overburdened. Volunteers can only reach a state of self-fulfilment when they have realized full potential. In other words, a person must feel that he/she has given everything available to the effort. Challenge your volunteers in your fundraising events. Most will rise admirably to the challenge.

Special fundraising events raise money, but such events can have much wider implications for any group.

Increased public awareness of the existence of any group can encourage greater public participation. Most special events provide an excellent opportunity to socialize with potential new members and volunteers. People enjoying themselves are likely to feel good about the organizing body. They will want to be involved in future events. Special events provide an ideal opportunity to network with potential benefactors – people who may have the power to make a significant contribution to any organization. You will invite local dignitaries, businesspeople, celebrities and politicians to participate in your fundraising endeavours; special events are ideal opportunities to make informal approaches to such people. Networking is an essential element of fundraising. Success comes primarily from who you know, not what you know, and today, knowing the right person is more important than ever.

Many special events suggested in this book provide some sort of service to the public or community in addition to providing a charitable organization with an excellent opportunity for fostering good public relations.

Don't forget that special events, in one form or another, also enable an organization to take a greater share of the community purse than it might if fundraising was restricted to soliciting donations only. When you provide the public with products, services and entertainment, you raise money from sources otherwise serviced by the private sector.

KNOW THE COMPETITION

Every business, charity and not-for-profit group is in competition. Any individual's disposable income (once taxes, mortgage or rent are paid) is up for grabs. Food, clothing, heating and transportation usually have a higher priority than a charitable donation, although sometimes people's priorities can be manipulated. Gambling, for instance, in all its many guises, may even take precedence over the mortgage for someone who earnestly believes in the eternal triumph of hope over experience. Every cent your organization receives is money won from the purse of another organization or business. To believe otherwise would be spurious.

Assume that each person has three pockets into which all of his/her money is placed each pay day. The first, generally the largest, is claimed by the tax collector, mortgage lender, or landlord; the second is used for routine expenses; and the third, usually the smallest, contains whatever is left over from the other two. Leisure, pleasure, and savings – and charitable donations – all come from this third pocket.

An alert registered charity has the ability to take money from all three pockets. Donors issued with charitable receipts have contributed money that the government would otherwise have taken. Goods and services offered in competition with the private sector urge money from the second pocket (sales of cookies, clothing, speciality items and secondhand goods otherwise purchased through private sector stores). Finally, contents of the third pocket are available to charitable organizations in the form of donations, or fees for participation in leisure activities or special events which compete with commercially organized leisure industry entertainment.

Not everyone feels charitable toward charity and N.F.P. organizations. A volunteer-run secondhand store may put an existing privately owned store out of business. Work done by volunteers, or low paid charity staff, may infringe upon employment in the private sector. A charitable organization subsidized by grants and donations should always be able to provide products and services at lower cost than the private sector. It is never competing on a level playing field. In some sectors of the economy, specifically the theatre, the arts, and certain health services, the division between private sector and the charitable sector has become so blurred, distinguishing between them is well nigh impossible.

It is always difficult to evaluate the worthiness of one cause versus another subjectively. There is no question that charitable donations often end up in the hands of those organizations with the most passionate fundraisers, and not necessarily those with the most worthy cause.

KNOW YOUR COMMUNITY

A charitable organization's community is not geographic. It is a complex mix of society wherein which perception is as important as reality. People make donations and attend events for a wide variety of reasons. Knowing your community means knowing which segment of society will be most receptive to your requests, understanding what type of event will appeal to that group, and recognizing what works and doesn't work within that community. Look around. What are other similar organizations doing? Should you copy them? Should you try to win some of their supporters to your cause? Should you try to find out who their major donors are, so you can target these people with your requests? There is only a certain amount of money in the pot. If you take more, somebody else is going to get less. If somebody else takes more, you may be the one who will get less.

Be sensitive as to what is ethically and morally acceptable, and what is likely to cause annoyance or offence. I have included events in this book because they exist and because they have been used successfully for fundraising. I do not personally agree with each event, but I acknowledge that each can raise money in the right circumstances.

RESPONSIBILITIES AND LIABILITIES

Regulations regarding the holding of charitable events vary from province to province, and from community to community. Before arranging any event always check with relevant authorities to discover if a licence, permit or consent is required.

The Criminal Code of Canada, Provincial Acts and Municipal Bylaws take no account of the fact that an unlawful action may have been committed in furtherance of a worthy cause. When you organize an illegal event, or commit an unlawful act during a lawful event, then you must expect to be dealt with accordingly. Seek out and take good legal advice before organizing anything involving gambling or alcohol. Provincial regulations vary widely on these two subjects, and many municipalities have bylaws relating to when and where such events can be held. Events involving large numbers of people, children, and animals may all be subject to local or provincial laws. Make relevant inquiries before you waste time and money organizing something that cannot legally proceed.

Many events organized by charity and N.F.P. groups are inherently dangerous, leaving organizers, and their organization, vulnerable to litigation by aggrieved parties. Some, like fireworks displays, marathons and polar bear swims, have been responsible for numerous deaths and injuries to staff, spectators and participants in the past, and they will almost certainly be responsible for more mishaps in the future. Almost any event can turn into a tragedy, notwithstanding that all reasonable precautions have been taken. A child's car seat sold at a secondhand store may be an absolute bargain for the mother, but if it fails to perform, and a child is injured or killed, the seller may be held liable. Even bake sales can turn into a major disaster if the donor of a cake accidentally, or even maliciously, uses a poisonous ingredient. The organizer of any auction, garage sale or secondhand store could be held liable if any item is sold which does not satisfy Canadian safety standards or which causes injury. A donated television set, for example, may have been tampered with by the donor and although it is sold without any guarantee of performance, it explodes when connected to the power supply and injures the purchaser.

Many charitable events pose a particular threat because they include alcohol. Precedents set in Canadian courts have made it very clear that suppliers of alcohol can be held personally liable for any injury or damage caused by a person who has become inebriated, or drives a motor vehicle while impaired.

There can be no question that the executive and directors of any organization can be held liable for injurious activities of its members and there are numerous ways in which an aggrieved person can seek damages or compensation. Event organizers protect themselves as much as possible by taking out insurance, and insisting that all participants sign disclaimers.

Insurance policies that can be purchased to provide financial protection to people involved in charitable organizations vary, and any reputable insurance broker will be willing to provide information, and prices, in relation to the following:

General Liability Insurance providing coverage for accidents and liability in normal circumstances.

Errors and Omissions Insurance providing coverage should someone make an error or fail to carry out their responsibilities thereby leaving them open to lawsuit.

Special Event Insurance providing coverage for organizers, staff and volunteers against any liability as a result of the event. Every event can be insured, at a price, with the premium charged dependent upon a slew of factors including: type, location and venue, anticipated attendance, previous experience of organizer, history of previous claims, availability of medical facilities and staff, security facilities and staff, and the availability of alcohol. These insurance policies usually require the organizer to obtain disclaimers from participants in which the organizer is held not accountable for personal injury or damage.

Cancellation Insurance refunds losses and out-of-pocket expenses if an event has to be cancelled because of circumstances beyond the organizer's control: unforeseen illness of the star performer etc.

Weather Insurance refunds losses and expenses if an event has to be cancelled or postponed due to inclement weather.

Prize Insurance can be arranged to cover the value of a prize in certain competitions (commonly a hole-in-one in golf or a perfect game in bowling). Some specialized insurance companies will quote premiums to insure a major prize for almost any event where the probable outcome can be calculated.

DISCLAIMERS

Canada is, per capita, the most litigious nation in the world, and courts have proved particularly fickle in their decisions regarding the validity of disclaimers. The usual bone of contention is whether the signatory to a disclaimer was fully informed as to the potential risks involved in participation prior to signing. For example: the family of a runner who dies of a heart attack during a marathon would be unlikely to be successful in claiming that the organizer was in some way responsible for the death. However, if twenty minutes had elapsed before medical attention reached the victim, the family might claim negligence on the part of the organizer. Whether a disclaimer signed by the runner would protect the organizer in such circumstances depends on any number of factors including, one suspects, the disposition of the Judge.

Always obtain disclaimers from anyone participating in any event where there is known risk and even obtain disclaimers, if possible, in cases where there appears to be little risk.

"NOT-FOR-PROFIT" VERSUS "NON-PROFIT"

Many organizations and corporations routinely fail to make a profit and could be considered to be non-profit making entities. On the other hand, the term "not-for-profit" expresses in three words the intent of the organization and, in my opinion, more accurately describes the role of any philanthropic organization.

I hope you find this book enjoyable, informative and useful. I wish you the very best of luck in your fundraising endeavours. Everybody needs a little luck sometimes and luck has certainly played a very important role in making my life successful. I sincerely believe the harder I worked, the luckier I seemed to become.

TIPS AND ADVICE

Advance Sales

Whatever your event, ALWAYS, ALWAYS, ALWAYS, sell tickets in advance. Almost everyone asked will promise faithfully to attend your concert, luncheon, dinner, dance, or whatever else you arrange, but unless you sell people tickets and take your money up front, chances are your audience will not appear.

Selling tickets in advance provides many benefits:

• You can gauge potential turnout and decide whether to proceed with a potential money loser.

• Tickets are a form of advertising.

• Ticket holders, once committed, are more likely to encourage others to attend.

• Some people who buy tickets will not attend. Your gain and their loss.

• Money in hand is very useful to pay expenses prior to the event.

• A ticket purchase represents a commitment to attend.

Advance sales of tickets also solves the problem of you having to turn people away at the door. Parking, catering, seating, and washroom facilities cannot be suddenly doubled. Many events have been ruined because too many people have crammed into inadequate facilities.

Encourage advance sales by offering early-bird discounts, or entry into an early-bird raffle.

Always Have a Raffle for Every Event

Always consider turning the most valuable donation into a raffle prize. Use the advance sale of raffle tickets as a means of publicizing your event. A raffle can be held at almost every event, and a valuable raffle prize will encourage people to attend.

Angels

Many movie-makers and theatrical producers rely on "angels" for financial backing. Charity and N.F.P. groups can do the same. When planning a major event which has the potential to become a financial disaster, ease the risk by inviting corporate "angels" to put up part of the funding in advance. When your event is successful, you can repay the "angel" all of its seed money. Your backer loses everything only if the event is a total disaster. Potential losses to corporate sponsors will be ameliorated by tax breaks.

Alternatively, you can solicit help from a number of corporate sponsors so a loss, if it occurs, never becomes burdensome. Invite a number of "angels" to assume partial responsibility for any losses should they occur. Here's how:

In order to pay for the orchestra, celebrity singer and entertainers at your "Mammoth Midsummer Madness Ball," you may need to sell 5,000 tickets. If you sell 6,000 tickets you will make a handsome profit, but if you only sell 4,900 tickets you may lose a great deal of sleep. The answer: ask a number of corporate and individual supporters, in advance, to make up the shortfall, should one occur. Ask potential "angels," prior to making any financial commitment whatsoever, to accept liability for a certain number of tickets. Ten "angels," for example, could agree to cover the cost of 500 tickets each for a total of $5,000. Individual liability would only amount to ten percent of the value of unsold tickets. If the total loss is 100 tickets, each angel would be on the hook for the cost of just ten.

To ensure that no one is liable for substantial sums of money, decide beforehand on a cancellation cutoff point. Thus, if you have not sold 4,000 tickets by your cutoff date, the event should be cancelled.

Animals and Children

A favourite acting expression, "Never work with animals or children," arose because actors discovered through bitter experience that animals and children always steal the limelight. Fundraisers, however, should turn this fact to advantage. If you can safely involve animals or children in your fundraising event, do so. You will always attract more attention and therefore raise more money.

Young children, in particular, can dramatically increase the amount of money raised, particularly in door-to-door collections. If you are accompanied by a young child, people will give more and are much less likely to be aggressive or rude.

Annual Subscriptions

If you are not charging your members an annual membership fee, think seriously about doing so. Find out what similar organizations are charging. Make sure your fee schedule is realistic. Many organizations introduce very low initial fees to encourage membership. They then find themselves unable to raise rates because democratic organizations rarely come to consensus on significant fee hikes. You may feel your initial membership rate is heavy-handed, but go for it anyway. It is better to err on the high side. Later, you can always give a discount on joint or family membership, or a break to those temporarily unable to pay the full amount.

You can increase revenue from annual subscriptions, without upsetting your entire membership, by instigating a sliding scale whereby fees are levied according to members' ability to pay (or according to hierarchical position in the organization). Everyone should be required to pay a minimum fee, which can be set according to the type of organization. Certain members can subsequently be requested to make additional payment. Such members should be promoted within the organization by simply designating them "life" or "sustaining" members.

Whenever all organization members belong to the same profession, ascertain which fall within certain earnings groups. You can easily adopt a fee schedule whereby students, novices, professionals, part-timers, and the temporarily unwaged all pay relevant amounts.

General membership organizations can set their minimum fee, and then appeal to people's conscience to make additional payment. Consider adding the following to your membership appeal:

Annual membership fees $200

Members with family incomes in excess of $50,000 are requested to pay $300

Members with family incomes in excess of $100,000 are requested to pay $400

Executive members, voting members and members afforded special privileges can all be asked to pay higher annual subscriptions.

Ask

However simple it may seem, the easiest way to raise money is to ask for it. If you believe passionately in your cause, you will have no difficulty requesting donations from friends, colleagues, relatives and acquaintances. Always ask for a specific amount which you believe people can afford. Remember, if you ask for a small donation you will probably be given a small donation. If your initial request is rebuffed, do not be disheartened. Ask again. It is often less embarrassing for a potential benefactor to make a donation than refuse a second time. In any case, a second request cannot be less successful than the first.

Awards and Certificates

Keep your staff and volunteers motivated by offering awards, certificates and incentives. They will be more productive. Ask sponsors, donors and suppliers to give awards to your staff. Such gifts can be much more valuable to you in the long term than a cash donation. A major corporate sponsor with a close affiliation to your organization may be prepared to present an entire range of awards to your staff and volunteers as a way of gaining publicity.

Award Ceremony

Perhaps you could invite a corporate sponsor to hold an annual award ceremony to specifically honour the work of your staff and volunteers. The publicity potential is considerable, particularly if the sponsoring corporation were to use its own publicity machine to promote the event.

Awareness Week

Are you a small organization, hiding away in a third floor office, wondering why you get little public support? Just remember, the squeaky wheel gets the grease.

Once a year you can turn yourself into a high profile organization by: borrowing a storefront for one week and setting up a display which outlines your work in the community; inundating the local press with details of your members, volunteers and their roles; holding an open public meeting; having all of your staff and volunteers handing out information leaflets in public places; visiting schools and colleges to address the students; or holding a public collection.

Maximize your efforts during that one week, and by week's end everyone in your community will know who and what you are.

Work with all of the other charity organizations in your community to create an annual "Charity Awareness" week, as you demonstrate the variety and scope of work carried out by local charity and not-for-profit organizations.

Involve the local press, television and radio by arranging "Charity Awareness" days featuring your charity and N.F.P. groups at various locations like the local library, shopping mall, high school etc. Charity awareness weeks, although not direct fundraisers, help each group achieve the recognition required before the public will donate funds. Don't forget to place collection boxes at all strategic locations during your promotion.

Be Realistic

No one can realistically expect every new fundraising event to be an immediate success. In fact, I can only remember two first time events which wildly exceeded everybody's expectations. One, a rally of steam-driven vehicles, was expected to attract 5,000 people. Over 100,000 showed up. The other event was a half-marathon in a small town which attracted more than four times the anticipated entries. A new product in the private sector normally takes three to five years to become established, and nearly 90% of all new products fail altogether. Survival in the private sector is very difficult. More than 80% of small businesses fail within the first three years.

Fundraising events and campaigns take time to develop. Like products and businesses in the private sector, the best or most worthy events do not necessarily survive.

Beware the Con-Artist

Raising money is difficult. Don't lose what you've worked hard to achieve. Many charities and N.F.P. groups have been defrauded of large sums by clever con-artists. Some criminals have no conscience at all and will steal from the easiest target. While every organization can expect to be the target of a petty criminal from time to time, a large scale fraud can bankrupt. The PONZI scheme is the most common fraud and, like most confidence tricks, acts on the victim's greed. A professional fundraising company guarantees to double an organization's funds within a specific period of time through a mail or telephone solicitation campaign. The organization is asked to pay start up fees, $750,000 for example, and is guaranteed a cheque for $1,500,000 three short months later. Everyone is overjoyed when the campaign is declared a huge success and the promised cheque arrives.

The confidence trickster now solicits several other charities in the area offering to provide a similar service. The offer is very tempting, particularly insofar as the first charity is happy to confirm exactly how their resources doubled in such a short period of time. After a dozen or so other charities have paid "seed" money, the fundraising company quietly disappears with the funds, and without a trace.

Remember, if an offer seems to good to be true, it probably is.

Canadian Donor's Guide

The donor's guide published annually in April, lists thousands of charity and N.F.P. groups seeking public donations. Written to provide estate lawyers and accountants with details of charitable organizations, the guide also prints advertisements. Some organizations pay for large solicitations in the guide in the hope of attracting major donors. Others are simply listed by name and address.

For information about the guide write to P.O. Box 744, Station A, Toronto, Ontario M5W 1G2, or Phone/Fax (416) 961-6776.

Captive Audiences

One of the biggest problems facing any event organizer is how to entice enough people to attend. One way of avoiding this problem is to hold your event in or nearby a popular location, or alternatively, to arrange the event to coincide with existing custom and practice.

Always try to identify those locales which attract crowds. Arrange events accordingly. Some venues are popular because of their proximity to other amenities. Some may have good parking facilities; others may not.

Another way to capitalize on a captive audience is to arrange the type of event that people would normally be attending at a specific time: New Year's Eve celebrations, Burn's Night Dinners, and Canada Day fireworks displays are good examples.

Car Parking

Can you charge a car parking fee at your event? If you can – do it. After all, commercial ventures nearly always charge for parking.

When another organization is holding a major event in your community, offer to organize staff and run the car parking service. Most organizations are short staffed, particularly when hosting a major event, and most are glad of assistance. If another organization is reluctant to lose possible funds, offer to split the parking revenue with them.

Don't forget to raise substantial sums by operating a car park whenever a major commercial event is being held in your area.

Suitable events would include a royal visit, a gala performance by an international singing star, or a mega-fireworks display. Any nearby land or space is suitable as long as the owner will permit you to use it. Charge commercial parking rates.

Celebrities

If you are looking for proof that celebrity patronage can be of assistance to your fundraising campaign, consider Christopher Reeve, the actor who portrayed Superman in the movie of the same name. Paralysed by a spinal injury in 1994, he has since, tirelessly championed the cause of those charities devoted to spinal injury research. Reeve has, both directly and indirectly, raised millions of dollars for spinal injury research, and has raised public awareness to the point where, today, few people are unaware of the problem.

Celebrity Endorsements

Celebrities can endorse your organization in three helpful ways: in writing, in an audio cassette, or through video. Any acknowledgement of your work by a well-known personality can enhance your fundraising abilities, especially if yours is a small or lesser known organization.

Once you have identified suitable celebrities, send out a letter which outlines your objectives, together with copies of any relevant information bulletins, and a request that the celebrity assist your organization. Genuine admiration of the person is essential. Make the celebrity feel that he/she has been especially chosen as the only person in the world who can make a difference to your group.

Choose the type of endorsement you need: it is easiest initially to ask for a written endorsement, a few words like: "I congratulate the (Stray Groundhog Society) for the excellent work that they do in the field of (preserving groundhogs)." You will then append this message to all of your appeal literature.

Next, ask your supporter to make a short audio cassette wishing your organization well, and congratulating it on the work it is doing. This tape can be edited (subject to the speaker's approval) and played on local radio stations or at public meetings during fundraising efforts. You can also use direct quotes in your literature.

A video cassette appeal should be your ultimate goal. Several seconds of public broadcast by a well-known celebrity praising your organization can do wonders for any appeal. And don't forget that, with permission, you will have the option of using the audio track for radio advertisements and text transliteration for your literature.

Celebrity Patronage

Every organization needs credibility and while this can only be truly achieved by giving your members and the public the service they demand, you can certainly enhance your credibility by securing the endorsement of a celebrity patron.

Many patrons are patrons in name only, being happy to lend their name to support a cause because it is something they believe in. Other patrons become deeply involved in assisting the organization which bears their patronage. A good example is Princess Anne, the Princess Royal, who is the patron of hundreds of charity and N.F.P. agencies. Her tireless work on behalf of "Save the Children" is legendary world-wide.

Ensure that your organization looks credible. If you don't have a celebrity patron, maybe it is time that you did. Consider writing to the Governor General first, then work your way down.

Celebrity Attendance

Virtually any fundraising event can be enhanced by the presence of a well-known celebrity, yet few organizations bother asking celebrities for help. When you contact a celebrity asking for support of your cause, he/she can say either "yes," "no," or "maybe." You have nothing to lose and everything to gain – so ask.

Ask your members if they know anyone famous, or, if they know anyone who knows anyone famous. However tenuous the link may be, it is always easier to get what you want if you can personalize your request.

Here are some questions to ask yourself, your committee and your members:

- Who do you know?
- Who have you met?
- Who can you blackmail?
- Who will be in town at the time of your event?
- Who needs publicity?
- Who has recently become famous?
- Whose parents live in your community?
- Who was born or went to school in your community?

- Who is connected with your community in any way?
- Who would want to be associated with your cause?
- How much are you prepared to pay to entice a celebrity?
- Who suffers from . . . (the subject of your cause)?
- Who has a relative who suffers from . . . ?

Who to ask? Absolutely anyone who is a public figure. Stars of stage, screen, TV, singers, dancer, ballerinas, sports personalities, Prime Ministers, Presidents, CEO's of major corporations, Members of Parliament, authors, artists, columnists etc.

Celebrity Awards

• **CATEGORY:** GENERAL • **GROUP SIZE:** MED./LARGE •**TIME FRAME:** 1 YR+ •**TIME OF YEAR:** SPR./SUM./FALL/WINT.

Celebrities may show support for an organization by donating an annual award to be presented in their name, with the resultant ceremony beneficial to both the celebrity and the organization.

The type and value of award depends on the status of celebrity, and the perceived worthiness of the charitable organization: many awards consist only of a trophy, while others combine a trophy with a cash prize or bursary. Terms and conditions under which an award is to be presented need to be worked out mutually between your organization and the award sponsor. These may vary from year to year. Celebrity awards are often given to those persons who have made major contributions to the work of an organization during the preceding year, even though there is no reason why an award cannot be used to reward someone for his/her civic duty, even though that person is not necessarily connected with your organization.

Any organization can ask any celebrity to favour it with an award of this type, and any celebrity closely connected to an organization should want to present the award. Celebrity awards can be used as fundraising tools in a number of ways. It is reasonable to expect the celebrity to present his/her award personally to the first recipient. This event should cause considerable interest in your organization, perhaps even providing an excuse for a charity dinner and gala ball. The award ceremony should be well publicized in the media. The prestige and public awareness should make it easier to attract attention for a gala celebration from major sponsors. Each anniversary on which the award is presented provides opportunities to hold more fundraising dinners or dances, and these could become significant annual media events in their own right. Presenting your celebrity award to another celebrity, assuming he/she meets your criteria, is guaranteed to attract media attention, and ensure that your gala awards ball or whatever is a sell out.

Celebrity Clothing

• **CATEGORY:** GENERAL • **GROUP SIZE:** MED./LARGE • **TIME FRAME:** 1 YR + • **TIME OF YEAR:** SPR./SUM./FALL/WINT.

Clothing takes on an entirely different aura once it has been worn by a celebrity. Princess Diana's collection of dresses which was auctioned in 1997 fetched $6 million (US) for two British charities. If your organization has celebrity patronage, make sure that it is a recipient of castoff garments. You will need to raise this point specifically, as your patron is unlikely to realize the potential value of the unwanted vestments.

Celebrity Sporting Paraphernalia

• **CATEGORY:** GENERAL • **GROUP SIZE:** SM./MED./LARGE • **TIME FRAME:** 1 YR + • **TIME OF YEAR:** SPR./SUM./FALL/WINT.

Collections of equipment and clothing used by famous athletes are always valuable, and are frequently given to charities upon request. Write to sports clubs, sports stars and club managers requesting signed bats, balls, hockey sticks or whatever for use at auction. Be persistent. Don't take "no" for an answer.

Alternatively, you might also consider collecting sporting paraphernalia from the soon-to-be-famous. Try to spot young up-and-coming sports stars; ask them to sign any of a number of items: jerseys, shoes, or equipment. Usually your quarry will be highly flattered. Next, you wait and if you've backed a winner, your charity will benefit.

Celebrity Autograph Session

• **CATEGORY:** GENERAL • **GROUP SIZE:** SM./MED./LARGE • **TIME FRAME:** UP TO 1 YR. • **TIME OF YEAR:** SPR./SUM./FALL/WINT.

Ask celebrities to donate time to autograph photographs, books, and calendars for your organization. Many celebrities are willing to spend a few hours with their fans for a good cause. Don't always think in terms of only one celebrity: perhaps you might bring together several stars from a hit show or all the members of a great sports team. Charity autograph sessions also provide excellent photo opportunities for both the stars and your local or national media.

Celebrity Mementos

• **CATEGORY:** GENERAL • **GROUP SIZE:** SM./MED./LARGE • **TIME FRAME:** 1 YR + • **TIME OF YEAR:** SPR./SUM./FALL/WINT.

How do other charities and N.F.P. groups come upon autographed memorabilia from stars and celebrities to feature at auctions, raffles, and other successful events? They asked!

Your appeal should be hand-written, on letterhead paper and might read something like:

Dear Burt,

Margery Jones, who you may remember sat next to you in grade 10 at Newtown High, sends her regards and has suggested I write to you because she believes that you will be keen to help. Margery is a member of (association) because she suffers from (ailment) and she is no longer able to read or write. She has fond memories of the time spent together with you in class and often talks about the things that you did together. I know she is extremely proud of having known you.

Margery, and many other people suffering in the same way, need support at this difficult time in their lives. Margery would never ask you for help for herself but she believes that you may be able to help others by donating an autographed (whatever) that can be auctioned at a special event in December of this year.

Of course, Margery would love to see you again and we would be thrilled to have you attend our holiday fundraising auction on 21st of December. We know how busy you must be. Perhaps you would be kind enough to send us an autographed (whatever). This would make a great difference to our auction and would mean a great deal to Margery. We do hope that you can help in this way.

Yours Sincerely

You may wish to enclose a recent photo of Margery, together with one of the celebrity and Margery at school together, if available. If Margery can make the appeal herself, it will be even more effective.

Request exactly what would assist you most. Don't be vague by asking your donor to send just "anything." Be imaginative, creative, and even funny. You may receive nothing, but you will get absolutely nowhere if you don't ask. As before, if no reply is received, don't hesitate to ask again. Once offended, twice shy.

How much would a school notebook penned by Marilyn Monroe in grade 5 (Norma Jean Baker) be worth today? If her teacher had realized her future potential and kept a memento, would this not be very valuable? Your mission is to spot people who are up-and-comers and start collecting anything belonging to them. This is not easy or even rewarding in the short term, but don't dismiss the idea altogether. Young performers and athletes are easily flattered, and will readily give away signed artifacts that might in time be worth thousands of dollars.

The best person to solicit autographs, memorabilia and personal items from a celebrity is another celebrity. If you are lucky enough to count a celebrity amongst your supporters, ask him/her to make requests for you. They will have much greater success than you will.

Celebrity Doodles

• **CATEGORY:** GENERAL • **GROUP SIZE:** SM./MED./LARGE • **TIME FRAME:** UP TO 1 YR. • **TIME OF YEAR:** SPR./SUM./FALL/WINT.

People will collect anything and spectacular sums have been paid for doodles of the rich and famous. Authenticated, autographed doodles, or pages of doodles, by a celebrity can become the centre-piece of any auction or raffle. An annual auction of doodles could attract significant public and media interest.

Celebrity Lip-Prints

• **CATEGORY:** GENERAL • **GROUP SIZE:** SM./MED./LARGE • **TIME FRAME:** 1 YR+ • **TIME OF YEAR:** SPR./SUM./FALL/WINT.

Autographs of celebrities are always worth something at auction, but an autographed set of celebrity lip-prints might be much more valuable. Prints taken from other parts of the anatomy, properly authenticated, can also make unique and highly saleable items. Fingerprints, palm-prints and footprints of the famous, or infamous, are always saleable. A full size superstar body-print would be worth a fortune, particularly if the star happens to be Madonna or Michael Jackson! An annual auction of celebrity prints could raise many thousands of dollars for your charity. Don't be shy, start asking today. Even a single celebrity print can be a great asset in any lottery.

Celebrity Challenge

• **CATEGORY:** GENERAL • **GROUP SIZE:** LARGE • **TIME FRAME:** UP TO 1 YR. • **TIME OF YEAR:** SPR./SUM./FALL/WINT.

In the 1970's a number of film and television celebrities challenged one another to a race from the top of the Post Office Tower in the heart of London, England, to the top of the Empire State Building in New York. They used various forms of transport, including supersonic jets and high-speed sports cars. The event received considerable media attention.

A similar contest can be used to good effect for fundraising and public awareness by any large charity group. If you are fortunate to have the support of a celebrity or sports personality, suggest that they challenge other celebrities to such a race. In Canada, a race from the top of the C.N. Tower in Toronto, to the top of the Calgary Tower, and on to the summit of the Harbour Centre Tower in Vancouver, would provide an interesting spectacle. Money could be raised by participants betting against each other, and by sponsorship.

Celebrity Board Games

• **CATEGORY:** GENERAL • **GROUP SIZE:** MED. • **TIME FRAME:** UP TO 1 YR. • **TIME OF YEAR:** SPR./SUM./FALL/WINT.

How much would you pay to play a game of scrabble or chess against your favourite entertainer, sports star, or politician? Many people will offer a significant amount for such personal contact. To make this event viable you need to encourage a number of local or national celebrities to participate. If you are successful in this regard, you can structure selection in a number of ways: a silent auction wherein the three highest bidders play with their chosen personality, or perhaps an entry fee for all participants with a draw or competition to decide who plays whom. Limit the playing time so that as many people as possible have an opportunity to partici- pate. The entry fee will depend on the notoriety of your celebrities.

Great care should be taken over the choice of games for such an event. Some sports celebrities, and a few politicians, might be reluctant to participate in games requiring strenuous mental activity. Whenever possible, use games which are relevant to the celebrities and your cause. Scrabble, for instance, is a good game for a litera- cy or education group where the focus is on spelling – and fun.

Celebrity House Party

• **CATEGORY:** GENERAL • **GROUP SIZE:** MED./LARGE • **TIME FRAME:** UP TO 1 YR. • **TIME OF YEAR:** SPR./SUM./FALL/WINT.

A celebrity fundraising party, held in the celebrity's own home, is usually an extremely successful event. Only a celebrity with a burning passion for your cause is likely to agree to such an undertaking. Organization, together with the choice of invitees, will almost certainly be out of your hands. You should be avail- able and willing to lend aid as requested, but normally, the host(ess) prefers to make all arrangements, including choice of theme, food and guests, and handing your group a handsome cheque at the finale. Be grateful for the money and hope that you get an invitation.

Celebrity Memento Auction

• **CATEGORY:** GENERAL • **GROUP SIZE:** LARGE • **TIME FRAME:** 1 YR+ • **TIME OF YEAR:** SPR./FALL/WINT.

Celebrity mementos are very collectable, and celebrity auctions are extremely popular. Begin assembling a collection of celebrity mementos, and with luck and persistence, you will compile an auction-worthy assortment within two years, although it might take considerably longer.

When considering appropriate celebrities, think of the following: stars of stage, screen, TV, singers, dancers, sports personalities, Prime Ministers, MPs and MPPs, CEOs, authors, illustrators, photographers, scientists, explorers, race car drivers, jockeys and so on. Don't forget the eccentrics as well, however bizarre or weird their particular accomplishments might seem. Bizarre sells. What to ask for? Absolutely anything, from autographed rolls of paper towels to an original drawing, even a horseshoe or bronzed golf clubs. Whatever you request, make sure that the provenance is thoroughly documented. Be original in your requests as well; a paper hat worn at last year's Christmas party (duly autographed), or a lock of hair, whatever. The date of the auction will depend upon the successful accumulation of sufficient material. This may take quite a long time, so it might be prudent not to provide benefactors with a firm auction date. However, most donors would like to know that their contributions are going to be useful and not merely stuck in a cupboard collecting dust. Careful wording such as, "Please help us with our projected Memento Auction, scheduled for December 18," may be the best way to phrase the request.

If there is no indication of a time frame, even an ardent supporter may be put off, and might instead deal with more urgent matters.

Celebrity Sales Assistants

• **CATEGORY:** GENERAL • **GROUP SIZE:** SM./MED./LARGE • **TIME FRAME:** UP TO 1 YR. • **TIME OF YEAR:** SPR./SUM./FALL/WINT.

Any event involving sales to the public can be enhanced if you have one or two celebrities acting as sales assistants. You can also ask celebrities to act as waiters, bartenders, auctioneer's assistants or general helpers at any event.

Celebrity Sports

• **CATEGORY:** FITNESS/SPORTS/GENERAL • **GROUP SIZE:** MED./LARGE • **TIME FRAME:** UP TO 1 YR. • **TIME OF YEAR:** SPR./SUM./FALL/WINT.

Many celebrities enjoy playing amateur sports, and some have achieved almost professional status. Charity sporting events of every kind can be arranged if a few celebrities agree to participate. Sometimes a group of celebrities (the cast of a musical or perhaps a group of actors filming in your locality), will field an entire team. A high profile celebrity can be a major draw to a sports event like a charity golf tournament. Comedian Bob Hope has been hosting such events for many years. Sports celebrities have also been amenable to charity matches, either in their own sport or a different one.

Celebrity Spouses

When any married person becomes famous, the spouse may be left in the shadows. Yet, for the fundraiser, spouses of celebrities can often be even more valuable than celebrities themselves. Spouses may be able to devote more time to your organization, and they might also have less competition for their patronage.

Always consider making an approach to a celebrity's spouse. Contact him/her directly. Make the spouse understand that you really want him/her to appear as your guest of honour, and that the invitation is not being issued in place of the more famous partner.

Many very successful fundraising groups are comprised entirely of celebrity's spouses who raise money for worthy causes. Seek support from any such organization at every opportunity.

Challenge Money

Fundraising for a new organization is usually much more difficult than raising additional funds for one already established. The reason is clear: few want to support an organization that may never raise sufficient funds to be viable. When seeking funds for a new group from a heavyweight sponsor, ask the projected donor to make a pledge of financial support on condition that a specified amount of funding will be forthcoming simultaneously from other sources. You then are under pressure to raise the other funds first, BUT you also have a selling tool because you will say to potential donors, "(Donor) has agreed to be a major sponsor, but only with your support."

Change Booths

Revenue generated at many events is directly related to the amount of small change people have in their pockets and purses. You can dramatically increase the take when you provide people with a change source for large notes, and a system for the use of cheques and credit cards to make purchases or donations.

We are living in an increasingly cash-less world. Even street musicians and taxi drivers accept Visa, MasterCard, and/or American Express.

Whenever you have organized a street procession or carnival, and intend to collect small change, put a pickup truck in the middle of your parade and have people with bags of coins in five dollar amounts offering to make change for the crowds.

Charity Performance

• **CATEGORY:** GENERAL • **GROUP SIZE:** MED./LARGE • **TIME FRAME:** UP TO 1 YR • **TIME OF YEAR:** SPR./SUM./FALL/WINT.

Any public entertainment can be turned into a fundraiser by addition of the magic words, "Charity Performance in aid of . . . ." Contact theatres, stadiums, ice rinks, concert halls, opera and ballet companies, and any other public entertainment venues you can think of. Ask if a charity performance for your group is possible in return for the publicity and goodwill that such an event would engender. Holding a performance in aid of a specific organization should guarantee a full house and considerable media attention. Once the event has been arranged, it is in your interest to sell all of the tickets. You may be fortunate enough to receive all revenues from such an event, but it is more realistic to expect only a percentage.

Costume Events

Whenever you are organizing a charity or N.F.P. event, never overlook the possibility of livening it up by inviting guests to wear costumes. Prizes can be awarded to the most appropriately dressed person or couple.

Desperation

An appeal to an individual, group, or the general public, based on the premise that unless donations are received IMMEDIATELY your organization may be forced to close its doors, can work to rally immediate support. Certain people, however, will be turned off by such an appeal, thinking your group is already doomed and further donations a waste of money. "Desperate" appeals are judgement calls and, probably should only be used if your group really is desperate.

Edible Models

When raising money for a new building, why not have a large edible model of the proposed structure crafted in sugar and almond paste, chocolate or other suitable material. Built to scale, and created by a culinary artist, the model could be raffled, or auctioned to the highest bidder after being displayed in a prominent location.

The Fundraiser's Equation

Apply this equation to any proposed event or campaign:

E + E + E = F

ENOUGH people with ENOUGH money and ENOUGH desire = FUNDS

Can you attract ENOUGH attendance, considering location, time of season or week, and type of event? People may travel hundreds, or even thousands of miles to attend certain events, but few would walk half a block to a rummage sale on a Wednesday afternoon in the middle of January.

Can you attract people with ENOUGH money to pay what you ask? A $500 a plate celebrity dinner may be an organizational coup, but if yours is a community where only a handful of people can afford to attend, the dinner will be a failure.

Will people really have ENOUGH desire to help your organization by participating?

If your answer to all three of these questions is "YES," then go ahead.

Goals

Setting a goal or target is very important when fundraising; it can also be a way of raising money in itself.

Every event should have a monetary goal, although few event organizers actually know how much they really want to raise each time. The usual target is "as much as possible," but the problem with this method of accounting is that any amount of profit will be considered a success. Volunteers and members need to know what monetary amount is expected of each of them. Otherwise, they will be happy to stop working as soon as they think they have made a profit.

Set an attainable target for each event. Make it clear to all that until that target is reached, the event will be considered a failure. Do not be tempted to set the target too high, because if nobody thinks it can be achieved, everyone will give up without really trying. Set a realistic target. You will always raise more money this way.

Glamorous Goals

Members of the public are more likely to donate toward the purchase of a new, highly technical and extremely expensive piece of equipment, whether necessary or not, than they are to donate money for 500 new bedpans. Every fundraiser should try to set a glamorous goal whatever the event. Capital projects, such as the building of a new community theatre, are usually much more likely to receive a more positive response than an appeal to run a shelter, or provide food to poor families.

Information Books & Pamphlets

• **CATEGORY:** GENERAL • **GROUP SIZE:** SM./MED./LARGE • **TIME FRAME:** UP TO 6 MTHS. • **TIME OF YEAR:** SPR./SUM./FALL/WINT.

Books and pamphlets offering useful advice and information to your organization's clients and members should be sold whenever possible. Most charities and N.F.P. groups have a tendency to offer such documents free of charge, but many people are more than willing to pay when asked. Always have a realistic price printed on the cover and charge those who can afford to pay.

Insured Prizes

Prize insurance does not raise money, but it can substantially increase the amount of money raised at certain events.

Often the number of event participants, and entry fees, are determined by the value of the prizes offered. The greater the prize value, the more attractive the event. When your event is one in which there is no certain winner, consider offering a very substantial cash prize (and take out an insurance policy to cover the possibility of someone actually winning).

For example, let's say you hold an apple peeling contest to break the world's record (which at last check was 173 feet of continuous peel – Note: All world record citations are copyright of *Guinness Book of Records*). To make this a major event, you will need to encourage wide participation. You might take a chance and offer a prize of $100,000. Probability says there would be little risk of a winner in this event, but if there was, your organization would probably go bankrupt. Minimize this risk by contacting a number of insurance companies, and requesting they quote a premium for indemnifying your organization against anyone breaking the world's record and claiming the offered prize. Insurance companies make money by taking calculated risks. Each company would calculate the odds of such an occurrence (in this case almost nil) and quote a premium accordingly.

Events at which insurance indemnification can be used successfully include golf tournaments with hole-in-one contests, bowling for a perfect score, or any attempt to break an existing world's record. You will probably be required to pay for the services of an independent scrutineer.

Internet

The tremendous promotional potential of the Internet has yet to be fully exploited. If your organization does not have a Web-Site, or at least an information page, it should establish one. Use the Internet to provide information to clients, to promote all of your fundraising events, to make requests for donations and assistance, and to seek out products to sell as part of a fundraising campaign.

Author's Note – When I searched the Internet for related topics while preparing the final draft of this book, I discovered more than 50,000 pages and sites related to fundraising products, services, solicitations and advice. Working eight hours a day, five days a week, and allowing one minute to access each site plus an additional minute to discover what information is available, I calculated that it would be possible to access all of this information in 40 WEEKS.

Liabilities

Operating any commercial venture, whether or not for charity, carries obligations, responsibilities and liabilities. It is important that you and your staff are fully aware that your organization can and probably will be held accountable for any injury or mishap that might occur on the event premises. Do not assume that an aggrieved person will not sue a charity or N.F.P. group for damages.

For any event involving the possibility of injury or damage, you must insist that all participants absolve your organization from liability. They do this by signing a release form. Persons under 18 must also obtain a signed release from a parent or guardian.

Here is one suitable format:

In signing this release, I acknowledge that I understand the intent thereof, and I hereby agree to absolve and hold harmless the (. . . organization), corporate sponsors, co-operating organizations and any other parties connected with this event in any way, singly or collectively, from and against any blame and liability for any injury, misadventure, harm, loss, inconvenience or damage hereby suffered or sustained as a result of participation in (. . .event) or any activities connected therewith. I hereby consent to, and permit, emergency medical treatment in the event of injury or illness.

In addition to the above disclaimer, it may be wise to include a short statement to the effect that an entrant permits his/her name and photograph to be used for publicity purposes without charging royalties or fees.

"Location, Location, Location"

This well-known maxim applies to fundraising events as much as it does to real estate. The success of almost every event depends on its location. When you are counting on large crowds, you need to be close to an urban centre, or the activity itself must provide a compelling reason for people to attend. Be realistic when choosing the venue. Ensure that it is easily accessible to the type, and numbers, of people that you are hoping to attract.

Sometimes, the choice of a strategic location may enable you to cash in on crowds drawn to another event. People flocking to, or from, a major tourist attraction, or even a major fundraising event, may be waylaid by your roadside sale of pumpkins or trees. Signposts directing people toward refreshments, rummage sales, car washing and a hundred other events may catch people's attention, and detain them so they can spend their money.

Major Donors

Almost every charity and N.F.P. group seeks support from major donors. What constitutes a major donation to any particular organization obviously depends on the size of both the donation and organization, but it is not uncommon for today's organizations to target individuals believed capable of donating $100,000 or more. Today, there are many people who could easily donate a million dollars to a single charity if they decided to do so, and some individuals have personal fortunes greater than the GNP of many small countries. By the year 2000, it is estimated there will be more than 3 million millionaires in North America. Pro rata, wealthy people tend to donate far less to charity than middle income earners, but they remain obvious targets for fundraisers because it is much simpler, and cheaper, to concentrate on extracting a large sum from one person than smaller sums from thousands of others.

The successful cultivation of wealthy supporters can make life a lot easier for any fundraiser, but it may take several years to extract a substantial donation from just one wealthy individual.

Begin with a list of potential donors – people on your mailing list, or known to you or a member of your executive, people you believe are capable of making substantial donations. Stockbrokers, successful business people, lawyers, doctors, and people who have inherited wealth are prime targets.

Refine your list in any way that you can to exclude people who, for one reason or another, are unlikely to offer assistance.

Discuss the people on your list with members and supporters until you can be fairly certain that the people you are going to approach will not be offended by a request. Then ask, and ask with a particular cause in mind. "We need $50,000 for a specially equipped vehicle," or "We want to build a new wing and need half a million dollars."

Study the potential donor's reaction, but don't be dissuaded by a look of surprise. If you believe that your donor has the means to provide the requested money, explain the potential benefits: "Naturally we would want to name the building in your honour if you would help us in this way."

Concentrate on the potential donor's self-interest and ego, but do not try to make him or her feel self-conscious about having so much money. Desperate appeals can be successful, but they can also be counter-productive. Obsequious pleading is likely to be as embarrassing to the potential donor as it is to you. Be business-like, confident, genuine; you may get what you want.

Multiple Objectives

Whenever you are raising money for charities, consider whether you can achieve other objectives at the same time.

Here is an example:

A service club decides to raise funds to build a house to be used as accommodation for families who are temporarily home-less as a result of a disaster, fire, earthquake, flood etc.

Primary objective: Raise $250,000.

Potential secondary objectives:

- Encourage other groups to build additional houses
- Provide work for recently released prisoners
- Obtain publicity for your organization
- Obtain publicity for the project by building the house in an unusual or interesting way
- Encourage youth organizations to participate in peripheral projects like landscaping or tree planting

Opportunist

Anyone truly serious about raising money must seize any opportunity that may arise. After a particularly heavy snowfall, for example, go door to door and offer to dig out neighbours' drive-ways for suitable donations.

Pain & Suffering

People are funny. Most feel they have given more if a little pain and suffering was involved in the process. Ask anyone who has completed a marathon for charity why he/she did not simply donate the entrance fee and spend a pleasant day fishing. People feel they have accomplished something when they are forced to make an effort. Never try to make participatory events simple and/or painless. The challenge is what attracts people, not ease of winning.

Piggybacking

Piggyback your advertising or event with another organization. You can share costs and save both groups time and money.

Find a noncompetitive charity or corporation with an advertising idea or theme similar to yours. Approach it about splitting advertising costs and ways in which the ads might be improved. Two heads are better than one. Your ideas are fresh, and may carry a different point of view. Alternatively, their advertisement might be geared to a particular market or group, which can be to your advantage, offering connections and outlets unfamiliar to you. Don't forget that your organization has similar connections to offer your advertising partner.

Piggyback your new event onto an existing one, particularly if you are concerned about the success of your new venture. Look around to discover what other groups are doing. Find an event that is compatible with what you are planning to do, and approach the organizers to suggest combining their event with yours to everyone's mutual advantage. Most events have a cyclical popularity and you are looking for an existing event which is fading but not completely defunct. By adding your event as a new dimension, everyone benefits. Piggybacking on an existing event also provides two groups of supporters and volunteers working together, thereby enabling you to run your event with a smaller work force than one needed if you were working alone.

Talk to other groups and organizations when you plan to send out mailings. The cost of mailing two flyers will be the same as one as long as the weight is not excessive. Sharing costs and mailing lists results in a larger mailing, with a potential for greater response, for less cost than a single mailing.

UNICEF has been incredibly successful in linking their annual door-to-door fundraiser to Halloween. Easter Seals is another organization which profits from a link with an annual event. How can your organization benefit? In what way can you link your event to a well-known annual celebration or festival?

Prizes

Corporations of all sizes have reasons for wanting to give away products or services. Sometimes they seek publicity, or a tax reduction, and sometimes they are happy to get rid of old or unsaleable stock which can be written off at full value even though it may appear unsaleable. Your task is to obtain prizes. Begin by ASKING, ASKING, and ASKING again. Be persistent and make a variety of requests in several different approaches. The personal request is usually the most effective, particularly when made by one of your members who just happens to work for the target company. Decide beforehand what you are going to request rather than simply asking for "anything." Do not be shy. Always ask for much more than you expect to receive. You may strike gold and be given everything you ask for. If you ask for something small, you will probably get something small.

Refreshments

• CATEGORY: GENERAL • GROUP SIZE: SM./MED. • TIME FRAME: UP TO 4WKS. • TIME OF YEAR: SPR./SUM./FALL/WINT.

Providing refreshments at any event is a profitable enterprise, yet many organizations fail to take advantage of this fact. Whenever you attract a group of people together for whatever function, always consider what refreshments you can sell. If you don't provide them, your guests will invade the local store for cans of pop and cookies.

At Other Events

• CATEGORY: GENERAL • GROUP SIZE: SM./MED. • TIME FRAME: UP TO 4WKS. • TIME OF YEAR: SPR./SUM./FALL/WINT.

Once your group has invested in the basic equipment necessary to provide refreshments for all of your own functions, consider the fact that you also have the ability to raise money by providing services at other non-organization events. Advertise whatever services you have to offer. Write to other clubs and organizations in your area and send them a brochure outlining your full range of services. Many groups welcome the chance to free themselves of the task of providing refreshments, but are reluctant to hire professionals because of the high cost. Additionally, they may view the potential profit made by a private company as a loss to charity. As long as your group offers reliable and reasonably priced service, it can make risk-free profits on a regular basis.

At Meetings

• **CATEGORY:** GENERAL • **GROUP SIZE:** SM./MED./LARGE • **TIME FRAME:** UP TO 4WKS. • **TIME OF YEAR:** SPR./SUM./FALL/WINT.

Many organizations feel they must provide free refreshments at meetings and seminars. While this costs little, money is being diverted from your organization's main purpose. Always invite guests and organizational members to make a refreshment contribution and make sure you include ALL guests, even your visiting Member of Parliament, mayor or national president.

School Children

School children are very good at collecting money, although usually in fairly small amounts. Schools or groups of schools can become involved in fundraising for a single project when properly approached. Some school fundraising campaigns have had national collections. You will need to establish support for your cause from school principals and/or boards of education. Your cause must be one that will attract sympathy from children. Teacher involvement is also vital. Actually, most campaigns begin with the dedication of a single teacher who inspires his/her class or school.

Self Interest

More people give to charity out of self interest than for any philanthropic reason. Even people with a genuine desire to help do so with their public image in mind. Awards, rewards, publicity, added sales, tax advantages, and public acclamation all act as spurs to pry open the public's purse. Usually, the greater the reward on offer, the more generous individuals and corporations are likely to become.

For any event to be successful as a fundraiser, it is essential that it should cater to the hopes and desires of potential donors. Promises of wealth, fame, popularity, happiness, accomplishment, fullfilment and public acclaim are positive motivators. Negative motivators can be just as successful. These include embarrassment, either real or potential, fear of disapproval and fear of ostracization.

To be successful in fundraising, seek to motivate people's self interest at every opportunity.

Service Clubs

Most service clubs exist to raise money for charity and N.F.P. groups, and obtaining ongoing support from an organization such as the Lions or Rotary International can make a significant difference to the fortunes of any charitable group. Make sure that you get your share of their funds. Ask and keep asking. Previous refusals do not necessarily mean future refusals. Infiltrate service clubs with your own members, or try to recruit an existing service club member to your board. Fundraising events jointly organized with service clubs can be especially beneficial. Many service club members are business people, or people in management, with access to resources and facilities not normally available to charity groups.

Many service clubs are affiliated with national and international organizations, with the ability to galvanize widespread support. Some service clubs support charities at a national level, encouraging each chapter to raise money and provide support at the local level. Some clubs remain loyal to a single charitable cause for many years, while others will entertain proposals from new charities on a regular basis. Try to discover the criteria used by each service club for allocation of funds at all levels. Target those that fit the profile of your organization.

Members of service clubs can also make a significant difference by acting as volunteer workers. Service club members seek to serve their communities and are usually willing to lend a hand at almost any event. Members can also be very useful in providing advice and information to event organizers. Your fundraising may be made easier if you network with service club members whenever possible.

Signposting Your Events

Whatever the event, never miss the opportunity of attracting passing trade (unless you've been lucky enough to sell out in advance). However much time and money have been spent on advertising, remember you will reach only a small proportion of possible patrons. Many who have seen your advertisements and said, "I'll go to that," will soon forget. Signposting on event day is essential, and should be as widespread as possible. Keep the notice simple and include only your event, day, time and location, and greeting. For example:

LAWN MOWER RACING

2:00 p.m. SATURDAY May 4

CENTRAL PARK

EVERYONE WELCOME – FREE ADMISSION

Include an arrow to indicate direction if necessary. Never print "TODAY" on your signs. The world is littered with signs indicating that something is occurring today: who knows when today is, was, or will be? Make sure you collect your signs immediately after the event.

Simultaneous Scheduling

In many multi-branch organizations, the fundraising program is determined by local chapters without consultation. Each branch advertises its functions and bears the full cost of producing literature, programs, tickets, and other administrative necessities. Sometimes, it can be much more effective, and efficient, to coordinate a local event schedule so it coincides with similar events of other branches. Let's say the individual branches of one national charity hold ten kilometer walks, once a year, all on different dates. These walks are unlikely to attract media attention and are not likely to raise enough money to warrant widescale advertising. What if all 300 branches of an organization were to hold all ten kilometer walks on the same day, in communities across the country. The situation would be entirely different. Even ten branches of an organization within a single metropolitan area can gain significantly by coordinating events in this way. Simultaneous scheduling benefits include: national media advertising and coverage; sponsorship by national companies; cost saving in program printing and application forms; volume discounts on the purchase of equipment and products.

Spokesperson

Many highly successful fundraising campaigns have centred around a single person who, in the public's eye, personifies the object of an organization's goals. If you can find a suitable spokesperson able to attract media attention and public compassion, then you may be able to captivate the hearts, minds and pocketbooks of the public, in addition to cementing public awareness of your goals. Lou Gehrig is a perfect example of someone who made a significant difference to the visibility and fortune of a specific charity. Joey, the muscular dystrophy child, is another.

Sponsorship

Many fundraising events require sponsorship to succeed because most events do not attract large audiences. Individual and team participants must be encouraged to obtain sponsorships from family, friends, and colleagues for any event involving a challenge or contest. Sponsorship pledges should be based on the successful completion of the event, although it is much easier from an organizer's standpoint to insist that entrants collect sponsorship money in advance, and hand it over to the organizers as entrance fees.

Whenever you ask someone to sponsor you for an event, it is normal for that person to want to see what amount others are giving. Always fill in the first few lines of your sponsorship form with those supporters who are pledging reasonably large sums.

A special prize should be awarded to the individual or team raising the greatest amount of money for any sponsored event. This prize should be almost as good as that given to the event winner, because even a team with no chance of winning the main competition can still be competitive. Remember, your goal as organizer is to raise as much money as possible. Thus, the greater the incentive to obtain sponsorship, the greater the amount of money that will be raised.

To increase the amount of sponsorship money individual entrants raise to enter an event, offer a range of incentives. For example: raise $200 and receive an event sweatshirt. Raise $400 and receive a corporate sponsor's prize package worth $75 in addition to the event sweatshirt. Raise $1,000 and receive a corporate sponsor's prize package worth $200, an event sweatshirt and two tickets to the celebration dinner.

Prize packages can be offered at any number of levels, and can contain any products that the corporate sponsor will donate. When you cannot find a corporate sponsor willing to offer such incentives, prizes can be purchased. Choose items that people will want to win. Make the awards relevant to the people you are hoping to attract to your event.

Table Sales

Selling individual tickets for any event can be time consuming and often frustrating. Why not sell tickets to corporate sponsors, major donors and institutions in table-sized blocks of eight to ten or more. If you suspect your event will be really popular, then consider selling tickets only in blocks. Such a confident approach may actually encourage sales, as potential purchasers may not want to be left begging for a last minute seat at some other person's table.

Wherever crowds of people gather at an event organized by a charity or N.F.P. group (or any other), always consider setting up a table to sell products relevant to your group, in addition to providing information, seeking new members, and soliciting donations. Tourist attractions and major sporting events often provide suitable venues for table sales.

Thanks a Million

Every donor deserves to be thanked for support, and a thank you letter is the minimum reward any person should receive. It is often impracticable and expensive to send individual letters to every donor, especially those who have given a small amount. One solution is to include a thank you at the time the money is raised. Also, all products should have a thank you slip attached. Thank you notes for people attending events can be prepared in advance, and handed out at the appropriate time.

Thank people who do not expect to be thanked and thank people who do not deserve to be thanked. Someone refusing to give a donation will be astonished to receive a warmly worded note of thanks for the time taken to listen to your request. A volunteer or staff member who knows he or she did not pull his or her weight during an event or campaign may redouble efforts when an effusive thank you letter is received.

Thank You Letters

Everyone who helps your group in any way deserves a thank you letter. It is good manners to say thank you, and it also provides an ideal opportunity to request more help or money. One suggestion for a thank you letter follows:

Dear . . .

On behalf of everyone at the Displaced Ear Society of Saskatchewan, I would like to thank you for the fabulous donation which you so kindly gave last week. Although the campaign has another week to run, I am sure that you will be pleased to hear that we have already raised more than three-quarters of our target figure. Did you know that we are holding our annual "Blue Nose Day" on the 5th of November? I have taken the liberty of reserving four Blue Nose tickets for you and three of your friends. Perhaps you would like to pick these up from our office, at your convenience. "Blue Nose" tickets are particularly good value at just $5 each, and I am sure that "Blue Nose Day" will provide much amusement to you and your friends.

Thank you once again for your valuable support.

Yours sincerely

President

Time Limits

Whenever a fundraising campaign requires volunteers or staff to request donations, establish strict deadlines. The creed of many fundraisers is "never put off to tomorrow what you can put off to next week." Asking for money is not easy – at least not as easy as finding excuses not to. When you place a time limit on results, you encourage your staff and volunteers to make prompt requests.

Timing

Timing, next to location, is the most important aspect of fundraising. A poorly timed event can be a total disaster, even though the same event might have been a glittering success a week or two earlier. Take for instance the case of the cyclist who in 1996, setout to raise $3,000 for charity by crossing a frozen Lake Simcoe, Ontario. His attempt might well have succeeded, had he not chosen to set off on a day when a blizzard reduced visibility to a few yards. His rescue operation cost in excess of $13,000.

Many challenging, sponsored events fail because of weather conditions or other uncontrollable factors like earthquakes. Other events have failed because an organizer did not take into account the fact that most of the proposed attendees would be on vacation or participating in some other event.

Once I organized an event, in conjunction with the British Broadcasting Corporation, on board a cruise ship, to raise money for disabled children. Bands, celebrities, magicians, and performers of all types provided entertainment. Numerous fundraising activities were arranged, including kidnapping the captain to make him walk the plank into the ship's swimming pool. Timing for the two-day charity cruise had to coincide with the plans of the BBC which had arranged to broadcast live radio and television programs from the ship. Unfortunately, this meant that the cruise took place in the North Sea, in November. Only a very small percentage of charity cruisers emerged from the experience in a healthy state. I learned a valuable lesson: plan every event to please the people expected to support it.

Many small organizations plan their events around members' availability. Unfortunately, this is not an effective strategy. Most fundraising events are forms of leisure and/or entertainment: thus they are most likely to be successful at those times when people are free and in a mood to enjoy themselves. Weekends and holidays are obvious times for fundraising events but you have a problem if your staff and volunteers are not prepared to work at these times.

As a general rule, January is a bad time to organize almost any event. Most people have spent more than intended over the holidays, and winter weather can cause havoc for events requiring a large attendance. July and August fundraisers suffer, except in tourist areas, from the summer vacation exodus. December is an excellent time for most events, BUT remember that every other charity and N.F.P. group will also be holding events and collections on a similar schedule.

Planning

Careful planning of all your events can greatly increase the amounts raised at each and can allow you to use one event to publicize and improve the next. Remember, everyone attending an event is a supporter of your cause, and will be pleased to know about ways in which he/she can help in the future.

One special events fundraising timetable might look something like this:

April – Home show and country craft fare

May – House-to-house collection

July – Celebrity garden party

November – Stocking filler (gift sale with grand raffle)

Now, consider making some minor changes, using each event to publicize the next:

How about holding your house-to-house collection just prior to the Home Show in late March or early April. Print one side of your collection envelopes with an advertisement for the Home Show, and equip each of your collectors with a stack of Home Show tickets and discount coupons. When each envelope is collected, your collector can point out the advertisement and ask if the householder has already purchased tickets. Offer tickets to anyone who does not already have them. Don't forget to distribute discount coupons with each purchase, AND to any person who will not commit to a purchase, but may later decide to go.

Sell tickets for the celebrity garden party at your Home Show, and offer four tickets as a major prize in the Home Show raffle.

The celebrity garden party may attract many influential people in your society, so make sure you approach each of them with a request for items to be donated for the grand raffle at your Christmas stocking filler.

Look at your own event calendar, and see how you can use one event to aid the next.

Unique Requests

When asking for donations of memorabilia, or event prizes, always ask for something unique. Anyone can give money, but unique and personalized items can be much more valuable, and can stimulate interest in your event.

A primitive painting by the four-year-old son of a celebrity, or an autographed photograph of the Prime Minister's pet dog should be relatively easy to obtain. The more outrageous or amusing your request, the more likely you are to receive a response. Teeth marks captured in playdoh, or some similar substance, could create interest.

United Way

The United Way organizations should be considered primary sources of funding for eligible charity and N.F.P. groups. The sole purpose of the United Way is to collect money on behalf of member groups, and to re-distribute it fairly within the criteria laid down by its executive. Find out whether your organization qualifies for funds, and, if so, apply.

Unusual Places

Holding any event in any unusual location will draw attention. Try to be creative in your choice of venues, and consider places which can never be used again. Bridges and highway intersections before they are opened to traffic, swimming pools prior to being filled for the first time, newly constructed animal cages in a zoo – these all make good locations.

Sometimes even the most unlikely places, like sewage works, police stations, hospitals, car factories and power plants can be fascinating to an audience. People are naturally curious about other people's lives, work or environment. Give them a great view.

Persuade administrators of unusual places to have an open house for charity, where you can solicit donations from the public in lieu of an entrance fee. Provide stewards and/or guides. The more unique the place, the better the turn out. A subterranean tour of a major city, like Toronto or Quebec, would probably attract considerable attention, and the cost to your organization would be minimal.

Almost everyone loves to ride in an unusual vehicle, and many people will cherish memories of such occasions for a long time. Steam engines, fire trucks, police cars and horse drawn sleighs have always provided excitement to people whose daily lives do not include such opportunities. Rides in giant earth moving machines, race cars, cranes, tunnel diggers, Hummers, tanks and personnel carriers may all be possible to arrange, with the right contacts. Giving someone a ride costs the vehicle operator little or nothing, but can be a big attraction for charity dollars. One Russian company is currently offering rides in the most advanced Mig military jet fighter. (A five day package including four hair raising flights can be purchased for $15,000 (US) and there is no shortage of takers.)

Always consider including an unusual ride in any raffle, lottery or auction. Invite owners of unusual vehicles to offer rides at fetes, carnivals and fairs.

Volunteer Rewards

Volunteers donate time to help charities and N.F.P. groups for any number of different reasons, but any organization which rewards its volunteers is more likely to recruit and maintain a solid volunteer base than those which do not.

Recognition is reward. Volunteers should be recognized at every opportunity. Never forget to thank volunteers publicly at every event. Recognize your volunteers in the organization magazine and/or literature, and it's always a good idea to have a Volunteer of the Month section, with specific commendation and photographs.

Volunteers should be afforded special privileges whenever possible. Free or cheap tickets to events, discounts on merchandise and favourable rates on services can all be afforded to someone who has given time and effort to the success of your organization.

Employment opportunities are perhaps the best way to reward some volunteers. Whenever a salaried position becomes vacant in your organization, give your volunteers first consideration. Loyalty and dedication are often more valuable employee assets than university degrees.

Volunteer Recognition Dinner

• **CATEGORY:** GENERAL • **GROUP SIZE:** SM./MED./LARGE • **TIME FRAME:** UP TO 1 YR. • **TIME OF YEAR:** SPR./SUM./FALL/WINT.

Hold an annual dinner to recognize and reward all of the volunteers who have helped your organization over the last 12 months.

You may wish to seek outside sponsorship to cover food costs and/or award and prize costs. Sell tickets to paid staff and volunteers' relatives. Raise additional money through traditional events like raffles and auctions.

Wealthy Fundraisers

Some, if not a majority of the most successful fundraising campaigns have been orchestrated by very wealthy people. There are reasons for this: wealth attracts wealth. Wealthy people are not embarrassed about asking for large sums of money. A wealthy fundraiser does not feel intimidated when dealing with high ranking executives or industrialists. A wealthy fundraiser can lend considerable credence to any campaign. Last, but not least, should fundraising efforts fail miserably, you can always ask your wealthy fundraising chairperson to offer a decent donation to make up for the shortfall.

Always try to appoint as fundraising chairperson the wealthiest person within the organization.

What if You . . . ?

Many ideas in this book rely on the "What if" statement to some degree. What will you donate if I bungee jump? What will you give to charity if the president jumps into an ice-covered swimming pool?

"What if" challenges can be used to raise money in many ways. A sports celebrity can be challenged to make a donation if he/she achieves a certain goal. (What if a professional golfer were to land a hole-in-one at PGA tournament? Would he or she pledge half of the prize money to charity? What if a baseball player were to hit through the cycle (single, double, triple and a home run in one game)? Would he or she be prepared to give $10,000 to charity?)

People can be asked to participate in any number of "What if" challenges. Devise the challenge and write to as many people as necessary until you receive acceptance.

What Will the Money Do?

When asking people to donate money, you should be able to tell them what you are going to do with it. Although most money collected by most campaigns simply disappears into the general account of an organization, it is often much more productive from a fundraising standpoint if the donor can be told precisely how his/her donation will be used. Many donors are concerned that the money they give will only be used to line the pockets of executives and administrators of an organization. When you quantify actual amounts to be used for specific items, and present the potential donor with a comprehensive list, then he/she will certainly feel more comfortable, and may be more generous.

YOUR ORGANIZATION

Book

• **CATEGORY:** GENERAL • **GROUP SIZE:** MED./LARGE • **TIME FRAME:** 1 YR+ • **TIME OF YEAR:** SPR./SUM./FALL/WINT.

The history and people of your organization may well be of interest to its own membership as well as to the general public. Writing a book is hard work, time consuming and mentally demanding, but your organization could gain considerable financial benefits, and increase public awareness of its cause, from the publication of such work. If you are fortunate to count a well known author among your supporters, he/she may be prepared to provide you with advice and a forward, or even help you with the book.

Client-Based Fundraising

• **CATEGORY:** HEALTH RELATED • **GROUP SIZE:** MED. • **TIME FRAME:** 1 YR+ • **TIME OF YEAR:** SPR./SUM./FALL/WINT.

Many organizations cater to clients who can also be part of the fundraising team. Many clients derive great pleasure from participating in the process. Donors are inclined to be even more generous when the contributors can help in this way.

Clients have assisted in fundraising with the following:

Choirs of Hearing Impaired or the Physically Challenged

Handicrafts and Product Manufacturing

Some organizations have developed product manufacturing companies, utilizing client labour to the point of being able to compete in the general marketplace. Arc Industries is a successful example of such an enterprise.

Entertainment

The Canadian "Famous People Players" group is an inspirational example of success in this vein.

Celebrity Performers: Disabled

• **CATEGORY:** HEALTH RELATED • **GROUP SIZE:** SM./MED./LARGE • **TIME FRAME:** UP TO 1 YR. • **TIME OF YEAR:** SPR./SUM./FALL/WINT.

Some performers have become celebrities in spite of their disabilities. Any celebrity who has overcome the challenges which face your client base should be invited to perform on your behalf. Don't expect them to perform for free.

Computer Screen-Savers

• **CATEGORY:** GENERAL • **GROUP SIZE:** MED./LARGE • **TIME FRAME:** UP TO 6 MTHS. • **TIME OF YEAR:** SPR./SUM./FALL/WINT.

Money can be raised in one of two ways from computer screen-savers. You can produce a screen-saver program which encourages people to think about your organization (and be responsive to appeals), or you can permit private companies to advertise on your computers.

Environmental organizations are likely candidates for the successful development of individual screen-saver programs. Fish, birds, insects and animals have long formed the basis of screen-saving images, and coupling these with a few words about the work of an organization or a simple logo, can heighten awareness of any computer operator, making he or she more receptive to solicitation. The screen-saver should be distributed as a premium gift or an inexpensive prize. It can also be given in return for a donation.

Any organization with a substantial number of computers can raise money by allowing private corporations to use its computer screens as advertising tools. Hospitals, schools and other educational establishments are particularly desirable targets for screen-saver advertisers. A fee of four dollars per screen, per month, appears to be the usual rate.

Conventions

• **CATEGORY:** GENERAL • **GROUP SIZE:** LARGE • **TIME FRAME:** 1 YR+ • **TIME OF YEAR:** SPR./SUM./FALL/WINT.

Annual conventions, whether regional, national or international, provide a major source of funds for many charity and N.F.P. groups. Properly organized, there is no reason why a convention should not make money, although this has not always been the case.

Public awareness and the opportunity to honour and reward major sponsors are aspects of an annual convention that should not be overlooked. If your group does not hold a convention, you should attend several arranged by other N.F.P. groups and talk to the organizers. Arranging an initial convention is a mammoth task which should not be undertaken lightly, or without proper research. Subsequent conventions can be easier to arrange as long as the first was successful.

Flags

• **CATEGORY:** GENERAL • **GROUP SIZE:** LARGE • **TIME FRAME:** 1 YR+ • **TIME OF YEAR:** SPR./SUM./FALL/WINT.

Does your organization have its own flag? If not, design one, or hold a design competition. You can either make flags in-house or have them made professionally to be sold to your members. Proudly fly your flag at all of your offices, and all events.

Longest Letter

• **CATEGORY:** GENERAL • **GROUP SIZE:** LARGE • **TIME FRAME:** UP TO 1 YR. • **TIME OF YEAR:** SPR./SUM./FALL/WINT.

Encourage people to contribute their thoughts about a specific subject in a letter, which you plan to be the world's longest. Obviously, the subject would be one which concerns your particular organization. Sufferers from a specific disease, their loved ones, caregivers and supporters might all be asked to write and donate one page. A multi-chaptered organization could circulate copies of the letter, making it the task of each chapter to add at least 100 pages. Members of the general public could also be invited to add thoughts. Each person adding a page should be requested to make a donation to your cause.

The result should be publicly displayed and/or put onto CD ROM's and sold to interested parties.

Membership Privileges

What discounts or privileges can be obtained from corporate supporters to enhance the value of someone becoming a member of your organization? Any charity or N.F.P. group with a large membership should be able to negotiate substantial discounts and valuable privileges with numerous product and service providers. Hotels, restaurants, car rental companies and travel agencies are always willing to discuss group discounts based on the number of potential customers they may attract. Goods and services provided by your own organization should always be made available to members at a reduced rate. Membership rewards encourage new members and help retain existing ones.

Named in Honour

• **CATEGORY:** GENERAL • **GROUP SIZE:** SM./MED./LARGE • **TIME FRAME:** UP TO 6 MTHS.• **TIME OF YEAR:** SPR./SUM./FALL/WINT.

Any building, garden, room or hall may be named after a major benefactor or any person nominated by a benefactor. Every significant room in the administrative offices of a charity or N.F.P. group, for example, could be named after a major donor, with the names changing over the years as donors change.

An entire building might be named for eternity after an original benefactor (only if he/she supplied most of the funding). It may be more appropriate to name your building only for a specified period of time.

Traditionally, structures have usually been named in honour of an organization's founder or other significant people in an organization's history: you may find it more financially advantageous, however, to name these locations after major donors.

Newsletter

Newsletters are a popular sources of information, rivaling general interest magazines and local newspapers. Focuses range from special interest groups on learning disabilities to the general interests of car enthusiasts. Chances are if something is of interest to you, it will be of interest to others. The range of topics is staggering. Look to your group for a source of inspiration.

Your organization's newsletter can pay for itself, or even make a profit, by carrying appropriate advertising and/or by subscriptions. If you do not make a profit, a newsletter provides long-term gains from enhanced public awareness and recognition. Don't forget to consider putting your newsletter on the Internet.

Open House

• **CATEGORY:** GENERAL • **GROUP SIZE:** MED./LARGE • **TIME FRAME:** UP TO 6 MTHS. • **TIME OF YEAR:** SPR./SUM./FALL/WINT.

If your organization is large enough to enjoy the luxury of its own offices or headquarters, make sure that you hold an annual open house. Invite the public to come and meet you, your staff and volunteers. Provide refreshments, and lots of information and advice. Give your visitors ample opportunities to make donations, and be sure that all local politicians – your mayor and Member of Parliament – are aware that they are expected to make suitable contributions as well. If your offices are poorly furnished and equipped, then all the more reason to hold an open house. Show the public what your working circumstances are, and expect sympathy as well as money.

An open house is also an ideal fundraiser for a theatre or opera house, as people can wander backstage, poke their heads into the wardrobes and get the feel of standing in the wings. Backstage staff can supply technical demonstrations of sound, lighting and scenery changes: the wardrobe coordinator can talk about design while displaying costumes, and some of the actors could hold a short rehearsal of an up-coming performance.

Opening Ceremonies
• **CATEGORY:** GENERAL • **GROUP SIZE:** SM./MED./LARGE • **TIME FRAME:** UP TO 6 MTHS. • **TIME OF YEAR:** SPR./SUM./FALL/WINT.

An opening ceremony of any building relevant to your organization should always be viewed as an excellent fundraising venue. Corporate sponsors and major donors can all see the physical benefits of their support. Others who have been less generous in the past can be encouraged to offer assistance (if you make sure that you specifically invite people who did not give enough in the first place, and you put them on the spot by publicly asking for support).

Postage Stamps
• **CATEGORY:** HEALTH RELATED/GENERAL • **GROUP SIZE:** LARGE • **TIME FRAME:** 1 YR+ • **TIME OF YEAR:** SPR./SUM./FALL/WINT

The Post Office is constantly seeking new designs for postage stamps and it has, from time to time, issued stamps depicting the roles of charities. Will Canada Post issue a set of stamps for your organization? It costs you nothing to ask.

The Post Office will, under certain circumstances, use a cancellation stamp which bears a charity message. Contact Canada Post to find out if they will do this for you.

National Day or Week
• **CATEGORY:** GENERAL • **GROUP SIZE:** LARGE • **TIME FRAME:** 1 YR+ • **TIME OF YEAR:** SPR./SUM./FALL/WINT.

The designation of a particular day, or week, in celebration or remembrance of any subject can galvanize members and supporters across the country, arouse considerable public interest, heighten awareness, disseminate information, and provide numerous fundraising opportunities.

One way of raising money for a major organization involved in literacy, The Literacy Council, would be to designate a National Reading Day so as to raise public awareness of literacy, and to encourage non-readers to seek help. The funding necessary to advertise and promote such a day should be sought from all levels of government, publishing companies, booksellers and immigrant support organizations. Target the print media.

Once the day has been designated, use the occasion to raise additional revenue for your organization. Şeek corporate donations and grants. Hold fundraising campaigns in offices and factories nation-wide. Design book-shaped collection boxes and distribute them throughout your organizations. Hold spelling bees, read-a-thons, mammoth book sales and book collections. Invite well-known authors to participate in day-long book readings. Encourage publishers to release a new book on National Reading Day, donating a percentage of that day's sales to enable someone to be taught to read.

Red Nose Day (and its ilk)

• **CATEGORY:** HEALTH RELATED/GENERAL • **GROUP SIZE:** LARGE • **TIME FRAME:** 1 YR+ • **TIME OF YEAR:** SPR./SUM./FALL/WINT.

Every year for one day, a British charity encourages people to walk around wearing silly plastic noses to show support for its organization or groups of organizations. However stupid this may sound, it has been a huge success, and people have even put noses on their cars and pets. Noses of all sizes are sold by the various charities, and fines are levied against office and factory workers not wearing a nose. One television channel devotes itself entirely to comedy programs, and people spend all day telling jokes. The entire populace becomes involved one way or another. Some Canadian organizations have started selling red noses, as well, and the potential exists here for the concept to develop into a major annual event.

If not red noses, start something similar. What about "Big Ears" day, with everyone wearing huge plastic ears to show that they really do listen.

Ribbons

• **CATEGORY:** GENERAL • **GROUP SIZE:** SM./MED./LARGE • **TIME FRAME:** UP TO 6 MTHS. • **TIME OF YEAR:** SPR./SUM./FALL/WINT.

Different coloured ribbons have come to mean different things and are used by a number of charitable groups for recognition and fundraising. Select a colour that no one has yet chosen and announce to the world, or your local community, that this colour stands for your organization. Have a ribbon day, or week, and sell short lengths of appropriately coloured ribbon. It is simple, but it works. Child Find sponsors an annual green ribbon day and receives strong support from Canadians each year.

Song for (Your) Charity

• **CATEGORY:** GENERAL • **GROUP SIZE:** LARGE • **TIME FRAME:** UP TO 1 YR. • **TIME OF YEAR:** SPR./SUM./FALL/WINT.

A great deal of money has been made internationally by famous singers and groups performing special songs to raise money and awareness for particular causes. Almost everyone remembers the 1980s hit song, "Feed the World," which netted millions of dollars for famine relief in Ethiopia. Singers, songwriters and professional musicians require constant publicity. If your cause is a universal one and you have the right contacts within the music world, your organization can raise substantial sums of money by commissioning and performing a relevant song.

Alternatively, you might ask the public to write a song commemorating your charity. Charge a small fee to each competitor, and offer a prize to the winner. People usually enter competitions like this for publicity, rather than the prize money. Stage a gala performance for the best 20 songs, with celebrity judges to pick the winner. The winning song should be used by your organization and, if possible, recorded by a well-known singer, and sold to the public.

Theme: Animal

If your organization doesn't have an animal in its logo, invent one. Use the logo at every event by hiring or volunteering someone to show up in a furry animal suit. This always attracts attention, and kids love to put coins in animal shaped collection boxes. Stuffed toys depicting your logo can be sold at any event, as can posters displaying your animal logo.

Training Courses

• **CATEGORY:** GENERAL • **GROUP SIZE:** SM./MED./LARGE • **TIME FRAME:** UP TO 6 MTHS • **TIME OF YEAR:** SPR./SUM./FALL/WINT.

Many charity and N.F.P. groups hold training courses, or sessions, for their volunteers or workers, and there is no reason why students should not pay something for the instruction. St. John's Ambulance or Red Cross first aid courses make this standard procedure. Bear in mind that graduates of volunteer and charity training programs are never slow to put course information on their resumes to enhance potential opportunities.

Year 2000

• **CATEGORY:** GENERAL • **GROUP SIZE:** SM./MED./LARGE • **TIME FRAME:** 1 YR+ • **TIME OF YEAR:** WINT.

Preparations are well under way to celebrate the advent of the third millennium. Huge opportunities exist for organizations to mark this unique occasion and every charity and N.F.P. group should already be making plans. If your community has not already commenced preparations, you have an opportunity to arrange, co-ordinate and promote all of the events, in addition to taking the lion's share of the proceeds. Don't delay, start today.

ADVERTISING & PUBLICITY

Ad Books

• **CATEGORY:** RELIGIOUS/GENERAL • **GROUP SIZE:** MED./LARGE • **TIME FRAME:** UP TO 1 YR. • **TIME OF YEAR:** SUM./FALL/WINT.

Commercial advertisement books have provided stable funding for church and political groups for years. Businesses and corporations purchase space in a booklet or magazine, copies of which are then circulated throughout an organization's membership and/or distributed at events. Many groups use the books to advertise up-coming events, in addition to promoting their cause. Others simply publish a book full of paid advertisements. A wide range of commercial sponsors and supporters will help generate a handsome profit from an ad book.

Ad Subsidies

Public support of charity and N.F.P. groups can be beneficial for many people or corporations willing to subsidize print or media advertisements which encourage people to support your organization. Often, the advertisement merely signs off with words like, "A.B.C. Corporation is proud to sponsor 'The . . . Society.' Please join us in supporting this worthy cause." Such an advertisement satisfies both parties.

Advertising Packages

Many direct mail companies stuff envelopes with advertising material and special offer coupons, distributing them either on a community-wide basis, or nationally, through the postal service. It is often in the interests of these firms to demonstrate a caring attitude toward the communities they service. What better way for them to do this than include your N.F.P. material free of charge in their packages.

Should a direct mail house be reluctant to put your message in their package, perhaps they might be prepared to place a simple, one line solicitation on their envelope: *"Please support . . . Charity"* is all that is required. Actually, any company with a large mailing list, not necessarily a direct mail house, would be able to do this for you. Utility companies, telephone and credit card companies all send out vast numbers of envelopes every day. Seek out such a partner. It might even promote your mega-events from time to time. The cost of printing a line like, "The Arts Association, Million Dollar Lottery – Call (888) 111-2222," on each envelope is relatively minor when compared to the potential audience base.

Advertising on Promotional Material

Many businesses produce regular releases of promotional material delivered through the postal service, through private delivery services, or as inserts in local or national newspapers. If you know a company whose products and services are compatible with the objectives of your organization, and which regularly sends out mass mailings of promotional material, approach its public relations manager. Ask if the firm will include details of your organization's events, appeals for assistance and general information with its own material. Additional costs would be small and could be offset against taxes. Benefits of such advertising can be considerable for both parties.

Private business can also be encouraged to advertise on your organization's promotional material. Whenever your association prints flyers, newsletters, posters etc., it creates the opportunity of recouping some, if not all, of its print costs by selling space to appropriate commercial advertisers. When printing any promotional material, it is sensible to seek out a commercial sponsor. Sponsors can defray the cost by charging it to advertising and receiving a tax benefit.

Cheques

If your group is going to be presented with a sizeable cheque, arrange for press coverage and have a giant, duplicate, cheque produced which can be signed in public. Tell the donor that the presentation will be publicized: the donation may be increased, and others, seeing the press report, will also be encouraged to give.

Cheques are written instructions to a bank to transfer money from one party to another. They are normally written on pre-printed slips, but not always. With the cooperation of a bank, a major benefactor can write a cheque on something unique. A donation to a zoo could be written in vegetable dye on the side of a baby elephant. Imagine the press coverage as the cheque is taken to the bank for cancellation.

Designed Messages

Specially crafted visual images can attract members, donors and clients. Encapsulate your message in a picture. Have it painted onto interesting objects like coffee cups and frisbees. Ensure that it gets the maximum possible attention.

Gaining Public Awareness

Any fundraising event requires public attention to succeed. Publicity and promotion are of paramount importance and you should gear your primary efforts towards these areas. Most poorly supported events suffered a lack of public awareness. Here are some ideas for ensuring you receive the publicity your deserve.

- Create a catchy title
- Make the event unique
- Demonstrate public relevancy of your cause
- Arrange for celebrity attendance
- Ensure "live" television or radio coverage
- Be outrageous by billing your event as "The Biggest . . .," "The Best . . .," or "The Ultimate . . . ."

Giant Signing

• **CATEGORY:** GENERAL • **GROUP SIZE:** MED./LARGE • **TIME FRAME:** UP TO 4WKS. • **TIME OF YEAR:** SPR./SUM./FALL/WINT.

Why not invite thousands of people to sign their names on a jumbo jet, train or bus for a fee. A unique redecoration scheme, this event would gain maximum publicity both for you and your corporate sponsor.

Graffiti

Graffiti used to draw attention to crises or perceived injustice can be particularly effective. Slogans sprayed onto walls, buildings and vehicles are attention-grabbers, much more so than artistically designed, carefully produced advertisements. Witty or controversial slogans are best. Graffiti is a criminal offense when done without the consent of property owners, so only spray your own walls unless you have permission to spray elsewhere.

Letter Writing Campaigns

Small organizations keep their work in the public eye by writing frequent letters to the "Correspondence" editors of local newspapers. A letter from your president, for example, thanking your supporters may find its way into print, just as letters from satisfied clients praising the work of your organization are likely to do so. Asking satisfied clients to write their local paper may not be easy, but anybody who really appreciates your work will not be offended. Persons who have taken the trouble to write a thank you letter directly to your organization would probably be flattered when contacted and asked to send a similar letter to the local press.

Make the Event Newsworthy

Everyone is familiar with the expression, "Dog bites man is not news. Man bites dog is news," yet fundraisers are constantly surprised when newspaper editors and TV producers show little interest in their "37th Annual Craft Fair" or "Giant Garage Sale."

If you require publicity for your event, and who does not, YOU HAVE TO BITE THE DOG!

Whatever the occasion, however complex or simple and mundane, you must enhance the news-worthiness and attendance of the event by doing something different, or at least by explaining or making it seem that you are doing something different.

Newspaper Coverage

An advance press release to the print media should be sent out at least one month prior to publicity expectations. Follow this up with a phone call a week later to the print editor delegated to cover the story. It is quite likely that no one has been given the assignment but the editor may be reluctant to admit this fact and supply a name. It is often necessary to become a nuisance. Everyone knows the squeaky wheel gets the grease.

Search out print media with free classified sections. Find out your local media's policy on providing free space for charity and N.F.P. announcements.

Painting

Imagine a jumbo jet painted entirely with your organization's logo and fundraising message. Why not approach major airlines with your idea. Would they do it? They paint their aircraft regularly, so why shouldn't they show their support for a worthy cause at the same time. Similar paint jobs might be done on a number of vehicles and vessels:

Trains

Either the whole train or a carriage could be decorated on your behalf.

Trucks

Many trucks carry advertising space on the sides and rear. Ask your local trucking company to put your message on its vehicles. Even shipping containers hauled by trucks can carry an appropriate message.

Buses

Bus companies often make money be renting out advertising on their mobile billboards. Ask a local bus company to donate space to your organization. You might also contact a company advertising on local buses and ask it to include a message about your organization in its next advertisement. School buses are an ideal canvas.

Cars

Does your organization have company cars? Why not use these vehicles as moving billboards. Have them professionally painted.

Buildings

Fundraising messages on the outside of a prominent building always receive attention. Will someone let you paint his/her building? Ask.

Billboards

Billboard advertising is expensive and possibly inappropriate, however you may be able to have your message painted on the billboard frame or supports. Alternatively, corporate sponsors may be willing to include a reference to your organization in their billboard advertisements.

Pickets

Pickets carrying placards never fail to get the attention of media and passers-by. Why not picket your own premises? A group of your friends and supporters marching up and down with well-designed, pungently effective slogans can do wonders for your campaign.

Programs

• **CATEGORY:** GENERAL • **GROUP SIZE:** SM./MED./LARGE • **TIME FRAME:** UP TO 6 MTHS • **TIME OF YEAR:** SPR./SUM./FALL/WINT.

Event programs are an effective method of raising additional revenue. Programs also provide an excellent means of fundraising at events where admission is free or where an event is advertised as "Free." Any event where attendees might find it essential to possess a program should have the entry fee amalgamated with the program cost. Staff and volunteers, normally used for selling tickets, checking tickets, and guarding the exits against gate-crashers, can now be used to sell programs. Most people will happily buy a program because it has cost them nothing to attend the event.

Free programs given to your event supporters will require sufficient advertising sales to cover the cost. If you have difficulty finding advertisers from among your supporters, consult the printer who may also have a list of potential advertisers. Alternatively, private marketing companies will find advertisers, arrange both layout and printing and present you with the final product, providing that your order is sufficiently large. Remember when you do it yourself, you can be selective as to which advertisements appear in your program. You will also make a greater profit.

Souvenir

• **CATEGORY:** GENERAL • **GROUP SIZE:** SM./MED./LARGE • **TIME FRAME:** UP TO 6 MTHS. • **TIME OF YEAR:** SPR./SUM./FALL/WINT.

Certain events are of such significant historical importance that they can be commemorated by the production of a souvenir program. Do not miss a major fundraising opportunity. People will want to buy a program, whatever the cost, as long as your final product is well designed and authoritative.

Sponsored

An alternative to direct advertising is to ask supporters to be sponsors in return for an acknowledgement message: "*Joe Jones Automobile Sales is pleased to sponsor this program and wishes . . . organization every success.*"

Public Service Message

Check with all of your radio and television stations to find out which are required by the CRTC to provide "air" time for public service messages. Call each one to find out format and lead time required. Make sure that you request broadcast time to publicize all suitable events.

Publicity

A common adage in fundraising circles is that "Publicity does not raise money. Fundraisers do." I disagree. In 1996, a Toronto woman claimed that she had been robbed on the street. She also told the police that she was dying from cancer and that the heartless thief had stolen her son's bus ticket which was intended to take him to a relative's home following his mother's death. Within hours, media around the world were using the story as a headline. Donations from well-wishers started pouring in. A bank set up a trust fund which within a few days contained more than $100,000 worth of donations. The fund would have undoubtedly increased had not the "victim" been arrested shortly thereafter when it was discovered that her story was a complete fabrication.

Good publicity, in other words, is essential to the success of most fundraising events.

Radio Show Premiums

An infallible method of gaining publicity is to give local radio stations tickets to use as prizes for simple "on-air" competitions, as give-aways to the "nth caller."

Shop Window Displays

Landlords with vacant stores often allow charity groups to use their windows as an advertising medium as long as advertisements are removed on request. Create an imaginative display. Don't waste this valuable publicity space. Attract attention and persuade the public of the merits of your cause or encourage them to attend your upcoming event. Your display should be eye-catching. Perhaps you could use live models to create a tableau or a performance that will stop people in their tracks. If you can draw a crowd, a spontaneous collection is always a possibility.

T-Shirts

• **CATEGORY:** GENERAL • **GROUP SIZE:** SM./MED./LARGE • **TIME FRAME:** UP TO 6 MTHS. • **TIME OF YEAR:** SPR./SUM./FALL/WINT.

T-shirt printing kits are widely available. Make up your own logo to commemorate a specific event or to publicize your organization. Printed T-shirts can be sold at a profit and, when worn, serve as walking advertisements.

When a larger number of T-shirts is required, have them printed professionally. Your return on investment is less than that achieved through the do-it-yourself method but the process is much easier.

Make absolutely sure that you check and re-check design and wording before printing begins. Five-thousand T-shirts with a typo or incorrect message will not endear you to your executive.

• **CATEGORY:** GENERAL • **GROUP SIZE:** SM./MED./LARGE • **TIME FRAME:** UP TO 1 YR. • **TIME OF YEAR:** SPR./SUM./FALL/WINT.

Invite well-known personalities from all walks of life to dream up a signed T-shirt design. A relevant design, accompanied by an autograph, can be reproduced on T-shirts or other clothing linking the celebrity to your fundraising entity. Printed T-shirts can be sold at any event, or at retail through established clothing stores.

Television Advertising

Few charity and N.F.P. groups believe they can afford to spend money on television advertisements but we all know there are no gains without pains. If you believe firmly that your fundraising event will raise a substantial sum, then you should advertise. As a charity or N.F.P. group, you should also be able to negotiate a very competitive rate. Many television stations have difficulty filling advertising spots especially at off-peak times. Asking for a ridiculously low rate may be rewarding. Often television stations donate advertising time to charity and N.F.P. groups. Many community channels are required by law to do so.

Advertising Paid by Sponsors

Ask one of your corporate sponsors to mention your upcoming event in its TV advertising campaign.

"*We are proud to sponsor 'The Flat Earth Society's annual 'Round the World Race,' commencing June 5. Please support this worthy cause.*"

Television Publicity

Inviting a local TV personality to attend your opening gala as guest of honour, and to say a few words or to sign autographs, is an effective way of gaining advance publicity and on-the-spot TV coverage.

Most local TV stations present daily news segments from on-site locations. You should give the station maximum advance notice about your event, in addition to specifying why covering it would make great local interest. Remember, television producers are interested in visually interesting topics.

Infomercials

• **CATEGORY:** RELIGIOUS/GENERAL • **GROUP SIZE:** LARGE • **TIME FRAME:** UP TO 1 YR. • **TIME OF YEAR:** SPR./SUM./FALL/WINT.

TV infomercials offer a new and rapidly expanding development in promotional opportunities for charitable organizations. Prices for 30 minute television slots vary wildly, depending on the time of day, day of week, time of year and expected audience. Infomercials are not for the faint-hearted. Professionally produced promotional videos can each cost from tens to hundreds of thousands of dollars, although a simple emotional appeal by an eloquent speaker can be just as successful in raising pledges. Charity and N.F.P. organizations use infomercials to sell promotional items like books and videos. Other groups use them to solicit lifetime "Adoptive" parents for underprivileged children in third world countries.

Any organization can take advantage of the undoubted benefits of an infomercial by persuading a commercial sponsor to pay the costs. In return for buying the air-time, the sponsor would expect to promote its product/service and capitalize on the fact that it is supporting a charitable organization.

Careful selection of channel and timing of the infomercial is of vital importance to the success of any appeal.

Corporate Advertising

Many corporations spending large sums on television advertising can actually benefit by indicating an allegiance to a charity or N.F.P. group. Request that one of your affiliate corporations include a special advertisement in their next campaign pitching your organization, followed by a short statement to the effect: *"This message has been brought to you by the kind people at . . . company, makers of fine . . . ."*

Video

A short, informative, video about your organization is often a useful promotional tool. Well-conceived promotions will lend credibility to your cause, enabling you to make a fundraising pitch to several people simultaneously. Professionally produced videos are very expensive but perhaps someone in your group is involved in television production, or knows someone who is.

Event Video

Make a video of any event, and ensure that all participants receive significant camera coverage. Take advance orders, together with full or part payment, or use the video as promotion for future events.

Totally Naked Ballroom Dancing for All-Comers

Getting attention is what it is all about.

Ask the Toronto pop group *Barenaked Ladies* how they became famous. Undoubtedly because of their musical ability, but certainly the clever choice of name attracted public attention, and thus contributed in some measure to the group's outstanding success. For the record, *Barenaked Ladies* are not bare naked, nor are they women.

In 1996 an American baseball game was cancelled because too many people threatened to show up. Why? Organizers had announced all nude fans would be given free admittance.

Totally Naked Ballroom Dancing for All-Comers. A punctuation error. The title should read, "Totally Naked Ballroom. Dancing for All-Comers." All that is required is a room, music, and dancers. There you go.

ART

Art works provide many opportunities for fundraisers although paintings and other artistic pieces are only worth as much as a buyer is prepared to pay. Fundraisers need to bring the artists together with potential customers for financially rewarding encounters, both for the artists and the organization.

Exhibition

• **CATEGORY:** ARTS & THEATRE/SERVICE CLUBS • **GROUP SIZE:** SM./MED. • **TIME FRAME:** UP TO 1 YR. • **TIME OF YEAR:** SPR./SUM./FALL/WINT.

Many local artists are rarely exhibited because they don't work with a gallery, or because their framed body of work is not large enough for a full show. You can arrange an art exhibition for the general public with these artisans in mind.

A catchy title is important:

"PAINTINGS YOU CAN LIVE WITH"

"ART WITHOUT TEARS"

"ART-FULLY YOURS"

"AFFORDABLE REMBRANDT"

"ART IN THE PARK"

Contact local art groups, art colleges, universities and any known professional working in the field. Discuss the idea of an all-comers exhibition. This event provides a vehicle for raising money without massive effort and with virtually no risk of financial loss. Expenses to be considered are the hire of a suitable hall and publicity: if lucky, you will find a free venue. The artists themselves will have a personal stake in doing advertising for you. The more outrageous or contentious the art work to be exhibited, the more publicity you will receive, but there will be criticism. Be sensitive to the feelings of your supporters and members.

All should be invited to exhibit any art work within the bounds of good taste tolerable to your membership. Charge a small exhibition fee, an entrance fee and a commission on all works sold. Uxbridge, Ontario, recently staged a very successful two-day *Art in the Park* show underwritten by its local newspaper.

Annual Competition

• **CATEGORY:** ARTS & THEATRE/SERVICE CLUBS • **GROUP SIZE:** SM./MED. • **TIME FRAME:** 1 YR+ • **TIME OF YEAR:** SPR./SUM./FALL/WINT.

An annual art competition in your community encourages local artists to display their best works. It can also become an event attracting national or international recognition. Annual art competitions are also dandy fundraisers.

Your organization must set competition rules, but bear in mind, the fewer rules you have, the more artists will be eligible to enter. Keep the entrance fee low, but as a requirement of entry, you may wish to include a provision to the effect that all winning entries must be offered for sale by auction at the conclusion of the competition, with sales commissions paid to your charity.

Early publicity to the art world is essential. This requires both time and research. You will need to identify all art groups within a wide area, contacting them at least six to nine months in advance. These initial contacts should lead to other groups and individuals: you will need to be persistent to ensure as many artists as possible enter your event.

The best reward an artist can receive is "recognition." In addition to competition prizes and awards (which should, if possible, be obtained from local business donations), you should arrange for winning art works to be prominently displayed in the community. If a well-known art gallery exists within your catchment area, attempt to have works displayed there. Alternatively, you may consider the city hall, public library, or any similar civic location.

Once you have an idea of how many entries the competition is likely to attract, you can select a suitable venue. Publicity about the event is vital, but to a certain extent publicity will be self-generating, as artists and art students tend to network with each other.

Revenues will be generated from entry fees and commissions on sales, but don't overlook public interest. You might display all entered art work and invite the public to judge. Each art patron, having paid a small entrance fee, should be given a ballot and the opportunity to choose winners within each artistic category. This scenario avoids allegations of judgmental bias, and makes your art competition an interactive event for all concerned. It also eliminates the difficult task of securing professional judges to adjudicate the entries.

Art Sale

• **CATEGORY:** ARTS & THEATRE/SERVICE CLUBS • **GROUP SIZE:** SM./MED./LARGE • **TIME FRAME:** UP TO 1 YR. • **TIME OF YEAR:** SPR./SUM./FALL/WINT.

An art sale is perhaps a natural extension of an art exhibition, however, revenues will comprise commissions drawn only from what is sold. Art sale organizers must screen prospective entries carefully to ensure only art work with strong sales potential is accepted. Revenue generated directly correlates to the quality of the works presented and rate of commission charged. You might assess a flat fee for each piece entered, sold or not, but this may discourage artists. Persuading a nationally known artist to donate a work of art, and attend the sale in person, will help establish a successful event.

Permanent Art Gallery

• **CATEGORY:** GENERAL • **GROUP SIZE:** SM./MED./LARGE • **TIME FRAME:** UP TO 6 MTHS. • **TIME OF YEAR:** SPR./SUM./FALL/WINT.

Give local artisans the opportunity of displaying art work on the walls of your organization's offices in return for a commission on any resultant sales. Approach local art groups and artists: if your location is popular and well lit, you may find that your office becomes an art gallery with money-making potential for your organization.

Art Loans

• **CATEGORY:** ARTS & THEATRE/GENERAL • **GROUP SIZE:** LARGE. • **TIME FRAME:** 1 YR+ • **TIME OF YEAR:** SPR./SUM./FALL/WINT.

Although most famous works of art are displayed in public galleries and museums, there remain many private collections which rarely see the light of day. Borrowing such a collection for public view will enable any charity to raise vast sums of money. In 1995, the Art Gallery of Ontario secured the "Barnes Collection" of paintings on loan and raised more than $2.5 million in sponsorship and admission fees. High profile events of this nature require resources well beyond those available to most organizations. Publicity, security and insurance costs absorb considerable proportions of the generated revenue. Private sector, or even government sponsorship must be sought to cover such expense requirements.

Query organization members and affiliates to identify potential collections which would attract wide scale public interest. You will also need someone who is able to persuade the patron to allow the collection to be put on exhibition. This is a long term project, one that demands careful planning and exact attention to detail.

Rent a Masterpiece

• **CATEGORY:** ARTS & THEATRE/GENERAL • **GROUP SIZE:** LARGE • **TIME FRAME:** 1 YR+ • **TIME OF YEAR:** SPR./SUM./FALL/WINT.

Most people cannot afford to purchase a genuine "Old Master," so this fundraiser has immediate appeal. If your organization can secure donations of art, or assistance in purchasing some, auction each painting, sculpture, valuable antique, or what have you, at a private event, open only to organization members and supporters. The highest bidder per piece takes possession of the work for one full year, to return it for the subsequent year's auction. Special insurance must be arranged both by your organization and the winning bidder. It is calculated that the masterpiece will retain its full capital value or, appreciate in value while at the same time generating funds for your group.

The type and value of masterpiece should be specifically selected to suit your membership.

Cartoons

• **CATEGORY:** GENERAL • **GROUP SIZE:** MED./LARGE • **TIME FRAME:** UP TO 1 YR. • **TIME OF YEAR:** SPR./SUM./FALL/WINT.

Contact a number of well-known cartoonists and ask each of them to create a special cartoon for your organization. Then, have a limited number of prints made from each piece to be sold to your members and sponsors. The more celebrated the cartoonist, the higher print price you can charge. Hang the original in your head office or auction it off to raise more money. If you, or someone in your organization knows a cartoonist personally, then your chances with this solicitation increase considerably.

Carvings and Craftwork

• **CATEGORY:** GENERAL/ENVIRONMENTAL • **GROUP SIZE:** SM./MED. • **TIME FRAME:** UP TO 1 YR. • **TIME OF YEAR:** SPR./SUM./FALL/WINT.

Relatively small hand-crafted pieces of art can fetch considerable sums at auction because each piece is unique. Hand carved ducks, loons and geese are particularly sought after and would provide an excellent fundraising medium for an environmental group.

Any carving by a well-known carver will be of significant value. Sometimes this value may be increased by the addition of decoration by a well-known artist. For an even wider audience, consider having the decoration designed by a celebrity. Autographs of all contributors should appear on the finished product.

Other hand-crafted works can be treated in this manner: mail boxes and bird houses may be very suitable. They are fairly simple to make yet can be decorated very attractively. Pottery items including vases, plates and tiles are additional possibilities.

Ice Sculpture

• **CATEGORY:** FITNESS, SPORTS/GENERAL • **GROUP SIZE:** SM./MED. • **TIME FRAME:** UP TO 4WKS. • **TIME OF YEAR:** WINT.

Here's a "cool" event especially suitable for winter sport associations and groups. Ice sculpting contests can be held at a professional, amateur or "just for fun" level or maybe a combination of all three.

Professional ice sculptors require a large supply of pure, clean ice, free of air bubbles. Amateurs will use whatever they are given. Professional competitions will attract a great deal of attention but the prizes offered need to be particularly attractive in order to lure the best sculptors. Hold the event in a hockey or curling arena at the end of the season, or even outdoors, weather permitting. Entrants and sightseers should be charged admission and additional funds can be raised by auctioning sculptures and by selling hot food and drinks.

In addition to an ice sculpture competition for amateurs, think about exhibiting professionally produced ice sculptures as well. Charge admission to the exhibit or request donations.

Limited Edition Prints

• **CATEGORY:** GENERAL • **GROUP SIZE:** LARGE • **TIME FRAME:** 1 YR.+ • **TIME OF YEAR:** SPR./SUM./FALL/WINT.

Invite a well-known artist to produce a limited edition print for your organization. Choose a subject which appeals to your membership to secure a guaranteed sale. You will need to pay press set-up costs but sometimes even these can be negotiated. The prints are sold for the benefit of your organization which receives royalties on each sale, so you would expect to make both profit and royalty. The original art work should be sold at auction, used as a major raffle prize or displayed in a place of honour. This has been a very successful and popular fundraiser which supports art education and instruction in North Vancouver schools.

Murals

Brightly coloured murals painted on the sides of prominent buildings will readily catch the attention of passers-by and the media. Find a suitable and available building, buy twenty cans of paint, seek out a local artist sympathetic with your cause, draft up a bunch of volunteers, and in no time at all you can let everybody know what your organization is all about.

Be a Part of a Mural

• **CATEGORY:** GENERAL • **GROUP SIZE:** MED./LARGE • **TIME FRAME:** UP TO 1 YR. • **TIME OF YEAR:** SPR./SUM./FALL/WINT.

One way of raising money from your mural is by selling people the right to be one of the characters depicted therein. Imagine a huge crowd scene of 50 smiling faces – each easily recognizable, each one smiling because he or she has donated $500 to be permanently represented.

Fundraising from Commercial Murals

• **CATEGORY:** GENERAL • **GROUP SIZE:** SM./MED./LARGE • **TIME FRAME:** UP TO 6 MTHS. • **TIME OF YEAR:** SPR./SUM./FALL/WINT.

Many companies use murals as an effective advertising medium. Contact commercial organizations supporting your cause and ask them to incorporate a sponsor's message and/or fundraising solicitation into any mural they commission. There is no additional cost involved, and the benefits of public support of a worthy cause are far-reaching.

Pasta Pastiche (Noodle Art)

• **CATEGORY:** GENERAL/CHILDREN & YOUTH • **GROUP SIZE:** SM. • **TIME FRAME:** UP TO 6 MTHS. • **TIME OF YEAR:** SPR./SUM./FALL/WINT.

Pasta's great variety of texture, shape, size, and colour makes it a superb medium for creating works of art, elaborate pictures, models, and exotic statues.

Pasta art competitions can be held for fun at pasta parties or other suitable fundraising events, but there is no reason why a serious pasta art competition could not be organized with pasta as the only permitted medium. Professional and amateur artists would vie for a fitting trophy, and a substantial cash prize donated by a major pasta manufacturer. Money would be raised from corporate sponsorship, entry fees, an exhibition of works, and an auction of prize winning entries.

Photography

Photographic Competitions

• **CATEGORY:** GENERAL • **GROUP SIZE:** SM./MED./LARGE • **TIME FRAME:** UP TO 6 MTHS. • **TIME OF YEAR:** SPR./SUM./FALL/WINT.

Almost everyone owns a camera and photography competitions have considerable fundraising potential. Trophies and awards can be obtained from camera, equipment, and film manufacturers, as well from retailers, who have a vested interest in promoting sales.

A "members only" photography competition can easily be arranged at any time. You will need to select the relevant categories, define competition rules and invite all of your members to submit entries. A prestigious panel of judges will give your competition credibility.

A major photographic competition with a prestigious charity award should be a successful fundraising venue for any national organization. Obviously the competition theme should, wherever appropriate, reflect the work of the organization involved. A campaign to preserve specific wildlife species might be accompanied by a competition for the best photograph depicting said wildlife. Judges for such a competition need to be carefully selected. If you are lucky, you may even find judges who are also able to promote the competition; the editor of a national newspaper or magazine may be particularly useful.

Photographs

• **CATEGORY:** GENERAL • **GROUP SIZE:** SM./MED./LARGE • **TIME FRAME:** UP TO 6 MTHS. • **TIME OF YEAR:** SPR./SUM./FALL/WINT.

Always consider selling photographs of any event, either by employing the services of a professional photographer who would donate a percentage of sales, or by letting an enthusiastic amateur take photographs and orders on behalf of your group.

Photography Fee

• **CATEGORY:** GENERAL • **GROUP SIZE:** SM./MED./LARGE • **TIME FRAME:** UP TO 4 WKS. • **TIME OF YEAR:** SPR./SUM./FALL/WINT.

When fundraising for an unusual or visually appealing building, animal, or object, consider charging the public a fee for the right to take photographs. Most people will not object. Similarly, when staging an event which provides strong photographic subjects and variety, charge a fee to people who want to take either pictures or videos.

Quilts

• **CATEGORY:** WOMEN'S GROUPS • **GROUP SIZE:** SM./MED./LARGE • **TIME FRAME:** UP TO 1 YR. • **TIME OF YEAR:** SPR./SUM./FALL/WINT.

Quilts and quilting are part of Canada's traditional folkcraft heritage and are accepted as an art form. Many galleries hold exhibitions devoted exclusively to quilts. If the art of quilting is alive and well in your community, consider holding a range of quilting events, displays, exhibitions, seminars, and sales. Seek out a local quilter to design and produce a special quilt which reflects the work of your organization. You might even secure a sponsor to pay for the quilt in return for the publicity that it could engender.

The resultant quilt, as a centrepiece in an auction or charity sale, would raise a substantial sum.

You needn't stop at a single quilt though. If your organization has some talented quilters and others willing to learn, perhaps together they may be able to produce several desirable quilts quite inexpensively. Completed quilts can be sold at any organizational event, especially around holidays, or at craft fairs. Your group might even produce enough quilts to justify an annual quilt fair/auction. Mennonite auctions of handmade quilts in southwestern Ontario have been successful fundraisers for many years.

Remember the giant AIDS quilt assembled by thousands of people all across North America and beyond in support of AIDS research. That project attracted international attention, and even produced a successful, full-colour commemorative book.

Professional Sandcastles and Sculptures
• **CATEGORY:** GENERAL • **GROUP SIZE:** MED./LARGE • **TIME FRAME:** UP TO 6 MTHS. • **TIME OF YEAR:** SUM./FALL.

Sand sculptures are beautiful and attract considerable attention. If you have access to a sandy beach and can seek out an isolated area, a sandcastle exhibition or competition may be the perfect fundraising vehicle. Remember, you will need to work fast, as your sandy canvas is only available at low tide. Charge an admission fee for contest entrants and secure the services of a respected art connoisseur as judge. Why not include sand sculptures created by a professional? If an admission fee is not feasible there is no reason why you should not ask for donations. Sand sculptures can be a very useful added attraction to summer events like a salt (or fresh) water day celebration.

Don't forget you can also have sandcastle building competitions for children. Beach sand is free and plentiful and almost everyone can have fun building a sandcastle. Sandcastle competitions can be held on any beach during the summer. All you need is a roped off area and a prize for the best castle builder. Charge a small entrance fee or simply ask for donations. You will not make much money but you should have some fun.

Indoor Sandcastles
• **CATEGORY:** CHILDREN & YOUTH • **GROUP SIZE:** SM. • **TIME FRAME:** UP TO 6 MTHS. • **TIME OF YEAR:** WINTER.

As a way of warming up winter why not hold a sandcastle competition inside a shopping mall or other public building. A few tons of sand is all that is needed and parents will happily pay for their children to amuse themselves for a few hours.

Sand Monument

• **CATEGORY:** GENERAL • **GROUP SIZE:** MED./LARGE • **TIME FRAME:** UP TO 1 YR. • **TIME OF YEAR:** SPR./SUM./FALL/WINT.

A huge sand monument depicting something or someone relevant to your organization could be a real show stopper in a large mall or busy public building. Invite a corporate sponsor to employ a professional sand sculptor to create something that will stand for several weeks, or months, and gain a great deal of attention for your cause, in addition to donations. Monuments can be created out of many different materials, and a locally produced substance might provide a new start to an age old art. In Tibet, for example, it is a tradition for monks to make huge monuments out of butter which is donated by local herdsmen.

Rather than pay a professional sculptor to design a sand monument, you could instigate a competition. Invite students, artists, and the public to design a suitable monument and compete for an annual award. Once the winning design is chosen, the winning designer must create it. Charge a small entry fee for the competition and ask spectators for donations.

Sidewalk Art

• **CATEGORY:** GENERAL • **GROUP SIZE:** SM./MED. • **TIME FRAME:** UP TO 6 MTHS. • **TIME OF YEAR:** SUM./FALL/WINT.

Sidewalk artists produce amazing creations which attract much attention. When promoting any event, employ a sidewalk artist to create relevant scenes on the sidewalk adjacent to the premises where the event is located. Have volunteers standing by to collect donations while promoting your event to people looking at the sidewalk art.

• **CATEGORY:** GENERAL • **GROUP SIZE:** SM./MED. • **TIME FRAME:** UP TO 6 MTHS. • **TIME OF YEAR:** SUM./FALL/WINT.

When properly promoted and properly located, an annual exhibition of sidewalk art can become a major attraction. An indoor venue is probably most suitable, along with a midwinter time frame. Outdoor venues in the summer are acceptable in protected areas like the paved courtyard of an office complex. Invite a number of artists to participate, depending on the space available. A corporate sponsor should be found for each artist and asked to pay the artist a set fee. In return, the artist would produce one picture as advertisement for the sponsor and several other pictures of his/her own choosing. Each artist would be aware of the corporate sponsorship and each advertisement piece must be a prominent work. Charge the public a viewing fee to walk around the exhibits as they are created, or when complete. Alternatively, you can request donations. A holiday weekend in a tourist area would be a good time to hold this event.

Additional revenue can be generated by offering workshops to enthusiastic amateurs or by having a children's area where kids can chalk their own pictures for a small fee.

Studio Tour

• **CATEGORY:** ARTS & THEATRE/GENERAL • **GROUP SIZE:** SM./MED./LARGE • **TIME FRAME:** UP TO 1 YR. • **TIME OF YEAR:** SPR./SUM./FALL/WINT.

If your community is home to a number of artists, it may be possible to arrange an unescorted tour of artists' studios over a one or two day period. You will need the cooperation of between 12 and 20 artisans, each of whom would offer the public opportunities to see works being created, as well as the possibility of purchasing works directly from the creator. Include painters, potters, sculptors, glass blowers, ceramic artists, wood carvers, cabinetmakers and blacksmiths, candlemakers and/or quilters.

Sell as many advance tickets as possible, but also remember to encourage last minute visitors by allowing tickets to be purchased at any of the participating studios. Charge a fee for the tour and give each participant a map detailing studio location, brief details about the artist, and type of work, plus opening times of all studios.

Tie Designs

• **CATEGORY:** GENERAL/CHILDREN & YOUTH • **GROUP SIZE:** SM./MED. • **TIME FRAME:** UP TO 1 YR. • **TIME OF YEAR:** SPR./SUM./FALL/WINT.

Tie manufacturers are constantly seeking new designs and markets for their products. Why not suggest to a tie manufacturer that they sponsor a tie design competition for your organization or community. The manufacturer should be invited to provide prizes as well as money for advertising and administration. The company should also be encouraged to promote the competition through its own publicity.

Tie designs may be solicited from schools and colleges, from members of the public and from organizational members and clients. The number of entrants depends on the value of prizes and the amount of publicity the competition attracts. Charge each entrant a fee for participation.

Winning designs in each age group can be made into ties to be sold to your members and to the community at large. If the competition is focused on designing a tie for your community, sponsorship money should also be sought from the local municipality and Chamber of Commerce. Such ties would have a wider appeal and your organization should receive a commission from the manufacturer on each tie sold.

Torah Writing

• **CATEGORY:** RELIGIOUS • **GROUP SIZE:** MED. • **TIME FRAME:** UP TO 4WKS. • **TIME OF YEAR:** SPR./SUM./FALL/WINT.

Synagogues have been known to raise money by asking members to pay a significant sum toward the writing of a new Torah. Perhaps a fee of one dollar per letter could be sold in blocks of 50 or 100. Donors wishing to inscribe their letters personally should be given an outline to follow and asked to make an additional donation for the privilege of having their handiwork enshrined in the new document.

BUSINESS

Business Relationships

Cultivating a permanent alliance with a commercial enterprise will provide your organization with many benefits and can be accomplished on many different levels. Perhaps the simplest form of business partnership exists when a store or bank keeps one of your collecting tins on a counter. This provides minimal benefit to the business and therefore no incentive for the staff to encourage donations.

A better way of approaching business partnerships may be to analyze means by which your organization can assist a business and receive benefits in return. What assets do you have that can be of benefit to a commercial operation?

The major bargaining asset available to you is your membership and client base. The larger the group, the greater the potential benefit to a business operation. Your members and clients can be viewed as potential customers with the possibility of direct marketing, targeted advertising and/or preferential service, or they may be utilized in the marketing process as a focus group. Additionally, a commercial enterprise can enhance its public image by appearing philanthropic and, finally, it may be able to gain various tax advantages.

What benefits can you obtain from such a relationship?

There are numerous benefits achievable by adopting close ties with a particular corporation:

- Direct funding
- Indirect funding: Provision of goods and services
- Free advertising in promotional material, flyers etc.
- Assistance with raising money from the public with special promotions

- Prime collecting sites and display areas
- Use of facilities, personnel and equipment
- Encouragement to staff to support your organization

Some of these benefits are dealt with individually under separate headings in this book and any such benefit may be obtained individually from a private company, but here I am proposing that you consider forming a close alliance with a specific business from which both parties may accrue considerable benefit.

Best Method of Approach

After you have analyzed what assets your organization offers and what it requires from a business partner, you will need next to identify suitable candidates. Eliminate immediately those whose ideals are at variance with your organization. When you find a potential candidate, make the approach at the highest possible level, through personal contact if at all possible. Your opening gambit should be, *"This is what our organization can offer your organization...."*

Speakers

• **CATEGORY:** GENERAL • **GROUP SIZE:** SM./MED./LARGE • **TIME FRAME:** UP TO 6 MTHS. • **TIME OF YEAR:** SPR./SUM./FALL/WINI.

There are many advantages to inviting business leaders to appear as guest speakers at your most important membership meetings even though these individuals may not be directly involved in fundraising. Entrepreneurial business executives often seize the opportunity to address audiences of potential customers in a setting where they will be perceived as both caring and philanthropic. Any highly motivated businessperson may be interested in addressing your group, particularly financial planners and real estate brokers. Remember, however, that the art of fundraising is not in getting someone to speak to your organization but in getting them to say what will assist your organization. Be specific. Have a wish list but don't be disappointed if all you get is ten dollars in your collection box. Keep in mind the fact that once an executive has addressed your organization, he or she will probably feel some commitment towards it and can more easily be approached with a specific request at a later date.

Many successful business entrepreneurs are able to attract large audiences and, as a result, command substantial fees. Owners and CEO's of major corporations are frequently called upon as keynote speakers because they attract an audience of professionals and other businesspeople. If your group can develop a relationship with such a person, you might be in a position to solicit his or her services as a public speaker at least once per annum. Such a speech should be accompanied by a dinner, cocktail party, or even a corn roast, depending on the organization and speaker.

Funds would be raised primarily through entrance fees but additional money can be gained from a pre-speech silent auction and/or sales of charitable items.

Commercial Ventures

• **CATEGORY:** GENERAL • **GROUP SIZE:** LARGE • **TIME FRAME:** 1 YR+ • **TIME OF YEAR:** SPR./SUM./FALL/WINT.

Many charitable organizations support themselves wholly or in part by operating full-time commercial businesses. Many thrift shops, secondhand stores, commission stores and bookstores are owned by charity groups. Hospital foundations run flower shops, gift and supply stores and restaurants. Art galleries, museums and science centres derive income from operating stores selling models, educational materials, books, replicas and prints. Any number of businesses can be operated to raise money although organizations usually restrict their ventures to those which are closely connected to the organization's primary goals.

Most charitable groups operating businesses are afforded benefits rarely enjoyed by for-profit companies. These can include prime location, either rent free or very low rent, low overhead, a captive audience, and no competition.

If you can identify a need for a specific commodity or service within your community, or among your clients, then consider setting up a small business which would fulfill that need and, in time, make money for your organization. Be aware however that a large percentage of small businesses do fail; those that are successful take three to five years to make a profit.

Cash Register Receipts

• **CATEGORY:** GENERAL • **GROUP SIZE:** SM./MED./LARGE • **TIME FRAME:** UP TO 6 MTHS. • **TIME OF YEAR:** SPR./SUM./FALL/WINT.

Many Canadian supermarkets make donations to local charity and N.F.P. groups because shoppers have donated cash register receipts in favour of a particular organization. Other stores provide collection boxes so that donations can be made on the spot. Some stores even have collection boxes for a multitude of different organizations.

A participating store will donate a small percentage of its accumulated cash register receipt totals, in effect giving the customer a discount on all purchases, but paying that discount directly to the nominated organization.

Every charity and N.F.P group should take advantage of this system, and each should encourage all store owners to start similar programs.

Changing Places

• **CATEGORY:** HEALTH RELATED/GENERAL • **GROUP SIZE:** SM./MED./LARGE • **TIME FRAME:** UP TO 6 MTHS. • **TIME OF YEAR:** SPR./SUM./FALL/WINT.

Would you like to be president for a day? Would you pay to change your boring routine and switch places with someone who appears to have an exciting or powerful position? This is a fun activity for everyone involved. Ask company and organization heads to sell their jobs to the highest bidder, for just one day. Many people will see the political value of spending a whole day in the shoes of the boss and a substantial amount of money can be raised. Try operating the scheme city-wide or even publicize a national day for changing places. If nothing else, you should surely consider auctioning or raffling your own organization's presidential job for a day.

Commercial Organization of Charity Events

• **CATEGORY:** GENERAL • **GROUP SIZE:** SM./MED./LARGE • **TIME FRAME:** UP TO 1 YR. • **TIME OF YEAR:** SPR./SUM./FALL/WINT.

There are often considerable advantages to certain businesses when they assume full responsibility for the organization of specific charity fundraising events. For example, a fitness club allying itself to an organization raising money for research into heart disease could organize, advertise and complete all the arrangements for a number of annual events:

• Marathon for Heart

• Hearty Walk-a-Thon

• Healthy Heart Awareness Week, and so on

Each event raises money for the charitable organization, while simultaneously promoting and publicizing the health club.

Corporate Donations

• **CATEGORY:** GENERAL • **GROUP SIZE:** SM./MED./LARGE • **TIME FRAME:** UP TO 6 MTHS. • **TIME OF YEAR:** SPR./SUM./FALL/WINT.

Direct donations from businesses and businesspeople make up a relatively small proportion of non-foundation funding available to charitable organizations but, many of the ideas in this book rely on the support of private corporations in different ways. Corporations are reliable sources of assistance because of the self-interest factor. Any charitable organization with a large number of members and clients can have a significant impact, beneficially or otherwise, on a corporation's profitability.

Seek donations and assistance from those companies which benefit most from your organization. Ask yourself: Where do we, as an organization, spend money? Where do our members and clients spend money? Which companies benefit most from the existence of our organization? What can we offer a corporation in return? Can we promote their business in any way? Can we suggest to our members that they should use a particular company? Once you have identified any company that has a vested interest in your continued existence as an organization, ask yourself: Do any of our members work for that company? Who do we know who works for that company? Who could arrange a meeting with a decision-maker in that company?

It is very important to be able to identify, and deal directly with a decision-maker, otherwise you may spend hours, days or months, talking to the nicest, friendliest person on earth, who gives you the impression that the mega-donation you've always dreamed about is just about to fall in your lap. Then your next meeting is abruptly cancelled because your contact has been fired!

Deal with potential corporate donors as you would individual major donors.

Matching Donations

• **CATEGORY:** GENERAL • **GROUP SIZE:** LARGE • **TIME FRAME:** UP TO 1 YR. • **TIME OF YEAR:** SPR./SUM./FALL/WINT.

For each dollar donated by a member of the public, ask a corporate sponsor to provide a matching amount. Corporate sponsors can use this idea as advertising with greater impact than a simple donation. The sponsor will need to actively encourage people to donate; how it does so will depend on the particular business involved. A manufacturer, for example, could use specially printed labels on all, or selected, merchandise: "*GIVE A DOLLAR TO . . . AND WE WILL MATCH IT.*" A service provider might print a similar request on its invoices. Stores could agree to match donations placed in a collection box during a specified period.

Gifts In Kind

• **CATEGORY:** GENERAL • **GROUP SIZE:** SM./MED./LARGE • **TIME FRAME:** UP TO 6 MTHS. • **TIME OF YEAR:** SPR./SUM./FALL/WINT.

Sometimes services/donations may be of more value to a

charity or N.F.P. group than a monetary contribution. Consider asking a corporation to provide talented personnel. The services of a designer or bookkeeper may be particularly useful. Perhaps a staff member or student could even be seconded to your organization for a specific period or task.

The use of facilities, hosting of events on corporate premises, a loan, a gift of obsolete furniture and equipment – all can be valuable to a charitable organization. A business may also be able to assist with transportation, marketing, public relations, printing, or with photocopy and computer services.

Other companies may be willing to share expertise on accounting, iegal or business matters. Some might assign an employee to sit on your board.

Product Donations

• **CATEGORY:** GENERAL • **GROUP SIZE:** SM./MED./LARGE • **TIME FRAME:** UP TO 1 YR. • **TIME OF YEAR:** SPR./SUM./FALL/WINT.

Raising money is not easy at any time, but in today's economy it is becoming very difficult indeed. As a result, saving money becomes more important, and it is often easier to solicit product donations than cash.

Here's an example: Your organization needs a computer, preferably the very latest model complete with laser printer and a whole range of software. You may spend as much as $5,000 with a negotiated discount, and a dealer will be pleased to make $500 on the deal. However, a two-year-old model that will actually do everything you really need might be gathering dust at the back of the store. This machine is worth nothing to the dealer if he/she cannot sell it and the longer it remains on his/her shelf, the less likely the dealer is to find a buyer. Persuaded to give it to you, he/she can write-off its full value as a donation to charity and claim tax relief. Additional benefits result when you publicize the generosity of the dealer with a notice on the computer reading, "*Kindly donated by ....*" A useful rule in charity work is always solicit product donations prior to payment.

Products From the Manufacturer

• **CATEGORY:** GENERAL • **GROUP SIZE:** SM./MED./LARGE • **TIME FRAME:** UP TO 1 YR. • **TIME OF YEAR:** SPR./SUM./FALL/WINT.

Consider going directly to the manufacturer when you need to purchase products and supplies. Although many manufacturers do insist that all purchases be made through a wholesaler or retailer, others are pleased to sell products any way they can. You should be able to negotiate: a manufacture-direct price should always be lower than the retailer's price. Compare them. Remember, however, a local retailer may offer incentives and discounts in order to obtain publicity, or shift old stock. Sometimes it is good PR to purchase locally as long as the price is comparable.

Partnerships with Retail Stores

• **CATEGORY:** GENERAL • **GROUP SIZE:** LARGE • **TIME FRAME:** UP TO 1 YR. • **TIME OF YEAR:** SPR./SUM./FALL/WINT.

Retail stores can assist charities and N.F.P. groups in public awareness and fundraising, in addition to providing space for collection boxes. Retail chains can display posters in their stores and offices, act as collection points for entry forms, money or goods, sell premium items on behalf of an N.F.P. organization, and advertise the fact they support a particular charity. Few of the larger chains are prepared to undertake charitable assistance in this way, however, and in order to persuade management of a large retail group to support your organization, you will need a truly compelling presentation indicating to them what benefits can be derived from such a partnership. Major health charities should consider forming strategic alliances with drug store chains.

Redundant Stock

• **CATEGORY:** GENERAL • **GROUP SIZE:** SM./MED./LARGE • **TIME FRAME:** UP TO 1 YR. • **TIME OF YEAR:** SPR./SUM./FALL/WINT.

Many companies have redundant stock which they cannot sell. Identify those companies dealing in products which you and/or your clients can use. Write companies detailing what your organization needs or wants. Ask if they have redundant stock to fit your needs. Ask them to consider you in the future when such stock might become available. Check back every six months or so.

Product Donation Brokerage

• **CATEGORY:** GENERAL • **GROUP SIZE:** MED./LARGE • **TIME FRAME:** UP TO 1 YR. • **TIME OF YEAR:** SPR./SUM./FALL/WINT.

As business cycles and personal tastes change, organizations and individuals throw away appliances or supplies no longer in use, rather than searching out suitable recipients for donations. Some organizations no longer make donations perhaps because their offers were refused in the past, or the recipient had failed to collect items promptly.

If your organization can establish a reliable reputation for accepting and collecting unwanted products, it can become a preferred service provider, and receive all product donations within a geographic area. One enterprising N.F.P. organization in southern Ontario has essentially cornered the market in unsaleable items of clothing. When apparel manufacturers and suppliers have items for which there is no market, they call one number in southern Ontario and know that these materials will be collected and distributed to the needy and other charitable groups.

Consider how your organization might become a charitable donation broker. You may reap significant rewards.

Radio Request Show
• **CATEGORY:** SERVICE CLUBS/HEALTH RELATED • **GROUP SIZE:** LARGE • **TIME FRAME:** 1 YR.+ • **TIME OF YEAR:** SPR./SUM./FALL/WINT.

One popular radio show invites charity and N.F.P. groups to make on-air requests for assistance. Monetary requests are not permitted, but organizations ask for, and receive, all sorts of corporate sponsorship through transportation vehicles, equipment, and donations in kind. Such a show, hosted by a well-known personality, could be successful in almost any locale. The program should be a mix of music and request. Donors would be invited to phone-in "live" during the program. Many gifts are given by companies seeking publicity for their products, or good public relations. Others come from service clubs and community groups. Individuals are prepared to make donations of valuable items in order to be publicly acknowledged for their philanthropy.

Corporate Loans
• **CATEGORY:** GENERAL • **GROUP SIZE:** MED./LARGE • **TIME FRAME:** UP TO 1 YR. • **TIME OF YEAR:** SPR./SUM./FALL/WINT.

When capital funding is required, why not ask your corporate supporters for assistance, instead of immediately approaching a bank or other lending institution. Some corporations are either rich in cash or have access to funds at much lower interest rates than banks and with fewer restrictions. It is also possible that part of the funding required may be offered as a grant or interest-free loan.

Corporate Tie-Ins
• **CATEGORY:** GENERAL • **GROUP SIZE:** MED./LARGE • **TIME FRAME:** UP TO 1 YR. • **TIME OF YEAR:** SPR./SUM./FALL/WINT.

Sometimes with a new product launch, or when sales are lagging on an older product, N.F.P. groups and businesses work together to generate a publicity campaign around the fact that the manufacturer will give a donation to charity for each item sold. *"Buy this product and we will donate $1 to . . . association."*

In addition to such a pledge, the corporate sponsor may also print information about your organization either on the product packaging or in its advertisements.

Major corporations have been known to donate a percentage of the purchase price of a product to charity as a means of direct promotion. When a manufacturer solicits sales on a product claiming to alleviate the symptoms of a particular disease, it may be willing to support an organization funding services for people suffering from that disease.

Ethics of such commercialism are always subject to debate, but bear in mind that nearly all forms of charitable donations arise from some element of self-interest.

Market Research Surveys

• **CATEGORY:** GENERAL • **GROUP SIZE:** LARGE • **TIME FRAME:** UP TO 1 YR. • **TIME OF YEAR:** SPR./SUM./FALL/WINT.

Many leading businesses regularly carry out market research surveys by canvassing persons on their mailing list. Questionnaires sent to customers receive relatively few public responses because most people see no purpose or advantage in responding.

Ask major corporations to make a donation to your charity for each completed questionnaire returned to them by a certain date. Making this deal public by printing it on the questionnaire will give respondents an incentive to complete and return the survey within the specified time.

One Percent Day

• **CATEGORY:** GENERAL • **GROUP SIZE:** MED./LARGE • **TIME FRAME:** UP TO 6 MTHS. • **TIME OF YEAR:** SPR./SUM./FALL/WINT.

Would you pay an additional sales tax of one percent, one day a year, for charity? One percent is not much, but taken as a proportion of all money spent in a community on any given day, it can add up.

Approach your local Chamber of Commerce. Suggest that it and all its members collect a one percent sales tax from willing customers on a specified day (a Saturday just before a holiday would be most effective). The Chamber of Commerce could then decide which organizations would receive the resultant surtax funds.

An alternative idea would be asking local retailers to donate one percent of their daily receipts and advertise this fact as a goodwill gesture within the community. Each retailer would be free to choose which charity it wished to support. The total amount should be reported through the Chamber of Commerce so that maximum publicity is achieved.

One Cent Day

• **CATEGORY:** GENERAL • **GROUP SIZE:** SM. • **TIME FRAME:** UP TO 6 MTHS. • **TIME OF YEAR:** SPR./SUM./FALL/WINT.

Ask each customer to donate one cent to charity for every item that they purchase during a 24-hour period. Supply all stores willing to assist with special collection boxes and information sheets.

Big Round-Up

• **CATEGORY:** GENERAL • **GROUP SIZE:** SM./MED./LARGE • **TIME FRAME:** UP TO 6 MTHS. • **TIME OF YEAR:** SPR./SUM./FALL/WINT.

This fundraising event can be held at a single store, an entire mall or in every store in town. On a designated day, or week, all shoppers are asked to round-up their bill to the nearest dollar: the additional money is placed in a special charity collection box. Cardboard collection boxes designed to resemble longhorn steers would be very appropriate and, with a little ingenuity, they can be made to "Moo" with satisfaction every time a coin is dropped in.

Change to Charity Day

• **CATEGORY:** GENERAL • **GROUP SIZE:** SM. • **TIME FRAME:** UP TO 6 MTHS. • **TIME OF YEAR:** SPR./SUM./FALL/WINT.

Hold a special "Change to Charity" day throughout your community. Although many charitable collection boxes can be found year round on retail counters, many are ignored by most buyers. Distribute special boxes, inscribed with your organization's logo, to every retailer in your community, and for one special day each year, ask that all customers donate all of their change to charity.

You are more likely to gain retailer support when you concentrate solicitation efforts to one day – a busy Saturday perhaps. Publicity is important. Ensure that all local media will run a story about your "Change for Charity" event. Distribute larger than normal collection boxes that are prominently displayed. Include signs imploring people to donate. Thank each retailer a few days before your event, in writing, and ask them to encourage patrons to donate.

Overtime Pay

• **CATEGORY:** HEALTH RELATED/GENERAL • **GROUP SIZE:** SM./MED. • **TIME FRAME:** UP TO 6 MTHS. • **TIME OF YEAR:** SPR./SUM./FALL/WINT.

Many workers are reluctant to make charitable donations of more than a dollar or two from their hard-earned after-tax wages. They may, however, be persuaded to work a few hours overtime for charity, particularly if everyone else in the company is doing the same. The company calculates the value of all overtime donated individually and collectively, and makes a donation to charity in the same amount. The company must also remit to the proper authorities all unemployment/pension contributions. Workers benefit because they are able to make a substantial and worthwhile charitable donation without losing any regular wages. This idea may be particularly useful in a city or town based on one large industry. Remember, though, the employer should submit a listing of individual contributions included in the collective so that proper receipts can be issued. Overtime hours must still be reported in each employee payroll record, and the individual donations deducted at income tax.

Personal Computers

• **CATEGORY:** SERVICE CLUB/GENERAL • **GROUP SIZE:** SM./MED. • **TIME FRAME:** UP TO 1 YR. • **TIME OF YEAR:** SPR./SUM./FALL/WINT.

Computers, fax machines and other office machinery become obsolete very quickly. Almost all business concerns have old, but usable equipment available for the asking. If your organization has talented volunteers, it might generate revenue by refurbishing old equipment for resale to other smaller organizations like school and church groups. Office machines can be sold at auction or other events, or swapped for some other needed item. You might also advertise in computer magazines and newspapers to ensure a steady supply of equipment. And don't forget word of mouth.

Sponsored Events

• **CATEGORY:** GENERAL • **GROUP SIZE:** SM./MED./LARGE • **TIME FRAME:** UP TO 1 YR. • **TIME OF YEAR:** SPR./SUM./FALL/WINT.

Every charity fundraising event costs something to produce, and your organization is on the hook for this amount unless you arrange sponsorship in advance. Seek out corporate sponsorship for all events. The sponsor will be guaranteed the attendant prestige and publicity in return for paying all out-of-pocket organizational expenses of the event. Always seek sponsors who will clearly benefit from your organization's event. Sponsorship is a two-way street: both organizations should feel a sense of satisfaction from the partnership. A satisfied sponsor will be eager to sponsor the same event in subsequent years. Multiple sponsorship of charitable events by non-competing companies eases the financial burden on each while still delivering an excellent means for getting the most value from their donation.

Coupons from Gas Stations

• **CATEGORY:** GENERAL • **GROUP SIZE:** SM./MED./LARGE • **TIME FRAME:** UP TO 1 YR. • **TIME OF YEAR:** SPR./SUM./FALL/WINT.

"Receive $1 off your next purchase of 25 litres." Oil companies

often give discount coupons to their customers at gas stations to encourage product loyalty.

Contact the public relations department of those oil companies regularly operating such schemes in your area and ask if they would give a cash amount to your charity in return for each coupon collected. You would not expect the full face value of the coupons (as opposed to a regular redemption of same at the gas pumps), and the company would benefit from being associated with charity, particularly one with an environmental background. You could place collection boxes at each gas station, and drivers could choose between taking the discount or making a donation to your charity.

• **CATEGORY:** GENERAL • **GROUP SIZE:** MED./LARGE • **TIME FRAME:** UP TO 6 MTHS. • **TIME OF YEAR:** SPR./SUM./FALL/WINT.

Another way to benefit from gas station coupons is to request that the oil company make a small, charitable donation for each discount coupon redeemed. The customer would receive the full discount, coupled with the satisfaction of knowing that a few cents were donated to charity because he or she turned in the coupon.

Store Money

• **CATEGORY:** GENERAL • **GROUP SIZE:** SM /MED./LARGE • **TIME FRAME:** UP TO 1 YR. • **TIME OF YEAR:** SPR./SUM./FALL/WINT.

Certain retail stores issue in-house currency, or discount vouchers, as a means of discounting future purchases, and rewarding customer loyalty. Whenever purchasing goods for your organization at such a store, always ask if bonus currency is available as a form of charity discount.

Here are some other ways you may be able to take advantage of store money or coupons:

In Store Collections

Ask the retail management if they will permit you to put a collection box in their store, inviting customers to donate store money to your organization. Then use the money within the store to purchase office supplies or event prizes.

Collecting Campaign

If the store does not wish to have a collection box, you can hold your own "store money" collection campaign. Make sure that the community knows your organization is collecting store money to use for purchases just like any other consumer. Each time you engage in fundraising of any form, remind donors that store money donations are welcome. Publicize this fact in all of your literature and advertisements. Classroom collections may prove very lucrative, as school children are particularly enthusiastic at collecting store money.

Cash Redemption

Store money and similar discount coupons do not usually carry a cash redemption value, but there is nothing to prevent you from asking the store whether it would offer a cash value redemption for a particularly worthy charitable cause. Do not expect to redeem vouchers at full face value but even 50 cents on the dollar would be agreeable when you have assembled a sizable store money supply.

Store Bonus Points

• **CATEGORY:** GENERAL • **GROUP SIZE:** SM./MED./LARGE • **TIME FRAME:** UP TO 1 YR. • **TIME OF YEAR:** SPR./SUM./FALL/WINT.

Many stores offer regular customers a bonus in the form of collectable points or stamps. Some stores allow consumers to accumulate the bonus to be exchanged for premium items. Other stores permit customers to remit their points against the cost of further purchases. Either way, such points can be valuable to a charitable group for the purchase of essential items or prizes. Ask any store offering bonus points to adopt a scheme whereby customers can donate their points to your organization.

Super-Dollar Coupons

• **CATEGORY:** RELIGIOUS/WOMEN'S GROUPS/GENERAL • **GROUP SIZE:** MED. • **TIME FRAME:** UP TO 1 YR. • **TIME OF YEAR:** SPR./SUM./FALL/WINT.

Certain organizations (churches, schools and ethnic social clubs) have large numbers of members within a relatively small catchment area. Such memberships have considerable purchasing power, and when an organization is able to negotiate a discount with local businesses based on total sales to its members, it can save a considerable amount of money.

For example, if 500 members of one organization spend an average of $100 per week at a supermarket, they collectively spend $2.6 million per year. Each one percent discount of this amount, negotiated to be repaid to the organization, would amount to $26,000. Some organizations have negotiated ten percent.

Super-Dollar coupon schemes only work if most group members cooperate and prepay their purchases by buying Super-Dollar coupons either 3, 6, or 12 months in advance. Coupons are printed in amounts of $10, $20, and $50 and are then used as money in the participating store. The coupons are purchased from the store by the organization quarterly, semi-annually, or annually, with the discount applied at time of purchase. They are then distributed to members who spend them in the store as cash.

Participating stores benefit from this arrangement because purchases made by your members are paid for in advance, and customer loyalty is guaranteed, at least for the duration of the scheme. It is vital, however, that the participating retailer be a well established and healthy member of your business community or your group will find themselves with unredeemable supercoupons for which they have already paid the retailer.

Supermarkets are most frequently targeted for Super-Dollar programs because everybody buys groceries. Gas stations and restaurants have also been used and, with continued government deregulation, opportunities also exist for bulk purchase of local and long-distance telephone services and natural gas supply.

Supermarket Special Offer Coupons

• **CATEGORY:** GENERAL • **GROUP SIZE:** SM./MED. • **TIME FRAME:** UP TO 6 MTHS. • **TIME OF YEAR:** SPR./SUM./FALL/WINT.

Ask a major supermarket chain to offer a special charity promotion in conjunction with its regular promotional offers. An extra one-dollar-off coupon printed in flyers would encourage customers to donate the coupon to charity by paying the regular price when purchasing the promotion. The consumer makes a donation without additional expense, while the retailer pays the resultant benefit to your organization. This arrangement can sometimes be enhanced when a retailer, in return for positive publicity received by donating to charity, can be persuaded to give an additional 50% above and beyond the coupon value. The original donation was made by the customer, thus a further retailer donation might not seem unreasonable.

Shopping Cart Return

• **CATEGORY:** GENERAL • **GROUP SIZE:** SM. • **TIME FRAME:** UP TO 6 MTHS. • **TIME OF YEAR:** SPR./SUM./FALL/WINT.

When a supermarket uses buggies with a coin-activated locking system, have collection boxes at the cart return point. Make sure there is also a large sign: "If you don't need the 25¢, we do. Please give to . . . (organization name) and we will give it to someone in need." Ensure that someone is monitoring the boxes regularly. You might even ask the store staff for assistance in this regard.

Grocery Bags

A message to the world, printed on grocery bags, will keep any organization in the public mind. Grocery bags can carry any message the retailer wants. In addition to information about the specific store, there is no reason why a bag should not include the fact that the owner supports your organization. Competition details, collections and special events of your organization can all be printed on the bags at no significant additional cost to the retailer.

Environmental Bags

• **CATEGORY:** GENERAL • **GROUP SIZE:** SM./MED./LARGE • **TIME FRAME:** UP TO 6 MTHS. • **TIME OF YEAR:** SPR./SUM./FALL/WINT.

Don't forget the lasting and beneficial impact of advertising on environmentally responsible Buggy Bags. These fully reusable and recyclable plastic bags make an ideal printing medium. Cloth bags, which have been used for this purpose for some time, are no longer deemed appropriate by many environmental groups because of the high chemical and water requirements necessary for their production. Unlike regular grocery bags, which are simply given to customers, Buggy Bags can be sold to supporters and stores at a high profit margin thereby turning an excellent advertising medium into a major fundraising vehicle.

Garbage Bags

• **CATEGORY:** ENVIRONMENTAL/GENERAL • **GROUP SIZE:** SM./MED. • **TIME FRAME:** UP TO 1 YR. • **TIME OF YEAR:** SPR./SUM./FALL/WINT.

Garbage bags as a source of revenue for charity may at first seem unlikely, but the old saying, "Where there's muck, there's money," always holds true.

People buy garbage bags in order to throw them away and then they buy more. They become instantly obsolescent. When packed, they take little space, never rot, and can be stored almost anywhere. Garbage bags can be environmentally friendly and a good advertisement for any organization every time they are left at curb side awaiting pick up.

Choose biodegradable bags. Have them printed with the following:

WE ARE HELPING THE ENVIRONMENT

THIS IS A FULLY BIO-DEGRADABLE BAG

AND WE SUPPORT

(ORGANIZATION)

(Have your organization's logos printed as large as possible on the bags.)

Sell the bags in packs of 20/50 door-to-door, through your membership and at every event. If your group is part of a national or regional organization, sell the bags in bulk to other chapters.

CHILDREN'S EVENTS

Bubble Making
• **CATEGORY:** CHILDREN & YOUTH • **GROUP SIZE:** SM. • **TIME FRAME:** UP TO 4WKS. • **TIME OF YEAR:** SUM./FALL

Children of all ages love making bubbles and so do many adults. A few litres of soapy liquid and some bubble makers is all that is required. Hold competitions to see who can make the most bubbles from a single "dip," the biggest bubble, and the highest flying bubble. Bubble making contests are fun events that can attract good money when held in conjunction with regattas or perhaps summer fetes.

An alternate activity, often used at country fairs, is a bubble-gum blowing contest.

Cartoon Character Cut-Outs
• **CATEGORY:** GENERAL/HEALTH RELATED • **GROUP SIZE:** LARGE • **TIME FRAME:** UP TO 1 YR. • **TIME OF YEAR:** SPR./SUM./FALL/WINT.

Choose a well-known cartoon character and, with the consent of the copyright holder, use it in a charitable fundraiser where parents and children offer donations and, in return, have their name written on the character where it is then prominently displayed in a public place. You will need to print a significant number of identical cartoon characters to be sold in pairs; the purchaser keeps one figure and adds his or her name to the other, after which the figure is displayed prominently in a window or on a store wall.

Here are some examples:

A favourite bear character could have the inscription: *"(Donor's name) . . . can't BEAR to see animals suffer and supports (animal charity)."*

A duck character could be inscribed: *"(Donor's name) . . . goes QUACKERS in support of (any charity)."*

An octopus character might have the inscription: *"(Donor's name) . . . is getting his TENTACLES around (any charity)."*

The donor's personal copy should include a thank you. Each donor copy rewards the donor for the contribution and hopefully, if the donor is a child, he or she will want to see the personalized character hanging on the wall of a local store, library, or school.

Babysitting

• **CATEGORY:** WOMEN'S GROUPS/GENERAL • **GROUP SIZE:** SM. • **TIME FRAME:** UP TO 6 MTHS. • **TIME OF YEAR:** SPR./SUM./FALL/WINT.

This is a simple fundraiser which can be combined with another event particularly if your group is small and without the staff to organize a major event. A mobile children's play-area can be transported to any venue where there are children to be baby-sat for an hour or two. You will need a range of toys and sturdy, reliable playpens. At events organized by other charity or N.F.P. groups, your group can offer to look after the children, for a fee, so that working and visiting parents have time to participate freely. Your group, if well organized with strong childraising and communication skills, will soon find that its services are in demand and other event planners may well come to you.

A word of caution: Make sure that your babysitters are highly respectable and accustomed to working with children. Always ensure that the babysitter-child ratio is never less than 1:3. Remember, willing volunteers are not necessarily the most suitable persons for your task. Liability insurance is essential.

Children's Hand or Footprints

• **CATEGORY:** GENERAL • **GROUP SIZE:** SM./MED./LARGE • **TIME FRAME:** UP TO 6 MTHS. • **TIME OF YEAR:** SPR./SUM./FALL/WINT.

A public display of children's hand- or footprints is often a good, fun, community-oriented fundraiser.

Invite children (ages 10-14) to draw a silhouette of their hand or foot on a thin card, cut out the shape, write their name and age on it, and submit it to your N.F.P. group with a donation. The prints can be pasted on store walls, in shopping malls, public libraries etc., or hung as decorations in any public place. Both parents and children will have fun finding their personal silhouette alongside those of their friends.

One alternative to having children cut out the shape of their silhouettes is to supply ready made cut-outs, larger than real size, so that the child need only draw his/her hand or foot outline and add the name to complete the display. This method, however, also reduces the personal involvement and satisfaction derived from making one's own personal cut-out.

Another variation of this theme is to assemble a permanent collage of children's hand-prints on a newly painted wall. Invite all-comers to add their hand-prints, in ink or paint, together with name and date, for a set donation. Any wall might be suitable for this treatment, with the owner's consent, of course. Best bets are walls in public buildings or at the very least, walls in a building to which your members have regular access. This is a particularly good fundraiser for pre-school and junior youth groups.

Face Painting

• **CATEGORY:** CHILDREN & YOUTH/GENERAL • **GROUP SIZE:** SM. • **TIME FRAME:** UP TO 4WKS. • **TIME OF YEAR:** SPR./SUM./FALL/WINT.

Although face painting is usually done solely for fun, there is no reason why you should not be able to make a small amount of money at any event attended by a large number of children. You will need to establish a reputation for amusing, entertaining face painting creations, and once this is done, your services should be in demand at both private and public functions. Purchase the paints in bulk, and train a group of artistic volunteers. Be imaginative. Take photographs (you may even be able to charge a small fee for these). Major sporting events, fairs, fetes, and carnivals provide excellent venues for a face painting fundraiser.

Once you have established your organization's reputation for high quality face painting, then take it a step further by holding annual competitions. Hold a competition where children paint each others' faces and vie for a prize. Charge each child an entry fee equivalent to the cost of materials, plus a donation. Co-ordinate your contest with any major children's event.

Haunted House for Halloween

• **CATEGORY:** CHILDREN & YOUTH/GENERAL • **GROUP SIZE:** SM. • **TIME FRAME:** UP TO 6 MTHS. • **TIME OF YEAR:** FALL

Many N.F.P. groups raise money by charging a small fee for Halloween visitations to a haunted house. Any structurally sound old house or building can be suitable when filled with frightening models (ghosts, goblins, witches, bats, vampires, ghouls etc.) and spooky lighting. You must make sure, however, that all floorboards are secure, steps are safe, and the electric wiring is first-class. Your volunteer team can have great fun with the preparations for this event. It will test their theatrical skills as well. Charge a reasonable admission fee and have a howling good time.

Goody Bag Sales

• **CATEGORY:** GENERAL• **GROUP SIZE:** SM. • **TIME FRAME:** UP TO 4WKS. • **TIME OF YEAR:** SPR./SUM./FALL/WINT.

Goody bags are an ongoing fundraising success, particularly during holiday seasons. Schools and youth organizations are well suited for raising much needed money in this way. Sweets, cookies, and small novelty items are bought in bulk, and made up into attractive, reasonably priced packages for public sale. Boy Scouts and Girl Guides often make up Mother's Day gift baskets which they sell at the appropriate time of year.

Kite Flying

Kite flying can be inexpensive family fun while providing various ways to raise money.

Annual Kite Fly

• **CATEGORY:** FITNESS, SPORTS & SOCIAL/CHILDREN • **GROUP SIZE:** SM./MED. • **TIME FRAME:** UP TO 1 YR. • **TIME OF YEAR:** SUM./FALL

Annual kite fly days in a local park or open space provide a fun members' day out for all your supporters, and can also increase public awareness of your organization. You might begin by approaching a kite manufacturer, or importer, to bulk purchase a number of inexpensive kites which can be re-sold to members and spectators at a profit. Any kites left over should be kept for the subsequent year's event, or given away as consolation prizes. Persons bringing their own kites should be charged a small entrance fee. You can raise additional funds by selling appropriate refreshments, or alternatively, by allowing commercial kite suppliers to set up selling stalls and displays. You can do both too! Kite flying is an event for all age groups, so you also have the opportunity for a variety of ancillary fundraising attractions. Tethered balloon flights might be especially popular, as they would offer spectators the happy chance of viewing kites from the air.

In the spring, a Sikh kite festival, or Basant, might provide an excellent basis for a fun fundraiser. Kites of all types are flown and it is tradition for children to tie small pieces of sharp glass shards to each kite and attempt to cut the strings of opponents' kites. Alternatively, you might choose to pattern your fundraiser after the Singapore kite festival wherein all entrants must make their own kites both for racing and for contests in design and speed. Competitions are held between teams who vie for launch and retrieval speed, total height, and ability to make pinpoint landings.

These are sponsored kite flying competitions. Another competition would centre on who could maintain the longest continual flight time. For all these events each entrant should be sponsored by friends and relatives, and you should also consider a small entrance fee, plus the usual ancillary offerings.

Advertise the event as *"Come fly your kite for . . ."* and don't forget to invite the media.

Kite Sales

• **CATEGORY:** CHILDREN & YOUTH /FITNESS, SPORTS & SOCIAL • **GROUP SIZE:** SM./MED./LARGE • **TIME FRAME:** UP TO 1 YR. • **TIME OF YEAR:** SPR./SUM./FALL

Kites can be inexpensive and they are environmentally friendly, particularly when compared to balloons because of the re-use factor. Remember as well: kites use air and not helium for lift. Kites can also be imprinted with a simple logo or message. The next time your organization considers selling balloons to raise money, perhaps it might look at kites instead.

Learn-a-Thon

• **CATEGORY:** GENERAL/CHILDREN & YOUTH • **GROUP SIZE:** SM./MED. • **TIME FRAME:** UP TO 6 MTHS. • **TIME OF YEAR:** SPR./SUM./FALL/WINT.

Most any group of young people can become fundraisers by competing to learn while being sponsored for doing so. Hymns, poems, Torah verses, math tables, popular songs, or trivia tidbits can all form the basis of a learn-a-thon. Each participant should be sponsored by friends and relatives for the total number of poems, pieces of data, songs, verses etc., learned within a given period of time. A small prize should be offered to the most successful learner.

Lego™ Building

What family with children does not own Lego™ blocks? These ubiquitous building tools can be used for any number of events. Begin by assembling a vast collection of blocks. Hold Lego™ drives, Lego™ street collections, and Lego™ drop box collections. You may need a year or more to accumulate sufficient stock, but Lego™ is neither heavy nor ruined by damp conditions, so finding suitable storage space should not be a problem. Then you might consider any of the following:

Lego™ Building Competition

• **CATEGORY:** CHILDREN & YOUTH /FITNESS, SPORTS & SOCIAL • **GROUP SIZE:** SM. • **TIME FRAME:** UP TO 6 MTHS. • **TIME OF YEAR:** SPR./SUM./FALL/WINT.

Use your mega Lego™ collection to hold a week-long building competition during any school vacation period. Object: find the best Lego™ architects in your area. You will need suitable prizes for a variety of age groups and you should also award prizes for different structural categories: best house, best tower or best bridge, best castle etc. Don't forget a free-for-all category which allows contestants to build whatever they like. Charge a small entrance fee and charge extra for busy parents who want to leave their children in your care for the day.

World's Biggest Lego™ Construction

• **CATEGORY:** CHILDREN & YOUTH /FITNESS, SPORTS & SOCIAL • **GROUP SIZE:** SM./MED. • **TIME FRAME:** UP TO 1 YR. **TIME OF YEAR:** SPR./SUM./FALL/WINT.

How about creating a monster in a public place. A certain attention grabber. Can you collect enough Lego™ blocks to build a real giant? Your model should be a centre piece in any shopping mall and worth a healthy donation from the landlord. You might also solicit donations from passers-by through collection boxes (made out of Lego™). The construction piece itself might be one huge collection box.

Sales

Once you have collected all possible funds from competition or construction events, consider selling your Lego™ blocks. Box, bag, or bucket them attractively for sale at any suitable event, or save them for next year's competition.

Remember, if you sell off your collection, it takes time to assemble another.

Alternate Tip: Meccano™

Meccano™ can be used in place of any of the fundraising schemes involving Lego™. Meccano™, however, takes longer to assemble en masse and it is less popular.

Mad Hatter Tea Party

• **CATEGORY:** GENERAL/CHILDREN & YOUTH • **GROUP SIZE:** SM./MED. • **TIME FRAME:** UP TO 6 MTHS. • **TIME OF YEAR:** SPR./SUM./FALL

This is an excellent theme for any fundraising event staged for the benefit of a children's institution or organization: a giant tea party for youngsters and guests (stuffed animals, dolls, parents etc.), just like the one that Alice attended in Wonderland. All toys are admitted free of charge when accompanied by a paying guest. You need to be careful in your choice of venue – *easy cleaning* is an important term to remember. Cake and ice cream and kids always create a mess. All participants should be costumed, but there can only be one Mad Hatter. Charge a modest admission fee and invite the media. Don't forget photo opportunities for proud parents and relatives and remember to award prizes. For the record, Lewis Carroll's birthday is January 27.

Teddy Bear's Picnic

• **CATEGORY:** CHILDREN & YOUTH • **GROUP SIZE:** SM. • **TIME FRAME:** UP TO 6 MTHS. • **TIME OF YEAR:** SPR./SUM./FALL

An ideal event for small children. Consider charging mothers a fee for participation in a picnic where each child must bring his or her favourite teddy bear/stuffed animal. Be reasonable. This fundraiser succeeds through word of mouth and repeat customers. Your group will need to provide entertainment, a puppet show, magician, face painting, and a clown giving away favours of some sort. Appropriate food and drink will ensure a great time for the little ones. Well publicized Teddy Bear's Picnics have been known to attract thousands of children of all ages.

Children's Treasure Hunt

• **CATEGORY:** CHILDREN & YOUTH • **GROUP SIZE:** SM. • **TIME FRAME:** UP TO 4WKS. • **TIME OF YEAR:** SPR./SUM./FALL/WINT.

Organize a treasure hunt. It is an excellent way of keeping children entertained while simultaneously raising money for your group. You will need to determine the theme of your hunt, to secure appropriate treasures to be hidden (to be collected by each participant or merely to be found, with a notation made to this effect upon each individual seekers' scorecard). You also need to secure a suitable venue – indoors or out – which is large enough to allow large numbers of treasure hunters without one group following cheek by jowl upon its predecessor. What time frame will you place on the activity? How will you monitor it? – spotters, stamps or cards to be collected, signatures at checkpoints etc.? What about scorecards? Don't forget treasure maps, a vital element of any organized treasure hunt. Will you include both true and false clues? What about riddles, rhymes, or verse? Each participant should be charged an entrance fee, and if you have secured some really fabulous rewards for the winners (either singular – the first to succeed – or multiple – all who reach the end successfully), you may be able to levy additional charges at each check point, payment of which allows continuance of the chase. Use your imagination on this fundraiser. It should really be an exciting experience for your entire community.

Mud Play

• **CATEGORY:** CHILDREN & YOUTH /FITNESS, SPORTS & SOCIAL• **GROUP SIZE:** SM. • **TIME FRAME:** UP TO 1 YR.+ • **TIME OF YEAR:** SUM.

We all know that kids like mud and dirt. And indeed, the opportunity of smothering one's self and one's friends with mud without public penalty is tempting for adults as well. You will need a roped-off corner of a muddy field or stream bank, or even artificially created mud plots (lots of water applied to a soil on property with a sympathetic owner or landlord). Ensure that there are no sharp stones or broken glass. More water creates more mud and thus more mess and more fun.

Invite local youth/family organizations to rent time at your mud bath. Throw in a barbecue for adults and participants once they are cleaned up. Arrange muddy games, provide water guns or water-hoses and watch the children have the time of their lives. Don't forget the traditional tug-of-war. Arrange an entrance fee. Sell refreshments. You might even charge for towels and showers. Don't forget prizes and insurance. Pictures might also be a good bet.

Pumpkin Growing Competition

• **CATEGORY:** CHILDREN & YOUTH /FITNESS, SPORTS & SOCIAL• **GROUP SIZE:** SM. • **TIME FRAME:** UP TO 1 YR. • **TIME OF YEAR:** FALL

Canada has several established pumpkin growing competitions. Every year the number of people vying to grow the world's largest pumpkin increases. Why not hold a local pumpkin growing competition. This is a particularly good fundraiser for schools. Individual seeds should be sold in the spring, together with a simple instruction sheet. The competition should be held in the fall. Award small prizes for the biggest, heaviest, and best-looking pumpkins. Don't forget to liaise with local fairs, when available, and perhaps you could even auction winners to local supermarkets or fruit and vegetable vendors.

Pumpkin Carving Competition

• **CATEGORY:** CHILDREN & YOUTH /SERVICE CLUBS• **GROUP SIZE:** SM. • **TIME FRAME:** UP TO 4WKS. • **TIME OF YEAR:** FALL

An annual pumpkin carving competition as part of a Halloween fair or as a single event is always a popular fundraiser. The number and quality of entrants depends on the prizes offered. Charge a fee for each pumpkin entered, and a fee to visitors.

Pumpkin Sales

• **CATEGORY:** GENERAL • **GROUP SIZE:** SMED. • **TIME FRAME:** UP TO 6 MTHS. • **TIME OF YEAR:** FALL

For maximum profit, buy the pumpkins in bulk, or perhaps a farmer's entire crop. Use your volunteers to pick and transport them. Sell them in a variety of ways.

Take advance orders whenever possible. Get commitments and cash from people before they are tempted to buy elsewhere. You will need to start taking orders long before the first pumpkins appear in the stores. Set up a central sales point in a prominent location with advance signs advising the public that pumpkins will be available after a certain date and that all proceeds are to be used in support of your organization. And optionally, decorate a horse-drawn hay cart, load it with pumpkins and tour residential streets selling from door-to-door.

Pumpkin Festival

• **CATEGORY:** FITNESS, SPORTS & SOCIAL/SERVICE CLUBS • **GROUP SIZE:** SM./MED./LARGE • **TIME FRAME:** UP TO 1 YR. • **TIME OF YEAR:** FALL

Put together a range of events to form an annual festival. Here are a few ideas:

- Biggest and smallest pumpkin competitions
- Carving competitions for ugliest, most lifelike, most like the carver
- Best illuminated pumpkin heads
- Best pumpkin pie
- Pumpkin pie-eating contest

Combine these events with a pumpkin dance, best pumpkin costume contest, a pumpkin princess competition, hay rides, and a pumpkin dinner to make an unusual annual event with considerable profit potential.

Sunflower Growing Contest

• **CATEGORY:** CHILDREN & YOUTH • **GROUP SIZE:** SM.• **TIME FRAME:** /UP TO 1 YR • **TIME OF YEAR:** SUM./FALL

These contests are excellent participation events for children, and can usually be run in conjunction with elementary schools. Each interested child should be encouraged to buy the seeds, or alternatively, your organization could supply the sunflower seeds in the spring. All should be given instructions on planting and growing. Enthusiastic teachers and librarians can utilize the contest as an education lesson ensuring that all seeds are properly germinated before being taken home for planting.

Each plant should be judged in one of three categories: tallest, largest, or most seeds. Don't forget to display all entries before the public.

Read-a-Thon

• **CATEGORY:** GENERAL/CHILDREN & YOUTH • **GROUP SIZE:** SM./MED. • **TIME FRAME:** UP TO 6 MTHS.• **TIME OF YEAR:** SPR./FALL/WINT.

Incorporated with a national reading day, or alternative event, read-a-thons are excellent fundraisers. They also provide a useful method for keeping children quiet and absorbed. Ask parents, grandparents, relatives, neighbours, and friends to sponsor the reading activity (e.g., 30 minutes, $3.00). The event should be challenging. Any child who can easily read a book in 30 minutes receives little incentive from sponsorship based on reading a book an hour, unless the only concern is with raising money. Read-a-thons are currently popular local fundraisers in many areas but, because of their universal popularity on multiple levels, they deserve a wider clientele.

Alternative Sponsorship

• **CATEGORY:** CHILDREN • **GROUP SIZE:** SM./MED./LARGE • **TIME FRAME:** UP TO 6 MTHS. • **TIME OF YEAR:** SPR./SUM./FALL/WINT.

Carefully, diplomatically, and only under appropriate circumstances, you might consider asking parents able to pay for one child to pay the way for another, less fortunate, child at the same time. This is a valuable guideline to remember for any or all events, particularly if your organization is dedicated to providing services to children.

Sponsored Spelling Bee

• **CATEGORY:** CHILDREN & YOUTH • **GROUP SIZE:** SM. • **TIME FRAME:** UP TO 4WKS. • **TIME OF YEAR:** SPR./SUM./FALL/WINT.

Usually young people of any age and grade level delight in a sponsored spelling bee. Parents easily see the educational value of sponsorship, particularly if they are contributing an incentive for their child to spell a number of difficult words correctly. Other family members and friends can usually be persuaded to add to the contribution.

Clothes Day Theme

• **CATEGORY:** CHILDREN & YOUTH • **GROUP SIZE:** SM. • **TIME FRAME:** UP TO 4WKS. • **TIME OF YEAR:** SPR./FALL/WINT.

This fundraising activity should be school-sponsored. Students are invited to wear clothes denoting a particular theme. A sports theme like baseball, basketball, or football is appropriate. Alternatively, you might suggest that all children wear one particular colour, especially if that colour has some significance to your organization. The parents of each child would make a small donation to your group on the day in question.

Theme Park, Special Charity Day

• **CATEGORY:** CHILDREN & YOUTH /GENERAL• **GROUP SIZE:** MED./LARGE • **TIME FRAME:** UP TO 1 YR. • **TIME OF YEAR:** SUM./FALL/SPRING

The larger your organization, the larger the theme park you should seek out, and the greater the group discount you should negotiate. This is ideal for children's charities. You request that the theme park hold a special day for your charity/N.F.P. group. All members are admitted at a reduced rate, helpers/assistants at half price, and ten percent of the day's receipts are donated to your charity.

Stuffed Toy Animals

• **CATEGORY:** WOMEN'S GROUPS • **GROUP SIZE:** SM./MED. • **TIME FRAME:** UP TO 1 YR. • **TIME OF YEAR:** SPR./SUM./FALL/WINT.

Do you have a group of capable volunteers who enjoy sewing, making and selling stuffed toys? If so, this may be a marvellous fundraising opportunity. The market for stuffed toy animals is perpetual although certain designs hold the imagination, and the market, more than others. A captivating design is the secret to success. Gaudy colours, big eyes and floppy ears have historically constituted a large percentage of the requirements. Required materials cost little. One of the most sought after toys in 1997 was a small furry toy animal stuffed with dried beans.

Recycled materials are best if you have access to them. You must ensure they are clean and safe. Begin by cutting out patterns in bulk. Have your teams sew in small groups or individually. Stuffed toy animals can yield a high return on investment.

Toy Exhibition

• **CATEGORY:** CHILDREN & YOUTH • **GROUP SIZE:** LARGE • **TIME FRAME:** UP TO 1 YR. • **TIME OF YEAR:** FALL/WINT.

Consider holding an exhibition of new toys. Toy manufacturers and retailers would be appreciative because they can target customers directly. Samples of toys could be tested to destruction by hundreds of kids eager to try the latest offerings. Parents would be able to avoid the sort of hasty decision, usually later regretted, that always arises at holiday time. Charge exhibitors a reasonable fee, and solicit exhibits from local, regional, and national toy manufacturers or wholesalers. Charge admission for visitors. Do not admit unaccompanied children. Additional fundraising activities would include babysitting, refreshments, car parking etc.

Toys for Children

• **CATEGORY:** CHILDREN & YOUTH • **GROUP SIZE:** SM./MED. • **TIME FRAME:** UP TO 6 MTHS. • **TIME OF YEAR:** FALL/WINT.

Any group associated with a charity catering to the needs of children should consider organizing an annual collection of new toys to be used as presents. This is currently a popular custom around holidays and it fosters and encourages a caring attitude in all concerned, child and adult. Work with your local toy stores to invite parents and children to purchase additional toys for children who would otherwise go without. Support this effort with local collection boxes and an active publicity campaign.

Initially, toy retailers are the key to this campaign, but ultimately any retailer with sense will jump at the opportunity to participate in the event because it will increase sales. (Ask for a donation of several toys from each retailer in return for the privilege of participating, and make sure each is acknowledged personally in writing by your group and by support of local media.)

Collection boxes must be conspicuous. Ideally, they should be covered in decorative wrap and located in highly visible, convenient locations within each participating store. Alternatively, donors could also be invited to place gifts under a specially erected community Christmas tree provided it is placed in a secure location, like the centre of a shopping mall.

Publicity is of paramount importance. Your toy collection should be advertised in the local press (updated regularly with weekly results), as well as in toy stores, seasonal flyers, and in every neighbourhood. Encourage children to think of others (and make their parents re-think lavish family gift giving splurges).

Toy Sales
• **CATEGORY:** CHILDREN & YOUTH/SERVICE CLUBS • **GROUP SIZE:** SM./MED. • **TIME FRAME:** UP TO 1 YR. • **TIME OF YEAR:** FALL/WINT.

Regular collections of secondhand and damaged toys throughout the year can be beneficial to your organization. How to manage them? Street collections; drop boxes in public places like libraries; school collections where each child is asked to bring in toys of which they have grown tired. (To avoid complications, each toy should be accompanied by a written consent from the parent.) Ask all of your members to collect old toys from friends and family. Hold workshops where everyone can help to repaint, repair, and refurbish the donations. Then stage a giant toy sale prior to the holidays, or take over an unoccupied store and open a Santa's Grotto.

Teddy Bear & Doll Hospital
• **CATEGORY:** CHILDREN & YOUTH/HEALTH RELATED • **GROUP SIZE:** SM./MED. • **TIME FRAME:** UP TO 1 YR. • **TIME OF YEAR:** SPR./SUM./FALL/WINT.

Has your group ever considered running a hospital dedicated to the repair of broken or injured dolls and teddy bears. As an adjunct, you can consider setting up a booth for the adoption of donated dolls and teddy bears (and doll paraphernalia – dresses, hats, and brushes). You might consider asking a major toy company to supply the necessary repair materials on a concession or cost basis. You will need volunteers with sewing skills, equipment, and heart. Teddy bear repair is not simple, so remember to allow enough time for "surgical recovery" or your patrons will become impatient and disillusioned. Your hospital could open for just a few days annually, or perhaps even on a regular basis. Determine an admittance fee and additional surgical repair charges.

Zoo Spy

• **CATEGORY:** CHILDREN & YOUTH • **GROUP SIZE:** SM. • **TIME FRAME:** UP TO 1 YR. • **TIME OF YEAR:** SPR./SUM./FALL

This fundraiser works best when associated with an organization raising money for animals or children. Each youngster (up to age 11) is encouraged to seek financial sponsorship for a walking trip around your local zoo wherein he or she spots and correctly identifies specific animals. All participants receive a special zoo walking map listing the location of each animal. Each child might also be given a sticker book for collecting stickers (given out at each of the animal locations) to affix in their books. Sponsors might also be invited to donate a specific pledge for each sticker collected.

Admission costs to the event should be reasonable and should include a bag of candies, the zoo walking map, a free lunch, and admission to the zoo. There should be a separate entry fee for the parents and older children. Sideline children's entertainment, like face painting, clowns, bubble blowing or other similar activities are strong adjunctive fundraisers.

Contests

Children love crazy contests, and any one of these competitions can be staged as an ancillary event at a festival, fair or carnival fundraiser: best decorated bicycle, wagon, or baby carriage; peanut shelling (who can shell the most within a specified time period), ugliest bug contest, an so on.

COLLECTIBLES

Aluminum Foil

• **CATEGORY:** GENERAL/CHILDREN & YOUTH • **GROUP SIZE:** SM./MED. • **TIME FRAME:** UP TO 6 MTHS. • **TIME OF YEAR:** SPR./FALL/WINT.

Aluminum foil collection, as a fundraiser, is relatively easy because most aluminum foil is thrown into the garbage. All your group needs to do is to educate the public to throw the foil your way. Clean, recyclable aluminum is valuable, although its price fluctuates widely depending upon supply and demand. Enterprising fundraisers can protect themselves against these market shifts by securing storage facilities, and waiting until the price is right.

Many municipalities collect aluminum as part of a blue box recycling scheme. Any organization considering aluminum collection should be aware that creaming one of the most valuable waste products from the municipal recycling stream might not be universally popular.

Education starts in school and school is the place to begin this fundraiser. Involve as many schools as possible. Demonstrate to each school administrator the value of collecting aluminum foil as part of the recycling program. In many cases it may be appropriate to approach school boards initially, seeking their agreement. Your final pitch to individual schools can be less difficult if you are already armed with board approval.

As a charitable organization, you should cite direct advantages that foil collection will achieve. For example, proceeds from a monthly sale of ten kilos of aluminum foil can be used to feed a starving child or provide a week's shelter to a homeless person. Personalization of collection results offers considerable incentive, especially if your organization exists to aid less fortunate children.

Each school participating in your campaign should be given proper containers for foil collection. You should set up a regular redemption routine so that no container overflows. Bulk storage of the foil is a problem that must be solved because the larger the quantity of aluminum offered for sale at any given time, the better price you will receive from metal dealers who are not partial to half-truck loads. Aim towards a tractor trailer full of aluminum foil and you and the dealers will make money. Scrap foil recycling is not a high ticket fundraiser, but it can supply a regular source of revenue.

Bottles

• **CATEGORY:** SERVICE CLUBS/CHILDREN & YOUTH • **GROUP SIZE:** SM. • **TIME FRAME:** UP TO 4WKS.• **TIME OF YEAR:** SPR./SUM./FALL/WINT.

As many communities institute a regular recycling program, there seems to be less opportunity to collect the large numbers of bottles necessary to make bottle collection a worthwhile source of fundraising. Don't be discouraged. Door-to-door solicitation of bottles for recycling costs nothing (except volunteer time) and, in spite of present day procedures, can be surprisingly rewarding. Returnable bottles, on which the deposit can be recovered, are the primary targets of such a campaign, but you must be prepared to end up with many worthless receipts as well. Be sure that you can dispose of scrap through the recycling process. Nothing does a charity organization's image more harm than to be seen throwing bottles collected through a successfully organized campaign onto a garbage dump.

Bottle Deposits

• **CATEGORY:** GENERAL • **GROUP SIZE:** SM./MED.• **TIME FRAME:** UP TO 6 MTHS. • **TIME OF YEAR:** SPR./SUM./FALL/WINT.

An alternative method of raising money from returned bottles is to contact your local retailer, asking that it donate the refundable deposit to your charity whenever returnable bottles are returned. Often your retailer will need to contact his/her supplier who is the final purchaser of recycled containers so this method may need significant lead time. Another possibility is the establishment of a permanent collection box at the bottle return desk. If not feasible, perhaps occasional collections can be held with the consent of your retailer.

• **CATEGORY:** GENERAL • **GROUP SIZE:** MED/LARGE . • **TIME FRAME:** UP TO 1 YR • **TIME OF YEAR:** SPR./SUM./FALL/WINT.

You might want to consider inviting a local brewery to be philanthropic by offering to double the amount raised from returned bottle deposits. Suggest to the firm that it could hold a special promotion (one week each year), during which all customers returning bottles would be asked to donate the deposit to your N.F.P. At week's end the brewery would match all donations. This is a very good fundraiser for raising media attention.

Buttons

• **CATEGORY:** WOMEN'S GROUPS/GENERAL • **GROUP SIZE:** MED./LARGE • **TIME FRAME:** 1 YR+ • **TIME OF YEAR:** SPR./SUM./FALL/WINT.

At first thought the idea of making money by collecting buttons from old clothing may seem far-fetched, but I know of a charity which raised more than $1 million over a 12-month period by holding a national button collection in conjunction with a well-known children's television program. Buttons were collected by children, youth organizations, and schools country-wide. A transportation company offered free delivery of the buttons to a central depot.

Buttons were sorted by volunteers into various categories – antique, valuable metal, collectable, military, recyclable and scrap – and were then offered for sale at special auction. Those not sold were disposed of through various dealers.

This type of campaign had three major elements:

• novelty

• a good cause

• substantial publicity

Major national charities should have no difficulty in setting up the organization necessary to run a campaign of this nature. Real success needs public sympathy coupled with a readily identifiable goal.

Involvement of children and young people in a campaign of this nature and magnitude is essential. Cooperation of a national youth organization like the Boy Scouts or Girl Guides can be extremely advantageous. Most homes have old and forgotten buttons. Your organization's mission, should you choose to accept it, is to collect, sort and sell them.

Clothing Banks

• **CATEGORY:** WOMEN'S GROUPS/GENERAL • **GROUP SIZE:** SM./MED./LARGE • **TIME FRAME:** UP TO 1 YR. • **TIME OF YEAR:** SPR./SUM./FALL/WINT.

Manufacturers, retailers and members of the public throw away vast amounts of perfectly usable clothing daily. Often manufacturers and retailers are reluctant to give away (even to charity) new, unused, but unsaleable clothing in case it should find its way back into the marketplace. A few donate clothing in good condition to charity stores, but the majority of secondhand clothing is thrown into the garbage.

Consider setting up a clothing bank. You can achieve a number of goals: raising money; providing clothes for the homeless; sending clothes to a disaster area when required; and shipping clothes abroad to countries where there is desperate need. Your group will also aid the environment by reusing or recycling thus reducing the amount of waste going to landfill.

A clothing bank requires suitable premises: something like an unused warehouse or church basement. Your collection storage site should be rent free if at all possible. Clothing banks are long-term ventures. You do not want to move. Search for a permanent location which is unlikely to be sold or leased.

Approach local manufacturers and retailers. Ask them to donate unsaleable product. Publicize your clothing bank so that people will bring clothing to you. Ask other charity and youth groups to collect clothing on your behalf. Request that your local town or city council advise ALL householders to deposit clothing in your bank to reduce the amount of garbage. Don't forget it is in the government's own interest to do so. You will make money from the clothing bank by selling a proportion of the cotton and wool collected to recycling companies, and/or by selling clothes cheaply to the needy or trendy.

Coins

Money collection in any form is the obvious goal of any fundraiser. "Look after the pennies and the dollars will look after themselves": this saying is never more true than in relation to charity fundraising. Many professional fundraisers are scornful of "nickel & dime" events but they forget that the only reason most of these people have a job today is because volunteers have put their hearts and energy into countless such events in the past. Every cent counts! Don't hesitate to collect every one.

Penny Drives

• **CATEGORY:** GENERAL • **GROUP SIZE:** SM. • **TIME FRAME:** UP TO 4WKS. • **TIME OF YEAR:** SPR./SUM./FALL/WINT.

Collect as many pennies as you can. Encourage all of your members to do the same. This should be a minimum 12-month collection period with an annual prize for the largest accumulated collection. Over the long haul, who's going to miss a few pennies here and there. Witness all the "need a penny, take a penny" offerings at your local retailers. When 12-months worth of penny collections by a substantial group of people are toted up, you may be shocked to discover the results. School children can easily be encouraged to hold Penny Drives. School classes can compete against each other to collect the most pennies within a given time. And don't forget, as an added bonus, to check as many of the coins as you can. There are many rare pennies worth a whole lot more than one cent.

Obsolete Coins

• **CATEGORY:** GENERAL • **GROUP SIZE:** SM./MED./LARGE • **TIME FRAME:** UP TO 6 MTHS. • **TIME OF YEAR:** SPR./SUM./FALL/WINT.

All of us have a few obsolete coins lying forgotten in the bottom of a drawer or in an old box in the basement. Many of us have small collections of old coins accumulated during childhood, which we've forgotten about or in which we've lost interest. Why not start a long term project to collect old and obsolete coins. Begin by informing all your staff, members and volunteers that old coins can be valuable and that many have scrap value exceeding their face value. Encourage your associates to collect old coins at every opportunity. Announce to the press that your organization will accept any old or obsolete coins as donations and will issue receipts for the face value of the same. Add a line to every piece of literature that you distribute: *"We collect old coins for . . . . Donations welcome."*

Column of Coins

• **CATEGORY:** FITNESS, SPORTS & SOCIAL/GENERAL• **GROUP SIZE:** SM. • **TIME FRAME:** UP TO 6 MTHS. • **TIME OF YEAR:** SPR./SUM./FALL/WINT.

One method of collecting for charity in bars, restaurants and offices is to start a column of coins. You will need a disc of wood about the size of a tea plate with a foot-long length of broom handle attached to the centre like a small flagpole. Cut a slot in the top of the pole and insert a card with your organization's name and the words, *"COLUMN of COINS for (whatever)."* Place sufficient coins around the base to initiate the column collection and **watch how fast it grows**.

Silver Mountain

• **CATEGORY:** GENERAL • **GROUP SIZE:** SM./MED. • **TIME FRAME:** UP TO 6 MTHS. • **TIME OF YEAR:** SPR./SUM./FALL/WINT.

Build a papier-mâché mountain. Stick silver coins on to your structure with water-soluble glue. Place a few silver coins around the base as well to give people an idea of what is required. Set a display with proper signage and an explanation in a local shopping mall, perhaps in a large department store, or any reasonably secure place, and invite people to add their own coins to cover the mountain. The structure can be as large or small as you wish and, if tastefully done, might even become a permanent feature.

Foreign Coins

• **CATEGORY:** GENERAL • **GROUP SIZE:** LARGE • **TIME FRAME:** 1 YR+ • **TIME OF YEAR:** SPR./SUM./FALL/WINT.

Anyone travelling abroad knows that foreign coins collected have no value at home because banks will not exchange them, despite the fact that large denominations of some foreign coins can be worth five dollars or more. To change the coins to cash, you will need sufficient quantity and possibly a foreign exchange bureau, if the head office of your bank will not oblige. If any of your members travel abroad regularly, and are willing to make exchanges out of the country, you can use that alternative. Passengers arriving at international air- and seaports are usually only too pleased to donate their foreign coins to charity, given the opportunity. You can make this easier for them by placing large collection boxes at suitable locations. Collecting sufficient coinage from any one country to make an exchange worthwhile may take time but – time is on your side.

• **CATEGORY:** GENERAL • **GROUP SIZE:** MED./LARGE • **TIME FRAME:** 1 YR+ • **TIME OF YEAR:** SPR./SUM./FALL/WINT.

If access to an international port is not possible, you can hold a foreign coin collection drive in your community. Advertise the fact that you will accept any and all foreign coins for charity. You will be amazed how many people make donations. If you are unable to secure a worthwhile exchange on the collection, consider the scrap value of the coins. This often exceeds the face value.

Exchange Rate Differences

• **CATEGORY:** GENERAL • **GROUP SIZE:** SM./MED./LARGE • **TIME FRAME:** UP TO 1 YR. • **TIME OF YEAR:** SPR./SUM./FALL/WINT.

Sometimes merchants in a town on or adjacent to a national border will exchange coins from the neighbouring country at face value or par despite the fact that they may be worth substantially more. This happens often in Canada as American coins can be worth as much as 40% more than coins of the same Canadian denomination. Offer to purchase all American currency in Canadian funds at face value, and your charity will obtain a substantial increase in revenue received. Exchanging the currency should not present a problem because of the regular trade between the two countries.

World's Longest Coin Line

• **CATEGORY:** GENERAL • **GROUP SIZE:** SM./MED. • **TIME FRAME:** UP TO 6 MTHS. • **TIME OF YEAR:** SPR./SUM./FALL/WINT.

Check *The Guinness Book of Records* for the current world's record for placing coins in a single line. Can you beat that?

Probably not, but it doesn't matter. The attempt to break the world's record will encourage people to lay down their coins and, at the end of the day, all the coins belong to you. If you don't break the record this year, you can always try again next year.

The simplicity of organizing this event makes it suitable for any organization. You will need a very busy public place, a supply of double sided scotch tape, a few sign boards and a group of "minders." Simply ask every passer-by to add a few coins to the line.

World's Tallest Unsupported Coin Tower
• **CATEGORY:** GENERAL • **GROUP SIZE:** SM./MED./LARGE • **TIME FRAME:** UP TO 1 YR. • **TIME OF YEAR:** SPR./SUM./FALL/WINT.

Set a world's record with a tower of coins of truly epic proportions! There are a number of considerations before attempting this venture. You need to find a very public venue which is secure and vandal proof. It will take weeks or even months to accumulate sufficient coins for a record setting tower and during that time the tower will be growing daily little by little. The taller the coin tower, the more people will be encouraged to add coins, so you must devise a way of increasing the tower height without knocking the whole thing over. Best of luck.

Cutlery Collection
• **CATEGORY:** GENERAL • **GROUP SIZE:** LARGE • **TIME FRAME:** 1 YR+ • **TIME OF YEAR:** SPR./SUM./FALL/WINT.

One British charity raised several million dollars by holding a nation-wide collection of obsolete cutlery. The idea to donate metal came from a similar drive during the Second World War when the British government encouraged all residents to donate metal pots, pans and cutlery to be melted down and reused in weapons manufacture. Every household always has oddments of unused cutlery lying around in various drawers and cupboards. Many of these utensils are made from high quality steel, much of it plated with silver or gold, with high scrap value. People may also have valuable pieces of antique cutlery without realizing it. Your group would collect all unwanted cutlery items, identify and sort them into categories, and then sell them to the highest bidder. Potentially valuable pieces and sets should be sold at auction.

If you decide that the collection of cutlery should be nationwide, your national organization should be at the forefront of the operation, and should seek national publicity. Promote the collection at every opportunity, seeking assistance from professional organizations like teacher's federations and service clubs. Encourage other groups, particularly youth groups, to collect on your behalf.

Determine your central collection depot. Your suitable location need be only temporary so the owner of an empty store or warehouse may be willing to lend the premises in return for part payment of property taxes and insurance. Transportation arrangements can be a problem especially for a nation-wide drive. In England, a national carrier offered to deliver all cutlery packages, free of charge, in return for favourable publicity.

Local collections should be organized at the branch level and might well include street collections, cutlery mountains at shopping malls, and drop boxes at various locations.

Arrange, in advance, for an antique silverware expert to view all potentially salable items. These should be kept for auction. All other pieces should be sold to the highest scrap metal bidder, and there will likely be plenty of offers as soon as you announce the collection.

Postage Stamp Collecting

• **CATEGORY:** GENERAL • **GROUP SIZE:** SM./MED. • **TIME FRAME:** UP TO 6 MTHS.• **TIME OF YEAR:** SPR./SUM./FALL/WINT.

Cancelled postage stamps are valuable to collectors worldwide, and philatelist's supply companies purchase stamps in bulk in order to resell them to foreign collectors. Your group should contact offices or businesses which regularly receive large quantities of mail (government offices or utility companies are particularly suitable). Search and request that these organizations save their stamps for your charity or N.F.P. group. Make sure, however, that you've done your homework by locating buyers and determining their rates and requirements prior to starting a collection. The Canadian Guide Dogs for the Blind uses this fundraiser very successfully with the help of an extremely large group of dedicated stamp savers.

Recyclable Materials

• **CATEGORY:** GENERAL • **GROUP SIZE:** SM./MED./LARGE • **TIME FRAME:** UP TO 1 YR. • **TIME OF YEAR:** SPR./SUM./FALL/WINT.

Several of the ideas in this book use the recycling process as a fundraiser. Almost everything in this world is recyclable, and believe it or not, most garbage would be considered valuable somewhere around the globe. Challenge your members to identify recyclable materials and/or products not currently collected in your neighbourhood. Find a market for these goods. Perhaps you may corner the market, providing your organization has the resources to do so.

Signatures

• **CATEGORY:** GENERAL • **GROUP SIZE:** SM./MED./LARGE • **TIME FRAME:** UP TO 4WKS. • **TIME OF YEAR:** SPR./SUM./FALL/WINT.

Many people will sign just about anything, so why not charge them a small fee for the privilege. Giant cards are excellent for this purpose. Ask people to sign their names on a giant card for the holidays as a way of raising money for a hospital or home for the elderly.

Turn the foyer of your administrative building into a fundraising campaign by inviting every visitor to sign the wall, in addition to your visitor's book. Ask for a reasonable donation, and let every visitor know how committed you are to your cause. Would you prefer to have a pristine wall or a coffer full of funds? Regular visitors can be asked to add the names of family members or to immortalize a deceased loved one. Several thousand people can sign a ten-foot-length of wall using fine-tipped permanent markers, and the result will become a major focal point. You might want to reserve one area for celebrities and major donors.

When one wall is completely covered with signatures, start on the next. You may wish to repaint the first wall after a four or five year period and start all over again. Request signatures from everyone, including the mail carrier. Charge whatever fee you feel appropriate, or simply ask for a donation.

Record Signing

How many signatures can you affix to a single sheet of paper? Obviously, this will depend on the size of the paper, but by using an entire paper roll, donated of course, you might secure hundreds of thousands of signatures. Set a goal – have everyone in your city sign by suggesting that everyone whose name appears on the paper might well be participating in a world record. Tour the roll from school to school, with prior arrangements, and to busy public places. Ask corporate supporters to let you hold signing sessions in factories and offices. You should seek publicity at every opportunity. Ask the press to print details of times and locations of signings. Request a small donation from each person, and search out a suitable venue where the completed document can be displayed.

Signing Unusual Objects

If you are purchasing a new vehicle for your organization, why not let all donors sign their name on it in paint. Charge a reasonable fee (after all, the names will be seen by one and all for a considerable period). Don't forget that the floor, walls, and shingles of a new building can also be inscribed, for a small fee, by the donors who made construction possible. People usually enjoy seeing their names displayed in public given the opportunity.

Sponsored Collection

• **CATEGORY:** GENERAL • **GROUP SIZE:** SM./MED./LARGE • **TIME FRAME:** 1 YR+ • **TIME OF YEAR:** SPR./SUM./FALL/WINT.

Postcards, bottletops, matchbooks, coasters, paperback books, 78 and LP records, old shoes, posters, pens and pencils. What is collected does not matter as long as somebody will pay sponsorship money once a certain goal is reached. Determine that goal and begin collecting. Children can be useful allies in this campaign. Try to collect useful or recyclable objects, items that can be sold for cash, or items that can be put on public display.

Swaps

• **CATEGORY:** GENERAL • **GROUP SIZE:** SM. • **TIME FRAME:** UP TO 4 WKS. • **TIME OF YEAR:** SPR./SUM./FALL/WINT.

This is an entertaining and challenging contest, which also serves as a useful fundraiser. Give each of your members one toilet roll. Tell them they have 14 days to turn it into something of value to your organization. They can each achieve this goal by swapping the toilet roll for something else of higher value, then swapping that item for something of even greater value and so on. Usually, the more swaps achieved, the higher the resultant value. You will want to hold a formal ceremony at the end of your 14-day period wherein each member must appear with whatever objects he/she has secured. Items not essential to your organization can be auctioned, or sold for cash.

Vehicle Donations

• **CATEGORY:** GENERAL • **GROUP SIZE:** SM./MED. • **TIME FRAME:** UP TO 1 YR. • **TIME OF YEAR:** SPR./SUM./FALL/WINT.

Old cars and trucks, one-step from the junk heap, can be used to make money for any group. First you will need to come to an arrangement with the local junk yard to pay your group a minimum amount for all vehicles donated in the name of your organization. Next, mount a publicity campaign to persuade local owners to turn in their old jalopies: many will be able to receive a tax receipt for a nominal amount. The junk yard can help your cause by placing promotional signs around its area, in addition to talking to customers about signing over vehicles to your group. Don't forget, this fundraising scheme need not be limited to cars and trucks: anything of value capable of being scrapped (boats, aircraft, farm machinery etc.) can be treated in the same way as motor vehicles.

COMMEMORATION & RECOGNITION

Birthdays and Special Days

• **CATEGORY:** GENERAL • **GROUP SIZE:** LARGE • **TIME FRAME:** 1 YR+ • **TIME OF YEAR:** SPR./SUM./FALL/WINT.

Every birthday and special day celebration began somewhere and was dreamt-up by someone. Many of these special days have been in existence for a long time. Others, like Mother's Day, Earth Day and Secretaries Day, have become popular over the last sixty years. Devise a new anniversary day, one appropriate to the aims of your organization, and around which you can build a commercial enterprise. Start small but think big. National and local media love to cite commemorative special days, particularly when they carry somewhat eccentric names. Your "*Stephen Leacock Day*" could become an annual event world-wide.

Your Anniversary

• **CATEGORY:** GENERAL • **GROUP SIZE:** SM./MED./LARGE • **TIME FRAME:** UP TO 1 YR. • **TIME OF YEAR:** SPR./SUM./FALL/WINT.

When was your organization founded? What other anniversaries are specifically relevant to your organization? Anniversaries provide excuses for holding events, open houses or sales of commemorative products. If your organization has no distinct anniversary, create one.

Buttons, Pins & Badges

• **CATEGORY:** GENERAL • **GROUP SIZE:** SM./MED./LARGE • **TIME FRAME:** UP TO 6 MTHS. • **TIME OF YEAR:** SPR./SUM./FALL/WINT.

Buttons, pins and badges can be sold at a profit to raise money. They also promote public awareness when worn. Relatively expensive to produce in small numbers, they can be very cheap if purchased in large quantities. Be absolutely sure of your marketplace, however, before buying 50,000 buttons or badges to celebrate your 50th anniversary. Organizations frequently end up with large numbers of unsalable buttons, because of over optimistic sales forecasts and persuasion from eager manufacturers.

• **CATEGORY:** GENERAL • **GROUP SIZE:** SM./MED./LARGE • **TIME FRAME:** UP TO 6 MTHS. • **TIME OF YEAR:** SPR./SUM./FALL/WINT.

Contact a sports stadium or shopping mall to work with your group by offering incentives to people seen wearing your button. This idea can provide good publicity for all concerned. Advertisements stating *"On Saturday 5th November all stores in The Centre Mall will offer an automatic 5% discount to wearers of Canker Society buttons,"* or something similar, can only be beneficial to every party. A major prize could also be offered to a randomly selected person during the day or event.

Note: Be very careful in selecting the type of button produced. A 1974 Consumer Product Safety Commission (Washington, D.C.) promotion featured 80,000 buttons publicizing a toy safety campaign. The buttons were coated with lead paint, had sharp edges and parts that a child could swallow.

Commemorative Products

• **CATEGORY:** GENERAL • **GROUP SIZE:** SM./MED./LARGE • **TIME FRAME:** UP TO 1 YR. • **TIME OF YEAR:** SPR./SUM./FALL/WINT.

Significant anniversaries, major events and terrific achievements can all be commemorated with the sale of inscribed or printed products. Whether it is champagne glasses at a few dollars each, sweatshirts at $20 or silver cutlery sets at $1000, all will depend entirely on your membership and the event. A word of caution, however. There are thousands of organizations with boxes of unsold commemorative products stacked in cupboards and basements because of optimistic fundraisers who overestimated the market and failed to take orders and money up-front. Commemorative products will not keep beyond the event date.

Commemorative Days, Sites and Events

• **CATEGORY:** GENERAL • **GROUP SIZE:** SM./MED. • **TIME FRAME:** UP TO 1 YR. • **TIME OF YEAR:** SPR./SUM./FALL/WINT.

Is there something in your community's history (a building, road, field etc.) which should be commemorated? Do you or have you had someone connected with your organization whose memory should be preserved for future generations? Many communities all over the world attract tourists (and tourist money), because they have connections with famous or infamous events or people. Some communities have become famous purely through their association with mythical events as in Batouche, Louisbourg, or Rome's Fontana de Trevi. Other communities create events like the Oberammergau Passion

Plays or the Shaw Festival in Niagara-on-the-Lake, or Calgary's Stampede, or Bancroft's Rock and Gem celebration. Every commemorative event, celebration or parade, including even the Blarney Stone, was created by someone with imagination. Design your own event in history. Everyone has to begin somewhere.

Plaques
• **CATEGORY:** GENERAL • **GROUP SIZE:** SM./MED./LARGE • **TIME FRAME:** UP TO 6 MTHS. • **TIME OF YEAR:** SPR./SUM./FALL/WINT.

Commemorative plaques are often used effectively as fundraising tools, especially when raising money to renovate an old building or to build a new one. An engraved plaque, prominently displayed on the outside of a building or in a foyer, permits public recognition of an individual's benevolence. Some plaques simply laud the generosity of a benefactor; others commemorate the life or accomplishments of a benefactor nominated by a third party.

Plaques recognizing the value of an individual's donation may be arranged in such a way as to give prominence to major donors, or they may be colour coded to imply membership to a particular group. (Gold, silver, red and green plaques can all signify donations within a certain range.) If desired, the size of individual plaques may also be a way of denoting the donation value.

Plaques dedicated to the memory of deceased personae make moving and inspirational displays. Donations received for such plaques provide ideal fundraising vehicles for organizations dealing with terminal illness victims. Plaques commemorating the birth of a child or grandchild are also viable fundraisers, and help bring your organization supporters from a new generation. Plaques can also be sold to commemorate other rites of passage like baptism, graduation, coming-of-age and marriage.

• **CATEGORY:** GENERAL • **GROUP SIZE:** SM./MED./LARGE • **TIME FRAME:** UP TO 6 MTHS. • **TIME OF YEAR:** SPR./SUM./FALL/WINT.

Benefactors donating significant contributions to the construction of new buildings may also be immortalized in a foundation stone or perhaps through a specially commissioned statue. The expense of such recognition is justified by the generosity of the donor. The resultant publicity is beneficial to both charitable organization and benefactor. Always mention the manner in which recognition will be given when seeking major funding for building construction.

Walk of Fame
• **CATEGORY:** GENERAL • **GROUP SIZE:** SM./MED./LARGE • **TIME FRAME:** UP TO 6 MTHS. • **TIME OF YEAR:** SPR./SUM./FALL/WINT.

The freshly paved patio or forecourt of an office tower may not be located on Hollywood Boulevard, but it still can provide an ideal venue for your very own Walk of Fame. Invite supporters to have their hand-prints immortalized in pavement. Expect a major donation from each person honoured in this way. Alternatively, charge $20 for each hand-print. Why not invite selected people to make footprints in your pavement. The resultant "footscape" would certainly make a symbolic statement. Involve the public.

Gala Award Ceremonies
• **CATEGORY:** GENERAL • **GROUP SIZE:** LARGE • **TIME FRAME:** 1 YR.+ • **TIME OF YEAR:** SPR./SUM./FALL/WINT.

Many major charities derive substantial sums from national and international award ceremonies (Genies, Gemini awards, Junos or the MTV Achievement Awards). Any charity selected as "Charity of Choice" by the organizers of such a gala ceremony should be the recipient of a munificence of funds. Usually only "major league" charities are able to secure gala award patronage, however, there is no reason your organization should not put itself and its goals forward as a future potential for such an event, particularly if your mission has implications and benefits for a wide range of people on the national or international scene.

Memorial Service or Concert
• **CATEGORY:** GENERAL • **GROUP SIZE:** SM./MED./LARGE • **TIME FRAME:** UP TO 6 MTHS. • **TIME OF YEAR:** SPR./SUM./FALL/WINT.

The death of someone closely connected to your organization may be commemorated by a memorial service or concert, which, with the consent of surviving relatives, should be seen as a tribute to the memory of the deceased. The fact that the concert proceeds will be used to continue the work of the deceased only enhances the value of such an event.

People's Service Awards
• **CATEGORY:** SERVICE CLUBS/GENERAL • **GROUP SIZE:** SM./MED. • **TIME FRAME:** 1 YR+ • **TIME OF YEAR:** SPR./SUM./FALL/WINT.

People's service awards, when properly organized, can easily become an annual fundraising event to increase public awareness of your organization while simultaneously honouring the work of local citizens. We all know most residents of a community live their lives without public recognition or reward despite the roles they play. We also know that each community is sustained by the faithful service of its member citizens. By creating, maintaining and publicizing community public service awards, your organization can provide a much needed public service, while also establishing a fundraising opportunity.

Publicity is essential for the establishment of any permanent award of this nature. Publicity elicits candidates, creates interest, and establishes credibility. Timing is important as well. What is the most propitious time of year for a people's award candidate search and presentation? When will most residents of your community be available?

An initial announcement should be placed in newspapers at least six months in advance. It might read:

"THE _____ AWARDS"

Do you know someone who deserves an award for what they do in our community every day? Does your mail delivery person always have a smile and a cheery word; does the attendant at the gas station always wash your windshield and check under the hood; is your checkout supermarket cashier always helpful, friendly and right with your change? Many people make your life easier and more pleasant every day. We notice them, but almost never reward them.

(Our Organization) has decided to do something to acknowledge the work of all the unsung heroes in our community and on (September 23) at the City Hall (well-known celebrity) will present valuable awards to those members of the community who have been nominated for a _____ AWARD.

NOMINATIONS can be made by anyone and nomination forms are available at the following locations . . . .

OR you can submit nominations on the entry form printed below.

NOMINATIONS can be submitted in the following categories:

(Your committee can decide on what categories are appropriate. Remember, the only limitation is the number of prizes you are able to obtain.)

Follow-up publicity should be repeated as often as possible to ensure that at least three or four nominations per category are received. Make sure that nomination forms are on display in as many public places as possible. Publicity is essential because fundraising occurs only when as many people as possible pay to attend the award ceremony.

Once the competition has been announced, you will need to procure the awards, and there are a number of ways in which this can be done without having to pay for them. Convince your city or town council that people's service awards are good for the community, and that it is in the municipality's best interest to provide some awards. The Chamber of Commerce and local businesspeople, politicians and dignitaries and all the service organizations should be contacted as well. Each should sponsor an honorary award in your community. Your final awards should include something like the following:

The Town of _____ award for the Most Helpful Citizen

The Ronald Jones award for the Best Teacher of '98

The Rotary Club of _____ award for the Friendliest Supermarket Clerk ...

And so on.

Entry rules, selection of nominees and the choice of winners are to be decided by your committee.

The fundraiser and your organization should send each award donor ONE free ticket plus ten regular priced tickets. Suggest that each donor may wish to sell tickets to friends and associates.

Send each award nominee one free ticket with a congratulatory letter. Point out the fact that awards will be adjudicated by a panel of judges on the night of the awards ceremony. Make mention of the prize available to the winner. Note too that your organization has reserved ten tickets for friends and family of each nominee, and request confirmation of the number of tickets required for purchase. Do not forget to sell tickets to the public, to local Chamber of Commerce members, councillors and anyone else with an interest in this event.

Size and style of the ceremony will depend on the size of your community and the facilities available, but make sure that everyone gets his or her money's worth. Your awards gala should feature dinner, a danceband, an entertaining M.C., door prizes and a raffle.

Business Service Awards

Commercial businesses can also be recognized and awarded exactly as individuals are. Solicit nominations from the public, and from business employees, for a wide range of categories: best restaurant; most attractive store window displays; friendliest store; fastest pizza delivery; best bar; best chiropractor; and so on. Include a few funny categories such as the best-dressed or worst-dressed boss. Liaise with your local Chamber of Commerce to develop a category range which encompasses most business activities within your community. Solicit trophies and prizes, and set up an awards ceremony and/or dinner. As noted above, the ceremony is your fundraiser so you will want to create maximum publicity for maximum attendance.

Recognition Awards

• **CATEGORY:** GENERAL • **GROUP SIZE:** LARGE • **TIME FRAME:** 1 YR+ • **TIME OF YEAR:** SPR./SUM./FALL/WINT.

Bestowing honours on famous or influential people can be an excellent means of highlighting the work of your organization while also enabling it to raise considerable sums of money. Develop meaningful awards to be given annually to people in the public spotlight who have made significant contributions to your organization or to society in general. The awards themselves need not be highly valuable, but they must be prestigious. Again, fundraising is accomplished by persuading recipients to appear at a gala, concert or dinner so they can personally receive the appropriate recognition.

Street Names

• **CATEGORY:** GENERAL • **GROUP SIZE:** SM./MED./LARGE • **TIME FRAME:** 1 YR+ • **TIME OF YEAR:** SPR./SUM./FALL/WINT.

Ask a local developer if you can hold a charity lottery to name all the streets within a new development. If he or she is receptive, hold a raffle for each street to be named. The developer would receive recognition and additional on-site traffic. Your group would gain media exposure and, more important, funds. Publicity is easy and who knows what crazy and innovative results could occur. Reserve to the developer the right to veto any inappropriate suggestions.

• **CATEGORY:** GENERAL • **GROUP SIZE:** MED./LARGE • **TIME FRAME:** UP TO 1 YR. • **TIME OF YEAR:** SPR./SUM./FALL/WINT.

If no new developments exist in your area, focus on municipal streets by persuading your local municipal government to allow your organization to provide names for nonresidential streets and short stretches of access roads on an ongoing basis. Most communities must find names for new streets every year. With co-operation from your local government, your charity can turn this event into an annual raffle – or even a yearly auction – where streets on offer would be named by the highest bidders. Remember, a public raffle provides more people with a greater chance of winning, but it may generate less money than an auction. Winners should be allowed to name the streets after themselves, or other persons, places or things of their liking, as long as no conflict arises with an existing street designation.

CONTESTS AND GAMES

Bicycle Polo

• **CATEGORY:** FITNESS, SPORTS & SOCIAL/SERVICE CLUBS • **GROUP SIZE:** SM. • **TIME FRAME:** UP TO 6 MTHS. • **TIME OF YEAR:** SPR./SUM./FALL/WINT.

Bicycle polo is fun and can be a strong event in a community fair. You will need a football field and several teams of six cyclists with rugged bicycles and a willingness to ride and knock balls into a net. Invite local youth organizations, scouting groups, military cadets and the like to enter teams of cyclists equipped with hockey sticks. Charge an entry fee. Each team should be sponsored for a minimum amount. Rules should be flexible. You can make this a more serious event by featuring substantial prizes. Offer local and regional invitations to all-comers to provide teams. Again, charge an entry fee. Where legal, take bets on the winners.

Bodybuilding Competitions

• **CATEGORY:** FITNESS, SPORTS & SOCIAL/SERVICE CLUBS • **GROUP SIZE:** MED./ARGE • **TIME FRAME:** UP TO 6 MTHS. • **TIME OF YEAR:** SPR./SUM./FALL/WINT.

Bodybuilders and weightlifters are competitive people and a bodybuilding competition can become a very successful fundraising venue. Contact a local fitness club. Ask it to participate in a "Charity Lift" and to arrange a full day's worth of competition, displays and fun events. The club should provide the equipment and most of the publicity. Club members and non-members alike should compete as teams for a trophy, or as individuals for cash prizes (perhaps in the form of club memberships). Raise money from entry fees, sponsorship, gambling (where legal), and ancillary events. If there are several fitness clubs in your neighbourhood, consider intramural bodybuilding competitions.

World's Most Boring Person

• **CATEGORY:** GENERAL • **GROUP SIZE:** SM./MED./LARGE • **TIME FRAME:** UP TO 1 YR. • **TIME OF YEAR:** SPR./SUM./FALL/WINT.

Why not arrange a competition to discover the world's most boring person. There is currently no known record holder in this category, and there are no set rules for choosing one. Your organization should define rules, set a venue, date, and announce details to the press. Some people will go to extraordinary lengths to become world champions, and this idea is novel enough to attract attention.

Raise money by corporate sponsorship, entrance fees, audience ticket sales and ancillary events like draws and refreshment sales. Publicity for this type of event is often self-generating because journalists are constantly seeking something new. A successful "Most Boring Person" contest means more events in subsequent years.

People

• **CATEGORY:** GENERAL • **GROUP SIZE:** SM. • **TIME FRAME:** UP TO 6 MTHS. • **TIME OF YEAR:** SPR./SUM./FALL/WINT.

Glamorous grandmothers, beautiful babies, knobby knees, long legs and even heads of hair can all form the basis of a fundraising competition, when staged as a sideline to a major event such as a fair or carnival, or even on its own.

World's Worst

• **CATEGORY:** FITNESS, SPORTS & SOCIAL/GENERAL • **GROUP SIZE:** SM./MED. • **TIME FRAME:** UP TO 1 YR. • **TIME OF YEAR:** SPR./SUM./FALL/WINT.

Being the world's worst at anything can often be more rewarding than being the world's best. Remember Eddie "The Eagle" Edwards, ski jumper in the 1988 Winter Olympics. Eddie, who did not set out to be the worst jumper in Olympic history, became a worldwide celebrity. He was invited to appear on prestigious talk shows and was featured daily in almost every newspaper in North America and Europe.

Competitions to discover the world's worst singers, dancers, comedians, magicians, sportsmen and sportswomen of all types, musicians, orchestras – these can be good moneymaking schemes. They can also be a lot of fun for all concerned. Raise money from sponsors, entry and admission fees and (maybe even) from television companies wanting to cover the event.

Car Holding

• **CATEGORY:** FITNESS, SPORTS & SOCIAL/GENERAL • **GROUP SIZE:** SM./MED. • **TIME FRAME:** UP TO 1 YR. • **TIME OF YEAR:** SPR./SUM./FALL

This event provides a car dealership with superb publicity. Your group should have no difficulty in finding one to assist in all aspects of the car holding spectacle. A new car is the first requirement, and it should be provided by the dealer at less than cost. Next, you need a suitable venue where several hundred people can congregate on a weekend morning. What better place than a large car lot where the dealer has the opportunity of displaying stock. Sell tickets. The dealership can assist you with this as well. People visiting a car dealer are looking for a new car, and can usually be persuaded to take a chance on a free one.

Sell tickets as you would a draw. Each ticket entitles the holder to attend at 7:00 a.m. on the day of the event and place his/her hands on the car, or on a rope attached to the car. You may wish to have each ticket bear a "lucky number" for a subsidiary consolation prize draw. The price of the ticket should be such that most people will buy with no intention of actually trying to win the car ($20 perhaps).

On the day of the event, you will require a large empty space around the car and a number of ropes attached to various parts of the car. Have a supply of additional ropes ready. At the appointed time, each ticket holder grabs a rope or holds onto the car. Scrutineers disqualify anyone who loses contact. Refreshments can be provided by friends, or you can make more money by selling these as well.

As the day wears on, people will gradually drop out. Shorten the ropes and remove them until eventually only those holding the car remain. The last person holding on can drive the car home. Pray for heavy rain, a sharp frost, or you may find yourself still competing three or four days later. To keep the event relatively short, do not allow washroom breaks.

• **CATEGORY:** FITNESS, SPORTS & SOCIAL/GENERAL • **GROUP SIZE:** SM. • **TIME FRAME:** UP TO 4 WKS. • **TIME OF YEAR:** SPR./SUM./FALL/WINT.

There is no reason why the car holding principle cannot be applied to any solid object. To raise money at any event, simply produce a cake, bottle of whisky, or basket of fruit. Charge everyone in the room a few dollars to hold onto the item. You will be amazed how much fun people have, and how easy it is to raise money. Last person holding on, wins.

Car Wrecking

• **CATEGORY:** GENERAL • **GROUP SIZE:** SM. • **TIME FRAME:** UP TO 6 MTHS. • **TIME OF YEAR:** SPR./SUM./FALL

This event features teams of men and women competing against each other to demolish a car to the extent that every piece of it can be pushed through the centre of a car tire.

Arrange the competition as a light-hearted addition to a more serious motor sport, rally/race, or alternatively as part of a larger charity event such as a fall fair. Each team is required to pay an entry fee. Perhaps you can also obtain a minimum amount of sponsorship. Take bets where gambling is legal. Charge spectators an admission fee or request a donation. Make the rules available in advance, so there is no confusion. Make sure that all participants are dressed safely with gloves, goggles, and protective clothing. You will need to provide each team with a car ready for the wrecker's yard (donated either by local enthusiasts or perhaps an insurance agent). Events of this nature are inherently dangerous, so ensure that your organization is adequately protected by insurance, and elicit a written liability disclaimer from each participant beforehand.

Building Demolition

• **CATEGORY:** FITNESS, SPORTS & SOCIAL/SERVICE CLUBS • **GROUP SIZE:** SM./MED./LARGE • **TIME FRAME:** UP TO 6 MTHS.
• **TIME OF YEAR:** SPR./SUM./FALL/WINT.

Building demolition will work as a fundraising activity with any building due for demolition, but it is most effective when the building is relevant to your organization (the demolition of an old office block, for instance, to make way for a new hospital). Arrange with the demolition contractor to set aside 60 to 90 minutes for your event. Who knows? He/she might even forgo the normal fee for this purpose. Make sure that a senior operator or the contractor in charge is available to monitor controls on the demolition vehicle. Invite all your organization members, friends, local dignitaries, doctors and the public at large to bid for a chance to help operate the machine that swings the giant steel demolition ball into the building. Media will love the idea of the mayor or chief surgeon at the controls of a huge crane, even if the crane operator is actually pulling the levers. When a building is to be levelled by explosives, expect a very substantial donation from the person who wants to pull the switch. Don't forget insurance for all participants, viewers, and vehicles at an event of this nature.

• **CATEGORY:** FITNESS, SPORTS & SOCIAL/SERVICE CLUBS • **GROUP SIZE:** SM./MED. • **TIME FRAME:** UP TO 6 MTHS. • **TIME OF YEAR:** SPR./SUM./FALL/WINT.

Alternatively, challenge your local karate club to knock a building down within a specified period without using tools of any kind. Advertise the event "Karate Club to set demolition record!" and ask for donation pledges, payable upon completion. You will need a somewhat smaller structure than that suggested above, and you may wish to apply this scheme only to certain parts or areas of a building. You might also consider demolition solely with the use of hand tools, working through both sponsorship and pay-as-you-play financing. Insurance is important. Proper safety precautions are vital and make sure you have safety spotters well positioned throughout the event.

Charity Runs

A charity run has little or nothing to do with the physical act of running. A charity run is about getting from point A to point B, within a time frame, by using a designated form of transport and by completing a specific task. The winner is the first individual, or team, to arrive home having completed the task. Money is raised by charging an entry fee and/or requiring each team to obtain a minimum amount of sponsorship pledges.

The annual "Beaujolais Run" is one of the finest examples of commercial hype in existence. Every year thousands of people travel huge distances in order to be the first to lay their hands on a bottle of nouveau French wine. Charities in Europe receive very substantial sums of money from this commercial venture. Groups of otherwise sensible people use every means of transport imaginable to convey the first bottles of Beaujolais nouveau from the heart of France to their home towns, to be sold at ridiculous prices while raising money for charity. These transportation teams also raise additional funds from friends and family through sponsorship.

The Beaujolais run, as a charity event, is a recent phenomena. It reminds us that if huge numbers of people will go to extraordinary lengths to procure a bottle of overpriced, immature wine, maybe a similar event with Canadian flavour will be just as successful.

Lobster Run

• **CATEGORY:** GENERAL • **GROUP SIZE:** SM./MED. • **TIME FRAME:** UP TO 1 YR. • **TIME OF YEAR:** SPR.

The lobster season opens May 6. On that day, race to be the first to catch the new lobsters and deliver them, fresh and alive, to participating hotels and restaurants in your area, whereupon top chefs would compete to produce exquisite lobster dinners for a charity Lobsterfest Ball.

Salmon Run
• **CATEGORY:** GENERAL • **GROUP SIZE:** SM./MED. • **TIME FRAME:** UP TO 1 YR. • **TIME OF YEAR:** FALL

Different fish, different date.

Ice Wine Run
• **CATEGORY:** GENERAL • **GROUP SIZE:** SM./MED./LARGE • **TIME FRAME:** UP TO 1 YR. • **TIME OF YEAR:** FALL

Ice Wine is more rare and more expensive than Beaujolais nouveau. Produced in Southern Ontario, it is poised to become North America's Beaujolais! Publicity and promotion are required, as well as an agreement by wine producers to release new vintages at a specific time on a specified day each year.

Poker Run (or Bingo Run)
• **CATEGORY:** FITNESS, SPORTS & SOCIAL • **GROUP SIZE:** SM./MED. • **TIME FRAME:** UP TO 1 YR. • **TIME OF YEAR:** SPR./SUM./FALL/WINT.

Contestants in this event travel to a number of different locations before returning home. At each destination, each contestant collects a playing card (or set of bingo numbers) from a scrutineer. Points are awarded for speed and game scores. Runs of this nature are most successful when organized by those catering to the owners of a particular form of transport: bicycles, snowmobiles, sailboats, or even horses.

Cow Pat Toss
• **CATEGORY:** FITNESS, SPORTS & SOCIAL/SERVICE CLUBS • **GROUP SIZE:** SM. • **TIME FRAME:** UP TO 6 MTHS. • **TIME OF YEAR:** /SUM./FALL

Tossing dried discs of cow manure in Frisbee fashion is a popular competition at some fall fairs and festivals.

There is even a current world record for the event. A cow pat throwing contest is cheap and easy to arrange, requiring only the use of a farmer's field, the cooperation of a herd of cows, and several (at least 30) days of dry, hot weather to season the pats.

Domino Toppling
• **CATEGORY:** GENERAL • **GROUP SIZE:** MED. • **TIME FRAME:** UP TO 4 WKS. • **TIME OF YEAR:** SPR./SUM./FALL/WINT.

Domino toppling is a terrific and fun event, one which can be staged in any open, public space. Entrants are given a roped-off area and a pile of dominoes. Each is allowed a fixed period of time in which to stand on end as many dominoes as he/she can so that when the first domino is toppled, all others follow. Only those dominoes that fall are counted. Offer a prize for the person who sets up, then knocks down the most dominos during any one attempt during the day.

• **CATEGORY:** GENERAL • **GROUP SIZE:** SM./MED. • **TIME FRAME:** UP TO 6 MTHS. • **TIME OF YEAR:** SPR./SUM./FALL/WINT.

Domino toppling is an event which does have a world record for the number of dominoes successfully set up, and knocked down with a single push.

Your organization may seek to mount a challenge, particularly if you have a suitable venue, an area the size of a basketball court perhaps, and someone in your organization with infinite patience, a steady hand and several weeks' free time. Raise money by asking for donations from visitors who watch the setting up, and charge a substantial entrance fee for those who want to watch the toppling event itself. Make sure that you contact *The Guinness Book of Records* people before the attempt, so that you can comply with any rules and ensure that your record is recognized.

If dominos are not appropriate for your group, consider toppling books, videocassette cases and anything else that will stand on edge until knocked over.

Double-a-Dollar Challenge

• **CATEGORY:** CHILDREN & YOUTH/HEALTH RELATED • **GROUP SIZE:** SM./MED. • **TIME FRAME:** UP TO 1 YR. • **TIME OF YEAR:** SPR./FALL/WINT.

Double-a-Dollar is based on the fact that most young people are conscious of the need to help charities and N.F.P. groups, but are rarely given the opportunity to do something that will make a difference. This idea also develops business acumen amongst young teenagers while testing their ingenuity.

Working with the cooperation of school principals and teachers, offer a new loonie coin to each student at a local community high school. Each student accepting the coin, together with an instruction leaflet, does so on the understanding that he/she will attempt to double its value, by any legal means, within 21 days.

Invite corporate sponsors to offer trophies to each school, each to be awarded to the student making the most effective use of his/her dollar. Be clear at the outset that the only requirement of this event is that the dollar be returned in 21 days. Sponsors hope students will have at least doubled the coin in some appropriate manner. Entrepreneurial students may be able to generate significant increases.

Competition, and the desire to win should ensure that your organization more than doubles the dollars it invests in this scheme.

Duck Races

• **CATEGORY:** GENERAL • **GROUP SIZE:** SM./MED./LARGE • **TIME FRAME:** UP TO 6 MTHS. • **TIME OF YEAR:** SPR./SUM./FALL

Duck racing is a popular fundraising event in many communities where a suitable river or stream is available. Vancouver's Capilano River Canyon race is famous across the country. Individually numbered plastic ducks are sold to public supporters over a period of several weeks, although the ducks actually remain in possession of the fundraising group. On race day, the ducks are released into the river. The first duck to reach a finishing line is the winner and whoever holds that duck's number wins first prize. Secondary prizes are awarded accordingly.

The Capilano River organizers actually sell the ducks to entrants who can retrieve them after the race; other groups lease the ducks.

Water Traverse

• **CATEGORY:** GENERAL • **GROUP SIZE:** SM. • **TIME FRAME:** UP TO 6 MTHS. • **TIME OF YEAR:** SPR./SUM./FALL/WINT.

The Dutch have a popular sport which has evolved from the century-old skill of crossing water by the use of vaulting poles. Contestants in this event leap narrow waterways with the aid of a long pole which they hope will propel them across the water. Your organization can develop its own fundraising competition based on this sport, as long as access to a stream or river is available. Anyone not afraid of getting wet can participate. Fine those participants who fail to leap the water successfully, and/or take bets where legal. Charge admission.

Human-powered flying is an attractive alternative to jumping and can be utilized wherever there is a relatively narrow stretch of water: a river, canal, or small lake perhaps.

This should be an annual challenge event initiated by offering a substantial prize to anyone who can fly across a pre-determined waterway without motorized assistance. Additional prizes for the funniest, most unlikely, most inventive flying machine will add colour to your event, in addition to increasing the size of your potential audience. This is a fun fundraiser and should attract eccentrics as well as serious contenders. Charge an entry fee for each attempt, and charge spectators a fee to watch. Hard work is required in your first year as you attempt to drum up entrants. If, however, your group generates enough publicity, and all participants have a good time, you might have a major annual fundraiser on your hands.

One British seaside resort attracts entries from all over Europe to its annual jump-off-the-end-of-a-pier and attempt-to-fly event. A fifty-foot flight out over the ocean is about the best mark, so far.

Tug-of-War Across a River

• **CATEGORY:** FITNESS, SPORTS & SOCIAL/GENERAL • **GROUP SIZE:** SM. • **TIME FRAME:** UP TO 6 MTHS. • **TIME OF YEAR:** SPR./SUM./FALL

This event could be combined with mud playing, raft racing, or any other water event. Make sure all participants wear life jackets. Each member of a tug-of-war team should collect pledges. You will need to find a suitable stretch of water, a very long rope and several hundred protagonists. Teams can be made up of any number of people of either gender and the rules can be flexible to suit conditions. Water temperature might be ice cold or pleasantly warm, depending on when and where the competition is held. Funds are generated from sponsorship, entry fees, spectator fees, and sales of appropriate refreshments.

Pop Cans: World's Tallest Tower

• **CATEGORY:** GENERAL/CHILDREN & YOUTH /ENVIRONMENTAL • **GROUP SIZE:** LARGE • **TIME FRAME:** UP TO 6 MTHS. • **TIME OF YEAR:** SPR./SUM./FALL

Here is an opportunity to raise money and public awareness, to address environmental issues and to set a new world record. Build the world's tallest structure from used drink cans. This is an ideal fundraiser for an environmental group hoping to raise the profile of its recycling campaign.

A suitable venue is important: a public site, which can be protected, but which is in a central location. This type of event usually attracts press attention, and your organization should have no difficulty in obtaining publicity as soon as it announces that your community is going to assemble the tallest pop can tower in the world.

Cans can be collected in numerous ways: drop boxes at schools, supermarkets and advertised sites, as well as a huge box at the building site itself. An event of this nature always generates its own momentum. As people see the structure growing, they will donate more and more cans. Cleanliness is important so your group needs to make sure that all cans are empty and free of pop.

Design and building methods are crucial. Perhaps someone in your organization knows an architect or builder from whom you can obtain plans and suitable building methods. Construction itself can be undertaken by volunteers, or maybe a local engineering firm will do it for the publicity. Is there a military base or a college, or a university in your area? Experts from any of these institutions could be approached to design and build the tower just for the experience.

Raise money by requesting donations from spectators, and by selling the completed structure, at special auction, to the highest bidder with the proviso that the purchaser has to dismantle it and take it away for recycling. Additional funds can be raised by inviting passers-by – young and old – to paint their names on the cans which are then incorporated into the structure for everyone to see. Charge a small fee for each autographed can.

Dunking

• **CATEGORY:** GENERAL • **GROUP SIZE:** SM. • **TIME FRAME:** UP TO 6 MTHS. • **TIME OF YEAR:** SPR./SUM./FALL/WINT.

A dunk-tank, which drops unfortunate victims into a bath of water, ice or jelly, can be used to raise money at a variety of different events. Anyone in a prestigious or powerful position – a politician, surgeon or school principal – makes an ideal candidate/victim. The dunk-tank is usually activated when a thrown ball strikes a trigger mechanism which unhinges the seat on which the candidate/victim sits; a cool dunking follows. This provides competition because a victim's fate hinges on the aim of participants.

Eating Contests

• **CATEGORY:** FITNESS, SPORTS & SOCIAL/SERVICE CLUBS • **GROUP SIZE:** SM. • **TIME FRAME:** UP TO 6 MTHS. • **TIME OF YEAR:** SPR./SUM./FALL/WINT.

Eating contests are a glutton's delight, relatively simple to organize, and often most successful. All that is required is a venue, probably as part of a larger main event like a fall fair, and a large supply of food. You will also need plates, cutlery, napkins, sponges, and a large exhibition participation area.

An alternative and possibly a more politically correct eating contest is the "REALLY DISGUSTING FOODS CONTEST."

Your group will need to assemble a collection of totally disgusting looking, but harmless foods to be presented to each contestant who then places a value on each item: the less appealing the item, the higher its value. Friends and supporters of each contestant, and the general audience, make pledges to an M.C. who begins with contestant number one. When pledges for the first contestant exceed the value that person has placed on the food being served, the pledges are redeemed and the contestant does not have to eat the item. Failure to rally sufficient pledges means the contestant must eat the item under bid. The M.C. moves along to the second contestant, solicits more pledges and so on. Ask your kids for ideas on really disgusting foods.

All You Can Eat

• **CATEGORY:** GENERAL • **GROUP SIZE:** SM. • **TIME FRAME:** UP TO 4 WKS. • **TIME OF YEAR:** SPR./SUM./FALL/WINT.

Another eating contest involves local restaurants which offer "all you can eat" menus. Suggest a one hour charity eat-in at what would otherwise be a quiet time. Charge all contestants an entry fee equivalent to the "all you can eat" price, plus a donation to your organization. Have a prize for the person who eats the most in one hour.

World's Eating Record

• **CATEGORY:** FITNESS, SPORTS & SOCIAL/SERVICE CLUBS • **GROUP SIZE:** SM./MED. • **TIME FRAME:** UP TO 6 MTHS.
• **TIME OF YEAR:** SPR./SUM./FALL/WINT.

World's record eating contests are only possible when a specific food type is chosen to be consumed within a record time: the time taken to eat ten pounds of potato chips, for example. *The Guinness Book of Records* no longer publishes the results of eating competitions because of the difficulty in determining rules and verifying claims. *The Guinness Book of Records* only monitors a small number of eating records and these are over very short periods of time for health and safety reasons. There is nothing to stop you from organizing such an event of this nature anyway.

Records from *THE GUINNESS BOOK OF RECORDS* 1997 Ed. Copyright © Guinness Publishing Limited 1996
THE GUINNESS BOOK OF RECORDS is a trade mark of Guinness Publishing Limited.

Pie Throwing

• **CATEGORY:** GENERAL • **GROUP SIZE:** SM. • **TIME FRAME:** UP TO 6 MTHS. • **TIME OF YEAR:** SPR./SUM./FALL/WINT.

If you don't want to be accused of wasting good food, use artificial pies with shaving cream on top. Charge a small fee for the purchase of each pie: let participants throw at a variety of people targets (who will need to be prepared mentally and physically for some slapstick abuse). A successful event usually features one or more politicians or celebrities. Make sure you check the pies carefully immediately prior to the event to ensure that nothing heavy or sharp has been added to the mix. Also make sure that all targets have fresh clothing, and plenty of towels and sponges to clean themselves.

Pie throwing contests are often useful as added attractions at many events.

Gladiator Combat

• **CATEGORY:** FITNESS, SPORTS & SOCIAL/SERVICE CLUBS • **GROUP SIZE:** SM./MED. • **TIME FRAME:** UP TO 1 YR.
• **TIME OF YEAR:** SPR./SUM./FALL/WINT.

Gladiatorial events can be staged in a large hall, gymnasium or outdoors. You will need imagination, a great deal of foam padding, and crash helmets for all contestants. Check popular television programs like *American Gladiators* for ideas.

Invite numerous organizations to enter male and female teams for a fee. Your spectators are the general public who have paid to watch the fun. If possible, provide sets complete with podiums, scrambling nets and "death slides." Don't forget insurance, safety rules, and a waiver of liability from all contestants.

Egg Race

• **CATEGORY:** GENERAL • **GROUP SIZE:** SM./MED. • **TIME FRAME:** UP TO 1 YR. • **TIME OF YEAR:** SPR./SUM./FALL/WINT.

An egg race is an ingenious fundraising event especially suitable for university, college, and senior high school students and teachers.

Teams of four, each sponsored by friends and relatives, compete to transport an uncooked egg over a given distance without touching it, using only the materials provided (these, of course, are chosen to test the ingenuity of the entrants and at first sight may seem totally impracticable). It is up to the organizers to decide whether transport materials should be tested beforehand (so as to establish their feasibility). Suitable materials have included rubber bands, paper clips, candles, ball-point pens, teaspoons and similar small objects.

When there is more than one centre of higher education in your area, encourage each to enter at least one race team, or more if possible. A trophy, sponsored by local industry, should be awarded to the winning team by your charity or N.F.P. organization, and the event should be held annually.

An interesting egg race offshoot is the Hi-Tech Egg Race which maintains the basic egg race concept, but brings it up to date by inviting students and engineers to design and construct advanced machines capable of finding an egg, picking it up, transporting it over any number of obstacles, and depositing it safely into a pan of boiling water. Allow entrants at least a year to develop their robot, and place no conditions whatsoever on designs or construction. Invite a major egg marketing company to provide a suitable trophy and prize on your behalf. Publicity potential is considerable, particularly if the event is picked up by a respected television channel like *Discovery*.

Great Escape

• **CATEGORY:** FITNESS, SPORTS & SOCIAL/GENERAL • **GROUP SIZE:** SM./MED. • **TIME FRAME:** UP TO 1 YR. • **TIME OF YEAR:** SPR./SUM./FALL

How far do you think you could travel in 24 hours, without money or identification, while dressed in an ape suit? Would you be able to travel further if you were a pink Cinderella or an escaped convict?

Teams of two, three, or four persons, dressed in outrageous costumes, are all released from a specific location at the same time. Collectively, they have no money, credit cards, or identification. They can use any means whatsoever to travel as far as possible within 24 hours with two exceptions: they must not accept credit, nor can they use their own motor vehicles or those belonging to relatives and friends. Teams may, however, make travel plans in advance, providing they have not paid for the travel.

Every team arranges sponsors for each mile successfully travelled. Great Escapes have garnered much publicity and some, involving hundreds of teams, have participants who managed to travel more than 10,000 miles in the 24 hour period. A Great Escape can raise $10,000 – $50,000 or more. Start small, but think big. Arranging a Great Escape costs nothing, and your organization can begin with only a few participants. You may all be surprised at how this adventure can develop into a major annual fundraiser.

One variation of the Great Escape, specifying less distance to be covered and more suited to a small organization, requires teams of contestants to spend 24 hours travelling and collecting specific items.

Rules for this competition might specify: travel to as many towns with names commencing with "A" and obtain proof that you have been there. Or, for a hospital fundraiser: travel to as many hospitals as possible within the 24 hours and collect a signed tongue depressor at each. Or, for a religious group: travel to as many churches or synagogues as possible and collect a hymn sheet signed by a church official.

Sponsorship is based on the number of times that a task is completed, i.e., ten dollars for each town visited or tongue depressor collected.

Yet another variation takes teams, each member blindfolded, a preselected distance of, say, 160 kilometres from the starting point. Each team is taken in a different direction and all the teams are freed from their blindfolds and released at a prearranged time. Release points should be in relatively remote areas and, if possible, in the middle of the night. Each team must use its ingenuity, and without money or credit, return to the start point. First team home is the winner. Sponsorship is based on the following suggested scale.

Maximum time allowed = 24 hours

If team takes	Pledge of
24 hours.	$1
23 hours.	$2
22 hours.	$3
and so on.	

An average time should be about ten hours = $15

Guess

• **CATEGORY:** GENERAL • **GROUP SIZE:** SM. • **TIME FRAME:** UP TO 4WKS. • **TIME OF YEAR:** SPR./SUM./FALL/WINT.

This is a simple and popular idea for an office collection or charity shop counter. Cut a small hole in the lid of a sealed, but empty, jam jar. Place a few coins in the jar, then place it in a conspicuous position with a small sign reading:

"WIN HALF THE CONTENTS OF THIS JAR"

Guess how much will be in this jar when it is full.

Nearest guess wins half, the other half will go to

...charity."

To enter insert a coin, (minimum 25 cents), write your guess on attached pad. You can have as many guesses as you like, one coin per guess. The faster the jar is filled, the sooner we will know who the winner is.

Next to the jar, place a pad with three ruled columns for name, telephone number, and amount guessed.

Another simple way to raise a few dollars quickly is to make or buy a cake, and ask people to guess its weight. Each entry costs a dollar, and the best guess wins the cake. The same process can be used to raise money at any meeting or event by substituting any object of known weight for the cake. Note: When someone donates the cake or object, you will make 100% profit.

Making Faces

• **CATEGORY:** GENERAL • **GROUP SIZE:** SM./MED. • **TIME FRAME:** UP TO 6 MTHS. • **TIME OF YEAR:** SPR./SUM./FALL/WINT.

Most people are prepared to make fools of themselves to raise money for charity, and this type of competition provides ample opportunity to do so. Charge a small fee to each participant, either as part of a larger event or as a major competition. Each contestant will assume several contorted face postures. Select your judges carefully. Charge spectators a fee – perhaps you may chose to select your winner based on spectator approval. (There is a very popular annual world championship held in England where they use the term *gurning* for this event.) You may be surprised at the amount of publicity generated.

Laughing Contest

• **CATEGORY:** GENERAL • **GROUP SIZE:** SM./MED. • **TIME FRAME:** UP TO 6 MTHS. • **TIME OF YEAR:** SPR./SUM./FALL/WINT.

The funniest, longest, loudest, most infectious, and most ridiculous laughs all stand a chance of winning this competition. Your organization will need an indoor or outdoor theatre, and teams of comedians to keep contestants, and the audience in stitches for hours on end. Perhaps your group contains some amateur comics or standup hopefuls. Alternatively, you could stage a simultaneous comedy competition charging an entry fee for hopeful stars. Add crazy events like pie throwing, spaghetti eating, and face making contests to make a full day's event. Why not hold a "straight face competition" to discover who can keep a straight face the longest when confronted by barrages of stupid jokes, whoopee cushions, and other laugh-inducing antics. Last one to laugh is the winner.

Screaming and Noise-Making Contests

• **CATEGORY:** FITNESS, SPORTS & SOCIAL/SERVICE CLUBS • **GROUP SIZE:** SM./MED. • **TIME FRAME:** UP TO 4WKS.
• **TIME OF YEAR:** SPR./SUM./FALL/WINT.

Screaming contests combine well with laughing contests. Alternatively, a screaming contest can also be arranged as a major event. Award prizes for the longest scream; the loudest; shrillest; most bloodcurdling; most ridiculous or humorous; and so on. Sponsorship, in the form of prizes, is essential. Any number of related shouting and calling events can also be included: hog calling, duck calling, yodelling, and animal sound imitation.

Handshaking

• **CATEGORY:** GENERAL • **GROUP SIZE:** SM./MED. • **TIME FRAME:** UP TO 1 YR. • **TIME OF YEAR:** SPR./SUM./FALL/WINT.

An attempt on the world handshaking record requires considerable planning. Where can you find at least 20,000 people within eight hours who would be willing to shake hands with you, and make a donation to your organization at the same time? The potential reward for finding a suitable venue is considerable. You might achieve a world record and, if the average donation was a mere 50 cents, you would raise $10,000. A perfect location for such an endeavour is a major sporting event, if organizers would be willing to promote the attempt throughout the day.

Hay Bale Rolling

• **CATEGORY:** FITNESS, SPORTS & SOCIAL/GENERAL • **GROUP SIZE:** SM./MED. • **TIME FRAME:** UP TO 1 YR. • **TIME OF YEAR:** FALL

Canadian fields are littered with huge cylindrical bales of hay and straw in summer and fall. Have you ever wondered what it would take to roll one of those huge bales of hay over a one-kilo-metre course? In Tasmania, Australia, there is an annual hay bale rolling championship over a 164-foot course, but to date there appears to be no history of attempts of a one-kilometre event.

Your organization might consider staging a world championship hay bale rolling event over a record distance of one kilometre. Solicit farmers, weightlifters, firefighters, police officers and others to vie in a wide range of hay bale rolling competitions including an obstacle race, 50-metre sprint, and 4 x 100 metre relay.

As always, publicity is the key to any activity of this nature and when properly organized, there is no reason why you should not receive considerable media attention. Of course, should your group set a world record in one year, it will need to organize a similar event in subsequent years to give challengers an opportunity to break it.

Charge an entry fee for each team, an entrance fee for spectators, and make money from a barbecue or pig-roast, and rides in a horse-drawn hay wagon. The fundraising potential is enormous and so are the hay bales, which should be borrowed for the day from a local farmer. Make sure you ask him/her to deliver and collect.

And it may be wise to look into insurance. Those round bales of hay weigh several hundred pounds each.

Hands Around . . .

• **CATEGORY:** GENERAL • **GROUP SIZE:** SM./MED./LARGE • **TIME FRAME:** UP TO 6 MTHS. • **TIME OF YEAR:** SPR./SUM./FALL

Perhaps "Hands Around the World" is stretching it a bit far but a recent "Hands Across America" event involved more than 5-million people. By inviting people to link hands to show solidarity with your cause, you increase public awareness of your organization. Hold a collection while people are linked together. It's a captive audience, unlikely to run away. Your cause must be readily identifiable, and your group must provide something tangible to hold hands around, or across. Publicity will bring out supporters.

"Impossible" Journeys

• **CATEGORY:** GENERAL • **GROUP SIZE:** LARGE • **TIME FRAME:** 1 YR+ • **TIME OF YEAR:** SPR./SUM./FALL/WINT.

The Terry Fox Run was an impossible journey by someone totally committed to his cause. Terry's attempt to run across Canada from the Atlantic to the Pacific, has raised in excess of $47-million for cancer since 1981 and has immortalized the Terry Fox name worldwide. Paraplegic, Rick Hansen's "Man in Motion" fundraising venture in 1987 took him around the world in his wheelchair and raised more than $23-million. "Man in Motion" is still raising money ten years later, as are the commemorative Terry Fox runs each September.

Challenges

• **CATEGORY:** GENERAL • **GROUP SIZE:** SM./MED./LARGE • **TIME FRAME:** UP TO 6 MTHS. • **TIME OF YEAR:** SPR./SUM./FALL/WINT.

Why do people climb mountains? Run marathons? Why do people participate in difficult, dangerous and exhausting events? Humans have a constant need to prove themselves – to beat a record, or set a new one. Your organization may be able to turn ambition into a fundraiser by considering challenge as a money raising vehicle. The more unusual, difficult, painful, or dangerous the challenge presented, the more likely people are to enter and the higher the attraction for sponsors. Many spectators watch motor races because of the challenge and also because of the danger. This is true of boxing, and in hockey where many fans enjoy the fights more than the goals.

Challenges can be simple – a sponsored bungee jump, parachute jump, or stair climbing in a particularly tall building. To be newsworthy and financially rewarding, however, a challenge must be unique and interesting. How many? How far? How fast? – these are just a few questions which should be posed to discover an appropriate test. How many people can cross a lake in a bathtub? How far can a contestant carry a refrigerator? How fast can a person scramble down the side of a notable building? You be the judge.

Outrageous Challenges

• **CATEGORY:** GENERAL • **GROUP SIZE:** SM./MED./LARGE • **TIME FRAME:** UP TO 6 MTHS. • **TIME OF YEAR:** SPR./SUM./FALL/WINT.

Another off-the-wall idea. Imagine your local Member of Parliament sitting in a green jelly bath in the middle of a shopping mall because you raised $5,000 worth of donations in just four hours. How to achieve this? Find someone willing to make an outrageous commitment, and enough people who would like to see it done. This campaign works well within a closed community, hospital, school or factory. You will need a very persuasive charity proponent to ensure that the principal, CEO, or head nurse volunteers to perform whatever outrageous act is required, should the proper sum be raised.

Jigsaw Puzzles

• **CATEGORY:** HEALTH RELATED/GENERAL • **GROUP SIZE:** SM./MED./LARGE • **TIME FRAME:** UP TO 1 YR. • **TIME OF YEAR:** SPR./SUM./FALL/WINT.

Create the world's largest or most intricate puzzle to gain attention and raise money. Charge people for the privilege of helping to piece it together, and charge spectators a viewing fee. If you've set out to establish a record, do so, then sell each individual puzzle piece.

• **CATEGORY:** GENERAL • **GROUP SIZE:** SM./MED. • **TIME FRAME:** UP TO 1 YR./1 YR+ • **TIME OF YEAR:** SPR./SUM./FALL/WINT.

Jigsaw puzzles make ideal gifts for people of all ages. Create a range of puzzles which reflect the work of your organization, and have them made to suit different age groups. If you are short of ideas for suitable pictures – hold a competition. Sell the puzzles at every opportunity, and use them as prizes for competitions and events.

Karaoke Contest

• **CATEGORY:** FITNESS, SPORTS & SOCIAL/SERVICE CLUBS • **GROUP SIZE:** SM. • **TIME FRAME:** UP TO 4WKS. • **TIME OF YEAR:** SPR./SUM./FALL/WINT.

Consider holding a karaoke contest in any suitable lounge or bar. Charge a few dollars per song, and hold an audience collection. Alternatively, arrange a grand karaoke night especially for organization members and supporters, to raise money while everyone has a good time.

Kidnapping or Jail-'n-bail

• **CATEGORY:** GENERAL • **GROUP SIZE:** SM. • **TIME FRAME:** UP TO 4WKS. • **TIME OF YEAR:** SPR./SUM./FALL/WINT.

Who could you kidnap and hold for ransom? This must be a fun event with the full cooperation of your intended victim. Would local school teachers pay to have their principal returned? Kidnap someone in authority and demand that everyone involved contribute towards the ransom. A similar event, requiring the cooperation of local police, involves placing your victim in jail and inviting his/her supporters to raise sufficient money to post bail.

Look-Alike Competitions

• **CATEGORY:** ARTS & THEATRE/FITNESS, SPORTS & SOCIAL/SERVICE CLUBS • **GROUP SIZE:** LARGE.• **TIME FRAME:** 1 YR. +

• **TIME OF YEAR:** SPR./SUM./FALL/WINT.

Elvis Presley impersonators abound, as do competitions to find the perfect Elvis. A competition with a wider mandate may be successful. Why not conduct a nation-wide hunt to find people who most resemble well-known politicians, TV personalities, sports celebrities and stage and screen stars. You would attract considerable media attention, and maybe develop groundwork for an annual fundraiser.

Initially you will need a national campaign, sponsored by a TV network or newspaper chain. Look-alike candidates would be invited to submit photographs together with a reasonable donation to your organization. A panel of well-known judges would adjudicate the entries. Keep in mind the fact that regional competitions, at which members of the public choose candidates to progress to the finals, add momentum to any event of this type. Finals, involving winners from all regional events, would be held in a metropolis, providing excellent reason for holding a fundraising dinner, dance, and gala.

Your organization needs to ensure that the communication channels between it and the sponsoring TV or newspaper chain are very close, because an event like this is only successful with large numbers of applicants. Prizes offered should be generous and carefully planned to appeal to the maximum number of people.

Fundraising should occur at all stages, from the initial photograph submission, through the regional heats to the final event.

Open the Bank Vault

• **CATEGORY:** HEALTH RELATED/GENERAL • **GROUP SIZE:** LARGE • **TIME FRAME:** 1 YR+ • **TIME OF YEAR:** SPR./SUM./FALL/WINT.

Here's a spectacular event, sure to gain local and even national attention. Persuade a major bank to participate in a fundraising campaign wherein entrants attempt to correctly guess a seven-digit number that will unlock the bank vault. The lucky contestant wins its contents: a supply of money and valuable items totalling some very substantial sum. Everyone knows the odds against a correct guess (just under 10-million to 1) but you can protect your organization by paying insurance to underwrite the cost of the prize, should it be won.

Some of the prize funds, and all of the valuable items, should be bank donations, or donations from local/national corporations in return for publicity generated. Additional prize money can be paid out of entry fees which are charged to each competitor. If no outright winner emerges, the vault's contents can be doubled for a subsequent year's event, or divided among those who came closest to guessing the correct number.

Work with your bank to provide the means of collecting entry forms, and fees. Your sponsor should also aggressively promote the event to all of its customers, throughout all of its branches.

Paper Aircraft Flying

• **CATEGORY:** FITNESS, SPORTS & SOCIAL/GENERAL • **GROUP SIZE:** MED./LARGE • **TIME FRAME:** UP TO 1 YR. • **TIME OF YEAR:** SPR./SUM./FALL/WINT.

This event requires participation from local schools, colleges, universities, engineering establishments and members of the public. It is an event for inventors, aviators, designers, dreamers, and physicists, as all of these skills are needed to design and build paper aircraft. Why not make it a world record attempt by determining the details of the current world record holder. Offer a substantial prize for *any* successful attempt to set a new record. Obtain suitable prizes by approaching private aircraft suppliers: ask them to offer a hang glider, ultra light aircraft or even a small Cessna to the first prize winner. There is little likelihood of a world's record actually being broken in this challenge, but perhaps your dealer will take the risk. He/she would, in any event, receive considerable publicity. (Place the donated aircraft prominently at your event with a huge placard saying, "Donated by ... dealership.") Prize value will determine the number of entrants. Charge a set fee per entrant or, perhaps, require each entrant to be sponsored for a minimum amount. You must offer a trophy and prize to the winner, irrespective of whether the world record is broken. Remember to insure the aircraft supplier against the risk of someone actually breaking the world record and winning the plane. Rule #1 in this fundraiser: find a suitable and very visible venue – a field from a generous farmer, or even an unused runway at your local airport. Remember, you will want plenty of spectator space. Additional funds can be raised through the sale of refreshments, aviator memorabilia, books, magazines, and posters.

Paper Boat Design

• **CATEGORY:** FITNESS, SPORTS & SOCIAL/GENERAL • **GROUP SIZE:** SM./MED. • **TIME FRAME:** UP TO 6 MTHS. • **TIME OF YEAR:** SUM./FALL

An alternative, for locales by the sea or with lakes abundant in the area is the model paper boat sailing contest. Invite all-comers to design and manufacture paper boats. Award points for innovation, construction, sailing ability, and seaworthiness, plus any other features that come to mind. Make the event as simple or complicated as you wish, and arrange your prizes accordingly.

• **CATEGORY:** FITNESS, SPORTS & SOCIAL/GENERAL • **GROUP SIZE:** SM./MED. • **TIME FRAME:** UP TO 6 MTHS. • **TIME OF YEAR:** SUM./FALL

Can you design and build a boat entirely from paper, capable of ferrying a person across a lake or river. Offer a reasonable prize, and incorporate the sponsorship of your local CEGEPS, colleges or universities. This is a great event for students or apprentices. It is also a good event for teams of entrants, wherein each is sponsored to a minimum amount in order to enter. Raise additional funds from spectator fees. Don't forget the media, and make sure you have professional judges on hand, first, to ensure that no obviously unseaworthy craft puts to sea, and second, to determine the winners.

Toss-a-Toonie
• **CATEGORY:** GENERAL • **GROUP SIZE:** SM./MED./LARGE • **TIME FRAME:** UP TO 4WKS. • **TIME OF YEAR:** SPR./SUM./FALL/WINT.

One simple fundraiser at any arena event such as hockey, basketball, or baseball, is to invite the crowd to throw two-dollar coins onto the rink or playing field during the interval. Give people an incentive: provide targets. We all know the child in everyone comes to the fore when given something to hit. Award prizes for the person or persons with the most accurate throws. How do you know this? Hand out envelopes to all attendees asking them to write their name on the envelope before inserting a coin. They then toss the coin laden envelope into the ring. Large arenas and crowds should be provided with a *moving* target – a slowly moving vehicle festooned with buckets, perhaps. Anyone who pitches his/her envelope into a bucket can win a small prize, but one lucky winner should receive a grand prize for hitting the predetermined most difficult target.

Raising money at a swimming event in similar fashion can be achieved by handing out sealable plastic sandwich bags to all-comers and inviting everyone to write his/her name on the bag prior to inserting a coin and throwing it into the pool. Hitting the target is bound to be much more difficult – and more fun. Let people have as many tries as they please. You might also want to point out to interested bystanders and participants the fact that the more coins put into the bag, the straighter its course of fall through the water.

Quizzes

• **CATEGORY:** GENERAL • **GROUP SIZE:** MED. • **TIME FRAME:** UP TO 6 MTHS. • **TIME OF YEAR:** SPR./FALL/WINT.

Long before television quiz shows became vogue, people would meet regularly to participate in competitions. Any organization, large or small, can always raise money by organizing public quiz shows or similar competitions.

Although "Trivial Pursuit" is probably the most obvious quiz trivia game for use in the Canadian context, particularly because of its Canadian origins, there are numerous other possibilities. You may even decide to produce your own quiz, using local knowledge or specialty knowledge particularly pertinent to your organization. Good quiz and trivia competitions often provide fodder for books.

Board Game Competitions

• **CATEGORY:** GENERAL • **GROUP SIZE:** MED. • **TIME FRAME:** UP TO 1 YR. • **TIME OF YEAR:** SPR./SUM./FALL/WINT.

Some board games are recognized internationally (Snakes & Ladders™, checkers, Monopoly™, and so on) with championships at both the national and international levels. Consider holding area, regional, or even national competitions and finals for these games. Contact the governing body, or players' representative, for any game you consider suitable, and discuss the possibility of sponsoring a major tournament in your community. A charitable cause can provide the catalyst necessary to generate wide support for competitions of this nature, and usually the host organization is pleased to make most of the arrangements. Don't forget to seek corporate sponsorship from the game manufacturer or local supplier.

Keep your eye out for new board games entering the market, so that your organization can be the first to stage a competition. You may even be able to persuade the manufacturer or retailer to donate samples of the new games in return for publicity generated.

Singing

• **CATEGORY:** ARTS & THEATRE/GENERAL • **GROUP SIZE:** SM./MED./LARGE • **TIME FRAME:** UP TO 6 MTHS. • **TIME OF YEAR:** SPR./SUM./FALL/WINT.

Singing competitions can be held with opera, rock, rap, pop, or country & western themes. Competitions for soloists, group, and choirs give all singers an opportunity to display their talents. Usually people will pay to listen as well. The size and style of competition depends entirely on the size of your organization, its ability to provide worthwhile trophies and prizes, its choice of location, and its ability to advertise the event.

You can also stage wacky singing contests which ignore quality of voice, but highlight the sillier uses of sound: holding a note for the longest period of time, singing the highest note (or the lowest), the loudest, trilling, yodelling, or growling note, and so on. You might want to include a competition for the world's worst singer, or possibly even stage a completely separate "World's Worst Singer" event.

Frog Jumping

• **CATEGORY:** GENERAL • **GROUP SIZE:** SM. • **TIME FRAME:** UP TO 1 YR. • **TIME OF YEAR:** SUM./FALL

This is a competition for the highest and longest frog jump. You can sell frog toys, frog buttons, and serve "Mock Frog Soup" as sideline fundraisers, in addition to awarding prizes for the best frog costume and the most realistic frog impersonation. The Calaveras County (California) Fair and Jumping Frog jubilee attracts over 3,000 eager frogs and 45,000 interested spectators per annum.

Slug climbs and grasshopper hops, subject to participant's availability, are additional possibilities.

Stair Climbing

• **CATEGORY:** FITNESS, SPORTS & SOCIAL/SERVICE CLUBS • **GROUP SIZE:** SM./MED. • **TIME FRAME:** UP TO 6 MTHS.
• **TIME OF YEAR:** SPR./SUM./FALL/WINT.

Competitive group stair climbing, although popular in some areas, is limited as a fundraising event. Only a few people can race at a time, spectators have difficulty finding vantage points from where they can follow the event, and insurance companies are most unlikely to accept liability for accidents. A sponsored climb, however, is easier, and every year thousands of dollars are raised for charity by people sponsored to climb the stairs of the world's tallest free-standing structure, Toronto's C.N. Tower. If you have access to a similarly challenging set of stairs (water towers, offices etc.), you can organize an annual event along the same lines.

When arranging a stair-climbing race, locate the tallest structure in your vicinity, and obtain permission to use its stairs. Each racer must collect sponsorship pledges for the number of stairs or floors ascended. Arrange to have prizes for the first three racers to reach the top, as well as one for the person who takes the longest to complete the event. Some dedicated stair-racers have participated in these events while carrying washing machines, fridges, stoves, and other heavy objects, in order to make the challenge more difficult. Whether you permit such obviously macho behaviour is between you, the owner of your stair locale, and your insurance company.

There are many ways to make stair climbing fun, and worthy of sponsorship:

- A timed climb: the number of times up and down a short stairwell in a limited time
- Piggyback: partners carrying each other up and switching to come back down
- Balancing items: carrying various items in hands, on head, or on feet
- Upside down or walking on hands: go for the number of steps covered
- Backwards: climb the stairs backwards
- On hands and knees: this is actually a crawl so have plenty of kneepads available
- Costumed: wear outlandish clothes and costumes
- Stair climb on fitness club stair-climbing machines

Warning – stairs are dangerous. Take all appropriate precautions and get a cast-iron disclaimer signed by every participant. Have a medical attendant standing by.

Storytelling Contest

• **CATEGORY:** GENERAL • **GROUP SIZE:** SM./MED./LARGE • **TIME FRAME:** UP TO 1 YR. • **TIME OF YEAR:** SPR./SUM./FALL/WINT.

Storytelling is an art enjoyed by both young and old and a popular fundraiser, in all languages. Charge a token fee for entering the competition, and seek participants from all walks of life. The turnout for stories told in foreign languages may be a pleasant surprise. Admission should be free, but you can hold a collection and sell refreshments. Stories should be judged on best presentation, style, and imagination. During the competition, record the stories on tape to sell later, as many people are very supportive fans of the storytelling art, and collect whatever is available.

'Thons

• **CATEGORY:** ARTS & THEATRE/CHILDREN & YOUTH • **GROUP SIZE:** SM. • **TIME FRAME:** UP TO 6 MTHS. • **TIME OF YEAR:** SPR./SUM./FALL/WINT.

There is no question that almost any sport, pastime, hobby, or activity can become a moneymaker if it is turned into a 'thon. Very often events that would occur anyway can be turned into a charity event by the simple addition of the suffix 'thon. A weekly swim at the local pool can become a swim-a-thon, a school spelling test can be a spell-a-thon, an hour's quiet reading can be turned into a read-a-thon. Ski-a-thon, skate-a-thon, eat-a-thon, sew-a-thon, knit-a-thon, type-a-thon, wake-a-thons, radio-a-thons etc. – the list is almost endless. 'Thons are easy to organize, guaranteed to raise money and are fun for the participants.

World Records

• **CATEGORY:** GENERAL • **GROUP SIZE:** SM./MED/LARGE . • **TIME FRAME:** UP TO 1 YR. • **TIME OF YEAR:** SPR./SUM./FALL/WINT.

World record attempts usually guarantee exposure and publicity for any event or group. Here is a list of world record categories which can be used as sponsored events, spectator fee events, or events with entry fees for the participants. Check with *The Guinness Book of Records* prior to staging your event, so that you, and your partici-pants, know exactly what goal is to be exceeded.

- Largest Bonfire
- Tallest Maypole
- Longest Debate
- Tallest Snowman
- Most Dominos Toppled
- Tallest Scarecrow
- The Most Handshakes
- Most Scheduled Passenger Flights in a Day
- Largest House of Cards
- Longest Line of Coins
- Longest Single Apple Peel
- The Most Onions Peeled
- Longest Barrel Roll
- Pancake Toss
- Barrow Push
- Pram Push
- Most People on a Two-Wheeled Bicycle
- Fastest Bricklaying
- Largest Sand Castle
- The Most Shoe Shines
- Brick Throwing
- Largest Champagne Fountain
- Longest Escalator Ride
- Longest Egg & Spoon Race
- Longest Skateboard Run

One world record not to be equalled is that for eating; this is currently held by a Frenchman, who, to date, has eaten eighteen bicycles, fifteen supermarket buggies, seven televisions, six chandeliers, and a Cessna light aircraft.

DINNERS, DANCES AND PARTIES

Cruising Events

• **CATEGORY:** GENERAL • **GROUP SIZE:** SM./MED./LARGE • **TIME FRAME:** UP TO 1 YR. • **TIME OF YEAR:** SPR./SUM./FALL

Charity cruises raise significant money whether the vehicle of choice be a river boat, a lake steamer, or even a full-sized cruise liner. Hire the entire boat, or part thereof, organize food, music, dancing, gambling, and anything else that will help sell tickets. Any event held on dry land can be held on board a boat. The next time you're organizing a fundraiser, ask yourself, "Would this attract more people if it was held afloat?"

• **CATEGORY:** GENERAL • **GROUP SIZE:** SM./MED.• **TIME FRAME:** /UP TO 1 YR.• **TIME OF YEAR:** SPR./SUM./FALL/WINT.

Ship owners frequently offer special group cruise bookings with substantial discounts. Sometimes, they will also provide a number of free trips to disadvantaged people. Your group should forward a proposal to a local cruise company offering to purchase a large number of tickets at a discount rate, if the company, in return, will provide a certain percentage of free tickets for distribution to your disadvantaged clients. Sell the discounted tickets to your members at full price and use the free tickets to take people, who would not normally attend, on a cruise of a lifetime.

Charity Cruise

• **CATEGORY:** HEALTH RELATED/GENERAL • **GROUP SIZE:** LARGE.• **TIME FRAME:** 1 YR+ • **TIME OF YEAR:** SPR./SUM./FALL/WINT.

Why not rent a cruise ship to hold your own four- or five-day event dedicated solely to your cause. Such an undertaking takes many years to organize, but it can net a substantial sum. You will require an itinerary and schedule to attract large sponsors and generous philanthropists to your cause.

A major environmental organization could utilize this idea to educate supporters while introducing them to endangered plant and animal species or locales.

Cruise the Caribbean with superstars, celebrities, sports personalities, and high profile politicians as shipmates, each hosting elegant dinners followed by dancing to the sounds of top musicians. Fundraising events like designer fashion shows, art auctions, book signings, lectures and screenings would be held daily wherein your charity would be receiving an agreed percentage of the ship's revenues. A fundraiser's dream surely but charity cruises are staged many times in many locations every year.

Dances and Balls

• **CATEGORY:** GENERAL • **GROUP SIZE:** SM./MED./LARGE • **TIME FRAME:** UP TO 6 MTHS. • **TIME OF YEAR:** SPR./SUM./FALL/WINT.

Fundraising dances and balls come in as many shapes, types, and sizes as the dancers themselves, and because people have been dancing for charity for hundreds of years, it would be almost impossible to dream up a totally novel idea in this field.

Gala charity balls held in a fashionable club or ballroom, with several well-known bands and celebrity singers, can easily raise hundreds of thousands of dollars, while a hop in the high school gymnasium may net a couple of hundred. Additional revenues are raised from the sale of refreshments, door prizes, raffles, dance competitions, auctions of choice items and so on.

Here are some popular and successful dance schemes:

Seasonal Dances

Every season provides a new opportunity to hold a different dance: Winter Wonderland Balls, Spring Fever Hops, Midsummer Night Madness, Fall Hoe-Downs and so on.

Theme Dances

Theme dances are based on books, movies, historical events, myths, or anything relevant to the members of a specific organization. A Garden of Eden Ball to a Star Trekkies Trek: the possibilities are countless.

Anniversary Dances

Anniversaries particularly relevant to an organization are always excellent gala dates, but don't forget national, international, and local anniversaries: New Year's Eve, St. Patrick's Day, St.

Valentine's Day, and Halloween are anniversaries commonly used for dances. National holidays like Canada Day and St. Jean Baptiste Day are also popular.

Costume Dances

Masked balls and costume dances can all be extremely successful when staged in the right location at the right time. Allow guests to choose their own costumes or suggest an overall theme.

Cross-Dress Dance

A particularly appropriate fundraiser for gay and lesbian groups.

Era Dances

One popular method of selecting the style of a dance is to choose a specific decade, centring all music, costume, refreshments, and decor around that period. 20's, 30's and 40's dances are obviously popular with the older generation. Baby boomers would prefer the 60's and younger generations will undoubtedly expect music from the 70's and 80's.

Recycled Dance

• **CATEGORY:** ENVIRONMENTAL • **GROUP SIZE:** SM./MED. • **TIME FRAME:** UP TO 1 YR. • **TIME OF YEAR:** SPR./SUM./FALL/WINT.

As a means of publicizing a recycling campaign, hold a recycling dance. You will want to create an event that symbolizes the concept of recycling by promoting the use of recycled materials, wherever possible. Everything should be made from previously used products, except the food. Guests should be required to wear secondhand clothing or costumes made from waste materials. Many musicians are able to play instruments made from such things as old sinks, saws, and garden hoses – all recycled items.

Radio Dance

• **CATEGORY:** GENERAL • **GROUP SIZE:** SM./MED. • **TIME FRAME:** UP TO 1 YR. • **TIME OF YEAR:** SPR./SUM./FALL/WINT.

Local radio stations are always looking for ways to increase their listenership in the same way that charities need to increase public awareness. Broadcasting a charity dance, live on local radio, can benefit both organizations. Linking up with a radio station can provide several significant advantages: the station will usually provide the host, amplification equipment, and music. The event will receive considerable free advertising on the radio because it is in the station's interest to have a large audience.

More people will attend just because of the broadcast. Whenever you think of organizing a dance, talk to the programme manager of your local radio station first.

Dinners

Dinners traditionally provide an opportunity for any organization to raise money from supporters at least once per annum, and every charity and N.F.P. group, regardless of size, should hold such a dinner. This need not be a $1,000 a plate affair, and guest speakers are not required to be well-known celebrities or educators (although it certainly helps the bank balance if they are). The size, style, and cost of your annual dinner should reflect your membership and supporters. Use this event to reward special personal efforts as well as donors.

Some dinners work as fundraisers because of their exclusivity (locale, chef, guests, entertainment, and/or social advantage). Should this be the case with an event sponsored by your organization, make sure that the cover or ticket charge is appropriate.

Theme Dinner Parties

• **CATEGORY:** GENERAL • **GROUP SIZE:** SM./MED. • **TIME FRAME:** UP TO 6 MTHS. • **TIME OF YEAR:** SPR./SUM./FALL/WINT.

Most dinner parties can be enlivened with a theme. This might incorporate costumes, or fancy dress for all. Consider having a dinner cooked by gourmet chefs in front of your guests. Alternatively, how about singing/dancing waiters and waitresses. Perhaps your local theatre group could perform as bus persons.

Fundraising Dinner

• **CATEGORY:** GENERAL • **GROUP SIZE:** SM./MED./LARGE • **TIME FRAME:** UP TO 1 YR. • **TIME OF YEAR:** SPR./SUM./FALL/WINT.

A straightforward fundraising dinner holds no pretensions as to its raison d'être. You will gather together people who are believed to have the power and the money to back your organization (a relatively small group of 18 or 20). Following a gourmet dinner, with excellent wine, your president should give a short speech outlining the work being carried out by your group and how much money is required to continue the mission, turning when finished to a committed donor (one who has already agreed to give a substantial donation), and asking outright what amount the patron is prepared to contribute. Upon receiving a positive reply, your president should then query the other guests in turn. It is a brave soul who will answer, "Nothing."

Pyramid Dinners

• **CATEGORY:** GENERAL • **GROUP SIZE:** SM./MED./LARGE • **TIME FRAME:** UP TO 6 MTHS. • **TIME OF YEAR:** SPR./SUM./FALL/WINT.

Pyramid dinners are an excellent means of raising modest amounts of money for any organization, large or small. The pyramid begins when your president and each of the organization's executive members host a dinner party at home, to be attended by organization members and some guests. Everyone attending is solicited for a donation to the organization, in addition to being required to host a similar party. Guests at the second party are solicited for a donation and asked to host another party and so on. Set specific dates for fundraisers of this nature, or the prevaricators will win out.

Each party host should recover food and drink costs from donations received as they wish. Style and cost of the dinners, and the donations requested, depend entirely upon the means of the people involved. Pyramid parties gradually peter out, so do not be shy about reintroducing them after a respectable rest period.

Note: These pyramid parties also provide ideal opportunities for new member recruitment.

Anniversary Dinners

• **CATEGORY:** GENERAL • **GROUP SIZE:** SM./MED./LARGE • **TIME FRAME:** UP TO 1 YR. • **TIME OF YEAR:** SPR./SUM./FALL/WINT.

Almost any anniversary can be celebrated with a fundraising dinner. Think about all of the traditional celebrations – New Year's Eve, St. Valentine's Day, Halloween, Skull, and Ta Chiu. Also consider all anniversaries unique to your organization: Founder's Day; President's Night; and other significant milestones such as 50th anniversaries. Public holidays and national anniversaries such as St. Jean Baptiste Day, International Literacy Day, Victoria Day, Canada Day, and Mother's or Father's Day can also provide ideal opportunities to hold a special dinner, as many people already eat out on those occasions, and may welcome a chance to celebrate with a like-minded group.

Dinnerless Dinners

• **CATEGORY:** GENERAL • **GROUP SIZE:** SM./MED./LARGE • **TIME FRAME:** UP TO 6 MTHS. • **TIME OF YEAR:** SPR./SUM./FALL/WINT.

Many organizations use the dinnerless dinner idea as a means of soliciting funds by inviting donors to buy a ticket, and stay at home.

Printed invitations, designed to look like the genuine article with the recipient's own home address as venue, are dispatched to friends and supporters with wording somewhat like this:

The Canadian Association of Parsimonious Plumbers takes pleasure in inviting Mr. and Mrs. Joe Wrench to its 4th annual Dinnerless Dinner.

This year the event will be held at (Recipient's address).

Guest of Honour – Mr. Joe Wrench

Guest Speaker – Mrs. Joe Wrench

Dress Informal

Note – Due to the high cost of hiring a hall, the exorbitant food expense, and the substantial entertainment fees required, the Parsimonious Plumbers Association once again requests that you attend our annual fundraising dinner and dance by remaining in your own home, eating your favourite meal, and dancing to any music that you like. The Parsimonious Plumbers Fundraising Dinner will take place on Monday the 6th of June, or any other date suitable to you, and we are thrilled to be able to tell you that the Prime Minister of Canada will not be attending.

Please note that because of the cutbacks in costs outlined above, tickets for the Parsimonious Plumbers Fundraising Dinner have been reduced from $150 each to $20 per couple. We welcome your participation.

Breakfasts
• **CATEGORY:** GENERAL • **GROUP SIZE:** SM./MED./LARGE • **TIME FRAME:** UP TO 6 MTHS. • **TIME OF YEAR:** SPR./SUM./FALL/WINT.

People with busy social calendars may be more amenable to attending a charity breakfast than a dinner. The key to a successful breakfast lies in your choice of speaker.

Cocktail Parties
• **CATEGORY:** GENERAL • **GROUP SIZE:** SM./MED./LARGE • **TIME FRAME:** UP TO 6 MTHS. • **TIME OF YEAR:** SPR./SUM./FALL/WINT.

A charity cocktail party may be an elegant black-tie affair, or a casual and folksy gathering of organizational benefactors. Cocktails can be as lavish or restrained as your ticket price will permit. Do not spend a fortune on the food, as much of it will probably be wasted. Attendees of charity cocktail parties are aware that the purpose of the party is to collect donations to the cause. Most guests are happy to show their face and slip away after a short visit.

Frugal Meals
Most of us eat far more food than we really need and would benefit from eating an occasional frugal meal, particularly when we can do so in support of a charity for famine relief or the like.

Frugal feast

• **CATEGORY:** GENERAL • **GROUP SIZE:** SM./MED./LARGE • **TIME FRAME:** UP TO 1 YR. • **TIME OF YEAR:** SPR./SUM./FALL/WINT.

Holding a frugal feast is a terrific way of raising money for famine victims and it is an event which can be arranged at any level of charity organization. Your plan is to hold a charity banquet with all the usual trappings: formal dress, erudite speakers, suitable music and entertainment. The meal, however, should consist solely of inexpensive food staples – the source of nourishment for millions of poorer people around the world.

A sampling:

Root vegetable soup

Bread (no butter)

Boiled rice with vegetables

Plain fruit

Water

The food cost will be minimal for this event and, consequently, the profit potential is enormous. More important, the positive message your organization sends to its supporters, members, and clients will hold you in good stead for a considerable time.

Frugal Supper Swap

• **CATEGORY:** GENERAL • **GROUP SIZE:** SM./MED. • **TIME FRAME:** UP TO 1 YR. • **TIME OF YEAR:** SPR./SUM./FALL/WINT.

A popular method of accumulating food for food banks is to hold a "supper swap." Open a well-publicized soup kitchen one evening in a local church or school, and prepare a large quantity of soup and bread. Ask local families to visit your soup kitchen for dinner, bringing with them the quantity of food they would have eaten for supper had they remained at home. That family food is then swapped for bowls of soup and bread.

"Surprise" Frugal Dinner

• **CATEGORY:** GENERAL • **GROUP SIZE:** SM./MED./LARGE • **TIME FRAME:** UP TO 1 YR. • **TIME OF YEAR:** SPR./SUM./FALL/WINT.

If your organization holds regular dinner meetings, it can raise money once a year by arranging a surprise frugal dinner. Members should be alerted to the fact that one of their regular dinner meetings will be replaced with an offering of bread and soup, although costs to your members will remain at the regular level. The resultant savings are then donated to famine relief.

Charity Soup Kitchen

• **CATEGORY:** GENERAL • **GROUP SIZE:** SM./MED./LARGE • **TIME FRAME:** UP TO 6 MTHS. • **TIME OF YEAR:** SPR./FALL/WINT.

A charity soup kitchen invites members of the public to "EAT FOR CHARITY." Your soup kitchen should be set up in a reasonably high traffic pedestrian area – one which you have received permission to use. Bulk buying and food donations will enable you to produce a large quantity of soup cheaply, and most people actually eat very little. All persons are charged a set fee for the meal regardless of whether they have one helping or six. Promote the event heavily.

Soup (The World's Largest Bowl)

• **CATEGORY:** GENERAL/SERVICE CLUBS • **GROUP SIZE:** SM./MED./LARGE • **TIME FRAME:** UP TO 6 MTHS. • **TIME OF YEAR:** SPR./FALL/WINT.

A *souperb* idea for an inner city area which focuses attention on problems of unemployment and homelessness is to make, and sell enough soup for 5,000 people. Borrow a brand new cement mixing truck (in return for publicity). Beg, borrow or buy (only if absolutely necessary) the ingredients. You might consider inviting a celebrity chef to devise the recipe and oversee your event. You will need a large volunteer team to peel and prepare several tons of vegetables. Heat the soup mixture with steam lances and (with a little organization) you could put your group's name and city on the world map, in addition to feeding several thousand people. This event is ideal for groups and charities serving the needs of the less fortunate. Involve local politicians in the soup selling process. Don't expect 5,000 people to turn out just to pay two dollars each for a bowl of soup. You must arrange this event to coincide with another crowd-pleaser event, like a giant parade.

Medieval Banquets

• **CATEGORY:** GENERAL • **GROUP SIZE:** MED./LARGE • **TIME FRAME:** UP TO 1 YR. • **TIME OF YEAR:** SPR./SUM./FALL/WINT.

Authentically produced medieval banquets have high profit potential, but require considerable planning. Location is vital. In Europe, 13th or 14th century castles/chateaux with huge banquet halls are easily found. Not so here in Canada. You will need to be truly innovative in your selection and decoration of a proper site. Consult your local library for ideas on costumes, food, drink, and entertainment.

Picnics

Champagne Picnic

• **CATEGORY:** GENERAL • **GROUP SIZE:** SM./MED./LARGE • **TIME FRAME:** UP TO 1 YR. • **TIME OF YEAR:** SPR./SUM./FALL/WINT.

An elegant way of raising money from the more affluent supporters of your organization is to hold a champagne picnic by the riverside (if you have one) on a warm sunny afternoon. This might be a black-tie affair with food, waiters, and of course, wine properly chilled and set out in ice buckets. Guests could be conveyed in horse-drawn carriages or delivered by rowboat. Pamper your guests with sparkling wine and caviar, and expect them to pay handsomely for the privilege. All of these details can be carefully worked out and scheduled but you must never underestimate the vagaries of the weather.

Picnic with the Animals

• **CATEGORY:** CHILDREN & YOUTH/GENERAL • **GROUP SIZE:** LARGE • **TIME FRAME:** UP TO 6 MTHS. • **TIME OF YEAR:** SUM.

This is a dandy fundraiser for any zoo, particularly because it is aimed especially at families. The Metropolitan Toronto Zoo has been very successful with this event as thousands of people join them every year to picnic among the animals. The entrance fee for picnic participants should be less than normal as you want to encourage a large turnout. It may be possible to make arrangements with public transit to offer a special service from major population centres to the zoo. All kinds of special events can be arranged in conjunction with your picnic-rides, lectures, petting zoos, children's races, and so on. You will want to charge for refreshments, and souvenirs – T-shirts are always popular. Zoo picnics are also excellent vehicles for increasing zoo membership.

Picnic in the Park

• **CATEGORY:** GENERAL • **GROUP SIZE:** SM./MED./LARGE • **TIME FRAME:** UP TO 6 MTHS. • **TIME OF YEAR:** SUM./FALL

It usually costs very little to organize a picnic in the park: just a permit charge, although some communities place restrictions on numbers. Food and drink can be sold to picnickers, entertainment provided, and small fees charged for all sorts of fun things like kite hire, face painting, magic shows, balloon art, and puppet shows. Additional money can be made from sales of organization publications and arts and crafts.

Picnic in Unique Places

• **CATEGORY:** GENERAL • **GROUP SIZE:** MED./LARGE • **TIME FRAME:** UP TO 1 YR. • **TIME OF YEAR:** SUM.

How about a picnic on a skyscraper roof or on the roof of an airport terminal. Both provide interesting views. Other unusual picnic venues include: the middle of a new road tunnel before opening, a new sewage separation plant before the sewage begins to flow, the basket of a hot air balloon, the tops of haystacks, or even the deck of a tug or ferryboat. Be imaginative in your search; there are plenty of places to attract publicity and picnickers.

Parties

Special Event Parties

• **CATEGORY:** GENERAL • **GROUP SIZE:** SM./MED./LARGE • **TIME FRAME:** UP TO 4WKS. • **TIME OF YEAR:** SPR./SUM./FALL/WINT.

Events of national or international importance always provide opportunities to hold special celebration parties: federal or provincial elections, royal weddings, eclipses or comet sightings etc., always provide a focal point for gatherings at which money can be made either through the sale of refreshments, foods, memorabilia, or even from donations. Happy people always give more than sad people.

Sports Parties

• **CATEGORY:** SERVICE CLUBS • **GROUP SIZE:** MED./LARGE • **TIME FRAME:** UP TO 6 MTHS. • **TIME OF YEAR:** SPR./SUM./FALL/WINT.

Whether it is in celebration of the Stanley Cup, the Grey Cup, a World Series, or any other sporting clash, a special sports party is always an opportunity to socialize, have fun, and raise money all at the same time. One giant television screen or several smaller ones can provide all the entertainment necessary. Money can be made from sale of food and drink. Gambling, where legal, adds to the enjoyment but should not be confined to the outcome of the game. Take bets based on all kinds of statistics: total number of scores; number of players injured; number of errors (baseball); number of times a commentator uses a particular word or phrase; number of TV advertisements aired during the game; number of catches made by spectators; and so on.

Street Party

• **CATEGORY:** CHILDREN & YOUTH/GENERAL • **GROUP SIZE:** SM. • **TIME FRAME:** UP TO 4WKS. • **TIME OF YEAR:** SPR./SUM./FALL/WINT.

An impromptu street party is a quick and relatively easy fundraiser. You will need to select a suitable street, and organize events of all kinds geared both to children and adults. You will raise money by selling food and drink, face painting, sales of balloons and party hats, and by organizing silly games. The great thing about a street party is that no one has to drive home.

Mammoth Street Party
• **CATEGORY:** GENERAL • **GROUP SIZE:** SM./MED. • **TIME FRAME:** UP TO 1 YR. • **TIME OF YEAR:** SPR./SUM./FALL/WINT.

A mammoth street party involving numerous charities and N.F.P. groups can become an annual event for the whole town. Plan on music, theatre, street sales, exhibitions (old cars, motorcycles, juggling etc.), games, contests, and educational displays. Make sure there are vast quantities of all types of food and drink for all ages for sale. Hold the event in a main street so shopkeepers benefit from the increase in traffic. Everyone can have fun. Each charitable organization involved could operate its own display booth or stall, raising money by providing services or selling products.

Garden Party
• **CATEGORY:** WOMEN'S GROUPS/GENERAL • **GROUP SIZE:** SM./MED. • **TIME FRAME:** UP TO 6 MTHS. • **TIME OF YEAR:** SUM.

Charity garden parties are pleasant ways to raise money, given reliable weather and access to a suitable garden. These events can range in size from a few people to several thousand, depending on the cause and location. Garden parties are traditionally genteel and leisurely affairs where guests entertain themselves by engaging in conversation while nibbling on a selection of delicacies and drinking tea or wine. Such parties provide an ideal venue for initial overtures made toward potential sponsors and major donors.

The traditional garden party usually is set in an elegant, formal garden with large areas of relatively flat lawn. Borders and displays of sweet smelling flowers add to the ambience, and provide topics of conversation. The size, style and ticket price of your garden party will determine whether it is self-catered or requires the services of a catering company. Profit margins of self-catered parties can be very high, but you must maintain excellent service. If in doubt, employ a professional. Traditional garden party food usually consists of delicate sandwiches (watercress, cucumber), cream cakes, and soft fruit, like strawberries. Background music is often provided by a string ensemble. Whether the necessary equipment and furniture will be rented or borrowed depends on availability and the size of your party.

Period Garden Parties

Any historical period can be selected. I recommend either the Victorian era with authentic costumes, a violin trio and croquet on the lawn, or the roaring 1920s, featuring Edwardian costumes and ragtime music.

Themed Garden Party

• **CATEGORY:** GENERAL • **GROUP SIZE:** SM./MED./LARGE • **TIME FRAME:** UP TO 1 YR./1 YR+ • **TIME OF YEAR:** SUM.

Themes should suit the venue and/or the type of people most likely to attend. A garden party held on the lawns of an early church would be splendid if everyone were to be dressed in pioneer costumes. Other potential themes are:

- A Viennese Tea Party complete with cream cakes and Strauss waltzes
- A theme based on a movie like "Gone With the Wind"
- A Japanese Cherry Blossom celebration party
- A May Day party

Educational Garden Party

• **CATEGORY:** GENERAL • **GROUP SIZE:** SM./MED./LARGE • **TIME FRAME:** /UP TO 1 YR. • **TIME OF YEAR:** SUM.

Consider inviting a well-known gardening expert to attend and speak at your party. A popular TV or radio garden host, or a well-known author of gardening books, would be ideal.

Roof-Top Garden Parties

• **CATEGORY:** GENERAL • **GROUP SIZE:** SM./MED./LARGE • **TIME FRAME:** 1 YR+ • **TIME OF YEAR:** SUM.

Many office towers and apartment buildings have roof-top gardens which would provide an excellent venue. Parties held in these locations can even be held in the evening, or at sunset.

Gardener's Delight Garden Party

• **CATEGORY:** ENVIRONMENTAL/GENERAL • **GROUP SIZE:** SM./MED./LARGE • **TIME FRAME:** UP TO 1 YR. • **TIME OF YEAR:** SUM.

Ask a local garden centre to display a large selection of their plants throughout your chosen garden, thereby turning it into a showpiece. The nursery should have staff on hand to advise guests on gardening matters and, of course, to discreetly promote their products. The centre should also be very active in promoting the event, and may even give your organization a generous donation in return for the exposure.

Garden Fashion Party

• **CATEGORY:** WOMEN'S GROUPS/GENERAL • **GROUP SIZE:** SM./MED./LARGE • **TIME FRAME:** 1 YR+ • **TIME OF YEAR:** SUM.

Combine a summer fashion show and garden party for a really great event.

EXHIBITIONS & FAIRS

Air Shows

• **CATEGORY:** SERVICE CLUBS/GENERAL • **GROUP SIZE:** MED./LARGE • **TIME FRAME:** 1 YR+ • **TIME OF YEAR:** SUM./FALL

Charity and N.F.P. groups often benefit directly or indirectly from aeronautical (air) shows. Many of these events are organized entirely by such groups. As with any form of entertainment, however, an air show has to have a suitable venue, celebrity performers, and a fundraising procedure.

The choice of venue is the most important. The site must be near a major population centre to command a sufficient audience, but it cannot be in a position where spectators are able to watch free of charge. The display area must be safe and away from residential areas. Your local flying club probably has a suitable facility and you should consider approaching them to discuss the feasibility of staging a show before making any plans.

Celebrity performers, including military display teams like the "Snowbirds" and "Red Arrows," as well as commercially sponsored stunt flyers, are usually available for hire.

Money can be raised through admission fees, parking, peripheral events, corporate sponsorship in return for advertising opportunities, refreshments, sales of souvenirs, flags, paraphernalia, and so on.

If the logistics of organizing an air show or display appear daunting, consider approaching several other N.F.P. groups with the idea. Each organization would then assume responsibility for one specific aspect of the event and everyone would benefit.

• **CATEGORY:** SERVICE CLUBS/GENERAL • **GROUP SIZE:** SM. • **TIME FRAME:** UP TO 6 MTHS. • **TIME OF YEAR:** SPR./SUM./FALL

If an air show is already held in your area, ask its management to allow you to provide supplementary services or additional events as a fundraiser. You might also inquire about what happens to money raised at the show. Sometimes all or part of the profit from these events is donated to charity. If so, make sure show management is familiar with your organization and its goals.

Antiques Valuation Fair

• **CATEGORY:** SERVICE CLUBS/GENERAL • **GROUP SIZE:** SM./MED. • **TIME FRAME:** UP TO 1 YR. • **TIME OF YEAR:** SPR./FALL/WINT.

Many people own antiques and heirlooms, which may be valuable, and which they would like to know more about. And there is always the possibility that the piece of junk dug out of the basement is, in fact, some immensely valuable artifact. Most people enjoy showing off their prize pieces and appreciate the opportunity of viewing the prize possessions of others. Antique valuation fairs are perfect fundraisers for stable communities in which a wide variety of antiques and heirlooms might be found. They can be held in conjunction with a local museum, flea market or antique store.

To be successful, an antique valuation fair must attract a large number of people, each bringing items for experts to evaluate. A small fee, say one dollar per item, should be collected at the time of appraisal. Additional funds may be raised by selling refreshments, requesting a donation upon entry, and by asking participating dealers or stores to provide items for an antiques raffle. Antique valuation fairs may be combined with an antiques auction or a 50/50 auction.

Here are some brief ground rules, but it may be advisable to watch an episode of the televised *Antiques Roadshow* or attend an existing event to fully understand the concept.

You and your committee should approach a number of local antique dealers and antiques experts. Suggest to them that in return for spending one day evaluating antiques, giving opinions and advice, they will have the opportunity to view a large selection of heirloom articles not normally on public view. They also gain the opportunity to make offers on items, and will make numerous contacts. You may also offer them a free lunch and, if all else fails, agree to pay reasonable expenses and an honorarium. Next, find a convenient venue. Halls and indoor arenas are suitable as long as there is ample space to set up tables for the dealers and experts, sufficient room for line-ups at the various tables, and catering facilities.

Publicity is everything. Your event should have a notable name or catchy title, perhaps something like:

"Is Picasso in your attic or Wedgwood in your drawers?"

Publicize your event through newspapers, posters, and flyers, targeting groups of middle-aged and elderly people. Additionally, you should send special personal invitations to *over 60's* clubs, hospital staff associations, school teachers, women's clubs and church social clubs. These organizations should be sent blocks of free entry tickets even if you are not planning to charge an entrance fee. You may also want to consider targeting younger people, many of whom possess heirlooms without having any concept of their value.

Don't forget to alert your local or neighbourhood television station to this event. Perhaps it would even be prepared to pay for taping privileges.

Note: A televised series of North American Antique Roadshows is being shown on several public broadcast networks in Canada and the U.S. and the producers of such programs may be seeking venues for future programs.

You should categorize the specialists' areas of expertise (paintings, furniture, china, country collectibles, glassware, toys, tools etc.) and identify that specialty by colour code. Then, as people arrive with items for valuation, issue consecutively numbered colour coded tickets to ensure that everyone sees the correct appraiser, and that specialists confer with all visitors on a first-come-first-served basis.

Collections of Artifacts

• **CATEGORY:** GENERAL • **GROUP SIZE:** SM./MED./LARGE • **TIME FRAME:** UP TO 1 YR. • **TIME OF YEAR:** SPR./SUM./FALL/WINT.

You can always raise money if you have access to a collection of any kind, or if you can persuade someone to lend you one, whether it be a collection of models, vehicles, stamps, antiques, historical artifacts, photographs, tools, equipment etc. You should be able to raise money by mounting a display open to the public.

Collections of weird or unusual objects always attract attention. An exhibition of torture instruments or a collection of wooden legs or a display of objects made from wooden matchsticks – these might all be fascinating to some people. Contact avid local collectors or hold sponsored collections among your members. Really off-the-wall collections can be big moneymakers. Consider London's Tate Gallery which sponsored a wildly successful display of old bricks. Most visitors couldn't believe that an art gallery would mount a display comprised solely of old building blocks but they paid to come see for themselves.

Craft Workshop

• **CATEGORY:** ARTS & THEATRE/GENERAL • **GROUP SIZE:** SM./MED. • **TIME FRAME:** UP TO 1 YR. • **TIME OF YEAR:** SPR./SUM./FALL/WINT.

Nothing is more satisfying than watching someone else at work, particularly if the work is artistic and creative. A craft workshop assembles groups of craftspeople who are prepared to display their expertise in return for the opportunity of selling their products.

Craft fairs or workshops differ from craft markets, in that members of the public pay a reasonably large fee for a full day's attendance during which time they can learn how to create a number of different crafts.

A successful fair must attract a wide variety of craftspeople able to display their skills at a popular venue of your choice. Begin by contacting craftspeople and vendors to assess the practicality of the event within your community: call the various local craft organizations, and/or place advertisements in craft magazines. Personal visits to craftspeople are even more effective. Artisans have an active network, so word about your proposed event will spread quickly and potential exhibitors may contact you.

Venue selection depends on the types of crafts to be displayed. You must consult the exhibitors on their requirements: electrical, light, floor space etc., and bear in mind the safety aspect.

Publicize the event well in advance. Sell tickets throughout your organization and ask your participating craftspeople to display posters and sell tickets as well. You can raise additional funds by setting up your own stall with products made by your members, by selling refreshments, and by selling draw tickets to win prizes donated by the exhibitors.

Designer Show House

• **CATEGORY:** WOMEN'S GROUPS/GENERAL • **GROUP SIZE:** LARGE • **TIME FRAME:** 1 YR+ • **TIME OF YEAR:** SPR./SUM./FALL/WINT.

Many people enjoy visiting lavishly furnished, extravagantly decorated houses and the designer show house fundraiser has been very successful in raising large sums.

Locate a suitable property: a large, unoccupied house (probably new) on the market and proving difficult to sell. Secure the temporary loan of the premises by agreeing to pay heat, hydro, and insurance. Invite a number of interior designers each to decorate and furnish a room. Invite landscapers and garden centres to landscape the grounds. Your intention is to create a dream home, one which will attract considerable attention.

Participating designers benefit from the exposure of their work. They can claim material cost as an advertising expense. The property will be more salable after your showcase. Charge an entrance fee, sell refreshments, and hold a major raffle for designer-donated items or services. It might even be possible to offer the house as first prize in a "Dream Home" lottery.

Any "Designer Show House" should be a major attraction, especially on weekends, but to maximize profits, you will need to keep it open daily for several weeks. This requires a large number of volunteers to sell tickets at the door, to supervise visitors (preventing damage or theft), and to keep the house clean.

Publicity is essential and advance ticket sales are highly desirable. Local media, and perhaps even regional or national "home" magazines should find an event of this nature very attractive.

Displays in Stores or Shopping Malls

• **CATEGORY:** GENERAL • **GROUP SIZE:** MED. • **TIME FRAME:** UP TO 6 MTHS. • **TIME OF YEAR:** SPR./SUM./FALL/WINT.

These are funny, artistic, and/or topical exhibits in convenient public locations (municipal buildings, banks, shopping malls) which will attract attention and donations. Your display should be made of suitable materials and designed according to available space, costs, and artistic capabilities of your members.

Some ideas for suitable scenes include:

• Charity Work: A display which depicts the various achievements and goals of your organization

• Halloween Display: Pumpkins, ghosts, and spiders

• Easter Tableau: Perhaps with live baby chicks and a couple of baby rabbits if you really want to attract attention. Make sure your exhibit space is enclosed, secure, and protected

• Thanksgiving Scene: Carefully decorated fruit and vegetables might be a good idea for a food bank fundraiser. Can you obtain a giant vegetable or fruit as a centrepiece?

• Nativity Scene: For maximum attention and publicity make it a living Nativity with real people and real animals

• Chinese New Year: Dragon effigies would make sure-fire attractions

The most difficult aspect of this idea is obtaining permission to set up in a suitable locale, particularly at a busy time of the year. You will need to approach the landlord or owner with a superb plan, and a persuasive manner. If you outline an attractive display, which will not interfere in any way with local traffic, the owner may realize the value of additional attracted custom, and be pleased to assist. Raise funds by placing donation boxes in various locations around your display and/or having volunteers request donations from people passing by.

Everybody's Dog Show

• **CATEGORY:** GENERAL • **GROUP SIZE:** SM./MED. • **TIME FRAME:** UP TO 1 YR. • **TIME OF YEAR:** SPR./SUM./FALL/WINT.

There are plenty of dog shows for the dog elite, organized with rules and regulations that usually disqualify the average family pet without a woof! Why not organize a dog show for all dogs. Feature special categories not usually found on the canine show circuit: best dressed dog, dog which most resembles its owner, smallest dog, heaviest dog, most obedient dog, cleverest dog etc. Charge an entry fee per dog, and an admission fee for spectators. This should be a fun event. Contact pet food manufacturers and local pet stores. Offer selling space at the show in return for sponsorship money and prizes.

Everybody's Cat Show

• **CATEGORY:** GENERAL • **GROUP SIZE:** SM./MED. • **TIME FRAME:** UP TO 1 YR. • **TIME OF YEAR:** SPR./SUM./FALL/WINT.

Cat shows for Burmese and Siamese abound, but who cares about the average ginger Tom? You can. Organize your own cat show. Your special categories should interest and amuse people: best dressed cat, owner who most resembles his/her cat, fattest cat, heaviest cat, most colourful, fastest, oldest and cleverest cat, best yowl, fastest tail etc.

Hold a children's cat-costume contest, make up some "cat" games, and give prizes for the best cat-walk and the loudest, or most realistic, non-cat generated meow. Invite local artisans to sell cat art, and to make or sell cat crafts.

Charge an entry fee per cat, an admission fee for spectators, and an exhibitor fee for anyone selling products. Contact pet food manufacturers and local pet stores and offer selling space at the show in return for sponsorship money and prizes.

Publicize the event in local pet stores and veterinary clinics.

Talented Pet Show

• **CATEGORY:** GENERAL • **GROUP SIZE:** SM./MED. • **TIME FRAME:** UP TO 1 YR. • **TIME OF YEAR:** SPR./SUM./FALL/WINT.

Why not arrange a special talent show for all the non-dangerous pets in your neighbourhood. Judging can be based on talent: talking birds, begging dogs, or jumping rabbits. Include special awards for the most bizarre pet tricks, and for the pets who look most like their owners. Charge all spectators an entry fee. Invite pet food and animal paraphernalia manufacturers to set up tables to sell their products. Charge them for the space, and request prize donations.

Erotic Displays

• **CATEGORY:** FITNESS, SPORTS & SOCIAL/ARTS & THEATRE • **GROUP SIZE:** SM./MED. • **TIME FRAME:** UP TO 1 YR.
• **TIME OF YEAR:** SPR./SUM./FALL/WINT.

Though definitely not an event for the majority of charity or N.F.P. groups, erotic displays *have* been successful fundraisers. Staging one could certainly pull in the crowds for a fringe organization. A 1995 Toronto exhibition of naked couples in statuesque poses caused considerable excitement, and attracted international media attention, especially as some of the couples were same-sex partners. Paid attendance was substantial. Displays of erotic art and erotic photographs have also attracted large paying audiences in cities all around the world.

Fetes, Fairs, and Festivals

Traditionally, fetes are one-day events held outdoors, which combine any number of simple competitions with side-shows and entertainment, together with the sale of produce and refreshments. Fetes have been used to raise money for charities for hundreds of years, probably since medieval times.

All fetes are basically the same and people will patronize yours only if you have sold them the idea that yours is worth attending. Be creative, inventive, and even outrageous.

How about a "Midsummer Night's Fete" in December. Turn the heating up high and feature stalls selling summer drinks, barbecued ribs, ice cream, and cotton candy. Because traditional summer fruits and produce are available all year-round, you can sell these or use them as prizes. Furnish the hall with garden furniture and beach umbrellas. Ask all staff to wear shorts and T-shirts and, if you dare, hold a bathing suit beauty contest.

Fairs or festivals are held world-wide on all types of occasions and for all sorts of reasons. Many are specific to a particular region or country, and rely on specific local customs and conditions. Others can be successfully organized anywhere. Every fair or festival was started by someone or some organization to celebrate or commemorate something. Certain well-known festivals such as Thanksgiving, summer solstice, and Halloween have their roots in ancient religious and cultural rites and are used today by various groups as occasions for fundraising. The resurrection of an ancient festival could provide an interesting basis for a fundraising event, especially if the festival has some relevance to the organizing group. There are no set rules, and almost no limit to the possible themes. Organizing an annual festival/fair is a major undertaking but, when successful, can generate considerable income. Fair components, while always flexible, include side shows and entertainment, sports and games, food, and drink – all produced around a central theme. Money is generated in numerous ways. The organizing body can obtain sponsorship from advertisers and supporters; there are exhibitor fees, entrance fees, and additional funds accrue through the selling of services and products. Infrequent natural events such as the appearance of a comet, a solar eclipse, or an exceptional low or high tide could also provide reasons for holding a festival.

Natural Festivals

• **CATEGORY:** ENVIRONMENTAL/GENERAL • **GROUP SIZE:** SM./MED./LARGE • **TIME FRAME:** UP TO 1 YR. • **TIME OF YEAR:** SPR./SUM./FALL/WINT.

Celebrate Earth Day or Week, the end of winter, the start of spring, midsummer's day, the harvest, or any other significant natural event with a festival. Pageants and festivals are held around the world to mark passing of the seasons, arrival and departure of migrating birds and animals, the planting of seeds and harvesting of crops. Summer solstice is usually celebrated on June 21 in Canada, but celebrated on June 5 by people of the Taoist religion.

Seasonal Fairs

• **CATEGORY:** GENERAL • **GROUP SIZE:** SM./MED./LARGE • **TIME FRAME:** UP TO 1 YR. • **TIME OF YEAR:** SPR./SUM./FALL/WINT.

Spring Fairs: Celebrate the start of the new year with sales of seeds and seedlings. Nunavut's Toonik Tyme Spring Fair features snowhouse building competitions and dogsled races.

Maple Sugar Fairs: Feature demonstrations of sugaring at a sugar shack, with guided tours of the bush and huge meals of pancakes and sausages all covered with maple syrup.

May Fairs: These may include musical concerts, singing, and dancing. Art shows and strawberry teas will make this a success. What about dancing around a maypole on May Day? Ottawa runs its Tulip Fest celebration in May. Irish Maytime fairies stage their revels in May. Japan's Hollyhock festival is held in Kyoto each May.

Midsummer Fairs: What better way to spend a warm summer evening than with music, dancing, street theatre, and stalls selling ice-cold drinks and delicious food. Mahone Bay, Nova Scotia, holds its wooden boat festival with races, boat-building demon-strations, fireworks, music, and a trade fair in August. The Bunol, Spain, Tomatina festival also occurs in August when all residents of the town engage in frenzied bouts of tomato slinging.

Fall Fairs, Festivals, and Harvest Fairs: Arts and crafts made from leaves and fruit will make this fair a colourful event. Jams and preserves of all types will be in big demand. Fruit, vegeta-bles, and flowers can all be used in a wide range of competitions. Who can make the best scarecrow? Threshing festivals are pop-ular as well.

Oktoberfest: Beer and oompah bands are the mainstays of this festival which has enjoyed great success in Ontario and British Columbia.

Winter Fairs: Ice sculpting, snowman making, and lots of ski-ing and skating competitions. Hot soup around a roaring fire. Quebec's ten-day Winter Carnival is the world's largest.

Birthday and Anniversary Fairs

St. Valentine's Day Fair, Mickey Mouse Birthday Fair (November 18), Dr. Seuss Birthday Fair (March 2), Elvis Presley Birthday Fair (January 8), Mardi Gras.

Fairs and festivals with more unusual themes can be held almost anywhere:

Herb Festival
• **CATEGORY:** HEALTH RELATED/WOMEN'S GROUPS • **GROUP SIZE:** SM./MED. • **TIME FRAME:** UP TO 1 YR. • **TIME OF YEAR:** SPR./SUM./FALL

Herbs are "in." All kinds, not only for cooking but also for their medicinal and aromatic properties. There is a solid and growing industry developing around herbs, and herbalists, gardeners, aroma-therapist, potpourri producers, and manufacturers of herb-related products all need access to a public market place. Your annual herb festival can provide the venue.

Many herbs are easy and inexpensive to grow, thus, in addition to charging exhibitors a fee, and the general public an entrance fee, your organization's members should be able to grow all sorts of herbs and sell them at profit. Exhibitor's fees, collected in advance of the show, should cover most expenses. If sufficient exhibitors cannot be induced to attend, the festival can be can-celled without financial loss.

Publicity is essential, although many exhibitors can assist you in this regard with their newsletters and mailing lists. Herb festi-vals are still sufficiently unusual events and should attract considerable attention from the community. They also have the potential to be profitable ventures.

Psychic Fair

• **CATEGORY:** GENERAL • **GROUP SIZE:** SM./MED. • **TIME FRAME:** UP TO 1 YR. • **TIME OF YEAR:** SPR./SUM./FALL/WINT.

Flavoured with a large number of psychics, astrologers, sorcerers and seers.

Medieval Fest

• **CATEGORY:** GENERAL • **GROUP SIZE:** SM./MED. • **TIME FRAME:** UP TO 1 YR. • **TIME OF YEAR:** SPR./SUM./FALL/WINT.

Good costumes, an ox-roast and medieval music will make this fair a success. Archery, jousting, and horse jumping will also attract the crowds.

Miniature Fair

• **CATEGORY:** GENERAL • **GROUP SIZE:** SM./MED. • **TIME FRAME:** UP TO 1 YR. • **TIME OF YEAR:** SPR./SUM./FALL/WINT.

There are many extant collections of miniatures and models, some of which are commercially produced while others are one-of-a-kind. Your fair should bring together creators, sellers, and buyers in an extravagant setting. Attractions might include rides on miniature steam locomotives, miniature cycle riding and performances on miniature musical instruments.

New Product Fair

• **CATEGORY:** GENERAL • **GROUP SIZE:** SM./MED. • **TIME FRAME:** UP TO 1 YR. • **TIME OF YEAR:** SPR./SUM./FALL/WINT.

An annual showcase of newly invented, newly created, even weird, products, systems and services would provide a boost to the economy and enable inventors and entrepreneurs to meet with financiers and marketers. Sponsorship for such an event should be sought from government at all levels, together with Chambers of Commerce and economic development organizations. Innovation is the fuel of the economy. Charge an exhibitor fee and admission fees to the public and make additional money from provision of the usual range of exhibit services.

One of a Kind Fair/Bazaar

• **CATEGORY:** GENERAL • **GROUP SIZE:** MED./LARGE • **TIME FRAME:** UP TO 1 YR. • **TIME OF YEAR:** SPR./SUM./FALL/WINT.

An annual "One of a Kind" bazaar is really an elaborate craft fair coupled with art collections and showcases of designer clothing. The show must be restricted exclusively to the sale of unique objects, or it could degenerate into a second-rate craft fair.

Charge vendors for the use of stalls and tables. Charge visitors an entrance fee. Make sure that all members and supporters donate at least one unique item for your own stall. Ask every exhibitor to donate one item toward a grand raffle.

A Flower Fair

• **CATEGORY:** GENERAL • **GROUP SIZE:** SM./MED. • **TIME FRAME:** UP TO 1 YR. • **TIME OF YEAR:** SUM./FALL

Feature floral displays and competitions, as well as plant sales and offerings of seed and blooms. A parade of floats decorated with flowers would be an asset, as would informative lectures by well-known experts. Make sure you have prizes for all types of flower decorations.

Country Fair (held in the city centre)

• **CATEGORY:** FITNESS, SPORTS & SOCIAL/SERVICE CLUBS • **GROUP SIZE:** MED. • **TIME FRAME:** UP TO 1 YR. • **TIME OF YEAR:** SPR./FALL

Feature farm animals and have displays of milking, butter making, sheep shearing, horse shoeing, and many other country pursuits.

Cycle Fair

• **CATEGORY:** FITNESS, SPORTS & SOCIAL/SERVICE CLUBS • **GROUP SIZE:** MED. • **TIME FRAME:** UP TO 1 YR. • **TIME OF YEAR:** SPR./SUM./FALL

Why not hold a cycle fair for motorcycle enthusiasts of all ages. Feature a motorcycle marketplace, motorcross events, a motorcycle concours by category (touring, stock, Harley, sport, vintage, custom etc.), an obstacle course competition, and perhaps even exhibition cycling by professionals.

Produce Fair

• **CATEGORY:** WOMEN'S GROUPS/SERVICE CLUBS • **GROUP SIZE:** SM./MED. • **TIME FRAME:** UP TO 1 YR. • **TIME OF YEAR:** SUM./FALL

Local produce of any kind can be celebrated in an annual fair. Strawberry fairs, apple fairs, and blueberry fairs are all very popular.

Environmental Fair

• **CATEGORY:** ENVIRONMENTAL • **GROUP SIZE:** MED. • **TIME FRAME:** UP TO 1 YR. • **TIME OF YEAR:** SPR./SUM./FALL/WINT.

Today's growing awareness of the links between the environment, health and food provide an ideal opportunity for this event. Producers of organically grown produce and manufacturers of environmentally responsible products can be offered a forum to display and sell their goods while events and displays may be sponsored by government and recycling companies. One alternative to this concept is the Vegetarian Fair or Vegetarian Food Festival (Toronto has held one for the past 13 years).

Religious Festivals

• **CATEGORY:** RELIGIOUS • **GROUP SIZE:** SM./MED./LARGE • **TIME FRAME:** UP TO 1 YR. • **TIME OF YEAR:** SPR./SUM./FALL/WINT.

Almost every religious organization in the world celebrates festivals that encourage charitable donations. Some religions, Hinduism for example, exhorts the giving of gifts as a form of sacrifice. If you are fundraising for a religious organization look for ways in which you can turn a festival into a fundraising event. At Purim, for example, some Jewish communities have replaced individual food donations (Shelach Manot), with money donated to N.F.P. foundations which by combining several community donations can make a large donation to selected individuals, while retaining some money for their own fundraising purposes. Shelach Manot recipients are presented with one large gift rather than several smaller ones, and donors are not troubled with the task of choosing and delivering a number of small keepsakes.

Here is a sampling of festivals held around the world. Perhaps your group can adapt some of these celebrations for its own use:

• **Schaferlauf** (Shepherd's run) held in Germany in August, is a barefoot race to prove people can run faster than sheep.

• **Festival of the Floating Cup Leaves** (Loy Krathong) held in Thailand in November, features hand-made boats (of paper or leaves) which are floated on water by moonlight. Each boat carries a candle and a wish.

• **Navasard**, the Armenian grape festival, held in August, celebrates the first grapes of the season.

• **Belgium's Cat Festival**, held in May, features a massive parade of people dressed in cat costumes.

• **The Hopi Niman Dance** in July honours homeward bound Kachina spirits through a series of dances and children's gifts.

• **Norway's Potato Days** celebrates the harvesting of the potato crop.

• **Succoth**, the Jewish Feast of Booths (September - October) is a harvest celebration honouring the Jewish exodus.

• **Tano**, the Korean planting festival, in June, features young children in wrestling and swinging matches.

• **Morocco's Wax Festival** in November features thousands of wax carvings mounted on posts and carried in a large parade.

• **Mexico's Night of the Radishes** (December) has an annual radish sculpture competition and exhibition.

• **Ghana's Yam Festival** is held in September and the Gilroy (California) Garlic Festival in July.

- **The Chinese Lantern Festival** in February signals the conclusion of the New Year's celebrations with a children's parade.
- **The French Battle of the Flowers** in February features elaborate flowered floats, a parade, and several flower throwing matches.
- **Southern India's Pongal** ("It Boils") Festival in January celebrates the new rice harvest.
- **Chogna Coeba**, the Tibetan Butter Lamp Festival (March), centres around multi-coloured sculptures of iced butter which are paraded before crowds of people before being thrown into the river.
- **The Midwinter Ceremony** in January marking the Iroquois New Year is celebrated by False Faces who travel from house to house scattering ashes in preservation of good health.
- **Tu bi-Shevat**, the Jewish New Year for trees occurs in January/February.
- **The Japanese Hira Matsuri Doll Festival** is celebrated in March.
- **Yukon's International Storytelling Festival** is in July.
- During the **Klopfelnachte**, "knocking nights," German children dress in masks and serenade their neighbours with verse.
- **Iceland's Yuletide Lads**, all 13, descendants of Gryla the Ogre, begin their annual holiday visits to Icelandic homes in mid-December.
- **Mexican Christmas posadas** feature neighbourhood carolling, and finish with a festive party complete with piñata stuffed with toys and gifts.
- **Japanese Greenery Day** is April 29.
- **Mayday** on May 1.

Fireworks Displays

• **CATEGORY:** FITNESS, SPORTS & SOCIAL/SERVICE CLUBS • **GROUP SIZE:** SM./MED./LARGE • **TIME FRAME:** UP TO 1 YR. • **TIME OF YEAR:** SPRING/SUM.

As the financial mainstay of many local charity and N.F.P. organizations, fireworks displays continue to attract spectators on festive occasions. If your area has no annual display, then you should be able to lure a substantial audience for such an event. If you are concerned about attracting sufficient numbers to cover the cost of the fireworks, then begin the first year with a small display just for organization members, friends, and guests. Gradually increase the size and scope of your display until it becomes a major annual event. Charge an entrance fee and make money from selling refreshments. Don't forget to acquire the appropriate licenses for this event from municipal and/or regional authorities.

The Benson and Hedges Symphony of Fire competition held in Toronto every June has become an international event attended by hundreds of thousands of people – so the track record for this type of event is a successful one.

• **CATEGORY:** FITNESS, SPORTS & SOCIAL/SERVICE CLUBS • **GROUP SIZE:** SM./MED.• **TIME FRAME:** UP TO 6 MTHS.• **TIME OF YEAR:** SUM./FALL

Some service clubs and N.F.P. organizations raise substantial sums of money annually by selling fireworks to the public at appropriate times. Your organization may be able to raise money in this way subject to your local bylaws. Fireworks have a very high profit margin, and with a suitable sales location operated by a hardworking volunteer sales staff, you should be very successful. A 12-meter shipping container parked in the middle of a shopping mall parking lot for a few days provides a great store.

Ghostly Tours

Historical societies in particular can often raise money by catering to curiosity seekers interested in aspects of the supernatural. Some communities thrive on the notoriety gained by reputed sightings of ghosts and other supernatural or unexplained phenomena in the area.

Haunted Area

• **CATEGORY:** FITNESS, SPORTS & SOCIAL/ARTS & THEATRE • **GROUP SIZE:** SM./MED. • **TIME FRAME:** UP TO 1 YR.
• **TIME OF YEAR:** SPR./SUM./FALL/WINT.

Any historically significant location may be rich in stories about ghosts and unexplained phenomena. The University of Toronto, for example, offers a campus tour of its ghosts and ivory towers. Most ghost stories, particularly those relating to institutions like hospitals and universities, are the result of student pranks and fertile imaginations, however, a knowledgeable guide can make a tour of a "haunted area" both an enjoyable and eerie experience whatever the validity of the ghostly claims. Make money by charging a fee for the tour and by selling relevant maps or booklets.

• **CATEGORY:** FITNESS, SPORTS & SOCIAL/ARTS & THEATRE • **GROUP SIZE:** SM./MED. • **TIME FRAME:** UP TO 1 YR. • **TIME OF YEAR:** SPR./SUM./FALL/WINT.

Any reputedly haunted building attracts sightseers, and you will be able to raise money from time to time, if you are able to arrange with the owners or administrators to allow your group to conduct guided tours. Churches and the buildings associated with them are excellent candidates for reported ghostly sightings, although religious organizations are often ambivalent about such claims. Old public buildings like libraries, hospitals, universities and government offices frequently abound with myths and stories of ghosts. Private houses, usually old and large, can also be suitable venues.

To make a haunted house or building tour worthwhile, your group must assemble a great deal of information, essentially an entire history of the property, coupled with interesting anecdotes about previous occupiers and information about significant events in the community. The building's current owners or occupants will probably be able to offer information, and further research can be conducted at the local library, city hall, museum and/or historical society. Previous owners and occupants and longtime neighbourhood residents may also have interesting stories to tell. Remember, if you can't substantiate every historical fact, be creative. Who is going to know the difference?

Try to orchestrate the opening of your haunted house to coincide with a significant historical event, for maximum publicity. A talk by a psychic, or an experiment with a Ouija board, can add interest and excitement to the event.

Home Shows

• **CATEGORY:** SERVICE CLUBS/GENERAL • **GROUP SIZE:** SM./MED. • **TIME FRAME:** UP TO 1 YR. • **TIME OF YEAR:** SPR./SUM./FALL/WINT.

Home shows, large and small, have been around for many years – an indication of their success. Most, if not all, of the larger Canadian home shows are organized by private companies, but many small towns are capable of supporting a charity home show. People are always looking to improve their homes or are seeking new ones. A home show is one of the easiest ways for a charity to raise money with an almost guaranteed rate of success. You will require an indoor venue and a suitable date.

Sell space at the show to a range of local businesses providing materials, equipment, or services to home owners: builders, painters, roofers, landscapers, carpet, curtain, paint and wallpaper suppliers, interior designers, kitchen and bathroom specialists, garden suppliers, real estate agents, and new home builders.

Each vendor pays in advance for space, and each is charged according to the amount of exhibit size required. The primary responsibility of your organization is to attract public interest and attendance. The amount of advertising that you contract for depends on the number of paid-up exhibitors. Failure to publicize the event properly means low attendance, and your vendors will not be interested in taking part in any subsequent show.

Additional money will be generated from car parking and washing, refreshments, a raffle with prizes donated by the exhibitors, and a handicraft stall with items from your own members and friends. Spring and early summer are good times to hold a home show.

Model Exhibitions

• **CATEGORY:** FITNESS, SPORTS & SOCIAL/SERVICE CLUBS • **GROUP SIZE:** SM. • **TIME FRAME:** UP TO 1 YR. • **TIME OF YEAR:** SPR./SUM./FALL/WINT.

Model-making is a world-wide hobby as model trains, boats, planes, houses, furniture, and animals are popular across all age and social groups.

Model manufacturers often organize exhibitions for commercial exposure, but there are still ample opportunities to organize an event for charity. Contact local model making clubs and suggest that you would like to consider joint arrangement of an annual exhibition. Most modellers welcome the opportunity to display their models, and view the work of others. Commercial suppliers of materials, kits and completed models should also welcome the chance to display their wares, and attract new customers.

Your organization's role is to generate enthusiasm among the various modellers' groups and organizations, to arrange a location, to contact all possible interested parties and to advertise the event. You can charge commercial exhibitors a rental fee per square foot of space occupied; sponsors should finance the display of special models, as well as provide prizes for various competitions. Charge a public admission fee, and parking fees; run a raffle with prizes donated by each of the exhibitors; sell refreshments, and operate a play area where young children can be supervised while they make simple models.

Pageants

• **CATEGORY:** RELIGIOUS/GENERAL • **GROUP SIZE:** SM./MED./LARGE • **TIME FRAME:** UP TO 1 YR. • **TIME OF YEAR:** SPR./SUM./FALL/WINT.

Religious and historical anniversaries are celebrated all over the world through pageants and/or tableaux. Often there appears to be no real link between the pageant location and the site of the event commemorated, except in the pageant organizer's mind. Some pageants involve entire communities, with thousands of players, while others may display under ten figures. Nativity pageants and passion plays commemorating the birth and death of Christ are major fundraisers in the western world and can be produced by any religious or theatrically inclined group. Chivalry is another popular pageant topic, as is myth, and even war. Battle re-enactments attract considerable interest, from both participants and spectators. Pageants are great events for raising community spirit, and their all-ages appeal make them popular with participants.

Previews

• **CATEGORY:** GENERAL • **GROUP SIZE:** SM./MED./LARGE • **TIME FRAME:** UP TO 6 MTHS. • **TIME OF YEAR:** SPR./SUM./FALL/WINT.

A new shopping mall, retail shop, public building, bell tower, trade centre, convention centre, hotel, swimming pool – any new facility of any kind, even a new line of cars, a perfume, a cosmetic, kitchen equipment, computer, super highway, bridge – all can be previewed by "special" guests prepared to make a donation to charity. Watch for opportunities and contact owners or developers of such facilities (or products) immediately at each available opportunity.

Sports Cards Show and Sale

• **CATEGORY:** SERVICE CLUBS/GENERAL • **GROUP SIZE:** MED. • **TIME FRAME:** UP TO 1 YR. • **TIME OF YEAR:** SPR./SUM./FALL/WINT.

Sports cards hit a peak in the early 1990s, and like many of these childhood fads and crazes, they continue to remain popular. Millions of children, and many adults, have large collections of sports cards on which they will want to capitalize. Watch for a sign of a resurgence in sports card sales, and be ready to organize a suitable event. Find a large hall, with tables available for rental to both avid card dealers and avid collectors. Advertise in comic bookstores, card shops and malls. Charge each hungry card collector a small admission fee.

Carnivals

The term carnival is often interchanged with fete, festival, and fair. However, in this section, we use the term to denote an event involving a street parade of people or decorated floats.

Carnival Participation

• **CATEGORY:** GENERAL • **GROUP SIZE:** SM./MED. • **TIME FRAME:** UP TO 6 MTHS. • **TIME OF YEAR:** SPR./SUM./FALL/WINT.

If your community holds an annual carnival, participation in the parade each year will add to the public awareness of your organization, perhaps even providing an opportunity to raise funds. Although you are unlikely to raise much money, your members should enjoy themselves and your supporters will praise you for making the effort. If no local annual carnival exists, your group may want to consider starting one. One advantage of being the primary organizer of such an event is that your group can keep the lion's share of the profits (should they emerge).

Annual community carnivals come and go in cycles. To be continually successful, they require considerable organization, and healthy community spirit. Although most events of this type do well in their early years, enthusiasm gradually wanes and the carnival is disbanded. Carnivals fail for a variety of reasons including poor management, bickering among organizers, changes in demographics, and general lack of enthusiasm. If your community once supported a carnival, but let it lapse, maybe the cycle has come full circle and it is time for another. Ask around.

Wait a minimum of five years from the date of the last community carnival before renewing. It is generally unwise to involve any of the previous carnival committee members, although they will almost certainly offer their services and suggestions. Watch out for explanations of how things used to be done.

It is important to find a very good cause for the money generated from the first year's parade. You must have a specific tangible project: a new bus for the disabled, a dialysis machine for the hospital, a new wing on the women's shelter. People will support a carnival when they feel that there is a good and worthy reason behind the solicitation of funds.

Starting a carnival in a new community is much easier than reviving a failed one in an older community. This is because residents of a new community are always looking for ways in which they can come together in a neighbourly way and bond as a community. Solicit carnival support by talking to neighbours, friends and local businesses. You could have a carnival committee formed in no time at all.

Many carnivals are successful because they have a particular theme. Mardi Gras, Easter, Christmas, and other religious anniversaries are celebrated with carnivals around the world. Other well-known themes for carnivals include the seasons, especially spring and fall, Chinese new year, and non-religious festivals such as Halloween and Thanksgiving. Lantern festivals are particularly popular in China and other parts of Asia, and illuminated carnivals are well supported in the U.K. where floats are decorated with thousands of coloured lights (powered by massive generators towed behind).

Other potential revenue sources at a carnival parade include car parking services, security, providing refreshments, marshalling and childcare. Product sales to spectators could include flags, balloons, buttons, hats, and even, plastic rain ponchos. Photography services are good moneymakers too.

FOOD & DRINK

Apples

Apples are a universal fruit and can be used as a fundraising tool in many ways. No fall fair would be complete without an apple bobbing contest. Any suitable locally grown fruit or produce can be substituted for apples in most of the following events. Consider cranberries, strawberries, blueberries, tomatoes, peaches, potatoes, or maple syrup.

Apple Day

• **CATEGORY:** CHILDREN & YOUTH • **GROUP SIZE:** SM. • **TIME FRAME:** UP TO 4WKS. • **TIME OF YEAR:** FALL

An apple day is an ideal annual fundraiser for schools. Organizers should buy small apples in bulk and encourage each student to buy at least one. Apples are healthy and make a good mid-day snack. Apple days yield good profit margins and they are an effective means of raising a few hundred dollars from very little work. If you can find a local grower or supplier to donate the apples, you are guaranteed an even greater profit.

Apple Peeling Contest

• **CATEGORY:** WOMEN'S GROUPS/GENERAL • **GROUP SIZE:** SM./MED. • **TIME FRAME:** UP TO 4WKS. • **TIME OF YEAR:** FALL

Apple peeling competitions can be held on their own, in a community prized for its orchards, or they can be utilized anywhere as part of a fall event. The goal of the contest is to break the world record for the longest piece of unbroken peel taken from a single apple. The unbroken peel record, to date, stands at an incredible 173 feet (*Guinness Book of World Records*) and it should be noted that the chance of anyone setting a new record at your fundraising event is remote. This caveat notwithstanding, apple peeling contests are popular in areas noted for their orchards.

Make sure you get an official judge. Notify your local newspaper, and ask them to print a photograph of your winner. Charge an entry fee which includes the purchase of one apple and the loan of a knife. Entrants should be able to purchase as many additional apples as they want.

If you choose to make this event a major annual fundraiser, then you will need to offer a major prize for anyone setting a new world record. You could do that with the assistance of an insurance company. If you are using the contest as part of a fall fair or harvest festival, then choose a more modest reward for the winner.

Applefest

• **CATEGORY:** WOMEN'S GROUPS/GENERAL • **GROUP SIZE:** SM./MED. • **TIME FRAME:** UP TO 6 MTHS. • **TIME OF YEAR:** FALL

If you live in an area with many orchards, you could consider establishing an annual Applefest, in cooperation with your local apple growers. Use the world record apple peeling attempt as a centrepiece. The growers know that a reasonably sized, well publicized Applefest celebration would provide a major local market for their produce, and they should be only too pleased to provide all the apples you need. For smaller events you may need to purchase apples in bulk, but the rate of return on your investment will be considerable (For example: if you pay ten cents per apple you can probably sell each for 50 cents or even one dollar.)

An Applefest should include all kinds of apple events: apple throwing and catching competitions; apple bobbing; apple carving; apple peeling; apple decorating and even apple eating. Apple growers, commercial and amateur, can enter their biggest, best, most colourful and tastiest apples in a best apple specimen competition, and pies, cakes and other apple products should be solicited for a Best Apple Baking, Best Apple Butter, Best Cider or Apple Wine, Best Apple Pie, Best Applesauce, Best Apple Jelly contest and so on. You could also squeeze fresh apples to make pure apple cider, hold a "William Tell" archery competition (without a human target), and fly apple kites.

Apple Product Sales

• **CATEGORY:** WOMEN'S GROUPS • **GROUP SIZE:** SM./MED./LARGE • **TIME FRAME:** UP TO 4WKS. • **TIME OF YEAR:** FALL

Because apples are relatively inexpensive, they are an ideal ingredient for making jellies, chutneys and pies which can be sold at a considerable profit at any event.

Bake Sales

Bake sales are neither innovative nor particularly effective ways of raising large sums of money for charity and N.F.P. organizations, but they can provide a no-lose means to raise a little money for almost any organization quickly, on almost any occasion. Bake sales will form part of any fair, market or bazaar and can even be held at every regular meeting of a group or chapter.

The following are some suggestions for sweetening up an old idea.

Bake Your Own Bake Sale

• **CATEGORY:** WOMEN'S GROUPS/GENERAL • **GROUP SIZE:** SM. • **TIME FRAME:** UP TO 4WKS. • **TIME OF YEAR:** SPR./SUM./FALL/WINT.

Each donor is asked to identify a recipe which requires blending of all the dry ingredients with the addition of liquid as the final catalyst. Donors supply and mix all the dry ingredients and attach simple instructions, (i.e., add 1 egg and 1 cup of water and bake at 175 C for 20 minutes), to the mixture for the buyer. Cookies, muffins and many types of cake mixtures can be offered for sale in this way.

Competitive Bake Sale

• **CATEGORY:** WOMEN'S GROUPS/GENERAL • **GROUP SIZE:** SM. • **TIME FRAME:** UP TO 6 MTHS. • **TIME OF YEAR:** SPR./SUM./FALL/WINT.

This is simply a way of encouraging people to enter quality products into the sale by offering a number of prizes in different categories: the crunchiest cookies, the most attractive decoration etc.

It's Very Good For You Bake Sale

• **CATEGORY:** WOMEN'S GROUPS/GENERAL • **GROUP SIZE:** SM. • **TIME FRAME:** UP TO 6 MTHS. • **TIME OF YEAR:** SPR./SUM./FALL/WINT.

Replace all those sticky sweet offerings with really nutritious ones, each item to be accompanied by its recipe proving that it really is good for you.

Really Decadent Bake Sale

• **CATEGORY:** GENERAL • **GROUP SIZE:** SM./MED. • **TIME FRAME:** UP TO 1 YR. • **TIME OF YEAR:** SPR./SUM./FALL/WINT.

If yours is a registered charity, a donation of a cake worth ten dollars or more may be classified as a charitable donation for tax purposes: value of the cake, cost of materials, plus the labour and expertise involved in making it.

Thus, should a professional chef or baker spend ten dollars on materials, valuing time, utensils, and expertise at an additional $20, then he/she would be entitled to a tax receipt for a donation in kind of $30 (effectively making the donation of the cake free of cost). The more decadent and expensive the cake or bake product offered, the more the donor will benefit from tax relief, and the greater the benefit to your organization

Surprise Bake Sale

• **CATEGORY:** WOMEN'S GROUPS/GENERAL • **GROUP SIZE:** SM./MED. • **TIME FRAME:** UP TO 1 YR. • **TIME OF YEAR:** SPR./SUM./FALL/WINT.

The surprise in a surprise bake sale is that a selected number of the baked goods on sale contain small items of valuable jewellery. No one must know which items contain the jewellery until after purchase. This in effect turns the bake sale into a lottery, which can be even more financially rewarding, when the baked goods are auctioned to the highest bidders.

Combine a really decadent bake sale with a surprise sale to raise a considerable sum of money.

50/50 Bake Sale

• **CATEGORY:** WOMEN'S GROUPS/GENERAL • **GROUP SIZE:** SM. • **TIME FRAME:** UP TO 4WKS. • **TIME OF YEAR:** SPR./SUM./FALL/WINT.

The 50/50 bake sale encourages donors to enter goods because they will receive 50% of the proceeds, an amount which will almost certainly exceed the cost of ingredients.

Seasonal Bake Sale

• **CATEGORY:** WOMEN'S GROUPS/GENERAL • **GROUP SIZE:** SM./MED. • **TIME FRAME:** UP TO 6 MTHS. • **TIME OF YEAR:** SPR./FALL/WINT.

Seasonal bake sales can be held close to any festival and can include such things as Easter bunnies, gingerbread houses, Christmas cakes, pumpkin pies, Thanksgiving Day goodies, and delicacies for the Moon Festival.

Baker's Dozen

• **CATEGORY:** GENERAL • **GROUP SIZE:** SM./MED. • **TIME FRAME:** UP TO 6 MTHS. • **TIME OF YEAR:** SPR./SUM./FALL/WINT.

If you are operating a food bank, soup kitchen, or can use food for a charitable purpose, utilize the baker's dozen principle. Invite all bakeries and grocery stores regularly selling baked goods to participate by offering each customer a deal based on the following suggested advertisement:

BAKER'S DOZEN –
WHEN YOU BUY A DOZEN OF THESE ITEMS
WE OFFER YOU AN ADDITIONAL ITEM
FREE OF CHARGE OR, AT YOUR REQUEST,
WE WILL DONATE IT TO (.................................FOOD BANK)

Wine and Cheese Auction

• **CATEGORY:** GENERAL • **GROUP SIZE:** SM./MED.• **TIME FRAME:** UP TO 1 YR. • **TIME OF YEAR:** FALL

Wine and Cheese auctions are best held in the fall, when the wine and cheese buffs, and those who would like to be same, are looking for new discoveries to take into the holiday season. You should contact a number of wine merchants, inviting each to participate in your auction by supplying at, or near cost, a range of wines in case lots and a few bottles of excellent vintage wine. Combine these donations with a quantity of superb quality, whole cheeses, direct from the manufacturers or importers, and you have the basis for an excellent fundraiser. Local wines and cheeses should be offered wherever possible. Include unusual products such as unpasteurized and goat cheese for interest. Tasting will be an essential element of the evening, and tickets should be priced accordingly. You may also find it useful to secure the services of an expert wine taster/connoisseur who can discourse on the vintages at some length with your auction participants. Similarly, a cheese expert, or cheese maker, could provide information about the cheeses on offer.

Participating wineries, wine merchants and cheese suppliers should all be given an opportunity to advertise their full range of products to the audience as a way to reward them for their donation.

Note – Sale of liquor is governed by provincial legislation. Obtain appropriate legal advice prior to arranging such an event. Usually when liquor is offered for sale, or is advertised as such, the provincial statutes come into play, and permits may be required. Check with your local distributors.

Wine and Cheese Tasting

• **CATEGORY:** GENERAL • **GROUP SIZE:** SM./MED./LARGE • **TIME FRAME:** UP TO 1 YR. • **TIME OF YEAR:** SPR./FALL/WINT.

This is an elegant fundraiser which has been successful for generations. As above, consult with a number of wine producers and merchants who may be interested in supplying wine at a reduced price in return for the opportunity of making a sales pitch to your guests.

The presence of a celebrity, politician, or sports personality is important if you wish to attract persons from outside your immediate membership.

Charge an entrance fee sufficient to cover the cost of a minimum number of tastings, then charge for each additional glass. Alternatively, charge a substantial entry fee which more than covers the cost of wines consumed. Use organization volunteers as waiters and washers for maximum profit.

Make additional funds from a cheese and wine auction, a raffle, and from sales of cheese and wine. Don't forget to have appropriate palate cleansers on hand.

Wine: Special Blend
• **CATEGORY:** GENERAL • **GROUP SIZE:** LARGE. • **TIME FRAME:** 1 YR.+ • **TIME OF YEAR:** SPR./SUM./FALL/WINT.

Larger organizations can benefit from the sale of wine by having a vineyard prepare a special blend named accordingly, "Chateau ..." or "Vino de Casa ..." The wine should be sold by the case to members, clients, and friends of the organization, with a reasonable donation included in its price.

Wine: Private Label
• **CATEGORY:** GENERAL • **GROUP SIZE:** SM./MED. • **TIME FRAME:** UP TO 1 YR. • **TIME OF YEAR:** SPR./SUM./FALL/WINT.

When your organization is too small to justify the making of a special wine blend, consider having special labels affixed to a regular blend. Private labelling of the wine bottle adds a marvellously exclusive cachet to any vintage. Make sure, however, that what's inside the bottle is quality goods, or your organization will only ever be able to sell one private label. Select good quality wines, red, white and rosé. Don't forget the dessert wines. Be proud to sell cases to all of your members and supporters.

Winery Tour
• **CATEGORY:** GENERAL • **GROUP SIZE:** SM./MED. • **TIME FRAME:** UP TO 1 YR. • **TIME OF YEAR:** FALL

Wine connoisseurs and wine novices alike usually are delighted to participate in an extensive winery tour to view the wine making process first-hand and sample each vineyard's offerings directly on the premises. A day tour of selected wineries and vineyards in your region should be a very popular outing. You will need to provide bus transportation, and to include a mouth-watering lunch as part of the tour. Funds are generated through the ticket price, which should include a realistic donation. You will need a guide, and, if possible, a respected wine expert, to explain the intricacies of the process and answer any questions.

Beer Bash
• **CATEGORY:** FITNESS, SPORTS & SOCIAL/SERVICE CLUBS • **GROUP SIZE:** SM. • **TIME FRAME:** UP TO 4WKS. • **TIME OF YEAR:** SPR./SUM./FALL/WINT.

It is not a pretty sight, but if your membership enjoys a drink, hold a beer bash. Be sensitive in the choice of venue, and make absolutely sure that no one who is drinking is driving. Provide as much beer as people want and let them have a great time. Hold beer drinking competitions; beer sports and games; beer showers and beer throwing. Charge a substantial admission fee and be prepared to cleanup the mess afterwards. Just remember, beer isn't bought, it is only rented for a short time. Make sure you have adequate washroom facilities.

Chili Contests

• **CATEGORY:** GENERAL • **GROUP SIZE:** SM./MED. • **TIME FRAME:** UP TO 6 MTHS.• **TIME OF YEAR:** SPR./SUM./FALL/WINT.

Chili con carne is a favourite with all ages. It has no particular occasion or season, although some of the hottest days of the year seem to be the most popular times to eat chili. Everyone appears to have a best recipe. So put it to the test. Organize a "Best Darn Chili" contest. Charge all entries a fee for each pot. Judge on presentation, consistency, and seasonings. Alternatively, for the judging, you could sell the chili to the spectators giving each person a score card. Winners are chosen from the results of the cards.

Organizations in American cities attract thousands of entrants to chili competitions and there is an award for the U.S. national chili champion.

Recipes of entries may be published in a cookbook of the same name, "Best Darn Chili Recipes." Sell the book to members, family, friends and the general public. By taking pre-paid orders for the book during the event, you will cover the cost of printing, especially if it is done cheaply using a desktop publishing package. If you cannot get enough cookbook orders during the event, then do not publish.

Cookbooks

• **CATEGORY:** WOMEN'S GROUPS/GENERAL • **GROUP SIZE:** MED./LARGE • **TIME FRAME:** UP TO 1 YR. • **TIME OF YEAR:** SPR./SUM./FALL/WINT.

Many, many charity organizations publish cookbooks and make money from them. Cookbooks make relatively inexpensive presents, and the recipient knows immediately that the giver is a charity supporter. Canvas your members for their own favourite recipes and assemble these into an attractive package. For something entirely different, you might try the following:

- Favourite Recipes of a Television Host
- Sure-Fire Political Delicacies
- An Author's Recipe Book

- A Journalist's Cookery Guide
- 50 Favourite Meals of Canadian Sports Personalities

The process for compiling each book is similar. Choose your theme and assemble a list of persons linked to your organization in any way who could be potential recipe donors, or who would know potential donors. Ideally, you want people prepared to personally solicit recipes from a number of their colleagues. The captain of a hockey team, for example, could obtain most of the recipes needed for a book just by asking his or her colleagues and friends. Between 100 and 150 recipes is the standard amount for any charity cookbook.

Without suitable contacts, it will be more difficult to amass sufficient content. Begin with 50 names. An afternoon spent in your public library with *Who's Who*, and a helpful librarian should provide you a good start. Note names, titles, and addresses for each potential donor. Devise a letter setting out the goals of your organization, the financial plight you are in, and request a favourite recipe or two. Ask for consent to publish the recipe, together with the donor's name, purely for charitable purposes.

You can also try something entirely different along the following lines:

- The Young Person's Guide to Totally Disgusting Recipes

Every parent has at least one obnoxious recipe his/her child has dreamed up. Ask for suggestions if you need to.

- Survive-on-Five

Recipes and complete meal ideas that allow a person to eat on five dollars a day. Target the book toward the parents of students.

- A Cookbook for the Culinarily Challenged

Put together a book of very simple but effective recipes that anyone can make easily.

Recipe Competition

• **CATEGORY:** WOMEN'S GROUPS/GENERAL • **GROUP SIZE:** MED/LARGE. • **TIME FRAME:** UP TO 1 YR. • **TIME OF YEAR:** SPR./SUM./FALL/WINT.

If you are totally unable to come up with recipe ideas for a cookbook, why not hold a recipe contest. Scare up a suitable prize, dinner for two at one of the best restaurants in town perhaps, with the winning recipe being served as a "Chef's Special."

Invite everyone to submit recipes, each accompanied by a charitable donation. Ask your local newspaper to print the entry form, put up small posters in likely places, write to service groups, invite local politicians and celebrities to submit their favourite recipes, contact local 4H clubs, senior and church groups, as well as high school and youth groups. It doesn't really matter how good the recipes are, as long as each entry is accompanied by a donation, and the name and address of the entrant. Printing costs of the book will be covered by these funds.

Ask members and friends to test each recipe, decide on how your book will be organized, and only publish the best submissions. Invite a well-known local chef or cook to select the winner from a presented short list. Search out a local printer to help you compile and print the book. Each recipe donor should receive a brochure/order form describing the finished volume, and offering a small 10-20% discount on personal purchase of same. Sell books through your organization and local book stores.

Once a competition has been held, and the book published, why not arrange a celebratory dinner for all the "Authors" and their guests. Hold it at a local restaurant (perhaps with your chef judge), and invite all donors who have recipes in the book. Arrange the menu to include prize-winning dishes from each category, but do not disclose the names of the winners, or the menu, until the event takes place. Dinner guests will be eager to find out if they have won, and will therefore have a vested interest in attending the dinner. Charge all guests a set attendance fee which covers the cost of the meal plus a donation.

Cooking Race

• **CATEGORY:** GENERAL • **GROUP SIZE:** SM./MED./LARGE • **TIME FRAME:** UP TO 1 YR. • **TIME OF YEAR:** SPR./SUM./FALL/WINT.

This annual European fundraiser involves teams of catering students from various colleges. The event begins early in the morning with a fundraising breakfast attended by celebrity chefs. Each student team of four people is handed a package of ingredients. During the course of the breakfast, teams must devise a menu, using only the ingredients given, with an explanation to the audience of what they intend to achieve. Next, the teams set off, complete with ingredients, on a 26-mile bicycle race to the next venue where they must prepare the food.

On completion of the preparations, in front of an audience, participants run two miles (carrying the food) to the final venue where they must cook and serve the meal to the celebrity judges. Prizes are awarded to the best and fastest teams. Money is raised throughout the day, and everyone has a great time.

Bread Race

• **CATEGORY:** GENERAL • **GROUP SIZE:** SM./MED./LARGE • **TIME FRAME:** UP TO 6 MTHS. • **TIME OF YEAR:** FALL

This idea stems from an ancient ritual wherein a successful harvest was celebrated by baking a loaf of bread from the first wheat. The loaf must be made entirely by hand and baked in a handmade brick oven heated by an open fire. Participants require a field of ripe wheat, yeast, a pile of bricks, some large stones, and as many teams of three contestants as can be persuaded to enter. Members of youth organizations and high school students are ideal candidates, along with members of environmental groups and service clubs.

Begin the race with a two-kilometre run to a selected field where sufficient wheat to make a loaf must be harvested by hand. Contestants must then grind the wheat in a makeshift stone quern to extract the flour and make a loaf of bread. Each team runs to a second location to start the fire and build the brick oven in which to bake the bread.

Contestants are judged on both speed and the quality of the finished loaf. Raise money from individual sponsorship, entry fees, and an auction of the finished products.

Cotton Candy

• **CATEGORY:** WOMEN'S GROUPS/GENERAL • **GROUP SIZE:** SM. • **TIME FRAME:** UP TO 6 MTHS. • **TIME OF YEAR:** SPR./SUM./FALL

Smaller, local organizations, with a limited number of members and volunteers, can make a substantial amount of money from operating a cotton candy stall. Cotton candy machines are not expensive to purchase, and consist only of a heater, drum, and small electric motor. They require a supply of electricity, some sugar, and some sticks to complete the operation. Each kilo of sugar yields dozens of cotton candies.

Owners of a cotton candy machine will be invited to set up and sell at any number of events, particularly those with children: fairs, carnivals, birthday parties, fireworks displays etc. You may even be allowed to operate in the park on Sunday afternoons. The amount of money your organization makes from this venture is directly proportional to the amount of time that your members are prepared to invest.

Remember, cotton candy machines can also be rented on a daily or weekly basis, so any small group can test-market their skill at one or two events prior to making a firm commitment to purchase.

It is a good idea to check out your power source at any venue where your organization operates the machine. Cotton candy machines can require considerable electrical power.

Popcorn machines are a good alternative.

Jam & Jelly Making Party

• **CATEGORY:** WOMEN'S GROUPS/GENERAL • **GROUP SIZE:** SM. • **TIME FRAME:** UP TO1 YR. • **TIME OF YEAR:** SPR./SUM./FALL

This is a great event for whole families that offers a considerable profit potential for a small charity of N.F.P. group. Organize an annual jam weekend timed to coincide with the harvest of a local crop: strawberries, blueberries, raspberries, peaches, apples, plums, grapes, rhubarb, and so on.

Your organization will need to approach a farmer at least one year in advance, and arrange to purchase all, or part of his/her crop. Your group will pick the crop and take it away, thereby saving labour and transportation costs to the farmer in addition to providing the market guarantee. These factors should gain you a rock-bottom price. Negotiate with a wholesaler for sugar, jars, labels etc., and arrange to borrow a commercial kitchen not used on weekends, perhaps at a school or community hall. You will also need somewhere to store the finished product, although as much as possible should be sold in advance. Organize your members, their families and friends into teams to pick, clean and transport the fruit. Some will prepare and make the jams, others will apply labels. Still others can act as tasters.

Your aim is to produce small jars of very high quality jam to sell at a premium price. When properly organized, you can quickly establish an annual market for your product, one which provides a guaranteed annual source of funding (and a good deal of fun).

Corn Roasts

• **CATEGORY:** GENERAL • **GROUP SIZE:** SM. • **TIME FRAME:** UP TO 4WKS. • **TIME OF YEAR:** FALL

What would an early Canadian autumn be like without an old-fashioned corn roast? Few fundraisers are cheaper or easier to arrange. You will need barbecues, or even an open fire located in a park, garden, or even in a parking lot. You will need some sacks of corn, a little butter and salt, and some cans or bottles of soda pop, lemonade, or ice tea. Secure the services of a good cook. Charge diners a fee of two dollars and let everyone enjoy the feast. Corn roasts can be combined with any number of other fundraising events. Alternatively, they can be social events designed to get people together so that you can detail the work of your organization.

Ox Roast

• **CATEGORY:** FITNESS, SPORTS & SOCIAL/SERVICE CLUBS • **GROUP SIZE:** SM./MED. • **TIME FRAME:** UP TO 6 MTHS.
• **TIME OF YEAR:** SPR./SUM./FALL/WINT.

As part of a major community event, even a very small organization can raise a substantial sum by roasting a whole steer and selling slices in sandwiches. Allow one animal per a thousand sandwiches. You will need 100 loaves of bread and plenty of mustard. You will also need at least 1,000 hungry people, and the usual paraphernalia plates, napkins, forks, seasonings, a couple of good cooks (well versed in slicing up beef), a sturdy spit, and lots of garbage cans.

Pig or Lamb Roast

• **CATEGORY:** GENERAL • **GROUP SIZE:** SM./MED. • **TIME FRAME:** UP TO 6 MTHS. • **TIME OF YEAR:** SPR./SUM./FALL/WINT.

Like an ox roast, this feast is for smaller events. It can also be an effective means of raising funds at most outdoor events. Pig or lamb roasts do not need to be small events. One Chilean charity organizes an annual gala where barbecues are placed end to end, creating a spit over a mile long. Six thousand lambs are roasted at one go.

Boiled Dinners

• **CATEGORY:** GENERAL • **GROUP SIZE:** SM./MED. • **TIME FRAME:** UP TO 6 MTHS. • **TIME OF YEAR:** SPR./SUM./FALL/WINT.

One Texas charity holds an annual Shrimp Boil Dinner; you can also hold a Boiled Corn Beef Dinner for St. Patrick's Day or a Perogy Feast for a Ukrainian festival.

Pancakes

Pancakes are cheap, easy to make, and can be used as very effective fundraising tools at any event. Few people will pass the opportunity of spending a few dollars on a plate of pancakes and the profit margin is high.

Pancake Fest

• **CATEGORY:** GENERAL • **GROUP SIZE:** MED. • **TIME FRAME:** UP TO 1 YR. • **TIME OF YEAR:** SPR./SUM./FALL/WINT.

Create an annual two-day event based entirely around the humble pancake and put your town and organization on the map. Start with all the restaurateurs in the area and invite them to participate by offering special pancake menus throughout the fest.

Types of pancakes offered will depend on the culinary flair and style of each restaurant, ranging from the simple pancake with syrup, to the most elaborately decorated and lavishly stuffed, pancake à la king. A donation to your organization should be made by each restaurant for each pancake or pancake meal sold.

Perhaps your pancake fest could coincide with a significant local event, or the harvest of a local crop like peaches, strawberries, blueberries, or maple syrup. Arrange for any number of pancake events including a pancake race, pancake flipping, eating, throwing, and pancake decoration. Sell pancakes, crepes, and flapjacks with fruit or syrup and hold a competition for pancake recipes, later to be assembled into a book. Why not make the world's biggest pancake and top off the event with a pancake dance.

Hold a competition to find the person who can flip a pancake the most number of times within a specified time, say one minute. If there is a world's record then try to beat it, if not, then why not set one?

Pancake Race

• **CATEGORY:** GENERAL • **GROUP SIZE:** SM./MED. • **TIME FRAME:** UP TO 1 YR. • **TIME OF YEAR:** SPR./FALL

This is an annual Shrove Tuesday event staged in towns and cities across Britain. Teams or individuals run through the town tossing pancakes in a frying pan. Each runner must toss the pancake, successfully catching it a specified number of times (although verification often proves impossible). There are various categories of winner: first past the post, best overall team effort, best costume etc. Money is raised through team sponsorship and collections from spectators.

Perfect Pie Competition

• **CATEGORY:** WOMEN'S GROUPS/GENERAL • **GROUP SIZE:** SM. • **TIME FRAME:** UP TO 6 MTHS. • **TIME OF YEAR:** SPR./SUM./FALL/WINT.

This contest invites groups and individuals to submit pies, accompanied by recipes, and chances to win prizes donated by local hotels and restaurants. Decide on different pie categories and establish whatever ground rules you deem appropriate. Hold the event in a well-known hotel or restaurant and include respected chefs, food columnists, and cookbook authors in your line-up of judges. The idea is to create a prestigious annual event which will attract entrants from a large area.

Raise money by charging an entry fee for each pie, and a spectator entrance fee. Auction all of the pies at the end of the event, and publish a book of the recipes. Make sure your entry form includes a disclaimer giving you the right to publish the recipe.

Pot Lucks

• **CATEGORY:** WOMEN'S GROUPS/GENERAL • **GROUP SIZE:** SM. • **TIME FRAME:** UP TO 4WKS. • **TIME OF YEAR:** SPR./SUM./FALL/WINT.

Pot luck suppers are primarily social events, but there is no reason why your organization should not raise a little money at the same time. Simply ask attendees to donate a supper dish together with one bill (any currency, any denomination) taped to the underside. The bill's value depends on the generosity and financial standing of the donator. Hold an auction of the empty dishes at the end of the evening, making sure that no one is allowed to look underneath them. Each successful bidder gets whatever is stuck to the base of the bid-upon dish, and your organization gets the auction proceeds.

Pot Luck Lunches

• **CATEGORY:** GENERAL • **GROUP SIZE:** SM. • **TIME FRAME:** UP TO 6 MTHS. • **TIME OF YEAR:** SPR./SUM./FALL/WINT.

A simple and effective way of raising money from members and supporters at any event is to ask everyone to bring a boxed lunch. All lunch boxes are collected and each is auctioned, unopened, to the highest bidder. Anyone who might feel embarrassed at supplying light faire can always buy it back. The last person buying a lunch has no competing bidders and thus should be asked to pay the same amount as the penultimate bidder.

Pot Luck Parties

• **CATEGORY:** GENERAL • **GROUP SIZE:** SM. • **TIME FRAME:** UP TO 6 MTHS. • **TIME OF YEAR:** SPR./SUM./FALL/WINT.

Invited guests to this event arrive with a bottle of alcoholic drink instead of food. The host provides snacks, munchies, and dips. Anyone partaking of beverages makes a donation every time a drink is taken from the bar, so that the guests are, in fact, paying to purchase their own drink. The organizer cannot lose.

It is usually a good idea to have nominated volunteers pouring drinks, otherwise the size of the shots can increase alarmingly as the evening wears on.

Note: See the warning regarding alcoholic events.

Taste and Tell Parties

• **CATEGORY:** WOMEN'S GROUPS/GENERAL • **GROUP SIZE:** SM. • **TIME FRAME:** UP TO 1 YR. • **TIME OF YEAR:** SPR./SUM./FALL/WINT.

Invite group members to make a dish which they believe to be unusual or unique. A multicultural group makes this party especially fun as people of different ethnic origins should be encouraged to bring something reflecting their culture (or recipes handed down year after year, generation after generation).

Each party guest introduces his/her dish, explaining its origins and creation method. As an extra bonus, guests should provide a written copy of each recipe. Everyone wishing to taste the dish makes a small donation prior to doing so. Those wishing to purchase copies of the recipe should make an additional donation: one dollar a taste and another for the recipe are probably reasonable charges for most taste-and-tell parties.

Potato and Pasta Parties

• **CATEGORY:** GENERAL • **GROUP SIZE:** SM./MED. • **TIME FRAME:** UP TO 6 MTHS. • **TIME OF YEAR:** SPR./SUM./FALL/WINT.

Potatoes and pasta have many things in common and they are both ideal fundraising tools. Both foods are popular, inexpensive, plentiful, versatile, and virtually fat-free. Recipes abound for potato and pasta dishes and most can be cooked indoors by almost anyone at any time of the year. Build a party around the humble potato or plebeian pasta, and enable hundreds of people to enjoy themselves for just a few dollars. Any number of silly games can be enjoyed by guests: pass the potato, potato-sack races, the great potato hunt, potato peeling competitions, pasta art, pasta puzzles, and home-made pasta contests are just a few examples.

Potato and pasta parties can be arranged to suit a wide spectrum of society. One or many Italian chefs could, for example, produce an exquisite pasta meal for a $100 a plate fundraiser, and conversely, a thousand hungry students could be fed for as little as two or three dollars a head. Either party can be a satisfying, money-raising venture.

In addition to an entry fee, hold a potato or pasta collection in support of a food bank.

GAMBLING

Gambling events always require permits from municipal, and possibly provincial authorities. Make sure you have these in hand prior to announcing any fundraiser involving games of chance.

Bingo

• **CATEGORY:** GENERAL • **GROUP SIZE:** SM./MED./LARGE • **TIME FRAME:** UP TO 6 MTHS. • **TIME OF YEAR:** SPR./SUM./FALL/WINT.

Bingo has been popular for a very long time and is the fundraising mainstay of many, many charity and N.F.P. organizations. Worldwide, huge sums are wagered on bingo and millions of people derive pleasure from the game, which is inexpensive and easy to organize at any small gathering. Serious money can be raised from involvement with professional bingo organizations who will, in some provinces, arrange venues, and provide equipment and publicity in return for the use of the charity's license.

• **CATEGORY:** HEALTH RELATED/GENERAL • **GROUP SIZE:** SM. • **TIME FRAME:** UP TO 6 MTHS. • **TIME OF YEAR:** SPR./SUM./FALL/WINT.

Hospitals, nursing homes, and senior's residences are always grateful for volunteers who can amuse and occupy patients and residents. They usually do not mind if your group makes a small profit for charity, especially if they are offered a cut in the proceeds. Bingo sessions for patients may be run on hospital radio or in hospital lounges. Sell the cards to those who wish to participate and offer prizes to attract players. It is imperative that your group has clearance from local authorities prior to embarking on a venture of this sort, and it is equally important that your volunteers accept bingo applications only from potential players who will not be endangered or embarrassed in any way by playing the game. Failure to take these precautions can subject your organization to legal action.

• **CATEGORY:** GENERAL • **GROUP SIZE:** MED./LARGE • **TIME FRAME:** UP TO 1 YR. • **TIME OF YEAR:** SPR./SUM./FALL/WINT.

Many Canadian communities already have the game on television and in many areas all bingo profits and profits from other forms of gambling must be given to charity. Your group can take advantage of this craze. Liaise with local television stations to televise bingo one or two afternoons a week. Bingo cards can be sold on a weekly or monthly basis by news agents, charity groups, corner stores etc., and they can be delivered directly to elderly or disabled persons as the idea is perfect for the house-bound. If bingo is legal in your area, the reward could be a steady income with relatively little effort.

Casinos

• **CATEGORY:** GENERAL • **GROUP SIZE:** SM./MED. • **TIME FRAME:** UP TO 6 MTHS. • **TIME OF YEAR:** SPR./SUM./FALL/WINT.

People love to gamble, and a properly arranged Casino Night should never fail. There are even private companies who contract to make all arrangements, and provide all necessary equipment and expertise. Venue, volunteer staff, and the method of casino operation vary, but it is common for those charities most benefiting from the event to be responsible for advertising. If your group wants to operate its own casino, it is well advised to talk to other groups who have done the same before, and to make a visit to view one or more successful charity casinos to study methods of operation.

Before you even consider staging a gambling event, seek good legal advice. The law in relation to betting and gaming is complex and can vary considerably from province to province. Also consider whether it is morally acceptable for your organization to benefit from this type of activity.

Certain provinces permit professional gambling organizations to operate casinos, providing a percentage of the take is given to charity. When and where such a policy exists, it usually makes sense for a charitable organization to apply to be a beneficiary of gambling profits, providing that organizational membership is in agreement.

In both Ontario and Nova Scotia, gambling casinos provide many organizations with stable funding. Ontario plans to open 44 permanent charity casinos in 1998. Any registered charity can apply to hold its events in these casinos, receiving between 10% and 42% of the net profits, depending on the type of gaming. Experts project that Ontario will receive some $180-million annually from these charities.

Compulsive gambling is the dark downside of all legalized (and illegal gambling) operations. Both Nova Scotia and Ontario have encountered significant elements of their gambling populace in this category.

Win a Car with Dice

• **CATEGORY:** GENERAL • **GROUP SIZE:** SM./MED./LARGE • **TIME FRAME:** UP TO 6 MTHS. • **TIME OF YEAR:** SPR./SUM./FALL/WINT.

Popular in Europe for sometime, this event is extremely simple to operate and works on the laws of chance.

Determine the likelihood of anyone throwing six dice, simultaneously, with each dice landing with the number 6 on top. An insurance company, using this calculation, should insure you against the cost of a car should someone actually throw a 6 x 6 at your event. Your insurance premium will be based on the value of the car, plus duration of the event, plus the cost of employing an independent scrutineer who must be present at all times throughout the event. These odds are not difficult to calculate and any insurance company should be willing to quote a premium. Consult an insurance broker or shop around for the best deal.

While this event can be held on its own, success is more likely when it is held as a side show to a major fundraising event such as a car race day, or as ancillary entertainment at a commercial sports event.

Note: Dice for a Car might be seen as illegal gambling in some Canadian provinces; check with the authorities before planning such an event.

Horse Racing

• **CATEGORY:** GENERAL • **GROUP SIZE:** SM./MED. • **TIME FRAME:** UP TO 4WKS. • **TIME OF YEAR:** SPR./SUM./FALL

Betting on horse racing is not recommended as prudent use of charitable funds, although it has certainly been done successfully. Your organization's members and supporters can always place a bet in the name of your charity. A member's group might even hold regular sweepstakes, donating half of the winnings to your organization with the other half going to the winning ticket holder.

Lotteries and Raffles

Lotteries and raffles can assist charities in many ways, and there is no real difference between the two, although the term lottery is most often used to describe competitions offering large sums of money. Lotteries of any kind require extensive publicity, plus a solid and widespread network of ticket distribution. Make sure your organization has both these factors covered before embarking on any lottery promotion.

Lotteries

• **CATEGORY:** GENERAL • **GROUP SIZE:** SM./MED./LARGE • **TIME FRAME:** UP TO 1 YR. • **TIME OF YEAR:** SPR./SUM./FALL/WINT.

Many provincial and even national lotteries can only be operated legally if the proceeds are donated to charity. If such is the case in your area, make sure that your local lottery commissioners know of your organization's existence and cause. Apply for funds as often as you are permitted. As they say, if your cause is just, it should reap the reward.

Where legal, there is no reason why your organization should not set up its own lottery, although prize values offered by a small organization will seem insignificant when compared to national or provincial lotteries. Remember, the odds of winning a locally sponsored lottery are much higher and participants know exactly where their money is going.

Car Lotteries

The Real Thing

• **CATEGORY:** SERVICE CLUBS/GENERAL • **GROUP SIZE:** SM./MED. • **TIME FRAME:** UP TO 1 YR. • **TIME OF YEAR:** SPR./SUM./FALL/WINT.

The car lottery, mainstay of many charity and service organizations, has always held wide appeal. The prospect of owning a shiny new Buick, Jeep, Voyager, Saturn, Honda, or Lexus has enormous attraction for someone with a ten-year-old Chevette, although much less appeal to someone who already owns a new car. Car lotteries can always be successful for any organization with large membership as well as for a committed band of volunteers willing to sell tickets at every opportunity.

Here are some suggestions for spicing up the old idea:

"Limited" Lottery

• **CATEGORY:** SERVICE CLUBS/GENERAL • **GROUP SIZE:** SM./MED. • **TIME FRAME:** UP TO 1 YR. • **TIME OF YEAR:** SPR./SUM./FALL/WINT.

We know the odds of winning a car in a lottery depend on the number of tickets sold: to raise $30,000 for charity on a car costing $30,000, the odds of winning on a one dollar ticket must be at least 1:60,000. If on the other hand, tickets are sold at $100 each, the odds decrease to 1:600. Selling tickets at $100 each is not necessarily difficult if your organization can encourage groups of people to buy tickets collectively, holding a secondary lottery among themselves.

"Special Car" Lottery

• **CATEGORY:** SERVICE CLUBS/GENERAL • **GROUP SIZE:** SM./MED./LARGE • **TIME FRAME:** UP TO 1 YR. • **TIME OF YEAR:** SPR./SUM./FALL/WINT.

Anyone with enough money can buy a new car, so create a "special" lottery by finding a car both rare and desirable. Very attractive vintage cars can be purchased at quite reasonable prices if you shop around, and shopping around is the key to any special car lottery event.

"Celebrity Car" Lottery

• **CATEGORY:** SERVICE CLUBS/GENERAL • **GROUP SIZE:** SM./MED. • **TIME FRAME:** 1 YR+ • **TIME OF YEAR:** SPR./SUM./FALL/WINT.

Whatever happens to celebrity cars? – they can't all end up in museums and memorabilia exhibitions. Elvis Presley's limo or John Lennon's minicar are unlikely to come your way, but there is no shortage of previously owned-by-celebrity cars on which you might hold a lottery or auction. Start making enquiries today.

"Car and Chauffeur" Lottery

• **CATEGORY:** SERVICE CLUBS/GENERAL • **GROUP SIZE:** SM./MED. • **TIME FRAME:** UP TO 1 YR. • **TIME OF YEAR:** SPR./SUM./FALL/WINT.

Why not offer the service of a full-time chauffeur to the lottery winner of your new car. The chauffeur would be employed for the first week, month, or year of ownership, depending on what potential fundraising goal your group has established for the lottery.

Buy an Extra Ticket for Charity

• **CATEGORY:** GENERAL • **GROUP SIZE:** MED./LARGE • **TIME FRAME:** UP TO 6 MTHS. • **TIME OF YEAR:** SPR./SUM./FALL/WINT.

Some charities have been successful with campaigns to persuade veteran lottery players to increase their luck with the purchase of a lottery ticket for charity every time they buy one ticket for themselves. This idea has been especially attractive to those charities dealing with disadvantaged children, but the N.F.P. group must set up a fraud-proof system which enables people to donate a ticket to charity, without actual possession, so there would be no chance of theft or fraud.

1 (900) Lottery

• **CATEGORY:** GENERAL • **GROUP SIZE:** MED./LARGE • **TIME FRAME:** UP TO 6 MTHS. • **TIME OF YEAR:** SPR./SUM./FALL/WINT.

Modern telecommunications make it possible for people to participate in lotteries without ever leaving the comfort of their own homes. A 1-900 interactive telephone number enables a caller to enter his/her name in any lottery and pay the stake money on their telephone bill. Your organization could install a 1-900 number lottery system which would bill callers, say $4.99 a minute. A small percentage of the money would be assessed as costs and the remainder passed to your charity or N.F.P. organization. A pre-recorded message would inform callers about the organization, your lottery and its prizes, whereupon they would be asked to state name, address, and telephone number so that a lottery ticket could be mailed to them. The first minute of each call would entitle the caller to one ticket; callers could be allowed to remain on the line for as long as they wished, receiving one ticket for each additional minute.

A word of caution: 1-900 numbers are inter-provincial and can be accessed from outside of the country. Lotteries in one province or country may be unlawful in another and it is advisable to seek good legal counsel before embarking on a project of this nature.

The Perpetual Lottery

• **CATEGORY:** GENERAL • **GROUP SIZE:** SM./MED./LARGE • **TIME FRAME:** UP TO 1 YR. • **TIME OF YEAR:** SPR./SUM./FALL/WINT.

A perpetual lottery is exciting all year round. Tickets are sold with a draw held on the last day of every month of the year. Each ticket is entered into 12 consecutive draws, and because tickets are sold continuously throughout the year, the lottery continues on and on. Each ticket should cost anywhere from $100 to $1,000. Each month (for 12 months) the ticket represents a chance at the grand prize. Note: prizes must be worth winning and must reflect the cost of the tickets. A perpetual lottery, where legal, provides any organization with a continual and fairly reliable cash flow.

Raffles

Few people equate raffles with gambling, yet this is precisely what they are. The odds of winning any raffle can be calculated by dividing the number of tickets sold by the number of prizes to be awarded.

People buy raffle tickets for a variety of reasons, including politeness, the wish to make a donation to a specific cause, for the thrill of participation, or merely to get rid of the seller. Some people even buy tickets to win prizes, and this is the only group that you, as a raffle organizer, have any real control over. Three factors affect raffle sales: price of tickets, quality of prizes, and the number of tickets sold.

The easiest way to make money from a raffle is to canvas your supporters and sponsors for donations of prizes, and offer service prizes which cost only volunteer time and effort: a spring house cleaning, a year's free lawn mowing, and so on. One charity N.F.P. group calls this process time tithing. Raffle tickets are easiest to sell during a participation event, and should be considered as an automatic additional fundraiser whenever a large group of people is gathered together for a charitable cause.

Limit ticket sales to a specific number, and purchasers will know precisely what the odds of winning are. As long as the odds appear reasonably favourable, you encourage greater sales. By limiting ticket sales, you will know in advance exactly how much money is to be made when all tickets are sold.

One way of enhancing raffle ticket sales is to offer a significant prize – a house or a round-the-world trip. Remember, if your organization is paying for the prize, it had better be sure to sell enough tickets to cover the cost, and then some.

Alternatively, offer very unusual prizes, or desirable and hard to get prizes, or those normally unattainable at any price. Here are some examples:

• One day's full use of the president's private suite at a major sports stadium during a major game, including all meals, drinks, introduction to the teams and presentation of trophies

• Twenty-four hours use of a company's private jet, with pilot

• A day on the set of a major movie with a brief appearance in the finished film

• A guest appearance on a TV talk show or as an assistant on a "how-to" TV show

• Conduct a symphony orchestra

"Every Ticket Wins" Raffle

• **CATEGORY:** GENERAL • **GROUP SIZE:** SM./MED./LARGE • **TIME FRAME:** UP TO 1 YR. • **TIME OF YEAR:** SPR./SUM./FALL/WINT.

What if every purchaser of a raffle ticket knew that he/she was going to win when the ticket was purchased? Your charity will sell more tickets when it can give that guarantee.

Here's what to do. Approach local businesses requesting that each support your raffle by donating a prize and by offering discounts to unlucky ticket holders. Ask a hotel to donate an all-inclusive weekend package for two as a major prize in the raffle; then suggest that it also offer a special two-for-one rate, subject to restrictions, to holders of losing tickets. A restaurant might give a dinner-for-four as a prize, and then offer a "Buy one entrée, Get one free" midweek special to the raffle losers. Retail stores donating a raffle prize might offer a ten percent discount to those that don't win.

Consolation prizes should only be valid for a specified period following the raffle, 60 days perhaps. Each offering should provide the participating businesses with additional customers during that period.

Offer your incentives in one of two ways: draw up a list of all awards and give a copy to each ticket purchaser, or print details of one specific incentive on the back of each ticket. If ten businesses are offering incentives, print details of each on ten percent of the tickets.

Here is one suggested wording:

Congratulations. You may not have won
1st prize in our raffle, but you have already won
a weekend get-a-way* at a hotel at HALF PRICE.
Just call 1-800-555-1111 anytime between 30 June
and 30 September, 1997. Tell the operator that you
are holding this special ticket and that you want
to claim your consolation prize. You will immediately
be given full information about this fabulous offer.

*subject to certain restrictions.

OR

This is a winning ticket worth up to $25.
Congratulations! You are a winner when you present
this ticket at any of the following fine restaurants between
January 4 and February 28, 1999. You will receive
TWO entrées for the price of one.
Maximum value $25.
• The Mexican Hat, Main Street
• Rialto, Back Street
• L' Artichoke et Faison, King Street
• Hardy's Fast Foods any of the 26 locations

Certain restrictions may apply. Not valid on February 14

Always try to choose establishments which would appeal to the majority of your potential ticket purchasers, and offer a variety of styles and prices so that most people will see the advantage of purchasing a ticket.

No Win – No Pay Raffle

• **CATEGORY:** GENERAL • **GROUP SIZE:** SM./MED./LARGE • **TIME FRAME:** UP TO 6 MTHS. • **TIME OF YEAR:** SPR./SUM./FALL/WINT.

You may think that only an idiot would return the purchase price to losers in a raffle, but this apparently crazy idea just might work for you. It's simple to operate. Print on the ticket:

Guaranteed Money Back Offer
If this ticket doesn't win a prize in our grand raffle on
15 July, 1999, bring it to our office by noon on
the 20 July, 1999 and we will be happy to give you back
the purchase price, in full.
All unclaimed money will be used to help find a cure
for . . . (acute discombobulation).
Thank you for purchasing this ticket,
your support means a lot to us.

How many people would ask for a return of their money when confronted with a message like the above. Make sure your guarantee carries the following qualifications – "Only the price of one ticket will be refunded per person."

The money back guarantee is not a feasible gambit when individual raffle tickets are priced over $20.

Dream Home Raffle

• **CATEGORY:** GENERAL • **GROUP SIZE:** MED./LARGE • **TIME FRAME:** UP TO 1 YR. • **TIME OF YEAR:** SPR./SUM./FALL/WINT.

Owning a beautifully furnished and perfectly decorated home in an upscale neighbourhood is almost everyone's dream – and a good raffle possibility. Your organization should contact those local developers who are building new houses, stressing the amount of publicity they will receive if they can work with you to raffle one of their new homes. Discuss the value of such advertising and ask what it would be worth to each developer. You may be able to negotiate a very low purchase price, and your persuasive skills will be put to the test again as you seek out appropriate interior designers, furniture and appliance manufacturers to provide the goods and services necessary to put together an irresistible package.

Any home previously used as a designer show house is also an ideal property for a raffle because thousands of people will have had the opportunity of visiting the house with almost every visitor wishing that he/she could own it.

Other raffle ideas include:

Spend a Day With . . .

• **CATEGORY:** GENERAL • **GROUP SIZE:** MED./LARGE • **TIME FRAME:** UP TO 1 YR. • **TIME OF YEAR:** SPR./SUM./FALL/WINT.

Do not assume that famous people will always refuse. If you believe your cause is worthy enough, then just ask.

Vacation

• **CATEGORY:** SERVICE CLUBS/GENERAL • **GROUP SIZE:** SM./MED. • **TIME FRAME:** UP TO 1 YR. • **TIME OF YEAR:** SPR./SUM./FALL/WINT.

An additional two weeks paid holiday is a very desirable prize for many workers. A large company might operate an entire raffle based on time off work, with prizes varying from a single day to several weeks.

Out Of This World

• **CATEGORY:** GENERAL • **GROUP SIZE:** MED. • **TIME FRAME:** 1 YR+ • **TIME OF YEAR:** SPR./SUM./FALL/WINT.

Make sure that your organization is one of the first to offer a trip to the moon or a space walk as a major prize in a raffle. Write to NASA today and enquire as to when passenger trips will become available.

Double Prize

• **CATEGORY:** GENERAL • **GROUP SIZE:** SM./MED./LARGE • **TIME FRAME:** UP TO 1 YR. • **TIME OF YEAR:** SPR./SUM./FALL/WINT.

Offer a bonus to people selling your raffle tickets: have TWO first prizes, one for the winning ticket number and the other, of similar value, given to the person who sells the most tickets.

HOLIDAYS – CHRISTMAS AND EASTER

Christmas Trees

• **CATEGORY:** GENERAL • **GROUP SIZE:** SM. • **TIME FRAME:** UP TO 6 MTHS. • **TIME OF YEAR:** WINT.

Many Canadian households have decorated trees at Christmas, and Christmas trees are an ideal fundraising source: purchase in bulk, and sell them at a profit. Many service clubs raise money in this manner, either by taking advance orders, selling trees door-to-door or selling them in a public place. Profit margins vary considerably but, if you live in an area where evergreen trees are grown, your best deal is to cut and transport the trees yourself. For maximum profit seek out a landowner who is prepared to donate the trees.

Here are some other tree fundraising ideas:

Light Up the Tree

• **CATEGORY:** GENERAL • **GROUP SIZE:** SM. • **TIME FRAME:** UP TO 4WKS. • **TIME OF YEAR:** WINT.

A large Christmas tree in a public place always attracts attention when lit with hundreds, or thousands, of bulbs. Working with municipal authorities, seek out an appropriate location and erect a large, stately tree without lights, a few weeks before Christmas. Invite each passer-by to purchase a light bulb. Add bulbs to the tree as they are purchased, each with a Christmas tag bearing the name of the donor. Encourage community spirit. People will take pride in the fact that their bulb has helped light the tree. As additional encouragement, you might donate the decorated tree to the local hospital a few days prior to Christmas and/or remove all of the tags to use as raffle tickets, the chosen winner to receive a suitable prize. Prices for each bulb should depend on location, and range from one to ten dollars or more. Save all the bulbs for subsequent appeals.

Ask people to put presents under your tree. Begin by placing a few wrapped parcels to give people the right idea. Make suggestions about the types of presents most suitable. Obviously this event is most appropriate for organizations catering to the needs of children, and new toys are the prime target.

Decorated Trees

• CATEGORY: GENERAL • GROUP SIZE: SM./MED.• TIME FRAME: UP TO 6 MTHS. • TIME OF YEAR: WINT.

Beg, borrow or buy decorations and lights to decorate dozens of Christmas trees in a park or town centre. Hold collections from sightseers every evening and have collection boxes strategically placed during the day. Combine this event with evening carolling or a Nativity play.

• CATEGORY: GENERAL • GROUP SIZE: SM. • TIME FRAME: UP TO 4WKS. • TIME OF YEAR: WINT.

Alternatively, set up several hundred small Christmas trees in a public place and invite families to decorate them. Charge a fee and award a small prize to the winner. People will participate to have their tree shown in public. You will create goodwill and publicity.

• CATEGORY: GENERAL • GROUP SIZE: SM. • TIME FRAME: UP TO 4WKS. • TIME OF YEAR: WINT.

Not everybody has the time to decorate a Christmas tree and many would happily pay money to a charity to get the tree done. An advertisement such as, "Please Let Us Decorate Your Christmas Tree to Help Someone in Need This Holiday Season," will attract attention. The donor can supply his/her own tree and decorations or, for a price, your organization can supply the necessary materials. Visiting people in their own homes at Christmas gives your members and volunteers an opportunity to make good contacts.

• CATEGORY: GENERAL • GROUP SIZE: MED./LARGE • TIME FRAME: UP TO 6 MTHS.. • TIME OF YEAR: WINT.

Interior designers, artists, window dressers and art students can create beautifully decorated Christmas trees. Ask them to create trees in various locations around the town and solicit public donations at each location while people watch. Store windows, hospital atriums, and shopping malls probably provide the best display locations. Management of a large shopping mall might even deliver a donation in order to have the trees as an attraction during the holiday season.

You might also consider inviting a number of celebrities to decorate trees and donate them to your organization. Perhaps you could accumulate enough trees to hold an annual auction. A single tree makes an excellent centrepiece for a holiday raffle.

Pre-decorated Christmas trees can be auctioned, and they are ideal for a television auction. Consider asking all of the staff of a local television company to decorate trees and then devote a special program to selling them for your charity. This could become an annual ritual.

Lights

• **CATEGORY:** GENERAL • **GROUP SIZE:** SM./MED. • **TIME FRAME:** UP TO 1 YR. • **TIME OF YEAR:** WINT.

Illuminated houses, buildings and trees all attract attention at Christmas and some displays are so spectacular that thousands of sightseers flock to them year after year. Residents in some communities even hold competitions for the best illuminated house and local newspapers print details of the streets most worth visiting.

Why not put up a display of Christmas lights on a public building, or even your own offices. Hold a "Lighting Up" ceremony as part of a major event which might also include carol singing, craft sales, or a grand raffle. Santa Claus could be on hand to have his picture taken and hand out cookies.

If your town or city holds an annual ceremony to switch on Christmas lights, why not become part of the event. Liaise with the organizers about the possibility of holding a collection and announcing to the crowd that lights are being switched on to benefit your organization. Perhaps you can offer an incentive by arranging for one of your sponsors to give the tree, decorations, and lights on behalf of your organization.

Decorated Houses

• **CATEGORY:** GENERAL • **GROUP SIZE:** SM. • **TIME FRAME:** UP TO 4WKS. • **TIME OF YEAR:** WINT.

Some people go to considerable trouble to decorate their houses during the holiday season with thousands of lights. Maybe they would be happy to have you put a collection box on their front lawn: they might even agree to hold collections on your behalf. If you, or someone in your group, has a prominently located house, decorate it yourselves and raise money.

A Note of Caution: Neighbours do not appreciate congestion caused by constant streams of traffic, even when it is for a good cause. There have even been a few cases of municipalities threatening legal action where displays have caused serious disruption and annoyance. Check with your neighbours before commencing.

Santa Claus/St. Nicholas

A Santa costume costs very little to buy. Alternatively, it can be easily made by anybody with a sewing machine and basic dress-making skills. Santas are constantly in demand at holiday time and money can be raised in numerous ways, including straightforward street or mall collections.

Santa Present Deliveries

• **CATEGORY:** RELIGIOUS/GENERAL • **GROUP SIZE:** SM. • **TIME FRAME:** UP TO 4WKS. • **TIME OF YEAR:** WINT.

Advertise your service and arrange for a drop-off point where parents bring the gifts that Santa will deliver. Have an army of Santa's available for a few evenings during the holidays, especially December 24th. Charge extra for deliveries on Christmas Eve and Christmas Day.

Photos with Santa

• **CATEGORY:** GENERAL • **GROUP SIZE:** SM. • **TIME FRAME:** UP TO 6 MTHS. • **TIME OF YEAR:** WINT.

Although there are professional Santas who provide this service to malls each year, there is no reason why you should not approach mall management and offer to provide the service for charity. With enough volunteer Santas to provide a reliable service, you can make money.

Santa's Workshop

• **CATEGORY:** GENERAL • **GROUP SIZE:** SM. • **TIME FRAME:** UP TO 1 YR. • **TIME OF YEAR:** WINT.

A small workshop filled with toys, dolls and a few tools can be set up almost anywhere. Children of all ages will be captivated as Santa and his elves prepare gifts for Christmas. Charge a small fee for viewing, and a greater fee for a photo taken with Santa in his very own workshop. Sell inexpensive toys at a good price to raise additional money.

Sleigh Rides

• **CATEGORY:** GENERAL • **GROUP SIZE:** SM. • **TIME FRAME:** UP TO 6 MTHS. • **TIME OF YEAR:** WINT.

Buy or build a sleigh, and find a willing volunteer with a horse to haul it. Seek out a suitable venue with great scenery, maybe a tree farm. You will need plenty of snow, and some popular outdoor location where people naturally congregate. Combine this event with a winter picnic, an ice skating party, or a mass snowball fight around a roaring fire.

Carol Singing

• **CATEGORY:** RELIGIOUS/ARTS & THEATRE • **GROUP SIZE:** SM. • **TIME FRAME:** UP TO 4WKS. • **TIME OF YEAR:** WINT.

A well-rehearsed carol singing group, plying its art in a mall or busy shopping street, a week or so before Christmas, should always be able to raise a reasonable sum. Apart from a few practice sessions, no other organization is required. There is no financial outlay, and absolutely no risk, other than potential embarrassment.

Here are a few refinements to the craft:

- Dress singers in elegant Victorian costumes
- Team up with a few musicians
- Advertise time and location of each carol sing
- Approach hotels and restaurants, offering to sing at annual Christmas dinners
- Stage a sponsored carol singing

Hold a carolling marathon when you and some friends sing carols for 24 hours with sponsorship from colleagues, and family. Don't forget to solicit donations from spectators and passers-by.

Hold an annual black-tie carol concert or a Messiah sing-a-long. Your group will need the services of an orchestra, and at least one professional singer, together with a massive choir. You may well have to pay the professionals for their appearances, so target major contributors for sponsorship of the event. A less formal carol concert can be arranged with a local band and choir.

• **CATEGORY:** RELIGIOUS/ARTS & THEATRE • **GROUP SIZE:** MED. • **TIME FRAME:** UP TO 6 MTHS. • **TIME OF YEAR:** WINT.

Hold a carol singing competition and judge the following:

- The best overall performance by an individual, duet, quartet, or full choir
- Best unaccompanied individual, duet etc.
- Best self accompanied individual etc.
- Best organ or piano solo
- Best performance of a carol on a non-traditional instrument

Funds may be raised by charging each competitor a fee; entree fees for spectators; corporate sponsorship; and from the sale of refreshments and holiday gifts. Obtain trophies and appropriate prizes from corporate sponsors. Carol competitions can be arranged to suit a variety of age groups and capabilities, and provide an excellent venue for performances by people with disabilities.

• **CATEGORY:** RELIGIOUS/ARTS & THEATRE • **GROUP SIZE:** MED/LRG. • **TIME FRAME:** UP TO 6 MTHS. • **TIME OF YEAR:** WINT.

Hold a carol writing competition and be amazed at how many people enter. If you can persuade a radio or TV station to broadcast the winning entries, then you will receive additional publicity and even more entries. Offer prizes that will be attractive to your target group. Publicize the competition through holiday newsletters. Request a minimum donation with each entry and require each to be accompanied by a form giving you permission to use the carol and reproduce it for the benefit of your organization. Appoint an impartial panel of judges. One way to avoid criticism is to hold a public concert of all entries and allow the entire audience to vote. Use the entries from your carol writing to compile a book of carols to be sold throughout your organization.

Christmas Cakes

• **CATEGORY:** WOMEN'S GROUPS/GENERAL • **GROUP SIZE:** SM./MED. • **TIME FRAME:** UP TO 4WKS. • **TIME OF YEAR:** WINT.

Make your own Christmas cakes, or purchase them in bulk from a bakery to sell in any way that you can. Almost everyone buys a Christmas cake, so why not give people an opportunity to make a charitable donation at the same time. If you make your own cakes, try to be original. Above all, make sure that they taste good. Create demand for the future, so that people will order your cakes a year in advance – just to get one.

Christmas Cards

• **CATEGORY:** RELIGIOUS/GENERAL • **GROUP SIZE:** SM./MED./LARGE • **TIME FRAME:** UP TO 6 MTHS. • **TIME OF YEAR:** FALL/WINT.

Computerized desktop publishing software makes it possible for any organization to produce high quality personalized Christmas cards which can serve a dual purpose: raising money while spreading the word about your organization.

Design a good card, with an appropriate message, or find a talented artist who will donate a design. Solicit orders early in the year, before people can say they have already bought. Make sure all of your members, donors and clients buy at least one box of cards.

If you are unable to find suitable design ideas, hold a competition. Offer a prize and charge a small entry fee for each aspiring designer. If you count a well-known artist or cartoonist amongst your supporters, he/she might agree to design a special card for you. Frame the original and auction it at an appropriate event, and be prepared to offer the artist part of the proceeds. Don't forget holiday gift tags. These too can be specially designed and personalized.

Easter Egg Hunt

• **CATEGORY:** GENERAL/CHILDREN & YOUTH • **GROUP SIZE:** SM. • **TIME FRAME:** UP TO 4WKS. • **TIME OF YEAR:** SPR.

An egg hunt requires a field or public park where any number of wrapped, chocolate Easter eggs can be safely hidden to be discovered later by young children who will want to gather and eat as many as possible. Any area with good green growth, lots of lawn, trees and bushes, or even an old building (providing it is safe) will do. Don't forget to find several very good hiding places for especially large eggs.

Sell tickets in advance, and you will be able to budget your expenditures based on the results. You can then purchase a suitable number of eggs knowing that you have made a profit. Use a spectacularly large egg, to be placed on public display for several weeks beforehand, as your publicity focus. You might even ask a store owner to donate the display in return for your purchase of all the smaller eggs. Ask merchants to sell tickets for you.

Concentrate your publicity around day-care centres, kindergartens, elementary schools, and junior youth organizations.

You will need a team of people to hide the eggs, and they must be out at first light on the day of the event. At the appointed start-time, let ticket holders in by cutting the entrance ribbon, opening the gate, or whatever. People without tickets can pay at the entrance.

• **CATEGORY:** GENERAL • **GROUP SIZE:** MED./LARGE • **TIME FRAME:** UP TO 1 YR. • **TIME OF YEAR:** SPR.

For an adult variation of this hunt, fill a large egg with loonies, or even a quantity of gold jewellery. The hiding place will necessarily be much more difficult to find, perhaps hidden in an area consisting of several square miles. Security is a potential problem and you would be wise to post a guard near your hiding place to ensure that any person discovering the egg is a bona fide ticket holder. You should have no difficulty selling tickets with a valuable price at stake.

An EGGSTRAVAGANZA, or series of egg-related fundraising events held at Easter, followed by an Easter parade, can become an annual event for your community and a major fundraiser for you.

• **CATEGORY:** GENERAL • **GROUP SIZE:** SM./MED./LARGE • **TIME FRAME:** UP TO 1 YR.• **TIME OF YEAR:** SPR.

Raise money by charging an entry fee, asking for donations, or by selling eggs and egg products at a profit. Prizes of enormous Easter eggs should be awarded to the winners.

Here are some ideas for EGG events:

- Egg Rolling: entrants roll hard-boiled eggs down a hill, and the egg which rolls furthest without breaking is the winner
- Egg Word Making: an eggstraordinarily eggsacting and eggciting event
- Egg Shelling: how fast can you shell a hard-boiled egg? How many eggs can you shell in 30 seconds? Make sure that you have a reliable stopwatch
- Egg Eating: how many eggs can one person eat in 30 seconds? Raw eggs or hard-boiled, the decision is yours
- Egg Toss: this is a world record event. One person throws an uncooked egg and another has to catch it without it breaking. See the *Guinness Book of Records* for the current record distance
- Egg Decorating: contestants have a limited time to decorate an egg with paints provided
- Omelette Tossing: each contestant must make an omelette then run an obstacle course, tossing the omelette a minimum number of times during the race without dropping it
- Easter Bonnet Competition: best decorated, biggest, most original or any such category

Make more money by selling Easter cakes, Easter biscuits, Easter eggs and any other seasonal products.

LIFESTYLE

Fashion Party

• **CATEGORY:** WOMEN'S GROUPS/GENERAL • **GROUP SIZE:** SM./MED. • **TIME FRAME:** UP TO 1 YR. • **TIME OF YEAR:** SPR./SUM./FALL/WINT.

As an alternative to a formal fashion show, arrange a charity fashion party in a clothing store. Approach the retailer with the idea of such an event as a vehicle for introducing a new collection, or merely as a way of enticing potential new customers into the store.

Combine the store mailing list with your membership and supporter's lists to secure a wide range of people. Some attendees will come because the event is a charity fundraiser, others will be more interested in the new season's fashions.

Any charity or N.F.P. with an extensive membership list offers fashion retailers access to a large number of potential new customers. Ask the retailer to share advertising and administrative costs.

Ticket sales, which account for the majority of the funds raised, can be augmented with proceeds from a raffle or an auction of donated items. Your party should be a combination of events: part fashion show, part social gathering, and part a "try on" of selected merchandise. Serve light refreshments, but be tactful and make sure they are not a potential hazard to the fashions being presented. Suitable entertainment can also be included.

Fashion Shows

• **CATEGORY:** HEALTH RELATED/WOMEN'S GROUPS/GENERAL • **GROUP SIZE:** SM./MED./LARGE • **TIME FRAME:** UP TO 1 YR.
• **TIME OF YEAR:** SPR./SUM./FALL/WINT.

Whether a "formal dress" affair organized in conjunction with a major fashion house by the headquarters of an international charity, or a local store displaying winter stock to the local

Women's Institute in the Scout's Hall, the net result is the same – charitable fashion shows are successful and have been a fundraising mainstay for many years. The quality of fashions displayed and the effort put into ticket sales will determine the rate of success.

Determine your potential audience first, then decide on the type of fashions to be shown. Your group members will probably be selling most of your tickets to people similar to themselves. The fashions chosen should thus be relevant to this market, both in design and price. You may even want to use organization members as models.

The venue selected depends on the size and tone of your show. Selling two-dollar tickets for a fashion show in the high school gymnasium is easier than selling tickets for a $150 show in a prime hotel but, with the right fashions and a location suitable to your clientele, both events should succeed.

Consider raising additional funds by auctioning one of the exhibits, holding a draw, and selling refreshments.

Here is a list of possible show themes:

- Fashions for Physically Challenged
- Petite and Ultra-Petite Fashions
- Extra Large Fashions
- Fashions for Toddlers and Babies
- Teenager and Young Adult Fashions
- Baby-Boomer Fashions
- Fashions for the Over 70's
- Fashions for Mothers-to-Be
- Bridal Fashions
- Swim-Wear and Holiday Fashions
- Winter Holiday Wear
- Sleepwear and Lingerie
- Sportswear
- Gowns & Tuxedos

Hair Cutting

• **CATEGORY:** WOMEN'S GROUPS/GENERAL • **GROUP SIZE:** SM./MED./LARGE • **TIME FRAME:** UP TO 6 MTHS. • **TIME OF YEAR:** SPR./SUM./FALL/WINT.

Hairdressing schools frequently seek volunteers willing to have their hair cut by senior students (although some schools do charge a nominal amount for the service). Why not approach your local beautician's college and suggest a 'cut-a-thon' which would enable haircutting students to practice their skills while raising money for charity. Everybody wins in this arrangement as students gain experience. The hairdressing school receives publicity, members of the public get a hair cut and your N.F.P. group receives the money.

Also consider inviting professional hair stylists to cut hair for charity, for an amount considerably higher than the student cut fee. Contact local hair stylists and ask them to donate a few hours of their time cutting hair for charity. The event should be well-publicized, and they may feel the public exposure is beneficial as a vehicle for attracting new clients.

Make Overs

• **CATEGORY:** WOMEN'S GROUPS/GENERAL • **GROUP SIZE:** SM./MED./LARGE • **TIME FRAME:** UP TO 1 YR. • **TIME OF YEAR:** SPR./SUM./FALL/WINT.

Many women and some men enjoy the prospect of a complete new look, and a "One Day Make Over Event" usually attracts a ready, paying clientele. Beauticians and cosmetic companies may jump at a chance to be a part of this one-day event. Gather together beauticians, estheticians, and hairstylists, all of whom should be familiar with the aims of your charity N.F.P. group. Whether you have to pay for their services will depend on your contacts, your cause and the beneficial publicity that the participants are likely to receive. Invite a celebrity hair stylist to perform as a star attraction.

Sponsorship should be obtained from leading cosmetic and hair care product manufacturers and everyone should be charged an entry fee. Invite women's groups, other charity organizations, and the public at large. Promote the event in drugstores, and the offices of its participating practitioners. Distribute a very large number of "FREE" raffle tickets making holders eligible to win a free make over, free massage or free body care products on the day of the event. To win, the holder must be present at the event when the draw is made.

Head Shaving

• **CATEGORY:** FITNESS, SPORTS & SOCIAL/SERVICE CLUBS • **GROUP SIZE:** SM. • **TIME FRAME:** UP TO 6 MTHS. • **TIME OF YEAR:** SPR./SUM./FALL/WINT.

Head shaving is a weird and successful charity fundraiser. It is basically a challenge event initiated by any person willing to have his/her head shaved. Funds are collected as pledges from friends, relatives and colleagues. Alternatively there is the target collection, wherein the person who is willing to have his/her head shaved sets a target figure for his friends and colleagues to beat. When the required sum is raised, he/she loses their hair, and the money passes to charity.

Head shaving can also be a team "sport" when a group who has agreed to raise money for an organization in any way it can penalizes the person who raised the least amount by shaving his/her head. Alternatively, every participant in the event can have his/her head shaved except for the individual who raised the most money.

Beard Growing

• **CATEGORY:** FITNESS, SPORTS & SOCIAL/SERVICE CLUBS • **GROUP SIZE:** SM. • **TIME FRAME:** UP TO 4WKS. • **TIME OF YEAR:** SPR./SUM./FALL/WINT.

Growing a beard for charity is a popular fundraiser, and your members can instigate competitions to raise a few hundred dollars at any time. There are two methods:

The Individual Challenge

A well-known local figure makes a fairly outrageous challenge, i.e., that he not shave on every day that $100 is donated to a particular cause. His family, friends and colleagues conspire to raise daily pledges of at least $100 to ensure beard growth.

The Group Challenge

This involves any number of men: members of the same club, organization, colleagues at work, or friends. Each person pledges a sum to a charity based inversely on length of beard after 14 days. Anyone still clean-shaven after that period pays $100. Each millimetre of beard growth results in a five-dollar deduction from the original donation: thus a person who grows 20 millimetres of beard and has received pledges totalling $100, pays nothing.

Knitting

Knitting is a surprisingly consistent fundraiser. Almost every household has a bag full of unused wool stuffed in a cupboard somewhere. Your charity needs to ask for donations. Contact knitting and embroidery stores and ask them to donate dirty, damaged or unsalable stock. As a last resort, your volunteers can unpick donated clothing.

• **CATEGORY:** WOMEN'S GROUPS/FITNESS, SPORTS & SOCIAL • **GROUP SIZE:** SM./MED. • **TIME FRAME:** UP TO 6 MTHS. • **TIME OF YEAR:** SPR./FALL/WINT.

All organization members, friends, spouses, and children can participate in a sponsored knit: sponsorship to be based on the length of time, the amount of wool, or the number of 6"x 6" squares knitted in a day. A sponsored knit, in addition to raising money for your organization, must produce something worthwhile. Knitting blankets, mitts, gloves, or socks for the homeless or elderly will ensure maximum publicity and good will.

• **CATEGORY:** WOMEN'S GROUPS/FITNESS, SPORTS & SOCIAL • **GROUP SIZE:** SM./MED. • **TIME FRAME:** UP TO 1 YR. • **TIME OF YEAR:** SPR./FALL/WINT.

Why not combine a sponsored knit with an attempt to produce the world's longest scarf or biggest blanket. If your organization is regionally or nationally based, all branches could participate on the same day, with each branch sponsored to produce a huge knitted square made of numerous smaller squares stitched together. When completed and collected at organizational head-quarters, all of the squares would be sewn together to make a blanket the size of a football field. You might even set a colourful world record, especially if the blanket were to be designed in the form of a national flag or other recognizable symbol. When all the hoopla dies down, your gigantic bedding specimen could be dis-assembled into usable sized blankets for the homeless or needy.

• **CATEGORY:** WOMEN'S GROUPS/FITNESS, SPORTS & SOCIAL/ • **GROUP SIZE:** SM. • **TIME FRAME:** UP TO 1 YR. • **TIME OF YEAR:** SPR./SUM./FALL/WINT.

The next time you organize a craft fair, or sale of any kind, make it mandatory for each of your members to donate at least one knitted item. Many people can knit and lots of households have some oddments of wool. Baby clothes appear to be the most popular items with the highest profit potential.

• **CATEGORY:** WOMEN'S GROUPS/FITNESS, SPORTS & SOCIAL/ • **GROUP SIZE:** SM./MED. • **TIME FRAME:** UP TO 6 MTHS. • **TIME OF YEAR:** SPR./FALL/WINT.

Why not hold an annual knitters' fair. Invite suppliers of wool, patterns, knitting machines etc., to purchase space and to give exhibitions. Sell space to knitters who have garments, toys and novelties for sale. Make additional money from refreshment sales, a grand raffle, and door money.

Motor Vehicle Licence Plates

• **CATEGORY:** GENERAL • **GROUP SIZE:** LARGE • **TIME FRAME:** UP TO 1 YR. • **TIME OF YEAR:** SPR./SUM./FALL/WINT.

A recent innovation in certain provinces permits license plates to bear crests and inscriptions of selected charitable organizations in place of the lines extolling provincial virtues. A donation to the charity depicted is added automatically to the cost of the plate. There is no reason why all Canadian provinces should not adopt this scheme, and every major charity/N.F.P. organization should apply to have plates issued for its benefit.

Mystery Tours

• **CATEGORY:** FITNESS, SPORTS & SOCIAL/GENERAL • **GROUP SIZE:** SM./MED. • **TIME FRAME:** UP TO 6 MTHS. • **TIME OF YEAR:** SPR./SUM./FALL/WINT.

The once popular mystery bus tour seems to have disappeared with the rise of the automobile. Perhaps your organization can revive the idea and give your members a day out together without worrying about drinking and driving laws, or the possibility of getting lost. Arrange an interesting route with imaginative stops, good meals, and entertainment. You may have people begging for a seat on your next coach.

Especially for Seniors

Events for seniors are usually strong fundraisers, and with the greying of the North American population, the number of seniors continues to grow. Consider the following fundraising ideas especially for the seniors' market:

• A Seniors' Fashion Show

• An Olde-Time Vaudeville Show with a mix of music, singing, dancing, and outrageous comedy, and an emphasis on participation and fun rather than professional perfection

• Bus Tours to the theatre, horticultural centres, museums, or to view autumn foliage or sporting events

• Board Games Bonanza: set up a hall or even a large home with card tables and a variety of games. Be sure to include all the old favourites: Monopoly™, Scrabble™, chess, Battleship™, checkers, Snakes and Ladders™, and Trivial Pursuit™. While you're at it, also include some of the newer games. Remember, learning a new game is often just as much fun as playing an old favourite.

Singles

How about staging events catering to singles. Make sure the settings are conducive to mingling, as most persons attending will be searching for companionship. Singles often have considerable disposable income, and will certainly want to spend money to impress others. Here are just a few ideas for possible singles events:

Masked Ball

Pick a date that sounds good to you. Have all guests outfitted in full costumes. Remember, it is always easier to interact with strangers when you are hidden by a mask.

Viennese Ball

The Canadian Hearing Society has used this fundraiser for years and provides guests with a night of free ballroom dance instruction prior to the event.

Dance Workshop

Present various forms of dance styles – from the cha-cha to line dancing – demonstrated by professionals. Once the presentation has been completed, break into smaller groups to study each particular style in greater depth. Offer both dance presentations and workshops for one low price. Make sure to choose a venue that will accommodate the entire group together, in addition to several smaller independent units. Make sure the floor is suitable for dancing (and not too slick).

Sitting Services

• **CATEGORY:** GENERAL • **GROUP SIZE:** SM. • **TIME FRAME:** UP TO 6 MTHS. • **TIME OF YEAR:** SPR./SUM./FALL/WINT.

Any organization with a healthy band of trustworthy volunteers can arrange sitters, for a fee, and many organizations are uniquely positioned to provide such a service to their clients and supporters.

Baby-Sitting

An ideal fundraising operation for groups of responsible teenagers or young parents. Baby-sitting services can be offered on an occasional basis to permit parents to attend functions and events, or operated on a regular basis.

Animal-Sitting

Any responsible group of animal loving volunteers can offer this service.

Plant-Sitting

Fundraising for any small local group can be done by looking after house plants for vacationers, busy executives, or people who are hospitalized.

Dieting

Sponsored Diet

• **CATEGORY:** HEALTH RELATED/FITNESS, SPORTS & SOCIAL • **GROUP SIZE:** SM./MED. • **TIME FRAME:** UP TO 6 MTHS.
• **TIME OF YEAR:** SPR./SUM./FALL/WINT.

Organize a mass-sponsored community diet at almost any time, although January is probably a good time to start as most people have overeaten during the holidays and are beginning to worry about getting into spring fashions. Individuals can be sponsored by friends, relatives, or colleagues. An entire shift of overweight Toronto police officers raised a substantial sum by losing weight in this manner. They were sponsored as a group on the basis of total number of pounds lost. Because the entire group was involved, no one was prepared to let his/her colleagues down. Everyone lost weight and the charity was the big winner.

Distribute sponsorship forms calling for donors to pledge an amount for every pound lost by the dieter. It should be noted that more than 90% of dieters regain lost weight within a couple of years. This means that sponsored diet fundraisers could become biannual fixtures.

• **CATEGORY:** HEALTH RELATED/FITNESS, SPORTS & SOCIAL • **GROUP SIZE:** SM./MED. • **TIME FRAME:** UP TO 6 MTHS. • **TIME OF YEAR:** SPR./SUM./FALL/WINT.

Devise a fine system for each person who fails to lose a certain amount of weight over a certain period of time. Combine this with a sponsored diet and your organization will win whatever the result.

• **CATEGORY:** HEALTH RELATED/FITNESS, SPORTS & SOCIAL • **GROUP SIZE:** SM./MED. • **TIME FRAME:** UP TO 6 MTHS. • **TIME OF YEAR:** SPR./SUM./FALL/WINT.

There is an ongoing demand for slimming and diet materials of all kinds. The selection is enormous. Why not organize a special event where relevant products and services can be displayed, demonstrated, and sold – everything from diet aids and slimming foods to exercise machines, liposuction services and plastic surgery. A doctor and dietician could be invited to give seminars and advice and have the entire event sponsored by one of the many commercial weight-loss organizations. Use this fundraiser as an introduction to a sponsored diet. Note that some diet products can result in harmful side effects: your research should be thorough and care should be taken.

Plants & Gardens

Flower Sales

• **CATEGORY:** HEALTH RELATED/GENERAL • **GROUP SIZE:** MED./LARGE • **TIME FRAME:** UP TO 1 YR. • **TIME OF YEAR:** SPR./FALL

Several major charities hold annual sales of cut flowers. By purchasing in bulk, direct from the grower, it is possible to buy flowers very cheaply, but you need an army of volunteers for wide distribution. Advance orders, and bulk sales to corporations and societies can account for a large part of your market. Flower sales have proved to be very lucrative for the Canadian Cancer Society and others. Is there room for more?

Flower Shows

• **CATEGORY:** SERVICE CLUBS/ENVIRONMENTAL • **GROUP SIZE:** SM./MED./LARGE • **TIME FRAME:** UP TO 6 MTHS.. • **TIME OF YEAR:** SPR./SUM./ FALL

Horticultural society members and gardening clubs are clearly best suited to organize an annual flower show, but the proceeds from such a show can be made available to any worthy charitable cause. A flower show can be any size, compatible with local conditions and local growers. A mammoth show will attract competitors, exhibitors and spectators from all over. Flower shows can be very profitable, and they provide numerous fundraising opportunities through sponsorship, exhibitor fees, competitions, entrance fees, product sales and ancillary events such as raffles, auctions, and refreshments.

Bulbs

• **CATEGORY:** WOMEN'S GROUPS/GENERAL • **GROUP SIZE:** SM./MED./LARGE • **TIME FRAME:** UP TO 1 YR. • **TIME OF YEAR:** FALL/WINT.

Many organizations sell cut flowers as part of an annual fundraising campaign. There are, however, drawbacks to such sales. Unsold flowers cannot be kept, and any cut flower campaign can only last for a few days, proceeding despite weather, lack of sellers, or any other problems that might arise. Your organization may wish to consider selling spring bulbs instead. Bulbs allow the purchaser to grow his/her own flowers. Tulips, amaryllis, or narcissus are appropriate and popular choices. Buy the bulbs in bulk to resell individually, or in small quantities, at any suitable event. Profit margins can be very high, especially for an organization with the ability to buy bulbs in substantial quantities.

Packaging

• **CATEGORY:** GENERAL • **GROUP SIZE:** MED./LARGE • **TIME FRAME:** UP TO 1 YR. • **TIME OF YEAR:** SPR./FALL/WINT.

Purchase spring bulbs in bulk and repackage them in small bags pre-printed with information about your cause. For example: *Proceeds from the sale of these bulbs will help a blind person who will never get to see the flowers. Your donation will prove that he/she has not been forgotten.*

Development of a Special Flowering Bulb

• **CATEGORY:** GENERAL • **GROUP SIZE:** LARGE • **TIME FRAME:** 1 YR+ • **TIME OF YEAR:** SPR./FALL/WINT.

While packages of any kind of bulbs can be sold on behalf of charity, your group may wish to consider finding one specific flowering bulb which would become the unmistakable hallmark of your organization. Horticulturists are continually developing new varieties of plants and flowers, and the market is very competitive. The potential sales a national charity or N.F.P. group can offer a new bulb variety producer are considerable indeed. Most major producers would vie for the chance of servicing such a market.

Contact several of the largest Canadian bulb growers and outline your organization's desire to have a flowering bulb variety named in its honour. Ask them to submit possibilities.

Once you have chosen the appropriate bulb, you will need to market it. Begin with a media announcement to the effect that a new variety of bulb has been developed especially for (organization), and that your organization will hold a fall sales campaign.

Purchase the bulbs in bulk, prepackaged in specially printed bags of six or twelve bulbs each. Distribute the bags throughout your organization in time for the sales campaign. Alternatively, you may choose to allow each of your branches to order numbers of bulb packs direct from the supplier. The producer may continue to sell the bulbs through his/her own sales network, but you can request that a percentage of each sale be credited to your organization, particularly if your group has made a monetary contribution to the bulb's development.

Nothing happens overnight and it will take a few years for sales to develop. The market should be steadily increasing every year. With sufficient selling tools, the bulb sale could become a major fundraiser with a potential million dollar annual turnover.

Maybe your organization would rather have a new variety of flower developed.

Plant Naming

• **CATEGORY:** GENERAL • **GROUP SIZE:** LARGE • **TIME FRAME:** 1 YR+ • **TIME OF YEAR:** SPR./SUM./ FALL/WINT.

New plant varieties are being created all the time and horticulturists constantly search for appropriate names by which to sell them. Choose an appropriate plant, arrange with the grower to name it on behalf of your group and request that he/she donate one dollar from the sale of each plant to your cause. Your organization will, in turn, promote the sale of plants through its membership in addition to selling them at all your events. A large, widespread membership will allow you to make this new plant variety highly visible, bringing funds both to you and to the developer. Rose varieties are an excellent choice for this venture, but any popular perennial could do just as well. Geraniums, mums, and fuschias are always very fashionable and can be sold as either potted or garden plants.

• **CATEGORY:** GENERAL • **GROUP SIZE:** LARGE • **TIME FRAME:** UP TO 1 YR./1 YR+ • **TIME OF YEAR:** SPR./FALL/WINT.

If your organization is selling large numbers of bulbs, it should also consider selling special pots in which to grow them. The type of pot sold whether plastic with a stick-on logo, or glazed earthenware with a relevant motif – depends on your membership. Small bags of potting soil, also printed with logos and information regarding your organization, would complete the ensemble. Sell a set of two pots, six bulbs and sufficient potting soil together with a small instruction leaflet – a complete do-it-yourself spring flower display.

Gardens

Beautiful gardens attract gardeners and non-gardeners alike. Strolling through a well-manicured creation on a warm summer day can afford great pleasure, particularly if someone else has done all the hard work. If your organization has no access to a garden large or diverse enough to attract a wide tourist audience, it can still utilize the garden as a fundraiser's motif.

• **CATEGORY:** GENERAL • **GROUP SIZE:** LARGE • **TIME FRAME:** 1 YR+ • **TIME OF YEAR:** SPR./SUM.

A temporary or permanent garden especially created in someone's memory, or dedicated to a particular event, can attract considerable attention and donations. Consult your membership to discover whether there is someone or something you should be honouring with a memorial garden. Seek sponsorship from anyone who might benefit from such a garden (local businesspeople perhaps) and approach landscape designers and/or garden centres for assistance and materials (which they may be willing to donate in return for publicity).

If your organization does not own land, but still wishes to establish a memorial garden, contact your local or municipal authorities to see if you can adopt a corner of a public park or garden for that purpose. A carefully tended garden display with specially selected plant species can attract many visitors, reminding them of your cause. Donations could be given in cash or in pledges placed in collection boxes.

• **CATEGORY:** ENVIRONMENTAL/GENERAL • **GROUP SIZE:** SM. • **TIME FRAME:** UP TO 1 YR. • **TIME OF YEAR:** SPR./SUM./FALL

Does anyone in your organization, or connected to it have a garden that can be opened to the public for a day? Size is not important, but variety and design are. Perhaps your organization members have conifer collections or rose bowers, selections of peonies, or tulips, or hosta. How about exotic vegetable gardens, or ones devoted to shade or water plants. Publicity costs aside, viewing a private garden is 100% profit, as you charge visitors an entrance fee and raise additional funds by selling plants, cuttings, seeds, and possibly, light refreshments.

• **CATEGORY:** ENVIRONMENTAL/GENERAL • **GROUP SIZE:** SM./MED./LARGE • **TIME FRAME:** UP TO 1 YR. • **TIME OF YEAR:** SPR./SUM./FALL

Why not assemble a package tour of local gardens by selecting five or six of the most interesting plots belonging to members and friends. Choose a variety of styles including large and small gardens and perhaps an indoor garden if someone has a beautiful display of houseplants. Sell tickets in advance: each should entitle the visitor to enter all the gardens, in any order, at any time, over a two day period.

• **CATEGORY:** ENVIRONMENTAL/GENERAL • **GROUP SIZE:** SM./MED./LARGE • **TIME FRAME:** UP TO 1 YR. • **TIME OF YEAR:** SPR./SUM.

Combine a private garden opening and/or garden safari with a plant sale and raise additional funds. Ask all of your green-thumbed members and volunteers to grow a wide variety of plants from seed to be sold at your garden sale. Coordination is important. All plants need to be ready at the right time so that you have a good selection. Attempt to get a popular mix of flowers and vegetables plus shrubs and grasses. For maximum profits, ask your volunteer growers to provide seeds, soil and pots or, at the very least, buy them in bulk from a horticultural supplier. Try to establish a specific number of plants to be grown by each member. If your members have brown thumbs, you can always recommend that they purchase quantities in bulk from a reputable nursery. Whether you acknowledge the source of the plants is entirely up to you, but you must ensure that only high quality stock is placed on the sale table.

• **CATEGORY:** GENERAL • **GROUP SIZE:** SM. • **TIME FRAME:** UP TO 1 YR. • **TIME OF YEAR:** SUM.

An alternative to having a mix of flowers and vegetables at your sale is to have all members grow different varieties of a single plant species, geraniums or tomatoes for instance. You can then hold an annual geranium sale or tomato sale. Become known as a reliable supplier of dozens of different varieties of the same species – some of them probably available nowhere else.

Herb Garden

• **CATEGORY:** WOMEN'S GROUPS/GENERAL • **GROUP SIZE:** SM. • **TIME FRAME:** UP TO 1 YR. • **TIME OF YEAR:** SPR./SUM./ FALL

Most herbs are easy to grow, requiring only a small garden plot. Plant as many herbs as will comfortably fit in your location of choice. Have numerous pots of herbs for sale as well. People are fascinated by herbs, and a well-stocked herb garden is a popular visiting spot for gardeners and cooks alike. You can open your garden to public view several times during the year. Don't forget dried or preserved herbs; and seeds can be sold at a fall fair, holiday bazaar, or other suitable event.

Garden Design Competitions

• **CATEGORY:** GENERAL • **GROUP SIZE:** SM./MED./LARGE • **TIME FRAME:** UP TO 1 YR. • **TIME OF YEAR:** SPR./SUM./FALL/WINT.

Aspiring and experienced gardeners should be encouraged to design a memorial garden to honour your organization's work. Hold a competition. Once you've selected a winner, enlist the aid of local garden centres to bring the winning design to fruition. Charge entry fees and admission to see the completed project. Remember, the winning design must be particularly suitable to the people and services of your organization.

Lawn Mowing

• **CATEGORY:** SERVICE CLUBS/GENERAL • **GROUP SIZE:** SM. • **TIME FRAME:** UP TO 1 YR. • **TIME OF YEAR:** SPR./SUM./FALL.

Mowing lawns is a time-honoured money source, although your organization will need a willing band of volunteers with some reliable mowers – push, pull, and riding.

Have lawnmower, will cut! Many people happily pay to have someone cut their lawns and are even happier to donate to charity in return for the service. If your organization needs a few dollars immediately, be a good neighbour and raise money at the same time.

• **CATEGORY:** FITNESS, SPORTS & SOCIAL/GENERAL • **GROUP SIZE:** SM./MED. • **TIME FRAME:** UP TO 6 MTHS. • **TIME OF YEAR:** SPR./SUM./FALL

If your members have the time available, and commitment, then operate a lawn mowing service. Advertise and market the service wherever you can. Establish a name for quality and reliability. As an incentive to members and volunteer participants, pay all expenses plus a small amount of commission. Begin by having members use their own lawnmowers and cutting lawns in local neighbourhoods. Charge the same rate as commercial operators but give a receipt for tax purposes. If your venture is a success, invest in some machinery, and gradually develop the business into a full-time fundraising operation.

• **CATEGORY:** FITNESS, SPORTS & SOCIAL/SERVICE CLUBS/GENERAL • **GROUP SIZE:** SM. • **TIME FRAME:** UP TO 6 MTHS. • **TIME OF YEAR:** SPR.

Why not hold an annual lawn mowing day each spring to raise money. Choose a neighbourhood where every house has a lawn and set a target number, 500 for instance. Attract local media attention with a press release, "*The Big Brothers will attempt to cut 500 lawns in a day.*" Give details of the area to be worked, and request that everyone living in that area "donate" their lawns to the attempt. Mention that a cutting fee will be requested for each lawn.

Produce a leaflet which provides details of your event and requests householders' support. Deliver the leaflets throughout your designated area one week in advance. Organize your members into teams and allocate streets. Allow 20 minutes per lawn and expect each mower to cut 25 lawns. You will need 20 mowers and about 50 volunteers to cut 500 lawns in the city. Rural properties have more green space, and the time required per lawn will rise, as will the number of volunteers needed.

Depending on the neighbourhood and the lawn sizes, it should be possible to charge from $10-$50 per cut. A minimum of $5,000, less expenses, can be raised from cutting 500 lawns. Ask a neighbourhood gas station to provide gas in return for publicity on the leaflets, viz., "*Gas generously donated by . . . .*" Then you will have no expenses at all, just a group of very tired people at the end of the day.

Leaf Raking

• **CATEGORY:** FITNESS, SPORTS & SOCIAL/GENERAL • **GROUP SIZE:** SM. • **TIME FRAME:** UP TO 4WKS. • **TIME OF YEAR:** FALL

Every fall, country folk and city folk face the prospect of raking leaves. Your members could volunteer for this task – in return for a donation, of course. A project like this is particularly suitable for youth organizations, or even a group of young seniors, who would benefit from the exercise.

Be environmentally correct and raise twice as much money. Rake and collect your leaves, then compost them. The results can be sold the following spring. You will need a small lot for the composting, and advice from a local garden centre. Take orders for compost at the same time as you collect the leaves in the fall so, in essence, you're raising funds by storing leaves over the winter season.

Tree Growing

• **CATEGORY:** ENVIRONMENTAL/GENERAL • **GROUP SIZE:** SM./MED./LARGE • **TIME FRAME:** 1 YR+ • **TIME OF YEAR:** SPR./FALL

Grow common varieties of trees from woodland seeds, or from seeds purchased from an arboretum. Trees can be grown by almost anyone, and the saplings offered for sale at any appropriate event. The more exotic tree varieties will raise more money, but such seeds are more difficult to obtain and even harder to grow. Large numbers of saplings can be sold at environmental fairs, garden shows and similar events but future planning is essential, as we all know trees do not grow overnight.

Seek donated seeds, containers, and potting soil, and apply for grants from environmental groups if you intend making tree growing a major fundraising activity. Trees not sold to raise funds can be planted in deforested areas or a suitable public park as a means of engendering public goodwill.

Many people will pay to have a tree planted in memory of . . . or a tree donated by . . . . Charge for the tree and plaque plus a substantial donation.

Plant trees in parks, gardens and other public areas, wherever you can obtain permission. You may be able to completely reforest an area of parkland with donated trees.

The Printed Word

Readings

• **CATEGORY:** ARTS & THEATRE/GENERAL • **GROUP SIZE:** SM./MED. • **TIME FRAME:** UP TO 6 MTHS. • **TIME OF YEAR:** SPR./SUM./FALL/WINT.

Invite a well-known writer to read his or her latest book, or excerpts therefrom. You could even assemble a series of author readings. You will need a quiet location where listeners can enjoy a sense of intimacy with the reader, but you must make sure the author is not overcrowded by his/her audience. Charge a general admission, and make refreshments available. You must offer copies of the author's book for sale and, of course, invite your guest to sign autographs. The audience will probably want to ask questions, so time should be allocated towards the end of your event for that purpose. Author readings, properly promoted, are very strong draws, both when staged for adults and when staged as children's events. Make sure the author's publisher helps you with publicity. In addition to print advertisements, you will need radio announcements, flyers, and, if possible, notices in all your local retail outlets and public libraries. Authors are popular with all generations, and if you know an author whose works are particularly relevant to your organization, so much the better.

Book Sales – Secondhand

Many charitable organizations derive all of their income from sales of secondhand books, and there are few organizations indeed that cannot raise some funds in this way. Whether you are able to open a book store, hold an occasional book sale, or sell second-hand books as part of an annual fair, depends on the number of volunteers working on the project and their commitment. There is no shortage of used books. You have to collect and store them.

• **CATEGORY:** GENERAL • **GROUP SIZE:** SM./MED. • **TIME FRAME:** UP TO 4 WKS.. • **TIME OF YEAR:** SPR./SUM./FALL/WINT.

You can raise a small amount of money at every membership meeting simply by asking every member and guest to bring a book or magazine with them each week/month and ask each of them to buy one of the books for a small fee.

Auction

• **CATEGORY:** GENERAL • **GROUP SIZE:** SM./MED. • **TIME FRAME:** UP TO 4WKS. • **TIME OF YEAR:** SPR./FALL/WINT.

Auctions attract dealers and bibliophiles from all over but, prior to planning one, you must assemble a suitable collection of interesting books to sell. Most used books are not worth much more than the $.25-$2.50 they are usually tagged with at your local bookstore, so the only solution, short of buying entire libraries on the sly, is to collect and keep every potentially valuable book that comes your way. Bear in mind that many people have far more books at home than they really need or want and, when offered a good charitable cause through which these overstocked volumes can be disposed, owners become quite generous. You must set up an organized collection system. Most effective is the pre-announced, street by street canvas. (Target a number of streets and put leaflets into each mailbox at the beginning of the week, stating for example: *ANY OLD BOOKS? THE NEWTOWN SOCIETY OF RETIRED THESPIANS WILL BE COLLECTING BOOKS FOR OUR UPCOMING ANNUAL FUNDRAISING SALE. OUR VOLUNTEERS WILL BE COLLECTING ON SATURDAY AFTERNOON. IF YOU ARE GOING TO BE OUT PLEASE LEAVE BOOKS IN A BOX ON DOORSTEP OR WITH A NEIGHBOUR. THANK YOU FOR SUPPORTING OUR CAUSE.* Make sure that your volunteers do collect on the Saturday and, when you've collected enough, and have held your sale, make sure that each donor is personally thanked for his/her contribution.) Sort your book collection into three categories: rubbish to be recycled into pulp; books of minimal value to be sold in bulk to a dealer and, most important, books of potentially significant value for your auction. It may take you several years to accumulate enough good books to justify an auction but in the meantime you will raise some revenue from your sales to paper recycling companies and used book dealers.

If auctions are not your cup of tea consider operating a permanent bookstore.

Secondhand Bookstore

• **CATEGORY:** GENERAL • **GROUP SIZE:** SM./MED./LARGE • **TIME FRAME:** UP TO 1 YR. • **TIME OF YEAR:** SPR./SUM./FALL/WINT.

Any organization should be able to run a financially successful secondhand bookstore if it has rent free accommodation and a willing band of volunteers. Making money from a rented store with paid staff will be much more difficult. Collection and storage are not problems for an organization running a bookstore: customers bring in books and magazines, and either give, swap two for one, or sell them at a low price. They then buy other books. A perfect recycling scheme.

Annual Book Sales

• **CATEGORY:** GENERAL • **GROUP SIZE:** SM./MED./LARGE • **TIME FRAME:** UP TO 1 YR. • **TIME OF YEAR:** SPR./SUM./FALL/WINT.

Annual book sales require some suitable place to store books and a means of transport. Books are heavy, flammable and susceptible to damp. Hold sales at any convenient location at a propitious time during the year. An empty store in the weeks before winter holidays may provide a good venue for an annual event.

• **CATEGORY:** GENERAL• **GROUP SIZE:** LARGE • **TIME FRAME:** 1 YR+ • **TIME OF YEAR:** SPR./SUM./FALL/WINT.

At least one charity in the United States raises all its revenue from holding a mammoth annual book sale. Hundreds of thousands of books are collected, as publishers donate large numbers of unsold stock, libraries give out-dated books, authors donate autographed copies of their works and wealthy benefactors donate rare editions. Experts set aside first editions, antique and other valuable books for auction, while hundreds of volunteers categorize and value all others.

• **CATEGORY:** GENERAL• **GROUP SIZE:** SM./MED. • **TIME FRAME:** UP TO 6 MTHS. • **TIME OF YEAR:** SPR./SUM./FALL/WINT.

Whether you run a bookstore or hold occasional sales, you can always raise additional funds by taking a stall at any other organization's charitable event. Every charity and N.F.P. group should be able to muster enough secondhand books to take the occasional table at a bazaar, fete or fair.

Libraries

Private Libraries

• **CATEGORY:** GENERAL • **GROUP SIZE:** MED./LARGE • **TIME FRAME:** 1 YR+ • **TIME OF YEAR:** SPR./SUM./FALL/WINT.

Does your organization have access to a private library of unique or hard-to-find publications? Opening it to the public could, perhaps, be beneficial to all.

Many major corporations have large collections of material within their own particular areas of expertise. Most of these libraries are strictly for internal use, and many are only open to corporate employees because budget restraints do not allow the company to staff its library with knowledgeable personnel.

If you know of such a library in your neighbourhood, consider approaching the corporation to propose that your organization be permitted to staff and operate the library and open it to the public in return for a management fee. Arrange to charge the public for the use of any publication, or for information retrieval, and make additional money by charging for photocopying and research. Most of these libraries are reference libraries and books may not be removed from the premises, so photocopy fees can produce a tidy sum.

• **CATEGORY:** GENERAL • **GROUP SIZE:** LARGE • **TIME FRAME:** UP TO 6 MTHS. • **TIME OF YEAR:** SPR./SUM./FALL/WINT.

Many charities would be surprised at the number of books and publications they have amassed over the years and, while the tendency is to allow free access to interested parties, there is no reason why donations should not be sought, or fees charged.

Amnesty

• **CATEGORY:** GENERAL • **GROUP SIZE:** MED./LARGE • **TIME FRAME:** UP TO 1 YR. • **TIME OF YEAR:** SPR./SUM./FALL/WINT.

Ask public and private libraries to help themselves, and your group at the same time, by holding an annual amnesty week, during which time patrons with overdue books can return them to the library, paying a set fee to charity in lieu of the actual library fine outstanding. This procedure encourages people to return books that otherwise may never be recovered and it is guaranteed to raise money for the charity or N.F.P. group involved. One particularly amusing example of this project's successful appeal occurred in 1985 when the County Library in Winchester, England, finally had *A Book of Fines* returned by the Bishop of Winchester. One of his predecessors had borrowed the volume in 1650.

Magazine Recycling

• **CATEGORY:** GENERAL • **GROUP SIZE:** SM. • **TIME FRAME:** UP TO 6 MTHS. • **TIME OF YEAR:** SPR./SUM./FALL/WINT.

Have you ever wondered where doctors, lawyers and dentists obtain their waiting room magazines? How much does this service cost each practitioner per annum, and how much time does a highly paid receptionist spend keeping the periodicals sorted and replacing old or damaged ones?

Your organization can provide a periodicals service to all of the waiting rooms in your area and be praised for its recycling initiative at the same time. Establish a number of convenient drop-off points and invite the public to donate used, but not abused, magazines on a regular basis. Charge doctors, dentists, barbers and the like a modest monthly fee for supplying them with current magazines and for removing old ones – to be recycled of course.

Poetry Competition

• **CATEGORY:** ARTS & THEATRE/CHILDREN & YOUTH • **GROUP SIZE:** SM./MED./LARGE • **TIME FRAME:** UP TO 1 YR.
• **TIME OF YEAR:** SPR./SUM./FALL/WINT.

Poetry competitions can be held at any level and involve any number of people. How about a national poetry competition for elementary and intermediate students. Your organization and its work would provide subject matter for the competition and, with cooperation from the schools, public awareness of your cause would soar.

Encourage school participation by finding a benefactor to offer a substantial prize to the school of the winning child (something along the lines of a new library or computer laboratory, perhaps). Create a prestigious title like, "Young Poet of the Year." The sponsoring charity/N.F.P. organization needs to be a large one with members in each community, with a strong desire to raise money. Each poem submitted should be accompanied by a suitable donation.

Have your competition judged by a well-known author, once a screening committee has selected a shortlist of suitable entries. Publish winning poems wherever possible – in your newsletter, the local press, and in the national press and on the radio if possible. If you can arrange to hold this event annually, publish a compilation of the very best entries every few years, to be sold to contestants, their families, and friends. Dream up similar poetry competitions for smaller or larger groups of any age.

Short Story Collection

• **CATEGORY:** GENERAL • **GROUP SIZE:** MED./LARGE • **TIME FRAME:** 1 YR+ • **TIME OF YEAR:** SPR./SUM./FALL/WINT.

Contact well-known and up-and-coming Canadian authors, outline your cause, and ask for help in compiling a collection of original short stories. You will need to contact dozens and dozens of writers before you have enough stories to make a book.

Stress in your appeal the fact that this is a totally non-profit project with all receipts going to charity. Your request is for first-time, royalty-free publication rights only, and you are seeking stories which have a particular significance to your membership for a book whose sale would be primarily to your membership, although you might also seek distribution through regular publishing channels.

The World's Greatest Treasure Hunt

• **CATEGORY:** GENERAL• **GROUP SIZE:** LARGE • **TIME FRAME:** 1 YR+ • **TIME OF YEAR:** SPR./SUM./FALL/WINT.

There are very many avid readers of adventure stories, and movies like *Indiana Jones* attract a wide audience. Psychologists suggest that people enjoy adventure books and movies because their own lives are dull, and they secretly yearn to be involved in some great adventure. Your charity or N.F.P. group can create an adventure and raise a substantial sum of money at the same time. This fundraiser was wildly successful in England and was promoted to the public by the children's book *Maze*, published by Jonathan Cape.

Fill a chest with priceless treasures and bury or hide it. Once the chest is safely hidden in a location known only to one person, create an attractive adventure picture book which contains all the clues in encoded format, and either self-publish the volume, or find a reputable commercial publisher familiar with your cause. Generating public fervour to send hordes of people to book stores determined to buy the book, have an adventure, and find the treasure, is the key to any successful conclusion of this fundraiser. Bear in mind the fact that, as far-fetched as it seems, schemes of this nature have been successful both in the United States (where the book *The Ultimate Alphabet*, was published by Henry Holt & Company) and in the U.K, as cited in the instance above.

Only the author must know the whereabouts of the treasure and, at a well publicized ceremony, he/she should swear on oath before a high court judge, that the treasure chest has been hidden and that he/she will divulge the location to no one. A sealed envelope containing details of the location (only to be opened in the event of the author's death) should be ceremoniously placed into a secure vault. The treasure chest itself should contain nothing of value, only instructions on how the prize may be claimed. The finder will be required to explain how the clues were deciphered in order to disqualify someone who may have stumbled upon the chest by accident.

PERFORMING ARTS

Music

Gala Performances

• **CATEGORY:** GENERAL • **GROUP SIZE:** LARGE • **TIME FRAME:** UP TO 1 YR. • **TIME OF YEAR:** SPR./SUM./FALL/WINT.

When fundraising for a major charity, an annual gala performance of a play, opera, ballet, or movie is an absolute must. Such an event enables you to involve your most important patrons, sponsors, and donors and provides opportunity to network with many musical or theatrical talents, political and business movers and shakers, and philanthropists. Choose the production carefully: the opening of a new musical is often considered ideal. Begin inviting guests immediately. If you have done your homework, guests will not be deterred by high ticket prices. They are pleased to be present at an affair of such significance on the social scene. The more expensive the seat, the more exclusive the event and therefore the more desirable the ticket.

Out of Character

• **CATEGORY:** ARTS & THEATRE • **GROUP SIZE:** SM./MED./LARGE • **TIME FRAME:** UP TO 1 YR. • **TIME OF YEAR:** SPR./SUM./FALL/WINT.

Any orchestra, ballet company, opera and/or theatre group can help raise money by occasionally performing in an annual "blue-jean" performance of light-hearted, even comical, pieces. These can attract considerable attention, goodwill, and funds. Another spin on this idea is to hold a competition, raffle, or auction for guest spots during an "out of character" performance.

Music Festivals

• **CATEGORY:** ARTS & THEATRE/GENERAL • **GROUP SIZE:** MED./LARGE • **TIME FRAME:** 1 YR+ • **TIME OF YEAR:** SPR./SUM./FALL/WINT.

Music festivals are exciting and popular fundraisers; a good one can attract people from around the world. Most festivals rely on substantial corporate sponsorship, and any group considering the development of such an event needs to secure sound financial backing as the first priority. Festivals can be organized by any music oriented group although sometimes they may be more successful when organized to raise money for an unrelated entity. The Festival of Hope celebration, for example, raises money for cancer research.

When considering fundraising through a music festival, investigate those festivals already in existence to discover potential pitfalls. If a music festival is already functioning in your area, you will want to contact its organizers to determine if there is some role that your organization can play. Organizers of a festival whose attendance is flagging may be receptive to suggestions to bolster the event, even at the cost of sharing profits.

Organizers of any existing music festival may be receptive to fundraising requests from non-music charities, perhaps by dedicating a particular performance to charity and allowing a collection to be taken. Organizers may also be willing to make a donation to your cause in return for services provided by your staff and volunteers. Your organization's mailing list is a valuable tool which might be leased to festival organizers. You could also offer to include festival promotional material with your solicitation mail.

Sing-A-Long

• **CATEGORY:** GENERAL • **GROUP SIZE:** SM./MED. • **TIME FRAME:** UP TO 6 MTHS. • **TIME OF YEAR:** SPR./SUM./FALL/WINT.

How about an old-fashioned sing-a-long with total audience participation in the rendition of favourite songs old and new. Everybody is bound to have a good time. Your group needs to find a suitable venue, a pianist, and the use of a photocopier. Check your list of celebrity contacts. Music lovers of all types can usually be encouraged to join in an informal evening of song for charity. Well-known opera and musical choruses can be just as popular as rock, and easy listening favourites from the 60s and 70s. Some sing-a-longs can be quite spectacular. Imagine 500 people singing the "Anvil Chorus" or a thousand people singing Rodgers & Hammerstein's "Oklahoma."

Many serious musicians, and some non-musicians, can make music on a wide range of alternative instruments like bathtubs, garden hoses, beer bottles, saws, spoons and various parts of the human body. Artists are often eager to participate in charity concerts staged with these instruments. When properly organized, such events can attract considerable media attention, beneficial to musicians and fundraisers alike.

• **CATEGORY:** ARTS & THEATRE/SERVICE CLUBS • **GROUP SIZE:** SM./MED. • **TIME FRAME:** UP TO 1 YR. • **TIME OF YEAR:** SPR./FALL/WINT.

Concert organizers should hold auditions, select soloists and arrange the repertoire well before the concert date to ensure musical talent is available. Adequate rehearsal time must be allotted so that the final presentation is well organized and entertaining. An alternative concert held annually could become an amusing fundraising vehicle for a band or orchestra, and is likely to generate both goodwill and generous donations.

• **CATEGORY:** WOMEN'S GROUPS/FITNESS, SPORTS & SOCIAL/ • **GROUP SIZE:** MED./LARGE • **TIME FRAME:** UP TO 1 YR. • **TIME OF YEAR:** SPR./SUM./FALL/WINT.

An annual concert featuring alumni members is a great fundraiser for any institution of higher education. This event may become eagerly anticipated by all, and will cost virtually nothing to arrange.

Band Concerts

• **CATEGORY:** GENERAL/CHILDREN & YOUTH • **GROUP SIZE:** SM./MED./LARGE • **TIME FRAME:** UP TO 1 YR. • **TIME OF YEAR:** SPR./SUM./FALL/WINT.

Bands of all kinds are always looking for venues and audiences. Don't be greedy, don't expect them to perform for nothing just because yours is a not-for-profit organization. On the other hand, avoid committing yourself to paying a set fee irrespective of audience turnout. Decide on the type of concert you want to hold, then track down suitable bands. If your quarry is not interested in discussing a profit-sharing scheme, try other performers. Organizing concerts, especially those involving high-powered music and young people, requires considerable overhead payouts. Make sure that you can cover all of your expenses before agreeing to pay any band a fixed amount.

For small, local organizations, a concert involving the high school band, the police or military band and a couple of local amateur musicians may be as financially rewarding as hosting a rock concert. You can make a reasonable amount for your group with a lot fewer headaches.

Choirs and Instrumental Groups

• **CATEGORY:** WOMEN'S GROUPS/ARTS & THEATRE • **GROUP SIZE:** SM. • **TIME FRAME:** UP TO 1 YR. • **TIME OF YEAR:** SPR./SUM./FALL/WINT.

Your staff, members, and clients can all become members of a choir or group. An ability to sing and play is an advantage but practice makes perfect. No matter how large or small your organization, you can make money by performing in public. If the performers are good, hold an annual concert. If you are not too confident of your abilities, then give a few short performances as part of any other fundraising event, and judge audience reaction.

When your choir or group has become popular, make recordings of your work to sell at all events.

Church Organ Music
• **CATEGORY:** GENERAL • **GROUP SIZE:** SM. • **TIME FRAME:** UP TO 6 MTHS. • **TIME OF YEAR:** SPR./SUM./FALL/WINT.

It is now possible to have a church organ-computer link which allows the organ to play a wide variety of religious tunes without an organist. Visitors to your church can select music of their choice by means of a coin operated electronic switch, which also makes a simultaneous donation. If your organ is not computer-controlled, make sure that the church has cassette recordings and CD's available for sale to visitors and church-goers.

Concerts & Recitals
• **CATEGORY:** ARTS & THEATRE/GENERAL • **GROUP SIZE:** MED./LARGE • **TIME FRAME:** UP TO 1 YR. • **TIME OF YEAR:** SPR./SUM./FALL/WINT.

A large public charity concert given by a musical virtuoso, accompanied by an internationally renowned orchestra, may be the ultimate aim of every organization. Pull strings, talk to the right people and you may be able to make it happen. Alternatively, perhaps you can persuade a well-known musician to give a private recital to benefit your organization. Most virtuosos are booked a year or more in advance so, even if he/she is an avid supporter of your cause, you may have to wait a considerable time for a suitable date. Make the event prestigious by inviting a relatively small number of honoured guests, each of whom should be encouraged to make a major donation to your cause.

Buskers

Every major city can boast an eclectic assortment of buskers and street entertainers. Most are very talented musicians and performers who, for one reason or another, have not been able to break into the big time. Here are two ways in which buskers could be utilized in a fundraising campaign:

As a Crowd Gatherer/Pleaser
• **CATEGORY:** GENERAL • **GROUP SIZE:** SM./MED./LARGE • **TIME FRAME:** UP TO 4WKS. • **TIME OF YEAR:** SPR./SUM./FALL/WINT.

Buskers are particularly good at attracting and entertaining crowds. If you need to catch the attention of passers-by, a good busker will be a big help. Offer a reasonable hourly rate and use volunteers to solicit contributions from the crowd while it is being entertained. Remember, whenever you hold an event which will have line-ups, consider employing a busker to keep the waiting crowd entertained. Again, collect donations.

Busking Competitions

• **CATEGORY:** SERVICE CLUBS/GENERAL • **GROUP SIZE:** SM./MED. • **TIME FRAME:** UP TO 1 YR. • **TIME OF YEAR:** SPR./SUM./FALL

An annual competition for professional buskers, with prizes donated by a sponsor, can be very successful in some locations. The variety show competition allots each performer a specific amount of time. Auditions may be necessary in order to weed out any performer whose act could send the audience home, but boredom notwithstanding, any professional street entertainer should be allowed to participate. Each busker should pay an entry fee (lured by the promise of talent scouts in the audience), but the bulk of the fundraising should come from ticket sales and peripheral events.

Historical Re-Enactments

• **CATEGORY:** ARTS & THEATRE/GENERAL • **GROUP SIZE:** SM./MED. • **TIME FRAME:** UP TO 1 YR. • **TIME OF YEAR:** SPR./SUM./FALL/WINT.

If you are fundraising in support of an historical site, or if you have access to an historical site, consider an historical re-enactment as a fundraising tool. Whether a specific battle, landing/arrival, departure, peace treaty negotiation, other momentous occasion, or simply a re-enactment of everyday life from the past depends on the site and the facilities available.

Canada's history is dramatic, peopled with interesting personalities and, often, controversial events. Contact the local historical society, and conduct your own local research. Your organization may be able to recreate an event which generates good press plus cash. Charge admission fees and arrange numerous ancillary activities – craft fairs, parades, and concerts.

Movies

Premiere

• **CATEGORY:** HEALTH RELATED/GENERAL • **GROUP SIZE:** LARGE • **TIME FRAME:** UP TO 1 YR. • **TIME OF YEAR:** SPR./SUM./FALL/WINT.

Charity premieres are an excellent attention getter both for a major charity and for the movie studio. A blockbuster premiere can generate staggering amounts of money in a single evening.

Persuading a studio that your organization is worthy of star treatment is not easy. You are most likely to succeed when a new movie deals with an issue with which your organization is already involved. Find out well in advance when such a suitable movie is being made, or even considered, by writing a standard letter to all major and minor studios, advising them of your organization's existence. Offer to advise the studio on any relevant matter should it, at any time, consider a movie dealing with subject matter related to your organization's expertise. When you are representing a specific group of people, your letter should also mention the fact that you wish to ensure that members of your organization are correctly and compassionately portrayed. Request notification of any future plans for movies which might impact on your organization, even though its advice may not be required. Then wait and hope.

When a proposed movie features individuals or people who would in everyday life be clients or members of your organization, then you have an interest in ensuring the accurate and compassionate portrait of same. A minority financial stake in such a movie allows your organization some negotiating clout with the movie's producer, some limited editorial rights over contents and, of course, a share in the projected profits.

Group Patronage/Promotion

• **CATEGORY:** HEALTH RELATED/GENERAL • **GROUP SIZE:** LARGE • **TIME FRAME:** 1 YR+ • **TIME OF YEAR:** SPR./SUM./FALL/WINT.

If your membership is extensive and committed, consider guaranteeing movie theatre owners substantial membership turnout. This translates into profit for both the movie studio and your group.

• **CATEGORY:** GENERAL • **GROUP SIZE:** SM./MED./LARGE • **TIME FRAME:** UP TO 1 YR. • **TIME OF YEAR:** SPR./SUM./FALL/WINT.

When a movie is sympathetic to the goals and/or cause of your organization, your group has a vested interest in promoting it. When such a movie is released through a national cinema chain, ask the distributor for a donation of one or two cents per ticket sold, in return for which you will promote the film in every possible way through your membership: the larger your membership, the more attractive your offer will be.

If your group is small, you can still benefit from this idea when a suitable movie is scheduled by contacting your local cinema. Statements on tickets and in print announcing the fact that, "10% of the ticket price is to be given to . . . charity," make good publicity. And don't forget the fact that all your members, friends and families will be encouraged to attend.

Cult Movie

• **CATEGORY:** FITNESS, SPORTS & SOCIAL/ARTS & THEATRE • **GROUP SIZE:** SM./MED. • **TIME FRAME:** UP TO 6 MTHS.
• **TIME OF YEAR:** SPR./SUM./FALL/WINT.

Do you long to see Roy Rogers riding off into the sunset, Bob Hope on the road to Morocco or Charlie Chaplin in the gold rush? There are many people who may share your desires. These movies are still available but cinemas will not show them unless there is a guaranteed audience. Discuss with your local cinema manager the idea of holding a special charity performance two or three times a year showing movies of a particular genre. Offer to promote the performance through your membership in return for a share of the profits.

Alternatively, consider purchasing all of the seats for the performance, and reselling them through your membership. A block purchase of seats allows you to negotiate a good price and ensures the cinema owner will recover his/her costs.

Still another method for showcasing movies of a particular genre is for an organization to set up its own projectionist in a suitable hall. Copies of classic movies can be rented for a relatively small fee and many viewers will enjoy a nostalgic evening, thinking back to a time when movies were shown in village halls and school gymnasiums. Your organization might stage a successful 1940s or 1950s night built around the screening of a couple of suitable movie classics.

Murder Most Mysterious

• **CATEGORY:** FITNESS, SPORTS & SOCIAL/ARTS & THEATRE • **GROUP SIZE:** SM./MED. • **TIME FRAME:** UP TO 1 YR. • **TIME OF YEAR:** SPR./FALL/WINT.

Mystery murder games-cum-theatre shows are popular entertainment, and they offer any charity or N.F.P. group an opportunity of hosting an event which is fun for both participants and organizers. Murder mysteries are especially suitable fundraisers for theatre groups with a wealth of acting talent at their disposal. Select an appropriate venue. While a theatre or small hotel is perfectly suitable, something unusual – a ship, submarine, or abandoned warehouse – may be more appropriate. Vacant or empty movie or television sets also provide good locations. Using a hotel or restaurant means the event can be focused around a meal, with the use of facilities built into the meal ticket price.

Find a murder mystery that will work well in your selected location. Most fictional murders can be re-enacted without elaborate sets or equipment, and many of the parts can be assumed unwittingly by guests who become witnesses during the course events.

Your group might also consider crafting its own original fictional murder to fit the available talents and chosen venue.

Theatre

First Night

• **CATEGORY:** GENERAL • **GROUP SIZE:** SM./MED./LARGE • **TIME FRAME:** UP TO 6 MTHS. • **TIME OF YEAR:** SPR./SUM./FALL/WINT.

Many amateur and professional theatres find difficulty in selling out the first night of a new show. Your charity might consider buying all the opening night seats at a greatly discounted price, and reselling these tickets throughout your organization and beyond. Remember a sellout on the first night can be a huge thespian morale booster, and a fund booster for any organization. Hold a reception afterwards to introduce the director and cast.

Benefactor's Night

• **CATEGORY:** GENERAL • **GROUP SIZE:** LARGE • **TIME FRAME:** UP TO 1 YR. • **TIME OF YEAR:** SPR./SUM./FALL/WINT.

On occassion, an affluent philanthropist will buy up an entire theatrical performance, donating all the tickets to a specific charity which then can resell them at full-face value. A benefactor willing to do this is making a considerable donation both to the theatre and to your organization.

Sell the Performance

• **CATEGORY:** ARTS & THEATRE • **GROUP SIZE:** SM./MED./LARGE • **TIME FRAME:** UP TO 1 YR. • **TIME OF YEAR:** SPR./SUM./FALL/WINT.

One way of enhancing ticket sales for any theatrical presentation (or any other performance art) is to sell a complete performance to a private corporation which then uses the event to promote itself in various ways – giving tickets to its best customers; rewarding staff members; impressing potential clients; rewarding suppliers or servicing providers; and launching a new product or service (usually done at a reception before opening curtain, or at a party after the show).

If no single private corporation will purchase an entire performance, why not target a particular community sector by encouraging groups of people from the same profession to meet and mingle. A performance for those in the legal professional could be sponsored by three or four law firms. Real estate professionals could attend a special performance sponsored by several real estate brokerages, or investment counsellors a presentation sponsored by several investment houses.

Rehearsals

• **CATEGORY:** ARTS & THEATRE • **GROUP SIZE:** SM./MED./LARGE • **TIME FRAME:** UP TO 4 WKS. • **TIME OF YEAR:** SPR./SUM./FALL/WINT.

Many theatre-goers are quite willing to pay to observe a show in development. If you are fundraising for a theatre group, consider opening one night of rehearsal to the public for a nominal fee. Use this night to full advantage, and set up an advanced ticket sales table to gather support for the final production while your rehearsal audience is still humming tunes, and scenes are fresh in their minds. Make money by selling refreshments. Don't forget to circulate forms describing how to become a friend of your theatre group. A sufficiently impressed audience should be willing to pledge future support.

Remember to make the rehearsal night far enough down the rehearsal process so that a reasonably complete performance is offered. Don't make it so good, however, that patrons feel no need to view the finished product. Rehearsal nights can also be used to introduce the playwright and director, who discuss the play, as the audience meets the cast informally.

Subscribers (Theatre Groups)

• **CATEGORY:** ARTS & THEATRE • **GROUP SIZE:** SM./MED./LARGE • **TIME FRAME:** UP TO 1 YR. • **TIME OF YEAR:** SPR./SUM./FALL/WINT.

Join together with other theatre groups in your area to form a subscription series. Arrange for the production of four or five various types of plays during the season, and offer patrons a reduced subscription price for all five shows. Your savings should amount to one free show, and by combining groups, you will also increase overall audience and market awareness.

Televised Performances

• **CATEGORY:** ARTS & THEATRE • **GROUP SIZE:** LARGE • **TIME FRAME:** 1 YR.+ • **TIME OF YEAR:** SPR./SUM./FALL/WINT.

A publicly televised production can greatly enhance the prestige of any particular theatrical group. Persuading a television company to donate air time is never easy, especially when the production is likely to attract a fairly limited audience, but a TV station may become much more interested when the production is sponsored by a corporation who takes most of the advertising slots surrounding the program. Both sectors benefit when the projected viewing audience fits the corporate customer profile.

The rise of specialty channels and the projected future explosion of new networks provide greatly improved opportunities for this type of exposure.

Playwright's Contest

• **CATEGORY:** ARTS & THEATRE • **GROUP SIZE:** SM./MED./LARGE • **TIME FRAME:** UP TO 1 YR. • **TIME OF YEAR:** SPR./SUM./FALL/WINT.

Amateur and professional playwrights are constantly in search of theatres and groups to perform their work. A playwright's contest provides a forum wherein playwrights can have their work evaluated, but more important, someone must put on a performance of the winning play. If your group can ensure such a performance, it has the genesis of a successful annual competition.

Props and Locale

Many theatre groups do not perform all year long, and much of their theatrical equipment (sets, props, and costumes) lays dormant during the off-season. Performance materials like this should be rented out to other groups. If your group owns space in addition to usable material, that too should be leased to other groups for a nominal fee.

• **CATEGORY:** ARTS & THEATRE • **GROUP SIZE:** SM./MED./LARGE • **TIME FRAME:** UP TO 1 YR. • **TIME OF YEAR:** SPR./SUM./ FALL

All theatre, ballet and opera companies accumulate heaps of costumes and props which can be put on public display from time to time. Articles of particular interest, especially those worn or used by celebrity performers, can be used as the main attractions. Additional funds can be raised from sales of unwanted costumes or paraphernalia, old programs, posters and theatre memorabilia.

Non-Traditional Performances

• **CATEGORY:** ARTS & THEATRE • **GROUP SIZE:** SM./MED./LARGE • **TIME FRAME:** UP TO 1 YR. • **TIME OF YEAR:** SPR./SUM./ FALL

Any performance group can save money by using non-traditional stages or settings for its show. Try performing *The Pirates of Penzance* on a tall ship, either in harbour or while cruising offshore. *A Funny Thing Happened on the Way to the Forum* can be set in a real fair ground. Shakespeare's *A Midsummer Night's Dream* is often performed in suitable parks and gardens. Be creative in your selection of venue. One Canadian production of *Romeo and Juliet* was staged under a bridge. Ticket prices can usually be increased for shows staged in imaginative, and appropriate venues, or decreased to encourage widescale attendance at a large venue.

Memorabilia

• **CATEGORY:** ARTS & THEATRE • **GROUP SIZE:** SM./MED./LARGE • **TIME FRAME:** UP TO 6 MTHS. • **TIME OF YEAR:** SPR./SUM./FALL/WINT.

Theatrical souvenirs add a whole new dimension to the theatre-going experience. Consider selling T-shirts with logos, or shirts that commemorate a particular show. Opera glasses, theatre post cards, posters, scripts, and scores are other items to be sold at a profit.

Cast Recordings
• **CATEGORY:** ARTS & THEATRE • **GROUP SIZE:** SM./MED./LARGE • **TIME FRAME:** UP TO 6 MTHS. • **TIME OF YEAR:** SPR./SUM./FALL/WINT.

Wherever possible, recordings of amateur musical productions should be available to be sold on cassettes, CD's, or videos. Every cast member will buy at least one. Duplication of the tapes can be done on any good quality dual cassette player, and recordable CD's became available in 1997. The quality of the reproduction need not necessarily be its most important factor. Relatives of the performers are more interested in having a keepsake than an art treasure.

Remember to obtain written permission from the copyright owner of the material prior to reproducing any performance.

Meet the Stars
• **CATEGORY:** ARTS & THEATRE • **GROUP SIZE:** MED./LARGE • **TIME FRAME:** UP TO 6 MTHS. • **TIME OF YEAR:** SPR./SUM./FALL/WINT.

Theatre, opera, and ballet companies all raise additional funds by charging patrons to meet the stars of the show. Other charity groups can also benefit from this scheme with a little assistance from the theatre and stars in question. Ask the theatre to host a special "meet the stars" event on behalf of your organization. If the stars will cooperate, these meetings can be arranged either as dinner before or after the show, a dressing room visit, or even a few seconds on stage after the performance. All for an appropriate fee.

• **CATEGORY:** ARTS & THEATRE • **GROUP SIZE:** LARGE • **TIME FRAME:** UP TO 1 YR. • **TIME OF YEAR:** SPR./SUM./FALL/WINT.

Many charities will throw a "Meet the Stars" party at some important period in each theatrical season. This gives a large number of people the opportunity to meet the show's actors, and allows any organization to request considerable donations from the public. Usually, the complete cast of a show is invited as guests of honour.

Speaking & Speakers

Debates
• **CATEGORY:** GENERAL • **GROUP SIZE:** SM./MED./LARGE • **TIME FRAME:** UP TO 6 MTHS. • **TIME OF YEAR:** SPR./FALL/WINT.

The art of oratory is not lost, it has merely become television. Judging from the number of TV shows where hosts and guests heatedly debate politics, religion, and the world at large, there is no reason to believe that a live debate forum would not attract similar attention. Your key, of course, is to attract controversial speakers. Use your debate as a fundraising tool, not as a platform for discussions of your organization. Although membership might well be interested in hearing a politician attempting to explain why your funding has been slashed by 50%, neither the politician nor the public at large will want to attend a debate on that topic. Choose controversial topics and eccentric speakers to attract the most publicity.

Seminars

• **CATEGORY:** GENERAL • **GROUP SIZE:** SM./MED./LARGE • **TIME FRAME:** UP TO 6 MTHS. • **TIME OF YEAR:** SPR./SUM./FALL/WINT.

Teach your own seminars. Many charitable organizations are experts on topics of general interest. Offering seminars in your area of expertise raises money and increases public awareness at the same time. Seminars are also good events for the recruitment of new members.

Your program must be informative, educational and, above all, entertaining. Your speakers must be erudite and their presentations well-organized. Many committed and loyal members of charity and N.F.P. organizations are fully prepared to speak in public, but most of them are not good at it. Every seminar speaker must shine. One rambling dissertation can destroy a whole evening, day or weekend. Don't let it happen. Be firm.

• **CATEGORY:** GENERAL/CHILDREN & YOUTH • **GROUP SIZE:** MED./LARGE • **TIME FRAME:** UP TO 1 YR. • **TIME OF YEAR:** SPR./SUM./FALL/WINT.

Many business and community colleges offer courses involving social sciences and other topics which may relate to the work of your organization. Your expertise in these fields may enable you to offer fully prepared seminars or even courses to students of such programs. The teaching fees for such programs can be substantial. Do your homework well, and ensure that all course material is relevant, well prepared and professionally presented.

• **CATEGORY:** GENERAL • **GROUP SIZE:** SM./MED./LARGE • **TIME FRAME:** UP TO 1 YR. • **TIME OF YEAR:** SPR./SUM./FALL/WINT

If you feel your topic will not arouse sufficient interest, or if accomplished speakers well versed in your subject area are not available, do not despair. Your organization can still sponsor seminars. You will need a well-known speaker prepared to lecture in order to raise funds. Contact anyone you, or anyone your members, believe may be willing to help. As long as the seminar topic does not conflict with your organizational aims and objects, you should be on to a good thing.

Speaking Contest

• **CATEGORY:** GENERAL • **GROUP SIZE:** SM./MED. • **TIME FRAME:** UP TO 1 YR. • **TIME OF YEAR:** SPR./FALL/WINT.

Some people like to talk just to hear themselves talk. Others love the idea of speaking at any public forum. Why not give these budding orators an opportunity. Arrange a public speaking contest, and for a small entry fee, give all-comers the opportunity to speak for a limited time on a subject of personal choice. The audience will probably be largely composed of people waiting a turn to speak as well as those who have just spoken. A few people, however, will pay to be spectators. Arrange for a public speakers' club, like Toast Masters, or the local debating society to sponsor your event and award prizes. Contests of this sort are especially good for high school and university students.

Many would-be comedians would also love the opportunity to try out their skills on a captive audience. Why not let them have their 15 minutes of laughter for a fee, and if you can arrange television or radio coverage, so much the better. A well-known comedian or other celebrity should host the event. The very best prize that you could offer would be an opportunity for the winner to appear on television or at a comedy night club.

Talent Contests

• **CATEGORY:** ARTS & THEATRE/GENERAL • **GROUP SIZE:** SM./MED. • **TIME FRAME:** UP TO 1 YR. • **TIME OF YEAR:** SPR./SUM./FALL/WINT.

In lean times anybody with talent and ambition must get as much exposure as possible, and most entertainers participating in an organized talent contest will just value the chance to work. Offer prizes worked out in conjunction with a local television station or recording studio. Guarantee winners excellent exposure. Media coverage (local or otherwise), is a must to encourage participants and to ensure an audience. If possible, offer the possibility of recording contracts, TV auditions, night club appearances etc. Open the contest to all with performance talent: singers, dancers, magicians, acrobats, musicians, and specialty acts of any kind. Charge participants an entry fee and an admission fee to the public.

Alternatively, you may choose to focus your competition on one field – musicians, actors, or mime artists. This concentration will increase the level of competence required to win your competition.

Large organizations with many branches across the country or worldwide may wish to hold numerous local talent contests as preliminary events, arranging for the winners to advance to regional and subsequent national or even international finals.

Local contests attract large numbers of talented performers anxious to gain national recognition. Charge a fairly substantial entry fee for each local event and raise additional funds made from audience admission, refreshments, car parking etc. Let each local branch retain 50% of the profit from the event, passing the remaining 50% to head office. The head office would arrange the finals as a major competition sponsored by a television company, recording studio or other organization anxious to be associated with such an undertaking.

A major prize, provided by your sponsors, should be accompanied by a guaranteed television appearance, recording contracts and other suitable awards. This is a win, win, win project and it can generate substantial revenue annually for any organization with the ability to organize local contests in every community across the country.

RACES & MARATHONS

Pushing or Pulling

Bed Racing

• **CATEGORY:** HEALTH RELATED/FITNESS, SPORTS & SOCIAL • **GROUP SIZE:** SM./MED. • **TIME FRAME:** UP TO 6 MTHS. • **TIME OF YEAR:** SPR./SUM./FALL

Sponsored bed racing, especially when raising funds for hospitals and medical facilities, has been a successful venture for many charities. Bed races can be organized either as an endurance push with one or two beds, or as a multi-team race over a short course. An event of this nature is most successful (like most fundraising) when there is a specific goal.

The choice between a single and multi-team event depends entirely on your available resources: how many old beds you have, the number of people prepared to run, and so on. Bear in mind, the more participants you have the more money you are likely to raise. How about a challenge event among all of the hospitals and medical facilities in the area? Will non-medical personnel like the police and/or fire fighters be willing to support your cause by entering teams?

A multi-team event in the form of a series of short sprints can be held in any suitable public place or even on hospital grounds. Fundraising should be achieved in advance.

Sometimes, where there are a number of medical facilities within in a reasonably small area, a point-to-point race can be arranged. The course should take the racers past each of the facilities, where crowds of supporters can be encouraged to cheer their teams on while making donations.

An endurance run by just one or two teams can be held on a circuit in a very public place – a large parking lot in the centre of town, or around a shopping plaza (with the cooperation of the developer) would be ideal. A 20-kilometre bed push around a circuit on a busy Saturday attracts considerable interest, and generates substantial funds. An endurance run can also be organized over any distance on the open road.

Bus

• **CATEGORY:** FITNESS, SPORTS & SOCIAL/SERVICE CLUBS • **GROUP SIZE:** MED./LARGE • **TIME FRAME:** UP TO 1 YR. • **TIME OF YEAR:** SPR./SUM./FALL

How about setting a world record for pulling a bus the marathon distance of 26 miles using teams of men, women, or both. This is an event that has never previously been attempted, and maybe for good reason. Create your own rules as to the number of persons pulling the bus and the distance that each group will pull. Pulling at reasonable speeds over a distance of one mile on a flat surface should take about eight minutes with a team of eight strong people.

There are a number of ways in which you could arrange this event in order to maximize publicity and revenue. The rules will vary accordingly. Here are some suggestions:

Members Only: use only your organization's members, each of whom should be sponsored by friends and family (at least fifty people will be needed for this feat).

Challenge Event: challenge other groups, organizations, police, fire, transit, and other workers to enter teams, each to pull the bus for each of the twenty-six miles, each with sponsors. You can add incentives by offering 50% of the total sponsorship money to the winning team's charity.

The bus company providing the vehicle can attract considerable publicity for itself and should be encouraged to provide a trophy for the winner.

For maximum publicity, and the opportunity to collect money from the public en route, pull the bus through the streets of your city, providing you can find a relatively flat route for 26 miles, and with the permission of the local municipality. Alternatively, hold the event in a large parking lot, racetrack, or similar arena. The more central and accessible the location, the better. Attention is an important element in this fundraiser.

Publicity about the event should be self-generating, particularly if you have twenty-six teams each pulling one mile.

Ensure that you notify *The Guinness Book of Records* and lay down a carefully planned set of rules so that other communities can challenge your record.

Alternative events along the same lines include:

Aircraft

• **CATEGORY:** FITNESS, SPORTS & SOCIAL/GENERAL • **GROUP SIZE:** LARGE • **TIME FRAME:** UP TO 1 YR. • **TIME OF YEAR:** SPR./SUM./FALL

How far can the entire crew of a jumbo jet pull their plane down a runway? Ask them to try it for charity, and ask all airport workers to sponsor them.

Train

• **CATEGORY:** FITNESS, SPORTS & SOCIAL/GENERAL • **GROUP SIZE:** LARGE • **TIME FRAME:** UP TO 1 YR. • **TIME OF YEAR:** SPR./SUM./FALL

How many "strongmen" would pay to make an attempt to pull a train? How many of their relatives and friends will sponsor them in the attempt?

Person Powered Grand Prix

• **CATEGORY:** FITNESS, SPORTS & SOCIAL/GENERAL • **GROUP SIZE:** SM./MED. • **TIME FRAME:** UP TO 1 YR. • **TIME OF YEAR:** SPR./SUM./FALL

Anyone who has pushed a car to start it up knows the effort required to overcome its inertia. Once moving on a flat surface, maintaining a car's momentum is not so difficult. Why not organize an annual Grand Prix where all races involve pushing, or pulling, cars around a short circuit. Invite a local car dealer to supply cars for the event, in return for the publicity, and then send out a challenge to your local sports clubs, service clubs, like organizations, and the public at large to enter teams.

Some possible events within your Grand Prix could be:

• The four-person, one-mile, four-seat-sedan sprint

• The 4 X 100 metre, three-person relay

• The four-person, five-mile minimarathon

Create your own rules, and assign your own race officials. You might also consider races for modified vehicles, those old cars stripped of excess weight, which can be pushed at greater speed.

Find a suitable venue. This event should be held on a large, flat, parking lot or wide street (blocked off with the permission of the relevant authorities). You will require sufficient space to mark out a circuit, and a spectator viewing area.

Try to obtain sponsorship from local car dealerships. The three components of this event are publicity, cars, and prizes. Car dealerships can provide you with all three items, and obtain good publicity for themselves at the same time.

Alternatively, there is no reason why you should not require each team participating to provide its own car for the race(s): this move is a must if no car dealers will supply vehicles. When a variety of different cars are to be used, you must consider rules regarding size and weight. For fast, exciting, racing you can permit teams to strip the cars of everything except bodywork and wheels. Or you can insist that all cars are road worthy.

You can stage a "special" event where the cars have to be driven once around the track carrying the entire team. At the end of the first lap the team has three minutes to remove as much of the vehicle as they choose, before pulling it a further ten laps.

Publicity should come in two stages. Advance publicity enables groups and organizations to put together teams and to arrange pledges of sponsorship. Invite as many different groups as possible to enter and especially invite the military, police, fire, and rescue organizations. Service clubs, car enthusiasts, and senior youth organizations are all likely entrants. Announce the event in your local press and, if the event is sponsored by a car dealership, ensure that the dealer gives you maximum publicity. Publicity to attract spectators should begin several weeks before the event.

Make race day a major attraction in your community by featuring heats and races, just like a regular race-day at the track. An entry fee, or a minimum pledge level, should be required from each team; spectators should be charged admission, or asked for a minimum donation. Additional funds can be raised through refreshment stands, program sales, side shows and betting (where permitted). To enhance attendance, combine this event with a vintage car rally, a used car auction, or a car dealer's fair.

Person-Powered 24-hour Le Mans Race

• **CATEGORY:** FITNESS, SPORTS & SOCIAL/GENERAL • **GROUP SIZE:** MED./LARGE • **TIME FRAME:** UP TO 1 YR. • **TIME OF YEAR:** SPR./SUM./FALL

The Le Mans, 24-hour motor race, is a gruelling annual event which tests the endurance of race cars and drivers alike. A person-powered Le Mans is exactly the same race (the driver who completes the most laps of the circuit in 24 hours is the winner), but with one not so subtle difference: person-powered cars are specially constructed of lightweight materials with no power or pedals. Each car is raced by a team of four persons who take turns pushing or riding in the vehicle with intermittent rest periods. Offer a major trophy to the winning team. Fundraising occurs as each team is sponsored for a substantial amount in order to enter the race, spectators pay an entrance fee, and your organization runs refreshment and entertainment facilities. Other, less demanding fundraising events can also be organized during this 24-hour period.

Car Racing

• **CATEGORY:** FITNESS, SPORTS & SOCIAL/SERVICE CLUBS • **GROUP SIZE:** LARGE • **TIME FRAME:** UP TO 1 YR. • **TIME OF YEAR:** SPR./SUM./FALL

Anybody can organize a car race and there are an almost limitless number of types and categories of cars to be raced. You will require the use of a racetrack of some description. Hold races for categories of cars not usually raced or over a course that is unusual in some way. Make sure that you have excellent liability insurance.

People race all types of vehicles and your organization might consider establishing an annual race for a specific model. The trick is to identify a particular model that would attract attention and publicity. Races for alternatively powered vehicles currently are very popular. How about dune buggies, or 4 x 4's, or even Hummers.

Charity Cup Race

• **CATEGORY:** FITNESS, SPORTS & SOCIAL/SERVICE CLUBS • **GROUP SIZE:** LARGE • **TIME FRAME:** UP TO 1 YR. • **TIME OF YEAR:** SPR./SUM./FALL

If there is a local automobile racetrack in your area, approach the management with the idea of holding an annual "Charity Cup" race. The cup, paid for by one of your patrons, donated by a local business or, as a last resort, purchased with charity funds, would be offered as a prize for the event, but no financial reward given because drivers would be racing for the prestige of winning the cup with all the profits going to charity.

Funds can be raised in the following ways:

• A proportion of the gate money donated by the management

• A race entry fee donated by the drivers/teams

• A spectator collection being taken up by your members

Car Obstacle Race

• **CATEGORY:** FITNESS, SPORTS & SOCIAL/SERVICE CLUBS • **GROUP SIZE:** SM. • **TIME FRAME:** UP TO 6 MTHS. • **TIME OF YEAR:** SPR./SUM./FALL

This obstacle race differs from most in that each team of competitors is required to *carry* a car over the course.

The obstacle course is yours to design but should resemble a horse show-jumping ring. The cars should be old and small, with engines removed. Teams race against the clock, or each other, and simply strong-arm the cars around the course and over obstacles without knocking them over. Make it funny with fancy dress. Raise money by "on course" betting (if legal). Ask local businesses to sponsor each car. Charge each team an entrance fee. Impose a fine for each fence knocked over etc.

Rallies

• **CATEGORY:** FITNESS, SPORTS & SOCIAL/SERVICE CLUBS • **GROUP SIZE:** SM./MED./LARGE • **TIME FRAME:** UP TO 1 YR.
• **TIME OF YEAR:** SPR./SUM./FALL/WINT.

Owners of old, unusual or interesting vehicles take great pleasure in showing off their treasures and, although there are a number of rallies organized by owners' associations, there is plenty of scope for new ones. A rally arranged for charity will encourage many people to participate who might not otherwise do so. Car and vehicle rallies can be organized in a number of ways to be both entertaining and profitable. Money can be made from entry fees, sponsorship, public attendance, parking fees, sale of refreshments, auctions of specialist paraphernalia, and fees from corporate exhibitors.

Arrange a massive car rally with various local automobile clubs, i.e., the Corvette Club of Ontario or the Classic Car Club. Approach any number of car enthusiast's clubs and organize all the events and prizes, and bring together thousands of car enthusiasts for a weekend of fun, entertainment and car-related competitions.

Swedish Style Car Racing/Endurance Rally

• **CATEGORY:** FITNESS, SPORTS & SOCIAL/SERVICE CLUBS • **GROUP SIZE:** SM./MED./LARGE • **TIME FRAME:** UP TO 6 MTHS.
• **TIME OF YEAR:** SPR./SUM./FALL/WINT.

The Swedes hold an annual car race/rally which is very successful, although it borders on the reckless. Starting in Stockholm, each team of three persons drives an automobile hundreds of miles north to the Arctic boundary of the country.

Each team pays an entry fee and lots are drawn to allocate cars which have been obtained from wrecker's yards (the only guarantee of roadworthiness is the fact that they are running at the start of the race). The Swedes seem to ignore insurance and licensing requirements. Designed to test the ingenuity, stamina, and perseverance of the teams in keeping the cars in motion, this race also tests driving ability in severe winter conditions.

Such events organized in North America are usually held on mostly private roads, or on logging trails in wilderness areas. The Michelin rally series in the Northeast and the Press On Regardless Rally in Michigan are two local examples of this endurance event. Here in North America the rally team is usually two, not three, persons.

Point-to-Point Rally

• **CATEGORY:** FITNESS, SPORTS & SOCIAL/GENERAL • **GROUP SIZE:** SM./MED. • **TIME FRAME:** UP TO 6 MTHS.
• **TIME OF YEAR:** SPR./SUM./FALL/WINT.

Each driver, beginning from a collective starting point, must navigate from unknown location to unknown location using only cryptic clues. As each clue is deciphered, the driver travels to the next point to pick up the next clue and so on. It is advisable to give each driver a sealed envelope containing details of the final destination. If the envelope is opened, the driver is disqualified, but at least he/she will find the way home.

Make sure, when planning your rally, that its size and style, and available prizes are all financially feasible, leaving a healthy surplus of funds for your organization. Would anybody enter a 3,000-kilometre, 5-day rally with a first prize of $10,000? Some people would almost undoubtedly, but the fundraiser's question is: would enough people enter to make the event financially worthwhile? A hundred entrants paying $100 each covers the prize value, but what about expenses involved in setting up the event, and the cost of publicity?

'Round-the-World Rally

• **CATEGORY:** GENERAL • **GROUP SIZE:** MED./LARGE • **TIME FRAME:** 1 YR.+ • **TIME OF YEAR:** SPR./SUM./FALL

Although it is certainly possible to actually travel around the world with the aid of a few ships, a 'round-the-world car rally is not that difficult. Most North American towns and communities were named by early settlers after the places they left behind, and many have European place names, or at least streets named after foreign cities and countries. The challenge for each driver would be to visit as many places with foreign names within a 24-hour period as possible, and to collect something in each place indicating the name. The winner is the person who goes to the most "countries." Alternatively, the rally could be run on a pre-selected route (by the organizers) travelling to these foreign locales, with the winner being the first to complete the route, mementos in hand.

Concours

• **CATEGORY:** GENERAL • **GROUP SIZE:** SM./MED. • **TIME FRAME:** UP TO 1 YR. • **TIME OF YEAR:** SPR./SUM./FALL

A wide range of interesting and amusing competitions can be held to entertain the participants and spectators at a concours but the primary purpose of such an event is to permit owners to display their vehicles, network with like-minded people, and raise money for charity. Usually each concours (d'elegance) relates to a specific automobile or even one specific model, but you may expand the concept as desired (Packard, Bricklin, Corvette, Porsche, Jaguar, Triumph).

Money can be made from admission fees and by charging commercial vendors for display space. A car trunk sale of specialty items may be particularly popular. A grand raffle and a memorabilia auction can raise additional funds.

Other potential themes for this event include:

Veteran Vehicle

Choose parameters that you think may be successful. Consult with owners of old and vintage vehicles, liaise with enthusiasts' clubs and hunt up the specialist magazines to bring together a large number of vintage vehicles.

Centenary Celebration

Hold a celebration in the year 2000 by bringing together 100 motor vehicles, one from each year of the 20th century.

Alternative Vehicle

Agricultural vehicles, steam vehicles, and solar-powered vehicles can also form the basis of a successful and unusual concours.

Caterpillar Racing

• **CATEGORY:** FITNESS, SPORTS & SOCIAL/SERVICE CLUBS • **GROUP SIZE:** SM./MED. • **TIME FRAME:** UP TO 1 YR. • **TIME OF YEAR:** SPR./SUM./FALL

However unlikely it may seem, one community in North America holds a major annual fundraising event based entirely on the ability of certain caterpillars to climb lengths of string.

Thousands of people turn out annually to bet on these little furry creatures as they climb a few inches. The entire community is involved in the event in a wide variety of ways, from providing refreshments; selling caterpillar toys; making and selling stuffed "woolly worm" caterpillars; setting up numerous side shows, all with the theme of caterpillars; and, of course, catching and racing caterpillars. The event is so popular that it even attracts international publicity.

Lawn Mower Racing

• **CATEGORY:** GENERAL • **GROUP SIZE:** SM./MED. • **TIME FRAME:** UP TO 6 MTHS. • **TIME OF YEAR:** SPR./SUM./FALL

With more and more people owning ride-on and powered mowers, you can organize an annual fun event to attract considerable attention. There are already a number of established mower race meetings in the U.S. over various classes and courses: ride-on mowers less than ten h.p.; standard models with blades removed; standard models with blades removed which are more than ten h.p.; walk-behind and power-assisted motors; specially prepared hot-rod mowers; and push mowers. You can set the rules, categories, and course. Offer prizes in each category. Ask mower dealers to donate a lawn mower or lawn related products. Raise money by charging an entry fee for each race. Sell display space to garden centres, lawn mower dealers and lawn care companies. Combine with your annual spring plant sale to make a major annual event.

Marathons

• **CATEGORY:** FITNESS, SPORTS & SOCIAL/GENERAL • **GROUP SIZE:** SM./MED./LARGE • **TIME FRAME:** UP TO 1 YR. • **TIME OF YEAR:** SPR./SUM./FALL.

Marathons have traditionally contributed huge sums toward charities and will undoubtedly continue to do so in the future.

Many marathons are organized specifically to raise money for charity and there are a number of ways in which you may benefit. Apply to the organizers for a donation from the proceeds. Offer to make your membership available to provide services during the race by acting as stewards, timekeepers, car park attendants, security patrol or even washroom attendants. (Someone has to do it and as large marathons will attract 20,000 participants or more, and 250,000 spectators, it's a big job.)

You can also raise money from someone else's marathon by operating services independently (by negotiating with a major corporation to borrow their corporate car park and opening it to the public on race day). Provide refreshments to spectators and/or runners. If one of your members or supporters has property overlooking the marathon route, consider asking if he/she will invite a few distinguished guests to take a ringside seat in return for substantial charitable donations.

• **CATEGORY:** GENERAL • **GROUP SIZE:** SM./MED./LARGE • **TIME FRAME:** UP TO 6 MTHS. • **TIME OF YEAR:** SPR./SUM./FALL

If organizing a marathon is inappropriate, you can always raise money by being sponsored to run in other people's marathons. This is particularly true if you hold a senior position within your own organization. The announcement, "President to run in Boston Marathon," may encourage many of your supporters to back you with a pledge. Consider entering your entire executive committee as a team, and solicit pledges from all members.

Handicap

• **CATEGORY:** GENERAL • **GROUP SIZE:** SM./MED./LARGE • **TIME FRAME:** UP TO 6 MTHS. • **TIME OF YEAR:** SPR./SUM./FALL

One way of raising more money from any charity or N.F.P. marathon event is to offer an advantage to those participants who enter the race with the greatest amount of financial sponsorship: for example, deduct one mile from the marathon distance for every $100 worth of sponsorship money raised by an individual, or $100 raised by each member of a team. Entrants have a choice – run fast or raise lots of money.

Note: Do not even consider offering this incentive with respect to any serious marathon run.

Half-Marathons

• **CATEGORY:** FITNESS, SPORTS & SOCIAL/GENERAL • **GROUP SIZE:** SM./MED. • **TIME FRAME:** UP TO 1 YR. • **TIME OF YEAR:** SPR./SUM./FALL

Half-marathons, or fun runs, usually garner more local support because of the shorter course. It is also easier to find a route. If your half-marathon is successful, you can always invite the really enthusiastic runner to go around the course again and complete the full distance. Alternatively, your people may wish to consider mini-marathons for these races, so all conditions – length, handicaps, classes etc. – are determined by the organizers. 10K or even 5K runs are very popular. For marathons with a twist, offer prizes for a variety of reasons other than pure speed:

• Biggest costume
• Funniest costume
• First person to run backwards all the way
• Heaviest weight carried the entire route
• Most stupid running technique
• The person who does the silliest thing throughout the race

There are no limits to the number of marathon categories. All you need is imagination and a little daring.

Funny Run

• **CATEGORY:** FITNESS, SPORTS & SOCIAL/GENERAL • **GROUP SIZE:** SM./MED. • **TIME FRAME:** UP TO 6 MTHS. • **TIME OF YEAR:** SPR./SUM./FALL/WINT.

Not to be confused with a fun run, the funny run awards two major prizes, in addition to first place: the funniest costume worn throughout the race and the person who runs the entire race in the funniest way. Use this competition as an adjunct to liven up any event. The distance depends on the age and capabilities of the runners.

Exercise Machines

How many fitness clubs operate in your area? Why not organize a competitive marathon on treadmill exercise machines between members of each of these fitness clubs. Each club must enter a minimum number of treadmills equipped with odometers. Assuming five machines per club, invite each institute to select their best marathon runners as participants. Offer a trophy to the winning club, whose runners complete the marathons in the shortest combined time. If possible, each team member should run at a different club. All the races should have a synchronized start time. Raise money from sponsorship and entry fees, as each team should receive substantial sponsorship from its own club, and fellow members, in addition to friends and families. This is a great event for live coverage by a local TV or radio station, particularly if they have teams of their own involved in the marathon. Also, provide audio or video links between the competing clubs.

• **CATEGORY:** HEALTH RELATED/FITNESS, SPORTS & SOCIAL • **GROUP SIZE:** MED. • **TIME FRAME:** UP TO 1 YR. • **TIME OF YEAR:** SPR./FALL/WINT.

Stage this event as a national competition and enable many thousands of people to participate without having to leave their home cities, linked by television and the Internet. Your goal would be to galvanize the imagination of millions of couch potatoes by having thousands of athletes simultaneously running marathons in fitness clubs and gymnasiums in hundreds of communities across the country.

Seek sponsorship from participating fitness clubs, treadmill manufacturers and from a sports speciality television channel. Each runner should also be sponsored by friends and supporters and the viewing public should be asked to call in with pledges. Sports personalities from all disciplines should be invited to act as hosts or to participate. Treadmill manufacturers might also be interested in supplying a large number of machines to a television studio where several invited athletes could participate (and from where the whole event could be coordinated). This competition provides excellent promotional opportunities for a major computer company as well.

Numb-Bum Competition

• **CATEGORY:** FITNESS, SPORTS & SOCIAL/GENERAL • **GROUP SIZE:** SM. • **TIME FRAME:** UP TO 6 MTHS. • **TIME OF YEAR:** SPR./SUM./FALL

An apt name for any number of possible events all based on the concept of sitting in one position for a long period of time, with money being raised by way of sponsorship for each hour completed. Pole-sitting is one example of a numb-bum competition. Here are some others:

- Bicycle or Motorcycle Marathon
- Pedal Car Racing: definitely a stamina event
- Horse Back Riding: just because you are prepared to ride a horse for 24 hours doesn't mean that the horse has to suffer. Use a relay of horses
  - Stationary Exercise Bike
  - Rowing Machine

Pigeon Racing

• **CATEGORY:** GENERAL • **GROUP SIZE:** SM./MED./LARGE • **TIME FRAME:** UP TO 1 YR. • **TIME OF YEAR:** SPR./SUM./FALL

Pigeon racing clubs exist worldwide, and each week there are dozens of races ranging from 100 to 1,000 miles. Pigeon owners race their birds for sport, winning substantial prizes, but there is no reason why they shouldn't race birds for charity as well. Contact your nearest pigeon club, or the national headquarters, and suggest an annual charity race for a trophy and prize.

Shopping Cart Racing

• **CATEGORY:** GENERAL • **GROUP SIZE:** SM. • **TIME FRAME:** UP TO 6 MTHS. • **TIME OF YEAR:** SPR./SUM./FALL

This event has the potential to raise substantial amounts of money when held annually. Teams of three persons, two runners and a rider, race shopping carts over a predetermined course. The event is usually sponsored by a local supermarket, which benefits from the publicity in return for the loan of the carts and a presentation of trophy and prizes. Race courses vary from three to seven km in distance, and money can be raised from a race entry fee, or from team sponsorship. To make the event more challenging, include an obstacle course in the route which requires teams to cross a river, negotiate fences, walls etc.

Raft Racing

• **CATEGORY:** FITNESS, SPORTS & SOCIAL/SERVICE CLUBS • **GROUP SIZE:** SM./MED. • **TIME FRAME:** UP TO 4WKS. • **TIME OF YEAR:** SUM./FALL

An annual raft race will provide fun for the contestants, entertainment for spectators, and cash for the organizer. A relatively calm and safe stretch of water is required, a river, lake or bay perhaps, and you will need a number of prizes for different competition categories. Invite numerous groups to enter teams, each of them being sponsored by friends, colleagues, and relatives. The British National Raft Racing Association has regulations establishing the different race categories and your group may wish to consult these rules before establishing the boundaries of your competition. Rafts are constructed inexpensively of plastic or steel drums and held together with rope. Some may be specially designed. Raft races are also successful when held in conjunction with established regattas.

Snowblower Racing

• **CATEGORY:** FITNESS, SPORTS & SOCIAL/SERVICE CLUBS • **GROUP SIZE:** SM. • **TIME FRAME:** UP TO 4WKS. • **TIME OF YEAR:** WINT.

Whenever the weather permits hold snowblower races. Use a local park as the venue and arrange trophies for winners. Create as many categories as you wish including: team snow blowing, relay races, speed trials, hill climbing, or straightness of lines. With mother nature's cooperation, you stand to have a good, fun event that raises a few dollars.

Wheelbarrow Grand Prix

• **CATEGORY:** GENERAL • **GROUP SIZE:** SM. • **TIME FRAME:** UP TO 6 MTHS. • **TIME OF YEAR:** SPR./SUM./FALL

Borrow wheelbarrows from local equipment rental outlets and/or from your membership. Hire them out to contestants. Participants may choose to bring their own. The course can vary: one section for endurance, one for obstacles, and one even cross-country or uphill. Your organization can decide what handicap will be carried in the wheelbarrows – a person, a load of bricks, or even a pile of manure.

Wheelchair Races

• **CATEGORY:** HEALTH RELATED/GENERAL • **GROUP SIZE:** SM./MED. • **TIME FRAME:** UP TO 6 MTHS. • **TIME OF YEAR:** SPR./SUM./FALL

Canada's Special Olympians have shown us all what a challenging and exciting sport wheelchair racing can be. Your organization might offer a sponsored race on closed streets of a town or village, around a paved racetrack, in a parking lot. Don't forget relay races. Beware of the specially adapted racing wheelchairs. They are fast. Competitions can be self-propelled or pushed. Your choice. Contact your provincial Special Olympics committee for help in this area.

SALES & AUCTIONS

Auctions

• **CATEGORY:** GENERAL • **GROUP SIZE:** SM./MED./LARGE • **TIME FRAME:** UP TO 1 YR. • **TIME OF YEAR:** SPR./FALL/WINT.

Auctions are always popular. In good times people have money to spend and enjoy the excitement generated at an auction. In tough times, people look for bargains. Auctions make money, they're fun to organize, and are immensely entertaining for the buyer (who hasn't heard of auction fever?), for the observer, and for the media. There is always the added bonus of a potential undiscovered treasure lurking in that assorted box of leftover gadgets next under the auctioneer's gavel.

Obtain the services of a professional auctioneer. Charity and N.F.P. groups often make the mistake of assuming that any enthusiastic amateur can be a successful auctioneer. This is simply not so. Professional auctioneers always raise more money overall because they understand how to pace an auction, which items to begin with and when to move into the higher price brackets. Auctioneers also serve to entertain the audience, often to such an extent that return engagements in subsequent years will be even more widely attended as word of mouth works its miracles.

Assembling sufficient items to make an auction worthwhile can be a major headache, particularly if you choose to hold a furniture sale. Storage, insurance, and security costs can make a huge dent in the projected profits, and for this reason most of the auctions we have suggested here do not involve large or cumbersome articles. The most profitable auctions are those where all of the items have been donated by benefactors and delivered to the auction room just a day or so before the sale. Canvassing for suitable articles may take a year or more and, while many people may be willing to donate, most will do so in order to quickly dispose of unwanted items. You will inevitably end up with a quantity of unsalable junk. Storage arrangements, where appropriate, should be made before canvassing begins.

Publicity is essential at both stages of an auction. First, it is necessary to inform as many people as possible of your intention to hold an auction, so that they may be enticed to donate suitable items. Second, the greater the number of people attending the auction, the more likelihood there is of reaching the highest possible prices.

Funds can be raised in a number of different ways. The primary source should be the income from the sale of donated items, but you can raise additional revenues from charging a buyers' registration fee, a fee for those wishing to preview the sale articles on the day prior to the auction, and from selling auction catalogues. More money can be made from the sale of refreshments, car parking and washing fees, and depending on the style of the auction, the sale of crafts, baked goods, farm produce, and products relevant to your organization.

Charity receipts for "Gifts in Kind" can be issued by registered charities for items donated to an auction, and at least one organization – the Canadian Opera Company – issues receipts on the spot for valuable items collected by their experts.

Here are some auction recommendations which have proven particularly successful for charity and N.F.P. fundraisers:

Furniture
• **CATEGORY:** GENERAL • **GROUP SIZE:** SM./MED. • **TIME FRAME:** UP TO 1 YR. • **TIME OF YEAR:** SPR./FALL/WINT.

True antiques are difficult to find. But a well-run furniture auction with a wide selection of material can net some pretty big money.

Bric-a-Brac
• **CATEGORY:** GENERAL • **GROUP SIZE:** SM. • **TIME FRAME:** UP TO 6 MTHS. • **TIME OF YEAR:** SPR./FALL/WINT.

An expensive form of garage sale where anything goes, although it can be more difficult to raise large sums with these sales unless a large quantity of materials is accumulated.

Chinese Auction
• **CATEGORY:** GENERAL • **GROUP SIZE:** SM./MED. • **TIME FRAME:** UP TO 6 MTHS. • **TIME OF YEAR:** SPR./SUM./FALL/WINT.

Chinese auctions differ from regular auctions in the method of operation rather than the type of goods on offer. A Chinese auction is really a series of mini-raffles where each winner receives the lot that was offered for auction. Begin by assembling all items and choosing a theme, if you wish to do so. Once the lots are assembled, produce a catalogue wherein each item has an individual number, and amalgamate any small lots into lots worth the bidding.

Begin the auction by selling bid slips to the assembled audience. Each slip can be priced at one dollar or more depending on the value of the lots on offer. Bidding slips can also be sold in advance. Bidders may purchase as many slips as they wish, and can be offered a discount rate for buying large volumes, i.e., 100 bidding slips for $90.

Bidders attempt to win each lot by placing a bid slip into a sealed container bearing the catalogue number of the desired item. One container is required for each lot. Once all the bid slips have been deposited, each container is opened and the winning ticket is drawn, as in a raffle. Bidders may place as many tickets as they wish in any container and can work to enhance their chance of winning any particular lot by placing large numbers of tickets in that lot's container. Other bidders may choose to spread tickets among any number of containers, trusting to their luck in the draw.

Servant Auction

• **CATEGORY:** GENERAL • **GROUP SIZE:** SM./MED. • **TIME FRAME:** UP TO 6 MTHS. • **TIME OF YEAR:** SPR./SUM./FALL/WINT.

This fundraiser always attracts attention. Servant auctions usually generate healthy returns, amid uproarious revelry, because the only expenses incurred are those for publicity and, when necessary, rental of a suitable venue. A wide variety of individuals should be asked to offer themselves on the auction block, each agreeing to work as required for a specified time, at any task, for any bidder willing to pay the required rate.

Seek volunteers from your organization, together with their friends, supporters, public figures, politicians, and even local celebrities. A local television personality, or a reporter or editor of a local paper, can make a significant contribution and should attract considerable publicity. Make it funny and make it fun.

Professional Services

• **CATEGORY:** GENERAL • **GROUP SIZE:** SM./MED. • **TIME FRAME:** UP TO 1 YR./1 YR+ • **TIME OF YEAR:** SPR./FALL

A well-patronized, professional services auction will provide a two-way benefit in terms of cash for your charity, and exposure for the professionals and craftspeople donating the time and services. Potential high bidding services include: accounting, financial planning, legal work, dental work, golf/tennis lessons with a professional, photography, secretarial services, carpet cleaning, lawn cutting, landscaping, chauffeur for a day, chimney sweeping, plumbing, services of an electrician, maid service, services of a hairdresser, a manicurist, a masseuse, painting lessons, cooking lessons and bridge lessons. Some more unusual professional services likely to catch the attention of the media might include plastic surgery, private investigation, fortune telling and flying lessons.

Bachelor and/or Spinster

• **CATEGORY:** GENERAL • **GROUP SIZE:** SM. • **TIME FRAME:** UP TO 1 YR. • **TIME OF YEAR:** SUM.

An auction of the region's most eligible singles to be purchased for a dinner date can be fun and entertaining. Perhaps a number of restaurants would donate dinners (for two) which could be auctioned to the lucky bachelor and spinster purchasers, thereby enabling your charity to make more money from the event.

Travel Auction

• **CATEGORY:** GENERAL • **GROUP SIZE:** SM./MED. • **TIME FRAME:** UP TO 1 YR. • **TIME OF YEAR:** SPR./FALL/WINT.

Most people like to travel and travel auctions with a diverse assortment of travel opportunities appeal to a wide spectrum of society.

Approach your neighbourhood travel agents, and all of the major airlines, cruise companies, rail companies, car rental firms, limousine services, taxi companies and bicycle, boat or balloon rental firms servicing your community. Ask each one to participate in a travel auction with the donation of a specific travel allowance relevant to their area of expertise. You are looking for items like airline tickets to some popular location in off-season, or less popular locations at any time, a time-share condominium slot, perhaps a guided walking tour with a local historian, a sightseeing flight in a hot air balloon or light aircraft, a Navy sponsored ride in a submarine, a trip in a flight simulator, hotel accommodation in a popular resort city, discounts on car rental rates, a limousine ride to the airport, a rickshaw ride around the city etc. Most travel-related businesses have pre-determined promotional budgets for these kinds of donations. If you can convince them your cause is worthy, and that a contribution to your cause will generate widespread positive publicity for their company, donations of the sort required for a travel auction should not be too difficult to obtain. One inducement you can offer these firms is the opportunity to set up display booths where they can sell their services at your event. Someone who has been unsuccessful in bidding for a holiday may be induced to purchase one.

Members and supporters of your organization can also offer travel prizes for this auction by donating the use of a cottage, time-share, or boat for a specified week. Any supporter with a boat or a plane could offer escorted trips lasting a few hours or even a few days, and anyone with a decent car could offer a chauffeured day-trip.

Use the idea of the "Every Ticket Wins" raffle as an excellent vehicle for increasing publicity and sales, particularly if you can convince travel companies participating in the auction to offer discounts and deals to holders of non-winning tickets.

Housework

• **CATEGORY:** GENERAL • **GROUP SIZE:** SM. • **TIME FRAME:** UP TO 1 YR. • **TIME OF YEAR:** SPR./FALL

A housework auction could be just the activity your community has always wanted but never knew it needed. Three groups of people are important for the success of this kind of event: professional housekeeping agencies; local celebrities including television personalities, politicians, the mayor, police chief, fire chief, head of your local car dealership, real estate professionals, doctors, editors of local newspapers etc.; and every member of your committee, including the president, and as many members and friends of your organization as are willing to offer their services. Approach the professional cleaning agencies in your area and ask that each company donate up to five-days free work in exchange for extensive publicity. Ask your local celebrities if they will donate a day's housework for your cause. Solicit pledges of time from every committee member and as many members and volunteers as necessary. Once you have secured the services of your houseworkers from the groups listed above, you then need to define your houseworking chores, hours, rules and equipment required. Publicity for a housework auction is vital. It must be publicity with humour, and should cover the event from its earliest stage right through to the completion of the assigned household tasks, preferably with pictures in the newspaper or on television. A housework auction can be a public event, held at a specified time in a hall or other suitable venue, but it is the type of event which is perfectly suited to local radio or television.

Articles Relevant to Your Organization

• **CATEGORY:** GENERAL • **GROUP SIZE:** SM. • **TIME FRAME:** UP TO 6 MTHS. • **TIME OF YEAR:** SPR./SUM./FALL/WINT.

An easy and very useful auction can be put together when you auction articles relevant to your membership, especially if you are raising funds for a sports organization. Hold an auction at the start of each season wherein some members can dispose of cast-offs, while others can equip themselves. This is a particularly effective vehicle for ski clubs, golf clubs, hockey teams, cottagers and even horticulture groups, among others. It also serves as an excellent beginning of season icebreaker.

50/50 Auction

• **CATEGORY:** GENERAL • **GROUP SIZE:** SM./MED./LARGE • **TIME FRAME:** UP TO 1 YR. • **TIME OF YEAR:** SPR./SUM./FALL/WINT.

50/50 auctions (or 60/40, 70/30 or any other combination) provide marvellous encouragement to people reluctant to enter items in a charity auction, particularly if you permit each donor to set his or her reserve on the selling price. This reserve price can work to your advantage because you know right away that the seller is willing to take 50% of the reserve. For example: on an item with a reserve of $50, the owner expects to be paid at least $25, and happiness is achieved as long as he/she receives the $25. This enables you to instruct your auctioneer to sell at any price above half the reserve, which gives good leeway for his/her selling spiel.

Dutch Auction

• **CATEGORY:** GENERAL • **GROUP SIZE:** SM./MED./LARGE • **TIME FRAME:** UP TO 6 MTHS. • **TIME OF YEAR:** SPR./SUM./FALL/WINT.

Auctions in Holland differ from those held elsewhere. In fact, they work in converse to auctions everywhere else in the world. They are faster, and the buyer must drop the bid at exactly the right moment, or lose all chance at securing the desired article. Dutch auctioneers begin the offer of each item by quoting the highest price that the seller expects to receive for his/her lot. Should that price not be met, the auctioneer drops the rate in preset increments until the article elicits a bid and is sold forthwith.

Here is an example:

- A fine 18th century French figurine – Who will pay $300?
- No takers at $300, any offers at $290?
- No takes at $290, well it's certainly worth $280.
- No offers at $280. Alright, will anybody give me $270.

One nod and the figurine is sold. The first person to offer the quoted price takes the lot.

Anyone who has not previously experienced a Dutch auction will be surprised at the level of tension and excitement generated by such an event.

Silent Auction

• **CATEGORY:** GENERAL • **GROUP SIZE:** SM./MED./LARGE • **TIME FRAME:** UP TO 1 YR. • **TIME OF YEAR:** SPR./SUM./FALL/WINT.

Silent auctions are easy to operate. Bids can be made by people unable to attend at the time of the sale, and you require no outside help, refreshments, and not even a large hall. Silent auctions, however, lack the excitement generated by a good auctioneer, and there is no auction fever to spur prices beyond rational limits. A silent auction simply displays items for sale and invites potential buyers to offer bids. These may be sealed, but it is more usual, and probably more effective, to have the bids publicly displayed so that potential bidders can see what has already been offered and can offer higher amounts on lots that they really want. All bids are made in writing prior to a designated deadline. Once the bidding is finished, auction officials scrutinize the numbers, awarding each lot to the highest bidder. Silent auctions work well with television or radio coverage and are often successful when the auction locale is not easily accessible to a large number of bidders. Silent auctions are used extensively to raise money for public television stations and are also useful for keeping people occupied at gala events and receptions while awaiting dinner or a speech.

Radio Auction

• **CATEGORY:** GENERAL • **GROUP SIZE:** SM./MED./LARGE • **TIME FRAME:** UP TO 1 YR. • **TIME OF YEAR:** SPR./SUM./FALL/WINT.

Radio auctions involve a specific daily radio program, which offers a different item for auction every day of the promotion. The items on offer are usually donated by a corporate sponsor who benefits from the resultant publicity. Listeners are encouraged to phone in with incremental bids until the end of the program, or a specified time-frame within the program, whereupon the auction closes and the winner is announced. This is an easy fundraiser which costs nothing to arrange. All you need is the cooperation of a radio station and a number of donors willing to offer valuable items. The lack of an auctioneer is mitigated by the on-air competition between bidders.

If a radio station is unwilling to devote so much air-time to your specific charity, perhaps it could be persuaded to auction one item on behalf of a different organization each day. Join forces with other groups and make a united appeal.

Television Auction

• **CATEGORY:** GENERAL • **GROUP SIZE:** SM./MED./LARGE • **TIME FRAME:** 1 YR+ • **TIME OF YEAR:** SPR./SUM./FALL/WINT.

Television auctions work most effectively when a number of charity organizations cooperate. Before contemplating a fundraising event of this nature, however, you will need to convince a community or public television station to provide you with 24 hours of continuous coverage at no (or minimal) charge. Once this hurdle has been overcome, you will want to work with your organizations setting up a schedule whereby each group is responsible for a specific time block, and for the articles to be auctioned within that time block. Each organization will set a deadline by which bids for its items must be received. Winning bids will be announced immediately after that deadline has been reached. Bids are tendered by telephone, or in person, by studio guests. Publicity should not be a problem because the television station will very likely have worked hard to ensure maximum audience participation.

Toy Auction

• **CATEGORY:** CHILDREN & YOUTH/GENERAL • **GROUP SIZE:** SM./MED. • **TIME FRAME:** UP TO 1 YR. • **TIME OF YEAR:** WINT.

Toy auctions should be held a few weeks before Christmas, and organized around a comprehensive collection of new toys purchased as surplus stock from suppliers, or donated by sponsors, retail and wholesale toy outlets or manufacturers. One variation of the toy auction is a 50/50 toy auction, an excellent recycling project, which enables some children to receive perfectly usable pre-used toys, while allowing the seller to recapture some of his/her initial investment on the purchase of new toys.

Tree-Crop Auction

• **CATEGORY:** GENERAL • **GROUP SIZE:** SM./MED. • **TIME FRAME:** 1 YR+ • **TIME OF YEAR:** SUM.

If you live in an area well-known for its fruit cultivation, you might introduce a tree-crop auction. Lease a large number of fruit trees from a local farmer on condition that the fruit from these trees will be picked on, or not later than, a certain date. The value of the trees depends on the amount and type of fruit borne by each, and the savings realized by the farmer by not having to employ workers to pick, pack and ship his/her crop. Apples and pears are most suitable for this venture because the fruit will last a long time once it is picked. Peaches, plums and other softer fruit would need to be frozen or preserved by the purchaser.

Each leased tree should be identified with an alphanumeric value and marked on a plan of the entire orchard. Next, auction each tree on the understanding that the purchaser must pick its crop on an appointed weekend, being careful not to touch or damage any surrounding trees. Crops not picked within the specified time revert back to your organization. You may wish to consider re-leasing the trees every year and establishing an annual tree-crop auction. Variations of this scheme could work on bush crops (blueberries etc.) or even selected vegetables, like corn. Once in a while, you might even find a farmer willing to donate the use of the trees if he/she has no particular interest in harvesting the crop for personal use.

Time, Talent & Treasure Auction

• **CATEGORY:** GENERAL • **GROUP SIZE:** SM. • **TIME FRAME:** UP TO 1 YR. • **TIME OF YEAR:** SPR./FALL/WINT.

This is an interesting event because the items to be auctioned are a combination of objects, services and works of art appealing to a wide audience. The "time" element of the auction refers to hours of work offered by a range of professional service providers. (See Professional Services Auction for suitable ideas.)

The "talent" element relates to the work of artists. Artists of all types can be invited to produce works of art according to their speciality: poets may write a sonnet, musicians write and play a tune, singers sing a song, actors perform a monologue or playlet, and so on. The performance, which can be done publicly, must conform to a time and place agreeable to the artist. Painters and sculptors should offer to produce a piece commissioned by the purchaser; its size and value would depend on the amount paid.

The "treasures" on offer can be real treasures: jewellery, antiques and works of art, or perhaps lesser treasures depending on what is available.

The success of a time, talent, and treasure auction depends entirely on the ingenuity of the service providers and artists selected, and the hype generated by a good auctioneer.

21st Century Auctions

• **CATEGORY:** GENERAL • **GROUP SIZE:** MED./LARGE • **TIME FRAME:** UP TO 1 YR. • **TIME OF YEAR:** SPR./SUM./FALL/WINT.

Don't wait for the future: you can take a major leap into the next millennium today with any auction if you make it a hi-tech affair.

Computerized Auction

Instead of having bidders flapping their hands, nodding their heads or waving numbered paddles in the air, why not let them make bids on-line through a computer.

Place tables around the auction room with seating for six or eight at each table; link each table to the auctioneer with a video monitor. The auctioneer controls all the monitors in the room through a central computer on which he/she can call up details of each lot in succession.

As the first lot is called and appears on each screen, bidders type in their bids and raise bids to beat previous ones. All the bids are displayed on the screen so everyone can watch the progression of the bidding. If the auctioneer wants to encourage higher bidding he/she can communicate with the audience either on-line or verbally. When the auctioneer is satisfied that the highest possible bid has been reached, the successful purchaser is declared.

Any person who cannot be present could make bids through an Internet link.

Telephone Auction

Another novel way of holding a hi-tech auction is to invite all bidders to make bids by phone. So many people have mobile phones that the idea is to set up a bank of bid takers at the auctioneer's table. Bidders on the auction room floor can telephone one of several numbers and talk to the bid takers directly. Bids increase by fixed increments and are displayed on a digital electronic display. Finally, only two bidders should be left on the phone and the lot is sold to the highest bidder. Anyone who does not have a personal phone can use a communal one provided on each table.

Treasure Hunts at Auctions

• **CATEGORY:** GENERAL • **GROUP SIZE:** SM./MED./LARGE • **TIME FRAME:** UP TO 4 WKS. • **TIME OF YEAR:** SPR./SUM./FALL/WINT.

If you are holding an auction of any type you can stimulate interest and increase the amount bid for items by "hiding" treasure in the lots.

Choose three items from your collection that are likely to cause some interest among the buyers and remove them from the catalogue. Next, secretly mark three of the lot numbers at random in the auctioneer's catalogue; one number near the beginning, one in the middle and one very near the end. Prominently display the three reserved items and start the auction by explaining that these three objects will not be offered for sale but will be given to whoever successfully bids for the secretly-marked items. The auction now becomes a form of lottery which will increase the amount of interest shown in every item until all three treasures have been won.

Bazaars

Bazaar is an oriental term for a marketplace and is normally used to denote an assembly of stallholders selling an assortment of items. Almost anything can be sold at a bazaar. Make money by selling space to stallholders, charging an admission fee and selling food, drink and products. All bazaars are fundamentally the same, but to encourage people to patronize yours, have an attractive theme and provide some entertainment.

Foreign Bazaars

• CATEGORY: GENERAL • GROUP SIZE: SM. • TIME FRAME: UP TO 1 YR. • TIME OF YEAR: SPR./FALL/WINT.

Consider holding an exotic, foreign bazaar. Stallholders should be suitably dressed in ethnic costumes, selling appropriate products, with decorations and entertainment reflecting the country or countries of choice.

Parisian Bazaar: French bread with cheeses and wines; artists wearing berets; an accordion band.

Turkish Bazaar: try to recreate the hub-bub of an eastern market with stalls crowded close together; serve Turkish coffee, or tea from a samovar; stallholders wearing Fez's; entertain with appropriate music and a bevy of belly dancers.

Austrian Bazaar: an oompah band with Tyrolean dancers; wiener schnitzel; apple strudel and cream cakes.

Scottish Bazaar: a pipe band with highland dancers; Haggis and whisky; stallholders wearing kilts and tam o'shanters; plaid decorations.

Now that you have the idea – here are some more foreign possibilities:

• Chinese Bazaar
• Japanese Bazaar

- Hawaiian Bazaar
- Mexican Bazaar
- Caribbean Bazaar
- Indian Bazaar

Ideas for costumes and decorations can be found at national tourist offices and can often be "borrowed" for a small fee from a local theatrical group. Posters, pictures, and travel guides can be obtained from travel agents, tourist offices, consulates, embassies, and local multicultural groups. Incidentally, a good first prize for your raffle could be a trip for two to the theme country: ask a travel agent to donate the prize in return for an advertising booth at the bazaar.

Seasonal Bazaars

• **CATEGORY:** GENERAL • **GROUP SIZE:** SM. • **TIME FRAME:** UP TO 1 YR. • **TIME OF YEAR:** FALL/WINT.

Haddassah and Christmas bazaars provide an excellent venue for the sale of holiday ornaments and decorations, food, gifts, and stocking-stuffers. Some appropriate music and entertainment can round-off a successful afternoon.

Bizarre Bazaar

• **CATEGORY:** GENERAL • **GROUP SIZE:** SM. • **TIME FRAME:** UP TO 6 MTHS. • **TIME OF YEAR:** SPR./SUM./FALL/WINT.

Most bazaars relate to a particular festival or season. Why not be bizarre and hold a bazaar at the wrong time of the year. How about a Valentine's Bazaar on October 14th?

Bring and Buy Sales

• **CATEGORY:** GENERAL • **GROUP SIZE:** SM. • **TIME FRAME:** UP TO 4WKS. • **TIME OF YEAR:** SPR./SUM./FALL/WINT.

Perhaps the simplest of all fundraising events for smaller organizations is the bring and buy sale. Donors bring items they have made or purchased and buy items other people have donated. It's easy, no risk, and guarantees a 100% profit. This event is ideal for churches, schools, amateur sports groups and similar organizations. Ask donors to put a realistic price tag on donated articles.

Sell the Boss

• **CATEGORY:** GENERAL • **GROUP SIZE:** SM. • **TIME FRAME:** UP TO 4WKS. • **TIME OF YEAR:** SPR./SUM./FALL/WINT.

Fundraising in offices, shops, and factories can become FUNdraising if the boss is a good sport. Sell the boss to the highest bidder and the purchaser can take him/her home to do eight hours of housework, gardening, or anything else agreeable. Will the boss do it? Ask in advance to avoid embarrassment.

Rummage Sales

• **CATEGORY:** GENERAL • **GROUP SIZE:** SM./MED. • **TIME FRAME:** UP TO 6 MTHS. • **TIME OF YEAR:** SPR./SUM./FALL/WINT.

Almost every organization has held a rummage sale. These can be staged almost anywhere, at any time and, in theory, cannot lose money. They do not, however, raise a lot of money, particularly when analyzed in relation to the time and effort involved. A large, eager, industrious volunteer force is required to track down and collect sufficient material for a worthwhile sale. If storage space is available, collections should be made year round. Toronto's annual Hadassah sale involves thousands of volunteers who work all year round to collect, itemize, and prepare stock for each event.

In some communities it may be worthwhile to place restrictions on a rummage sale, thereby giving it an air of exclusivity. You may wish to stipulate, for example, that all items for sale must have a minimum value of $25, with attendance by invitation only, with an admission ticket (fee $25) which would be redeemable against the purchase of a sale item.

Garage Sales

• **CATEGORY:** GENERAL • **GROUP SIZE:** SM • **TIME FRAME:** UP TO 6 MTHS. • **TIME OF YEAR:** SPR./SUM./FALL

For a small, local organization, an annual garage sale at the home of the chairperson or fundraiser is a sure-fire way to raise enough money for the office stationary. Ask each member to contribute any items he/she wishes. Ask clients, friends, and neighbours for contributions as well. Most of your sales will be within your organization, but make sure that you also get some local publicity. The effort involved is minimal, and you can't lose.

The amount of money raised in a single garage sale is unlikely to exceed a few hundred dollars, so when your organization needs more money, consider a mammoth garage sale. These events do not happen by accident. It may take teams of volunteers as much as a year to collect appropriate items and organize. Start collecting right now.

Fleamarkets

• **CATEGORY:** GENERAL • **GROUP SIZE:** SM. • **TIME FRAME:** UP TO 6 MTHS. • **TIME OF YEAR:** SPR./SUM./FALL

Fleamarkets are one of the simplest ways of fundraising, once you have found a suitable site – a parking lot, sports field, or other large, vacant, outdoor area, or, during the colder months, a large indoor arena will do nicely as long as you can control public entry. People with goods to sell load them into cars, trucks, vans, and trailers and drive to the sale site where each vendor has an assigned location to display his/her wares. Buyers wander from vendor to vendor checking what is on offer and bargaining with the vendors.

Fleamarkets eliminate the headaches of collecting, sorting and storing donated goods.

Publicize your event in as many ways as possible. Don't rely on a single advertisement in a local paper. Exaggerate the size of the sale – "*Hundreds of vendors!! Everything from armchairs to washing machines,*" etc.

Place posters in factories, staff rooms, street corners, electricity poles, and anywhere else to attract attention. Charge a set fee for each vendor and a small admission fee for buyers. You will need to cover advertising costs, but everything else is profit. Make more money by having a stand of your own, or by selling refreshments.

Consider adding a fleamarket to any fundraising event where you expect a crowd and have access to a private parking lot or similar area. Merely add the words, "Giant Fleamarket" to your advertisements. Rope off an area of your parking lot and charge vendors an admission fee. If no one turns up, you've lost nothing.

One variation of the fleamarket is the tailgate/car trunk sale wherein vendors sell directly from the backs of their automobiles and trucks thus eliminating the need for formal stands or display areas.

Charity Calendars

• **CATEGORY:** GENERAL • **GROUP SIZE:** SM./MED. • **TIME FRAME:** 1 YR+ • **TIME OF YEAR:** FALL/WINT.

How many times have you said, or heard others say, "I forgot all about your event this year?" Why not produce an annual charity calendar, funded by local businesses. You can sell in bulk to each of the other charity groups in your area and ensure the entire community is fully aware of your charity fundraisers.

Notify all charity and N.F.P. groups in your community of your intention to produce a calendar promoting all events, meetings, and fundraising campaigns for every organization in the area. Advise each organization how to advertise in your calendar, absolutely free of charge. In addition, be sure to let each group know it can raise money be selling calendars. How can they lose?

This idea is viable only if your organization pays nothing to produce the calendars, which means you must sell calendar advertising space to local businesses and to the town council. Commercial business should welcome the opportunity to support

EVERY charity and N.F.P. group in its community in one fell swoop. If you can't raise sufficient funds from business, approach your town council and request that it support the venture. A local printer might even absorb printing costs.

Once your organization has produced the calendars (at no expense to itself), it needs to sell them, cheaply and in bulk, to all participating charity and N.F.P. groups. Each should add a reasonable profit margin to the list price and resell to members, clients, and friends.

Don't forget to retail your charity calendars throughout your own organization. If your mailing list is particularly large, send each client, supporter, and friend a calendar with a donation request included.

Diaries and Daybooks

• **CATEGORY:** GENERAL • **GROUP SIZE:** MED. • **TIME FRAME:** UP TO 6 MTHS. • **TIME OF YEAR:** FALL/WINT.

Membership diaries are as old as the hills, but in these days of personal organizers and lap-top computers, it is difficult to gauge how much longer they will survive as a fundraising tool. The concept is simple, albeit outdated, and works on the premise that everyone needs a diary. Full production costs are recovered from the sale of advertising space to commercial sponsors, while the diaries themselves are sold or given to members and supporters. Many commercial printers will make all arrangements, and will find suitable advertisers using the name of the charitable organization as bait.

Secondhand Clothing Shop

• **CATEGORY:** WOMEN'S GROUPS/GENERAL • **GROUP SIZE:** SM./MED./LARGE • **TIME FRAME:** UP TO 1 YR. • **TIME OF YEAR:** SPR./SUM./FALL/WINT.

Many charity and N.F.P. groups like the Salvation Army and Goodwill operate secondhand clothing shops. Some are very successful. In challenging economic times, there is no doubt that secondhand clothing shops can provide a useful service to the public and make money for their sponsoring organizations. How you set up and staff such a store will depend on your organization, but here are some ideas:

The most profitable stores are those which are operated by volunteers out of donated rent-free premises. Finding and keeping volunteers who will work shop hours is difficult. Obtaining a rent-free store for a few weeks is never a problem, but loaning a storefront location permanently may challenge even the most philanthropic property owner. Secondhand stores are long term projects. You do not want to keep changing your place of business.

Some stores are operated on a purely commercial basis with paid staff and leased premises. Obviously, overheads are considerable, and therefore net profits drastically reduced, but from an organizer's point of view, these kinds of outlets are much easier to operate. Be absolutely sure of your market or you will lose money.

Consider compromising – it may be the best answer for the initial stages of any secondhand store operation. Negotiate with the owner of an empty store. Ask for an initial period of use rent free, say six months, with an agreement to pay a reasonable rent after that time, if the store is successful. Employ one staff member, part-time, on a very short contract, one month at a time. Have an agreement that, should the store be successful, you will renegotiate at the end of six months. Make sure that all of your members "volunteer" in the store on a regular basis. Do not let anyone escape his/her responsibility.

By proceeding cautiously you can evaluate, without great financial risk, the potential worth of a permanent secondhand retail outlet.

Commission Store

• **CATEGORY:** GENERAL • **GROUP SIZE:** SM./MED. • **TIME FRAME:** UP TO 1 YR. • **TIME OF YEAR:** SPR./SUM./FALL/WINT.

A commission store which sells secondhand items on behalf of members of the public, can be a very profitable venture. Commission is charged on each item, based on a pre-agreed percentage of the selling price. A small display fee should be charged for each item, whether or not it sells. Have a time limit policy in effect, which states that goods not sold within a specified period must be removed by the owner; otherwise, they become store property.

Catalogue Sales

• **CATEGORY:** GENERAL • **GROUP SIZE:** LARGE • **TIME FRAME:** 1 YR+ • **TIME OF YEAR:** SPR./SUM./FALL/WINT.

Fundraisers for major charitable organizations have the potential to raise substantial funds, on a continuing basis, by operating their own product marketing services.

If your organization has a large and committed membership, you have a potentially large customer base for ANY products, not just those specific to your organization. Compile a sales catalogue either annually or semi-annually for distribution to your supporters.

Feature items specifically relevant to your organization imprinted with your logo, or items generally in tune with the goals of your group. You must also feature a healthy mixture of both. The Western Wilderness Committee in Vancouver has used this idea as a successful fundraiser for some time, as has the Federation of Ontario Naturalists.

Encourage members and friends to purchase items through your catalogue by sharing a proportion of the profits with members' own local branches. Offer incentives in the form of gifts specific to your organization, and/or trophies and certificates commemorating commitment.

You can raise money by charging suppliers an advertising fee for each page of your catalogue taken (based on the number of catalogues to be distributed), and/or by taking an agreed percentage of each sale made. Make sure you factor distribution costs into your business plan and remember to charge for handling in addition to postage. All purchases should be prepaid prior to shipment. Leave a line in your catalogue for donations.

A Word of Caution: This type of fundraising is always likely to raise an ethical dilemma, as some people will question whether you should be promoting the products of private sector companies. My response has always been that ALL product sold or offered as a premium gift through a charity or N.F.P. organization will have been manufactured in the private sector. Someone is profiting from the sale whether an item bears your logo or not.

Multi-Level Marketing Sales

• **CATEGORY:** WOMEN'S GROUPS/GENERAL • **GROUP SIZE:** SM. • **TIME FRAME:** UP TO 6 MTHS. • **TIME OF YEAR:** SPR./SUM./FALL/WINT.

Perhaps one of the fastest growing businesses in North America at present is multi-level marketing (MLM), wherein a wide range of products can be purchased from a bulk supplier and each person in the distribution chain receives a commission on the products sold. If you are fundraising for a group with a stable membership and solid purchasing power, perhaps a women's group, a school support group or church organization, MLM can provide you with an ongoing source of revenue.

Contact a number of multi-level marketing companies and outline your proposal to sell their products through your organization. Once you find a suitable business partner, it will handle the logistics and supply you with all that is necessary. Your task will be to distribute catalogues, and encourage your members to buy for themselves, in addition to selling to their friends and family. Women's clothing, cosmetics and skin-care products appear to be perennially popular MLM items, however, some companies offer almost any product a householder may require. Be aware that some MLM firms require the purchase of an expensive sample kit, and this may expose you to unacceptable risk.

Designer Fashion Sale

• **CATEGORY:** WOMEN'S GROUPS/GENERAL • **GROUP SIZE:** MED. • **TIME FRAME:** UP TO 1 YR. • **TIME OF YEAR:** SPR./SUM./FALL/WINT.

Most larger cities have several resident fashion designers, some famous, others less well known. If each established designer, and all local design school students, were to donate a single garment or outfit to your organization, the result would rival any couturier collection and would attract considerable attention.

Discuss your project with design schools in your area and their students. Ask each student to create something special to donate to your fashion show and sale. You will probably need a year or more in order to gain sufficient support and interest, but a collection of several hundred fashion originals, some by well-known designers, could raise a substantial sum. Your goal is to hold a celebrity fashion show followed by an auction wherein your collection will be displayed and sold. Try to encourage the designer donors to attend.

Discount Coupon Book

• **CATEGORY:** GENERAL • **GROUP SIZE:** MED./LARGE • **TIME FRAME:** UP TO 1 YR. • **TIME OF YEAR:** SPR./SUM./FALL/WINT.

In good times and in bad, we all try to get a good deal on everything from a haircut to a three-legged table. A coupon book, jammed full of coupons which entitle the holder to valuable discounts on a wide range of products and services, is a reliable fundraiser.

Approach numerous retail companies, restaurants, and movie theatres and ask them to offer discounts on the goods and services they provide. Most businesspeople view a discount book as inexpensive advertising: unlike most other forms of advertising, there is no advance payment. Should the book prove unsuccessful, participating retailers will have lost nothing.

Once all the discounts have been arranged, print a book of coupons. This is a time-consuming and difficult process, which can be made easier if you use a similar format for each coupon, in addition to requiring each business to supply camera-ready art work.

Coupons can be straightforward, offering the holder ten-percent off everything in a store or they can offer specific rewards such as "buy one restaurant entrée and get a second free." Each business should stipulate special conditions relating to when the coupons can be used, how many times they may be used, and any minimum or maximum discounts applicable.

The finished book should be sold just about anywhere: to members, friends, family, at your place of business, and at all the stores and businesses featured in the book. Price your book somewhere between 5% and 20% of the total achievable savings.

Alternatively, ready-made discount books are available from companies who specialize in providing this service. Your organization will make less commission on the sale of the books, but will save itself a great deal of work.

Flags

• **CATEGORY:** GENERAL • **GROUP SIZE:** SM./MED. • **TIME FRAME:** UP TO 6 MTHS. • **TIME OF YEAR:** SPR./SUM./FALL/WINT.

Sell national flags at sporting events, celebrations, and any other suitable event. Make them, or buy them wholesale, direct from the manufacturer. Be conscious of the variety of nationalities likely to be attending any event, and have suitable flags available.

House-to-House Produce Sales

• **CATEGORY:** GENERAL • **GROUP SIZE:** SM./MED. • **TIME FRAME:** UP TO 6 MTHS. • **TIME OF YEAR:** SPR./SUM./FALL/WINT.

Small local organizations requiring quick injections of cash may find house-to-house produce sales very effective, assuming these are permitted by local by-law. Purchase produce directly from a grower, or wholesaler, and resell it to the public from the back of a hay cart. Ideally, try to obtain the services of someone with a horsedrawn cart to attract attention. The produce must be both cheap and timely. In addition to obvious favourites – pumpkins for Halloween, apples in the fall, or Christmas trees in December, consider selling strawberries, corn, potatoes, carrots, or onions, all of which can be purchased from growers for a few cents a pound. Revenues of $1,000 a day are not an impossible goal, with the right produce in the right area.

Kindling and Firewood

• **CATEGORY:** FITNESS, SPORTS & SOCIAL/SERVICE CLUBS • **GROUP SIZE:** SM. • **TIME FRAME:** UP TO 6 MTHS. • **TIME OF YEAR:** FALL/WINT.

Recycling wood into kindling for starting fires is an excellent means of raising money. Bundles or bags of kindling can be sold door-to-door, or through a local retail outlet. Market the kindling as "environmentally friendly" recycled wood.

Suitable, untreated, scrap wood is widely available, and often ends up in landfill sites. Factories and stores are usually happy to have you cart their waste wood away. Most industrial developments have broken pallets always available and most households have assorted wood piles in garages or basements. Knock on a few doors and ask for scrap wood. It should not take long to assemble a sufficient quantity to get started. Organize a "bring your own axe" weekend and hold a wood chopping party, complete with barbecue and campfire. Every bag or bundle of kindling assembled and sold will be pure profit for your organization.

One group of New Brunswick hydro workers, given the task of replacing thousands of old wooden hydro poles with new ones, volunteered to cut the old poles into fire logs on their own time. The results were bundled and given to various charities.

Commercial and government businesses frequently dispose of large quantities of scrap wood, and other materials, without any thought of the potential value of such items to a charity. Educate all your members to be on the constant lookout for opportunities to obtain valuable materials otherwise destined for scrap.

New Crazes

• **CATEGORY:** GENERAL • **GROUP SIZE:** SM./MED./LARGE • **TIME FRAME:** UP TO 1 YR. • **TIME OF YEAR:** SPR./SUM./FALL/WINT.

Remember the hulahoop, skateboard, or more recently, pogs, or inline skates? How about Dinopets? The introduction of a new sport, game, or fad always provides an opportunity to raise money because the inventor or manufacturer is eager that people should try it. It is also true that people are eager to try out new fads without excessive expense. Identify a new craze in its early stages. See if your organization can be part of the popularity build up.

An article appears in a national newspaper about a new fad: people spin plastic rings around their waists to have fun and lose weight. You would contact the newspaper and obtain the manufacturer's name and telephone number. Ask the manufacturer to send out product details and names of local suppliers, if any. Ask for a number of sample rings to be used for promotional purposes. If the manufacturer says no, negotiate with the local supplier. As a last resort, buy the samples. Let the public experiment with this new craze (for a fee), at any large and populous function. You may even be able to negotiate a special deal with the manufacturer or local supplier whereby your organization receives a commission for each sale made as a result of its efforts.

Note: buying inventory exposes any organization to the risk of losing money. Whenever possible, negotiate to obtain products on a concession basis.

Perhaps your group can design its own fad. "Pet Rocks" were once very popular and also very stupid. They made a great deal of money for the people marketing them. There certainly are other "Pet Rock" ideas freely available to innovative thinkers/designers. What about red maple leaves collected in the fall, laminated, or coated with clear polyurethane, and sold on behalf of any organization for Canada Day.

Novelty Sales

• **CATEGORY:** GENERAL • **GROUP SIZE:** SM./MED. • **TIME FRAME:** UP TO 6 MTHS. • **TIME OF YEAR:** SPR./SUM./FALL/WINT.

Selling balloons, flags, paper hats, masks, whistles, and other trinkets at charity events can be a good fundraiser. These items usually have a very high profit margin and a limitless shelf life. With a couple of clown costumes, and a stock of suitable products, you can raise money at any local event. Contact organizers of each charity affair, and offer your services, sharing a small proportion of your revenues if necessary.

Personalized Products

• **CATEGORY:** GENERAL • **GROUP SIZE:** SM./MED./LARGE • **TIME FRAME:** UP TO 6 MTHS • **TIME OF YEAR:** SPR./SUM./FALL/WINT.

Everyday lifestyle items that people find useful like coffee mugs, ball-point pens, scratch pads, table mats, and flower vases can be made, printed or decorated with your organization's logo and/or suitable commemorative inscription. Before ordering 5,000 mugs with your logo and motto, however, be absolutely sure that there are no plans afoot to change either within the next couple of years. Thousands of private companies target charity and N.F.P. groups with catalogues of personalized and premium products which may, or may not, be suitable. Be careful not to get talked into buying large numbers of items that you may never sell.

Because marketing ordinary lifestyle items like coffee mugs puts your group in competition with all other like-minded sellers of same, it might be more useful, albeit more difficult, to find a totally new and innovative product, for example a slidgett, wherein you can corner the sales market.

Advertise, "Attention all inventors – (. . .) is seeking to promote innovative products. Please send details of your household invention to . . . ." Having chosen a suitable slidgett you will need to carry out market research, arrange production, agree on profit levels, and market the product – all a major undertaking, but with enormous profit potential. The fact that your membership represents a worthwhile purchasing group is your attraction to the manufacturer.

Sales of Specialty Products

• **CATEGORY:** GENERAL/CHILDREN & YOUTH • **GROUP SIZE:** SM./MED./LARGE • **TIME FRAME:** UP TO 1 YR. • **TIME OF YEAR:** SPR./SUM./FALL/WINT.

Girl Guide Cookies have become so popular over the years that few people have not heard of them. Chocolate bars, peanuts, mints, and cakes are also staples of the charity sales industry. Find an established product that most people want or need, package it in a distinctive way, and use your entire membership as an unpaid sales force. The product should be reasonably non-perishable, relatively small, and inexpensive enough to enable your organization to work a substantial profit margin. If your organization has the resources available, why not consider manufacturing the product directly, so that go-between costs are eliminated. Manufacture by your organization would also allow it to sell the product to other charities as well.

Why not identify a suitable alternative to Girl Guide Cookies. Food manufacturers are constantly developing new products. The Canadian grocery trade is offered 12,000 new products a year and 90% of them are marketing failures. Write food manufacturers, large and small, and ask if they have a new product that could be marketed as a specialty item through your organization. Most companies will pay handsomely for such exposure. Alternatively, check the Internet. Your promotional product need not be food related. Thousands of companies are offering items which they deem to be suitable for fundraising sales.

Your membership is a valuable asset which can greatly assist the launch of any new product.

Manufacturing

• **CATEGORY:** GENERAL • **GROUP SIZE:** LARGE • **TIME FRAME:** 1 YR+ • **TIME OF YEAR:** SPR./SUM./FALL/WINT.

Cookies, cakes, candies, and chocolate bars have long been fundraising mainstays of youth groups in Canada, much to their manufacturer's delight. While there is no question that charity and N.F.P. organizations make substantial sums from the sale of such products, so do the manufacturers. Perhaps it is time for a charitable organization, or group of organizations, to start making products for other charitable organizations to sell. All of the profits would then be available to charity.

Product Parties

Gather together a group of like-minded people and give them a sales pitch they will find hard to refuse. This is the Tupperware™ marketing concept. Funds are raised through commissions on sales, the sale of refreshments, requests for donations and by operating a raffle with prizes donated by the sales company. Most relatively small and inexpensive merchandise can be sold in this manner: toys, books, lingerie, computer software and games, sports equipment, kitchen gadgets, workshop tools and equipment.

Some well established product parties include:

Kitchenware Parties
• **CATEGORY:** WOMEN'S GROUPS • **GROUP SIZE:** SM. • **TIME FRAME:** UP TO 6 MTHS. • **TIME OF YEAR:** SPR./FALL/WINT.

Yes, depending on your membership, you probably can still make money from plastic kitchenware.

Multi-Product Parties
• **CATEGORY:** WOMEN'S GROUPS/ARTS & THEATRE • **GROUP SIZE:** SM./MED. • **TIME FRAME:** UP TO 6 MTHS. • **TIME OF YEAR:** SPR./FALL/WINT.

If you can attract 100 or so guests to a product party, why not have a variety of different salespeople offer their goods. Consider combining cosmetics with sexy underwear, leisurewear with weight-loss programs, and kitchenware with household cleaners.

Principally Green Party
• **CATEGORY:** ENVIRONMENTAL/WOMEN'S GROUPS • **GROUP SIZE:** SM. • **TIME FRAME:** UP TO 6 MTHS. • **TIME OF YEAR:** SPR./FALL/WINT.

Environmentally friendly cleaning and household products can be sold alongside organic foods and non-polluting garden care materials.

A Heavenly Body Party
• **CATEGORY:** WOMEN'S GROUPS • **GROUP SIZE:** MED./LARGE • **TIME FRAME:** UP TO 1 YR. • **TIME OF YEAR:** SPR./SUM./FALL/WINT.

Cosmetics, skin care, and health foods together with aromatherapy and herbalism.

Jewellery Party

• **CATEGORY:** WOMEN'S GROUPS • **GROUP SIZE:** SM./MED. • **TIME FRAME:** UP TO 6 MTHS. • **TIME OF YEAR:** SPR./FALL/WINT.

The type of jewellery featured will depend entirely on the financial resources of the guests. One-of-a-kind designer pieces can be shown by the designers themselves, or a jewellery store can be invited to display a wide range of different styles. Costume jewellery, or handmade craft jewellery can also be offered where appropriate.

Saucy Sue Party

• **CATEGORY:** WOMEN'S GROUPS • **GROUP SIZE:** SM. • **TIME FRAME:** UP TO 6 MTHS. • **TIME OF YEAR:** SPR./FALL/WINT.

Sexy underwear, scanty swimwear, and marital sex aids.

LP Record Exhibition and Sale

• **CATEGORY:** FITNESS, SPORTS & SOCIAL/SERVICE CLUBS • **GROUP SIZE:** SM./MED. • **TIME FRAME:** UP TO 1 YR.
• **TIME OF YEAR:** SPR./SUM./FALL/WINT.

It has been said that standard LP record albums are dead, but many people still believe vinyl gives a better sound reproduction than CD's. Several present-day recording artists continue to publish their music on limited edition vinyl LP's, in addition to CD's.

An annual sale of vinyl records can provide the basis of an important fundraising campaign, when held in the right location. Organize your record collection by holding street-by-street solicitations or by visiting garage sales, rummage sales, and bric-a-brac auctions. Records generally attract little attention at such venues. Committed collectors are unlikely to attend unless they know that a specific collection is up for sale.

Once you have assembled a sizable record collection, ask an expert to look them over. Some older records are worth a great deal. Organize your sale in a suitable location, and rent tables to both collectors and dealers. Charge admission. You might choose to designate a musical theme such as jazz, classical, or rock & roll to attract really serious buyers.

Sports Accessory Sales

• **CATEGORY:** FITNESS, SPORTS & SOCIAL/GENERAL • **GROUP SIZE:** LARGE • **TIME FRAME:** UP TO 1 YR. • **TIME OF YEAR:** SPR./SUM./FALL/WINT.

A great deal of money is made from sales of relatively inexpensive sports items like golf balls, sports bags, and special clothing. Consider having an exclusive line of such products made, bearing your organization's logo. The owner becomes instantly identified as a philanthropist.

Clothing Sales

• **CATEGORY:** GENERAL • **GROUP SIZE:** MED./LARGE • **TIME FRAME:** UP TO 1 YR. • **TIME OF YEAR:** SPR./SUM./FALL/WINT.

All types of clothing can be purchased with logo and relevant charitable designs to suit your clientele. Sweatshirts, T-shirts, ties and sweaters are popular. Assess your sales potential realistically. Take orders and cash in advance whenever possible. Computer technology now permits the production of beautifully embroidered logos and motifs. Instead of pre-printed clothing, which may not sell, why not have garments embroidered to order, or purchase embroidered patches which can be sewn onto any item of clothing.

Scratch Pads

• **CATEGORY:** GENERAL • **GROUP SIZE:** MED./LARGE • **TIME FRAME:** UP TO 6 MTHS. • **TIME OF YEAR:** SPR./SUM./FALL/WINT.

Design a special scratch pad for your organization. Have it printed in quantity with a great slogan and your organization's name:

I bought this scratch pad from (The Demented Duck Society)

because: (Check one or more of the following)

I thought it was good value for $200	❏
My boss suggested it would be a good career move	❏
My boss was selling it	❏
My wife made me	❏
I am kind, warm-hearted and an easy touch	❏

Sell the pads everywhere. Distribute to all your branches.

Publicity Signs

• **CATEGORY:** GENERAL • **GROUP SIZE:** SM./MED./LARGE • **TIME FRAME:** UP TO 6 MTHS. • **TIME OF YEAR:** SPR./SUM./FALL/WINT.

Selling signs that publicize your organizational aims has a double benefit as you will profit from the sale of the sign, and receive free publicity whenever the sign is displayed. Design a sign people will want to display. Sell as many as you can.

"Do It" signs are designed for car windows or fenders and are intended to be controversial and to grab attention, viz:

"ARTHRITICS DO IT PAINFULLY"

"PORCUPINES DO IT CAREFULLY"

"DIVERS DO IT UNDERWATER"

"ROTARIANS DO IT IN A CIRCLE"

• **CATEGORY:** ENVIRONMENTAL • **GROUP SIZE:** SM./MED./LARGE • **TIME FRAME:** UP TO 6 MTHS. • **TIME OF YEAR:** SPR./SUM./FALL/WINT.

If yours is a "green" organization, encourage people not to use pesticides and herbicides on their gardens. Design a sign which enables homeowners to tell their neighbours they are not harming the environment. Such signs would be a welcome contrast to the signs used by chemical companies warning people to keep pets and children off lawns treated with deadly pesticides.

PESTICIDE FREE

OUR GARDEN IS SAFE FOR CHILDREN AND PETS

WE CARE ABOUT OUR ENVIRONMENT

& OUR FUTURE

WE SUPPORT (. . .)

Sell the signs door-to-door during your annual collection, and at any relevant event.

Souvenirs

• **CATEGORY:** GENERAL • **GROUP SIZE:** SM./MED./LARGE • **TIME FRAME:** UP TO 6 MTHS. • **TIME OF YEAR:** SPR./SUM./FALL/WINT.

Any physical object which has historic or sentimental value can be sold as a souvenir. Pieces of concrete from the Berlin Wall were highly sought after when the wall came down. If your organization is tearing down a famous (or infamous) building, or perhaps even cutting down a well-known tree, consider selling small pieces as souvenirs.

Almost anything can be divided into small pieces and sold. Each piece should be suitably inscribed, or mounted (maybe on an attractive stand). Old brick buildings are ideal for souvenir hunters, as each brick provides a simple memento which can be incorporated as a special feature in any wall.

COMMUNITY SERVICE

Car Pooling

• **CATEGORY:** GENERAL • **GROUP SIZE:** SM./MED.• **TIME FRAME:** UP TO 6 MTHS. • **TIME OF YEAR:** SPR./SUM./FALL/WINT.

One way in which any organization can demonstrate its concern for the environment, and fundraise at the same time, is to administer a car pooling scheme. Provide a central office where drivers with spare capacity can advertise, and where potential passengers can seek a suitable ride. Each potential passenger would pay a small registration fee regardless of whether he/she is successful in finding a driver. Start-up costs and out of pocket expenses should be sought from government agencies and corporate sponsors.

Car Washing

• **CATEGORY:** GENERAL • **GROUP SIZE:** SM. • **TIME FRAME:** UP TO 4WKS. • **TIME OF YEAR:** SPR./SUM./FALL

When holding any public event, do not overlook the possibility of raising additional funds from a car wash. Have a team in the parking lot ready to spruce up any dusty or dirty automobiles.

You can also raise money by operating a car washing service at other non-related events, although you may have to split the proceeds with event organizers. Very little organization is required to provide a team of volunteers with cleaning equipment. The only publicity necessary is done at the event itself.

If your organization includes some good-looking young women and men, choose a hot summer day and have them wash cars while wearing bikinis and swimsuits. Lots of soapy water will guarantee that everyone has fun.

What if you drove into an automatic car wash to find the brushes replaced by a bevy of furry animals or a bunch of clowns? Few people are likely to object, providing the car is washed properly and the proceeds used for charity. You will need cooperation from the car-wash owner and a team of volunteers wearing appropriate costumes. Very generous car-wash operators may agree to your organization keeping all the day's profits. Others may only agree to this event on a profit-sharing basis.

Clean-Up Campaign

• **CATEGORY:** FITNESS, SPORTS & SOCIAL/SERVICE CLUBS • **GROUP SIZE:** SM./MED. • **TIME FRAME:** 1 YR+ • **TIME OF YEAR:** SPR./FALL

Hold an annual, sponsored, clean-up of your town or area, with groups and individuals all vying for awards and prizes offered by the community, and local businesses.

Your primary purpose in organizing this event is to raise money, but when promoting a clean-up campaign, accentuate community goodwill and exercise. Warning: once you encourage 500 people to collect 20 tons of garbage from the neighbourhood, make sure proper arrangements have been made for its disposal. Involve your local government at the outset. Suggest that it assist you with costs. Invite a government representative to attend your meetings.

You will need the following: promotion of the event through community publicity; public acknowledgement and endorsement of the event by local government leaders; financial assistance to help defray advertising and other expenses; provision of certain equipment (rubber gloves and garbage bags); the loan of mechanical equipment and transport, together with operatives, in order to extract and dispose of the garbage.

In some neighbourhoods, you may be forced to deal with abandoned cars, or supermarket carts in a river or pond. You will need to ensure that equipment and trained personnel are available to handle such possibilities. Finally, encourage local government to provide trophies and certificates rewarding those who have donated time to the community in this way.

Once you have secured the backing of local government, turn your attention to local business and service clubs. You are looking for support in a variety of ways: businesses can provide awards in the form of products, and promote your event through their advertising media. Businesses will benefit by being perceived as environmentally responsible in assisting your organization.

Service clubs and young people's groups can form the backbone and will ensure the success of the project. Form "clean-up" teams from each of the service clubs in the area. Encourage other groups of responsible and caring citizens to form more teams. Encourage youth groups, teachers, school children, neighbourhood groups and other charity organizations to participate as well.

Hype the event. Major publicity will encourage more people.

Fundraising is done through sponsorship. Each team or individual seeks out sponsorship based on the number of FULL bags of garbage collected in a four-hour period. Bags are collected from various depots on production of a completed sponsorship form. Bags must be returned, within a specified time. Don't forget recyclables, especially metal. These can be sold to a dealer to raise even more money.

Dollar-a-Chore

• **CATEGORY:** GENERAL/CHILDREN & YOUTH • **GROUP SIZE:** SM./MED./LARGE • **TIME FRAME:** UP TO 6 MTHS. • **TIME OF YEAR:** SPR./SUM./FALL/WINT.

This concept involves volunteers doing household chores for a donation. This scheme is ideal for youth organizations as it encourages the work ethic. Most householders have a few jobs available – sweeping leaves, cleaning the car, garage or basement. Those householders who can't find work will usually give a donation anyway.

Publicity is necessary to make sure that everyone in your community knows that your organization's members will be knocking on doors and asking for a dollar-a-chore.

Equipment Rental

• **CATEGORY:** SERVICE CLUBS/GENERAL • **GROUP SIZE:** SM./MED./LARGE • **TIME FRAME:** UP TO 1 YR. • **TIME OF YEAR:** SPR./SUM./FALL/WINT.

Charity, N.F.P. and service organizations frequently find themselves in need of specific event equipment: collapsible tables, stacking chairs, crash barriers, tents, public address systems, kitchen equipment, and portable toilets. Why not let your organization rent such equipment to other clubs and organizations. Let the public know that you will keep such equipment for charitable purposes, and your organization may receive bankrupt stock and/or public donations.

You will need free, or inexpensive storage space, and access to suitable transport, although the latter could be rented. Seek suitable equipment. Initially, some items may have to be purchased, but once your venture becomes known, you may be surprised how easily useful equipment accumulates. Maintenance and repair of equipment will keep volunteers busy on a regular basis.

Prisoners

• **CATEGORY:** HEALTH RELATED/GENERAL • **GROUP SIZE:** SM./MED.• **TIME FRAME:** UP TO 1 YR. • **TIME OF YEAR:** SPR./SUM./FALL/WINT.

Prisoners' groups and even entire prison populations have been involved several times in raising funds for certain charitable causes. If you believe your cause would benefit in any way from the efforts of a prisoners' group, then ask. Most would welcome the opportunity to do something worthwhile with their time. Prison staff may be very supportive of any scheme which helps in prisoners' rehabilitation.

Shoe-Shine

• **CATEGORY:** GENERAL • **GROUP SIZE:** SM. • **TIME FRAME:** UP TO 4WKS. • **TIME OF YEAR:** SPR./SUM./FALL/WINT..

A shoe-shine service can be offered at almost any event. All you need is polish and a few brushes.

How many shoes can you polish, properly, in an hour or a day? Set a record and challenge others to beat it. For a truly novel prize consider asking Imelda Marcos to donate a pair of autographed shoes and have them bronzed and set into a trophy.

A record setting shoe shine is an excellent piggyback event for any major gathering where long line-ups are likely to occur. How many volunteers would it take to clean 10,000 pairs of shoes in two hours. Ask for a small donation from the owner of each pair.

Swap Shop

• **CATEGORY:** GENERAL • **GROUP SIZE:** SM. • **TIME FRAME:** UP TO 1 YR. • **TIME OF YEAR:** SPR./SUM./FALL/WINT.

This is an ideal venture for groups with semi-retired members, or reliable volunteers, and may work well in a collegiate setting. Open a shop where people can swap the things that they don't want for things that they do. Your shop need only be open evenings and weekends. It could be located in an old store or rent-free building.

Initially you will need to beg, or even buy, enough stock to fill the store. Stock non-perishable items like TVs, stereos, toys, tools, household equipment, bikes, furniture etc., much of which can be found at garage and rummage sales. The number of stocked items should remain fairly constant because each transaction is a swap. The shop manager should always try to end up with an item of higher value. Make money by charging a small administration fee for each transaction. Make additional money by holding regular auctions of the more valuable items.

Swap shops can be operated on the radio once a week, each Sunday morning for an hour, for example. People would call in to swap almost anything: cars, boats, holidays, equipment, and collectibles of all types. Swappers could also mail in requests. Prohibit the exchange of live animals, firearms, and illegal substances. Payment in cash should not normally be requested, as the idea is to swap one valuable item for another.

Specify that each request be accompanied by a ten-dollar donation to charity, paid by credit card on the spot for phone-in swappers, or by cheque if the request is mailed. Each caller, or swapper, should be permitted to give a brief description of the article together with an estimate of its value. Each should state what he/she wants in exchange, and provide a contact phone number. Allow an average of one minute of radio time per request. A charity should be able to raise $500 per hour, assuming ten minutes are allocated to commercial breaks and routine broadcasts like travel and weather updates.

One major charity could host such a program every week or alternatively, several charities could operate the program in rotation. Each charity would supply volunteers to open mail and operate the phone lines.

A weekend show on local or community television may be another venue for your swap shop. Each swapper would be charged a fee, based on the value, for displaying his/her goods and given a set time in which to offer the items for exchange. Cars, boats, and other large items could be assembled together in a parking lot and a whole segment of the show devoted to them.

SOLICITATIONS

Adoption

• **CATEGORY:** GENERAL • **GROUP SIZE:** SM./MED./LARGE • **TIME FRAME:** UP TO 6 MTHS. • **TIME OF YEAR:** SPR./SUM./FALL/WINT.

What is the object of your organization? If its purpose is to help specific persons, animals, buildings, trees, objects etc., then the first thing to be considered is adoption.

Many organizations, particularly those dealing with Third World poverty, use the idea of adoption to encourage long term financial commitment. Although adoption is usually associated with people, there is no reason why different groups, serving diverse functions, cannot use it as a means of encouraging donor loyalty.

Donors can usually be persuaded to adopt almost anything, but the scheme will only work if your organization deals with people or objects capable of being "adopted." You must judge carefully. Here are a few suitable adoption subjects for consideration: trees; historic buildings; animals; sufferers from certain diseases; elderly and/or disabled persons, or persons in need of some manner of help; works of art; books; antique objects; and so on.

How you encourage donors depends entirely on what, or who, your organization is trying to nurture or help. However, the most important factor is that the donor feels a sense of responsibility for the adoptee. He/she must derive some benefit from the adoptive action in order to provide on-going support. This benefit may be from feedback, personal satisfaction from knowing that one has made a difference in someone's life, or it may occur as a result of public recognition.

Corporations, service clubs, community groups and individuals can also be encouraged to adopt. Do not overlook the benefits of finding a lifetime sponsor, and you will never need to raise money for that purpose again.

• **CATEGORY:** GENERAL • **GROUP SIZE:** SM. • **TIME FRAME:** UP TO 1 YR./1 YR+ • **TIME OF YEAR:** SPR./SUM./FALL/WINT.

Individuals, corporations, or associations can also be encouraged to adopt your organization outright, solving some or all of your fundraising problems in one go.

First you need to consider why someone or some group would want to adopt your organization. Many people and groups recognize the benefits of being philanthropic because there are usually good promotion and advertising benefits and/or tax breaks. If your cause is genuine, and worthy of support, finding a lifetime sponsor should be a primary goal.

Associations

• **CATEGORY:** GENERAL • **GROUP SIZE:** SM./MED./LARGE • **TIME FRAME:** UP TO 1 YR. • **TIME OF YEAR:** SPR./SUM./FALL/WINT.

Professional associations, fraternal organizations, and industrial unions and/or affiliations are often receptive to requests from charity and N.F.P. groups. Many such organizations have committees set up specifically to find suitable recipients for their donations. All you need to do is ASK for help, and keep asking. Do not be deterred from making subsequent requests or proposals, even if you have previously been rejected. Only one or two charities are likely to benefit each year. Make sure that your group is known and you could be next. If you have a contact within such an association or organization, you will be in a much better position to know when solicitations should be made, and what would be the most effective proposal.

Banking on the Interest

• **CATEGORY:** GENERAL • **GROUP SIZE:** SM./MED./LARGE • **TIME FRAME:** 1 YR+ • **TIME OF YEAR:** SPR./SUM./FALL/WINT.

One fundraising idea, currently operated very successfully by a Canadian trust, solicits money from customers by asking them to donate a small proportion of the interest they receive on their accounts to a trust fund. The company, Canada Trust, then matches the contributions with an equal sum, and all of the money is made available to local groups and individuals for environmental projects. The trust fund is administered by local committees who receive applications from a diverse spectrum of environmental groups. Most customers donate as little as one percent of their interest, but the cumulative effect enables the funding of thousands of projects annually.

Consider approaching other trusts and banks with a similar idea. Ask them to support a range of charitable organizations which would include yours. Youth, disabled persons and poverty action groups could all benefit from this type of fundraising.

Bequests and Endowments

• **CATEGORY:** GENERAL • **GROUP SIZE:** SM./MED./LARGE • **TIME FRAME:** 1 YR+ • **TIME OF YEAR:** SPR./SUM./FALL/WINT.

There can be substantial tax advantages for certain people to give away their possessions while still living, even though the recipient organization does not receive anything until after the donor's death. Over the years, many organizations have benefited greatly from bequests of money, personal possessions and real estate. Occasionally, such bequests make headline news, especially when a small organization like a cat shelter becomes the sole beneficiary of a wealthy widow's estate, or a successful industrialist bequeaths property worth many millions of dollars to his/her university. Any charitable organization which intends to remain in existence for a long time should seek to inform its supporters about the value of bequests and endowments, and the methods available to arrange such gifts. Each situation is different. Seek advice from a lawyer and an accountant specializing in these matters.

At the very least, ask all of your members and clients to leave something in their will in recognition of the benefits and pleasure that they have obtained from your organization.

Life Insurance

• **CATEGORY:** GENERAL • **GROUP SIZE:** MED./LARGE • **TIME FRAME:** 1 YR+ • **TIME OF YEAR:** SPR./SUM./FALL/WINT.

Life insurance policies provide an excellent means of giving a substantial donation as a planned gift while costing the donor relatively little. The donor nominates your charitable organization as beneficiary, and pays the annual premiums, which are tax deductible. As a long term fundraising strategy, life insurance policies can provide any organization with the benefit of security, and the knowledge that the money will be forthcoming. The fact that premiums are not subject to income tax means that the government is, in effect, paying a substantial amount of the gift.

All life insurance policy premiums are calculated on the age of the insured and his/her expected life span. Average life expectancy in countries like Canada has been increasing dramatically in recent years. This trend looks set to continue into the next millennium, so a non-smoking 30-year-old male today might reasonably expect to live to be over 100. Although life insurance premiums should reflect this trend toward longevity, and be therefore less expensive, few organizations can realistically afford to wait 70 years or more to collect from a life policy. Instead, life insurance policies are used by many organizations as a form of collateral, held by a lending institute against a loan.

Note: Bequests of real estate, works of art and other valuable artifacts, together with the proceeds of life insurance policies, contribute significantly to many charitable organizations. Every fundraiser should be fully conversant with the regulations regarding such bequests, and should be aware of the advantages of securing such support.

Business Blitz

• **CATEGORY:** GENERAL • **GROUP SIZE:** SM./MED./LARGE • **TIME FRAME:** UP TO 6 MTHS. • **TIME OF YEAR:** SPR./SUM./FALL/WINT.

Hold an annual business blitz wherein teams of volunteers descend on all local businesses within a given area to solicit money directly from each company and its staff. You will require advance publicity, perhaps something like this:

ON TUESDAY (Date) THE . . . ASSOCIATION WILL BE
VISITING ALL BUSINESSES IN . . . AREA
TO COLLECT DONATIONS IN AID OF ITS WORK WITH . . .
PLEASE OFFER YOUR SUPPORT.

This idea should never be used by more than one organization in any given area, and in many communities it is already an established United Way fundraiser.

Buy-A-Brick

• **CATEGORY:** GENERAL • **GROUP SIZE:** SM./MED./LARGE • **TIME FRAME:** UP TO 6 MTHS. • **TIME OF YEAR:** SPR./SUM./FALL/WINT.

The sale of individual bricks to people donating funds to any building project is an ancient and very successful fundraising method. The brick becomes part of the building and the donor receives a "Thank You" certificate with a tear-off tax receipt. This fundraiser is so successful because it encompasses one of the most important features of charity fundraising, a tangible end product. Bricks should be sold at every opportunity, and donors given the opportunity of inscribing a personal name on each brick purchased, if so desired.

Sometimes, pictorial brick representations are sold in place of the real thing so each donor has a token "brick" to frame if he/she so wishes. A brick drawing can also be used as a receipt for tax purposes, with details of the organization, charity registration number and name of the donor being printed on the back.

Buy A . . .

• **CATEGORY:** GENERAL • **GROUP SIZE:** SM./MED./LARGE • **TIME FRAME:** UP TO 6 MTHS. • **TIME OF YEAR:** SPR./SUM./FALL/WINT.

Almost any relatively durable item can be "sold" to an individual donor when new facilities are under construction – or older buildings are being renovated. An inscription or plaque should be attached to the item to reward each donor's generosity. Some suitable examples include: a seat in a new or refurbished theatre, hockey arena or church; a bed for a women's shelter; a book in a school library; a chair for a senior's home.

Chain Letters

• **CATEGORY:** GENERAL • **GROUP SIZE:** SM./MED./LARGE • **TIME FRAME:** UP TO 6 MTHS. • **TIME OF YEAR:** SPR./SUM./FALL/WINT.

This direct-mail, chain-letter campaign is often likely to be much more successful than a general mailing because it works on two principles:

• It is easier to solicit money from people you know than from strangers

• People will give more easily when they know others are also giving

Compile a mailing list of all supporters, members, and organizational clients; you will write each a personal request as follows:

Dear . . .

As a friend I hope you will not be offended if I seek your support for a cause which I feel very strongly about, and with which I hope you can assist at this time.

The (Organization) which looks after the needs of (cause) requires financial support in order to (goal).

The following benefactors have all made recent, substantial contributions:

1) Name of a contributor.   2) Name of a contributor.

3) Name of a contributor.   4) Name of a contributor.

5) Name of a contributor.   6) YOUR NAME.

If you can help this very worthy cause, please send a donation to (Organization) and copies of this letter to 6 friends who you believe may wish to contribute to this cause as well. Please delete the name of the first contributor from the above list, and place your name at the bottom in the 6th slot.

We are extremely grateful for your help.

Ask each of your committee members, staff members, and volunteers to send six letters, each using the others' names to form an initial list. Each letter writer should give a donation, however small. If your organization has recently received a donation from a well-known personality, then add that person's name to each list in the third or fourth spot.

Charity Cheques

• **CATEGORY:** GENERAL • **GROUP SIZE:** LARGE • **TIME FRAME:** 1 YR+ • **TIME OF YEAR:** SPR./SUM./FALL/WINT.

Charity cheques are most suited to a national or international charity, insofar as you will ask a major banking institution (which supports your goals) to print one additional blank cheque at the back of each chequebook it distributes to its banking customers. This final cheque, which is accompanied by an information page about your cause and a space for a tax receipt stamp, should be made out to your organization, so that only the inclusion of an amount and donor's signature is required for the cheque to be valid. Any bank customer wishing to make a donation to your charity simply fills in the appropriate sum, signs the cheque, hands it in at any bank branch, and receives a cashier's stamp on the tax receipt.

Many banks which support a number of charities are unwilling to adopt a charity cheque scheme that favours one charity only. When this is the case, approach the bank with a suggestion that it should include a charity cheque with no prior designation in every bankbook. Thus donors can fill in the charity name of choice. Consider asking the bank to print a list of those charities which it supports, yours included, on the back of the cheque. Should the bank be reluctant to name specific charities, ask that it print a generic charity cheque in each bankbook, regardless, without a recommendation to any specific organization. Your group is bound to receive some donation fallout, in any case.

Charity Credit Card

• **CATEGORY:** GENERAL • **GROUP SIZE:** LARGE • **TIME FRAME:** 1 YR+ • **TIME OF YEAR:** SPR./SUM./FALL/WINT.

There is no reason why any of the major credit card companies should not issue a special affiliate card to members and supporters of a large charity organization, and it may well be sound commercial enterprise for them to do so. A Liver and Lung Foundation MasterCard™ would be acceptable in as many places around the world as any other credit card, in addition to offering the holder terms and rates competitive with other credit cards. The charitable organization should encourage all members, supporters, and the public at large to move to an affiliate card, and receive, in return, a commission on all transactions made. The Canadian Diabetes Association already uses this plan which is working to maximum effectiveness because donors and membership number at least half a million persons or more.

Collection Boxes

• **CATEGORY:** GENERAL • **GROUP SIZE:** SM./MED./LARGE • **TIME FRAME:** UP TO 6 MTHS. • **TIME OF YEAR:** SPR./SUM./FALL/WINT.

Collection boxes signal countless numbers of people for donations every day. Many organizations rely on collection boxes to provide a continual source of petty cash throughout the year, but there are drawbacks. Retailers must be persuaded to give up space; the boxes need to be emptied regularly, and, in some areas, they are frequently stolen.

Here are some ideas to help you overcome these problems, and to take a fresh look at collection boxes as a major fundraising source.

Highly Visible

Climbers climb mountains because they are there. The same is true of collection boxes. People who put money in collection boxes do so because the box is there, not because of any burning desire to help any particular charity. Unfortunately, most people are so focused on what they are doing that, unless someone draws attention to a collection box, most people don't see it. Make your collection boxes unmistakably visible in terms of size, shape, and colour. You will accrue another advantage: visible boxes are more difficult to steal and, if and when stolen, are immediately missed. Take a critical look at your current collection box – would you notice it at all in the daily course of events?

Challenging

The "challenging" collection box relies on the fact that most people are programmed to respond to challenge. I've seen marathon runners crawl painfully – feet blistered and bleeding – over a finish line just to say, "I made it." Don't disappoint. If the public wants a challenge, give it to them. The challenging collection box replaces several small collection boxes, and ideally should be made of heavy metal with glass windows. It should be placed in a prominent public place, or in the foyer of a major institution (with the owner's consent). Each box should feature a highly visible sign stating, *"FILL THIS CONTAINER FOR . . . ."*

Fascinating

The fascinating collection box is one where the coins do something other than simply drop into the bowels of the container. One example – the commercially available money box – has coins magically disappearing into a gas-fronted container. Another lets the coin travel around a clear plastic runway in ever decreasing circles before finally dropping. Whenever coins do something before entering the collection chamber, the donation amount increases dramatically.

Water Filled

Another popular idea is a water filled glass or plastic container with a number of small ledges beneath the water surface. The object of the "game" is to drop a coin into the water so that it catches on one of the ledges and fails to reach bottom. A small prize is usually offered to people who achieve this aquatic feat.

"World's Largest"

Imagine people travelling from afar for the privilege of putting money into your collection box. Imagine an entry in the *Guinness Book of Records* for "The World's Largest Collection Box." Imagine the publicity. Imagine the money.

Why not erect something the size of a large water tank, and place it strategically in the centre of your town or community. Decorate the container artistically to reflect the work of your organization. Speak to your municipal government: perhaps your box could become a permanent town feature. Think of intriguing methods in which money can be dropped in the container in a diagonal row of spiralling slots, each one inch from another running from a couple of feet off the ground right up to the top of the box. Challenge children to reach the highest slots. How about a giant conveyer to lift coins all the way to the top.

Funniest

A funny collecting box attracts children and adults alike. Make it a funny shape, a funny character or, in this age of talking greeting cards and noisy breakfast cereal, a box that makes a funny noise every time a coin is dropped.

Totally Amazing

Anyone familiar with the works of Rube Goldberg or Rowland Emett will know what is meant by a "Totally Amazing" collection box. These constructions are absolutely useless machines which whizz and whirr, spin round and round, up and down to attract a tremendous amount of attention. Each work can be decorated with an amazing array of very ordinary, brightly coloured objects and each is multitudinously more complicated than it needs to be.

If you have imaginative builders and tinkerers with spare time, and access to a workshop, create a collection box that "performs" in a totally amazing way every time it is fed a coin. (Examples of Emett's work can be found at the Ontario Science Centre in Toronto.)

Lucky

The lucky collection box is shaped like a wishing well or a "lucky" horseshoe. It sits on the counter of any retailer. Donors are invited to give a donation while simultaneously making a wish. The idea may seem corny, but if I were faced with a "lucky" collection box and a regular one, I know which would get my money.

The Reward

Collection boxes which offer a reward or prize to the lucky or skilful donor can be very attractive, as everyone likes to take a chance on winning something. Some organizations use collection boxes attached to a small tray of wrapped candies.

Collection Buckets

If your organization holds a number of annual events involving mass collections from large crowds – at parades or carnivals, for example – it may be profitable to invest in a set of collection buckets. Make additional money by hiring your buckets to other organizations holding similar events.

Find strong plastic buckets and design a simple metal insert to catch the coins. (The insert should be in the from of a shallow funnel with a hole in the centre and should clip onto the rim of the bucket.) Number each bucket and paste on each the logo of your organization. This professional look should impact positively on your collections.

Mailing Lists

A mailing list is profitable, useful, and essential for every charity and N.F.P. group. Apart from using the list for your annual funds appeal, you will ensure maximum attendance at every event by being able to contact all of your supporters directly. A personal invitation is always a much more effective tool than blanket advertising.

Creating your own mailing list can be done in a number of ways. You will need a computer to create and maintain the database file, and there are many inexpensive software programs available for this purpose. Your choice of system will depend on the anticipated mailing list size. See your local computer dealer for suggestions. Investigate what other, similarly sized, organizations have done. There is no need for you to reinvent the wheel. The purpose of your software should be to make your job easier and more effective, but beware, not all systems actually achieve that goal.

Unless you are starting a totally new organization, you already have a considerable list of members, clients, donors, friends, and supporters. Whether these contacts are listed together, or in separate files, depends on the size of your group and what you want to achieve. Sophisticated and expensive computer systems will enable you to mail information (newsletters, tax receipts, and appeals) automatically. Smaller, cheaper systems will keep a record of all supporters, and print labels for all mail-outs. A worthwhile mailing list may take a year or so to develop, but it pays handsome dividends in the long term.

• **CATEGORY:** GENERAL • **GROUP SIZE:** SM./MED./LARGE • **TIME FRAME:** 1 YR+ • **TIME OF YEAR:** SPR./SUM./FALL/WINT.

The ethics of selling information about organizational members is a matter for each individual organization to consider. Such sales generate good revenue, and, unless members have been told specifically that their names will be withheld, there is nothing unlawful in the practice.

Categorize your lists by sex, income, age, marital status, and property ownership. Mailing lists of 10,000 or more names can be sold to most marketing companies, and any number of organizations. You can contact interested parties through a "list broker." Prices vary from a few to 50 cents or more per name depending on the perceived value to the purchaser.

Alternatively, you can lease your mailing list to a company for "one-time use," or a specified number of uses, instead of selling it outright.

• **CATEGORY:** GENERAL • **GROUP SIZE:** LARGE • **TIME FRAME:** UP TO 1 YR. • **TIME OF YEAR:** SPR./SUM./FALL/WINT.

As you seek to increase your donor base, consider approaching list brokers with a view to purchasing commercial mailing lists. A good mailing list can make the difference between a successful fundraising campaign and a dismal one in almost every case. Specify your needs and goals precisely so the broker can find the perfect fit. A mailing list enables you to reach those people who are most likely to contribute. Lists can be rented for single- or multi-use.

• **CATEGORY:** GENERAL • **GROUP SIZE:** SM./MED. • **TIME FRAME:** UP TO 1 YR. • **TIME OF YEAR:** SPR./SUM./FALL/WINT.

Why not swap your list with another organization of a similar size. Most people who donate to charity give to more than one organization. Both organizations should benefit.

Direct Mail Campaigns

• **CATEGORY:** GENERAL • **GROUP SIZE:** MED./LARGE • **TIME FRAME:** 1 YR.+ • **TIME OF YEAR:** SPR./SUM./FALL/WINT.

Once you have obtained your mailing list, consider a direct mail campaign. A response rate of between two and four percent is the usual expectation from a successful campaign. During the first year of any campaign, however, it is quite normal to receive donations from less than one percent of the persons targeted. The quality of your mailing list, the worthiness of your cause, and the strength of your appeal will all impact on the amount that you receive. Direct mail campaigns go to the very heart of all effective fundraising: get someone's attention first, then ask for the donation.

Many books have been written on direct mail campaigns because of the popularity and power of this system. You should collect as much of this information as possible prior to commencing your own campaign. The research can be expensive and time consuming, but a properly run direct mail solicitation is very rewarding.

Most professional fundraising consultants specialize in direct mail campaigns and, for a fee, can provide any organization with a ready-made campaign package which requires only the input of a mailing list and personalized literature in order to proceed. Such services, however, are expensive; recouping the initial start-up fees may take several years.

Recognize that a direct mail campaign is a long-term project. Try to keep start-up costs to a minimum.

Before designing your direct mail piece, evaluate solicitations sent out by your competitors. Begin by asking all members to collect any direct mail they receive from other groups, as well as direct mail pieces from commercial entities. Imitation is the sincerest form of flattery. Select images, layouts, phrases, and ideas most appropriate to your organization, and incorporate them into your literature.

The proliferation of direct mail, often referred to as junk mail, leads many people to discard unsolicited items without a second glance. Although there is no way of ascertaining whether a person will make a donation if induced to open the envelope, we do know that unopened envelopes never elicit donations. Here are several ways to induce more people to open your envelopes:

• Disguise them as if they contain pieces of personal correspondence

• Hand address them. Potential donors may feel that they have been specially selected to assist if they receive hand addressed mail. (Larger organizations can cheat by using printer fonts which closely resemble handwriting, even to the point of simulating minor errors)

• Offer an incentive: "Your special gift enclosed," or "An opportunity you must not miss," printed boldly across the front may have some impact, although commercial direct mail campaigns have tended to spoil this approach with the use of such phrases as, "Congratulations, You Can Win Ten Million Dollars Just By Opening This Envelope." Few people now believe anything printed on the outside of direct mail envelopes

Studies have shown that people are more likely to open mail bearing a regular stamp rather than a bulk mail frank. There is, however, no way to determine which is the most effective. Just because someone is more likely to open the envelope does not mean he/she is more likely to make a donation.

Solicitation letters must immediately grab the reader's attention. Use of a person's first name, especially within the body of the letter, gives it a personal feel, although such familiarity can be overdone.

The key questions to be proposed and answered within your letter are:

"Who are we?"

"What do we do?"

"Why do we need your help?"

"What difference will your donation make?"

"What benefit will you, the donor, receive?"

"How can a donation be made?"

A sense of urgency, not panic, should be introduced into the request. Making a donation to charity is an emotional business. Unless someone takes action immediately, chances are that he/she will not donate to your cause – or some other equally worthy cause will grab their attention, and money.

Solicitation letters should be printed in large, easy-to-read type, and should be no longer than three or four pages in length. The use of highlights, underlines, and headings can maintain readers' interest, drawing attention to the more important sections. Colour makes a document more attractive, but adds considerably to production costs. Some potential donors can be turned off by the use of unnecessarily expensive paper and printing, although others may actually give more in the belief that they are funding a more professional, upmarket, organization.

Anything which gives your letter a personal feel is likely to be more effective: underlines which appear to have been made by someone using a pen without a ruler; splashes of coloured highlights that look as though they were made with a magic marker; a signature which appears absolutely genuine. Even a postscript can be a very good idea, especially if added in a style which makes it look hand-written. Few recipients are likely to believe that someone in a major organization actually sat down and wrote them a personal letter, but many may think that someone took the time to add a P.S.

Make it as easy as possible for people to donate, and request only sufficient information to enable you to collect the money.

A printed reply coupon should be included in the package and it should already bear the donor's name and address. To encourage people to donate a worthwhile sum, use boxes on the reply coupon to imply that a minimum donation is required. For instance:

I would like to donate: $50 ❑ $75 ❑ $100 ❑ $150 ❑ $200 ❑ Other ❑

Another effective means of obtaining a higher amount is to ask donors to pledge a relatively small monthly amount by means of a bank order or credit card:

I would like to support your work on a regular basis and I authorize you to deduct $10 ❑ $20 ❑ $30 ❑ Other ❑
from my bank account (please attach one cheque marked VOID), on the first day of each calendar month commencing .... 1997.

Or

from my credit card (Visa/M/Card/AmExpress) #____/ / / . Exp. date
on the first day of each calendar month commencing _____1997.

Suggestion: Some may find it more productive to simply ask for a specific donation within almost everybody's reach, especially if that donation can be equated with an identifiable goal. For example:

At this time we are asking you, and all of our supporters, to donate just $17.50 which will enable us to (feed a child for week). Please send your *donation of $17.50 by cheque in the envelope provided, or telephone your credit card donation to 1-800-111-2222.*

In recognition of the fact that most people have credit cards, and some people are more comfortable using the phone, fax or computer than a pen, why not encourage people to make an immediate donation.

Add the following to your reply coupon:

If you mail your donation today, we will be more than happy to pay the postage, BUT if you phone, fax or e-mail your donation, it will save you time, and will enable all of your donation to be used for a good cause immediately.

Telephone (800) 111-2222

Fax (800) 111-3333

E-mail: web.net @ fund.abc

All organizations state that donations received are spent on good works, but a genuine letter from someone whose life has been radically improved, or beneficially affected as a result of funding from your group has much more impact than any number of facts, figures, graphs and charts. Testimonials put human faces on any appeal, and bring potential donors into close contact with potential recipients. A copy of a genuine letter may be more believable than multiple quotes taken from several letters, and pasted on a bulletin board-type display.

The enclosure of a free gift in a direct mail package has two results. First, the promise of something free usually piques a recipient's interest at least enough to open the package. Second, any recipient who perceives that the gift has some value, may feel guilty about not sending a donation. Address labels, envelope stickers, bookmarks and inexpensive calendars, all bearing the organization's logo, are commonly given as free gifts, and many private companies specialize in producing a wide range of suitable products for this purpose.

Interactive gimmick gifts can also be effective in soliciting a donation. A paper jigsaw puzzle with a picture relevant to your organization's work may amuse people for a few moments, particularly if the message is appropriate. For example, "In the time it took you to do this puzzle another six people contracted (disease)." Any form of simple puzzle is likely to intrigue people and can be used as a lever as you unconsciously appeal to a person's conscience. "While it only took you a few seconds to work this puzzle out someone suffering from (disease) would never be able to do it."

CD's are another valuable direct mail tool, particularly as they are becoming increasingly less expensive to produce, once the original has been made. Most people today have access to a computer or a CD player and recipients of a gift CD could listen to the actual words of people aided by your cause or to the words of a celebrity praising your work, plus a carefully worded plea for support. Computer owners could also see pictures demonstrating your work, with a screen-saver program to constantly remind them of your existence.

The largest problem facing any fundraiser embarking on a direct mail campaign is the very real potential to lose a great deal of money. Total mailing costs per unit depend on quality, number of enclosures and method of mailing (bulk delivery or regular mail), but expect to pay an absolute minimum of one dollar per envelope, not including the cost of material design and the cost of developing your mailing list. Not all direct mail campaigns are successful, and, as previously mentioned, a response of less than one percent is common in the first year of any campaign. Ten thousand solicitations at one dollar per unit needs to garner an average return of $100 per respondent in order to break even: even a response rate in the order of 4%, with an average return of $25, would be insufficient to turn a profit. Payback comes in subsequent years when between 20%–40% of previous donors will re-donate, but even with these figures, it is obvious that the start-up costs of a direct mail campaign are usually too high for newly formed organizations.

Here are a number of ways to minimize potential revenue loss from your direct mail campaign start-up.

• Consider asking a non-competing entity to include your mail solicitation with its own. For instance, a company which sells products directly to customers might be sympathetic, and might actually benefit from enclosing your request with their direct mail literature. Ask your supporters and corporate sponsors to assist you in finding a suitable partner.

• Use volunteers to hand-deliver the mail.

• Consider selling advertising space to corporate supporters just as you would sell space on your brochures, programs and advertising material.

• Attempt to recruit new members by enclosing membership materials.

• Enclose your newsletter and information regarding your up-coming events with the appeal for funds.

• Promote products and services which can be purchased through your organization.

• Promote special offers, i.e., *"If you donate at any level during this campaign you will automatically receive one free ticket to our Celebrity Auction (Value $25) to be held on May 15."*

Good timing is essential. Everyone knows that a campaign in the weeks before the December holidays is likely to be particularly successful, but the competition for donations is fierce. January, July, and August are never good times to solicit donations.

One way to discover the most effective direct mail message for your organization is to test market a number of different approaches on a relatively small group of potential donors. Before incurring the expense of printing 10,000 solicitation letters, envelopes, the testimonial letter, means of reply and any device designed to encourage the recipient to open the envelope, use a computer and photocopier to print 50 copies of each. Then make alternate changes to the letters. Use stronger or weaker phraseology, change the font, add more information, underline different words, change the signature. Make 250 units in 5 batches of 50 (some in plain envelopes, some printed) and send all of them out to a cross section of potential donors. Keep an accurate record of which potential donors were sent plain envelopes, as opposed to printed, and who received one type of letter versus another. A 2% total response will only net 5 replies; if 3 or more replies come from one particular batch, you would be well advised to use that model for the full campaign. Like any form of test marketing, results can be skewed by factors beyond your control. Any sales executive can recount horror stories of products which were complete failures, despite exhaustive market research and successful test marketing.

Direct mail campaigns are most effective when they target individuals who have shown some prior interest in an organization, or are in some way affected by an organization's objectives. Up-to-date mailing lists developed over many years, from which no-hopers have been regularly culled, produce a significantly higher return than a random selection of names and addresses. In fact, the only time that a general mail-out may be effective, is in a crisis situation affecting an entire community. (For example, an appeal to save a hospital or school faced with imminent closure.)

• **CATEGORY:** GENERAL • **GROUP SIZE:** SM./MED./LARGE • **TIME FRAME:** UP TO 6 MTHS. • **TIME OF YEAR:** SPR./SUM./FALL/WINT

The Internet has spawned new methods of contacting potential donors and, in the fullness of time, e-mail campaigns may replace the traditional direct mail campaign. Thousands, even millions, of individuals and corporations can be targeted to receive the same e-mail solicitation at virtually no cost. E-mail addresses are available, free of charge, through on-line service providers. Lists of potential donors can also be purchased through list brokers.

Sometimes it is more productive to target businesses and individuals via fax. Computer-linked fax machines send the same request to any number of potential donors for a fraction of the money spent addressing and mailing envelopes. Anyone willing to make a donation can do so immediately by filling in a credit card donation slip and returning it by fax.

Note: There are government guidelines and regulations regarding the sending of unsolicited material by fax. Make relevant enquiries before starting a campaign. And be aware that many people are annoyed at receiving unsolicited mail in any form, but particularly by fax because your message prints on their paper.

Donor Rewards

Every donor deserves to be thanked for his/her contribution (whatever the amount given). Whenever possible, hand each donor a "Thank You" slip at the time they make their donation. Don't overlook the value of obtaining names and addresses of people who give larger donations. Decide on a dollar figure above which you will send a personal "Thank You" note, and add the person's name to your mailing list.

Printed certificates can be "awarded" to donors who give larger sums, and you can consider a range of beautifully designed certificates for levels of donation. Donation levels would be differentiated through the use of different colours and different quality. The highest "award" certificates might be printed on hand-laid vellum with gold borders. "Donor Award" certificates can work to create the illusion of an exclusive club.

Premiums

Many people can be encouraged to make a donation when they receive something of value in return. Your "Donor Gift" collection should include items particularly relevant to your organization or items that will enable each donor to gain prestige through possession. Limited edition prints and cartoons, donated to you by well-known artisans, make excellent donor award gifts, especially if they cannot be purchased through any other outlet. Confine the most valuable gifts to an exclusive group. Less exclusive gifts can be offered to those people who make smaller donations. Token gifts of a button, badge or tiny fluffy toy can be given to any donor, however small the contribution.

Discounts

Any organization which provides products or services for which fees are charged may find it appropriate to reward people making donations, above a specified sum, with a discount on those services. The donor, in effect, pays in advance for a portion of the goods or services he/she may, or may not, use during the year. Discounts should be carefully calculated so that the amount of the donation is likely to exceed the value of discounts given. The concept of this scheme follows the old adage, "A bird in the hand is worth two in the bush."

Halls of Fame

Fundraisers

Honouring your staff in a public arena is an excellent way of showing appreciation for their loyalty. Offer your fundraising staff, especially volunteers, some sort of recognition and reward as incentives. A place in perpetuity in the organizational Hall of Fame costs little but means a great deal to the recipient. A photograph or even an artist's portrait of your staffer, accompanied by a few well chosen words, encourages others to greater achievements in addition to spurring the individual so honoured. Your hall of fame should be set up in the most conspicuous place to let everyone know who your hardest workers are.

Donors

A donors' Hall of Fame, with a hierarchy of pictures, will reward the most benevolent while encouraging others. Donors at the top of your donation tree should have their portraits painted, framed, and hung in a prominent place. Lesser mortals can be photographed and placed wherever there is space. Pictures of lapsed donors should be quickly removed as an incentive to others to make their pledged donations on time. Alternatively, recognition of donors' generosity can be published through the use of commemorative plaques.

Dress Up or Down Days

• **CATEGORY:** GENERAL • **GROUP SIZE:** SM. • **TIME FRAME:** UP TO 4WKS. • **TIME OF YEAR:** SPR./SUM./FALL/WINT.

Whether people dress up or down depends on what the normal etiquette is for work or meetings. Give employees and volunteers an option to do either in return for a small donation. Create a regular event, like Dress Down Friday, and raise money on a continuing basis.

Elevator Fees

• **CATEGORY:** GENERAL • **GROUP SIZE:** SM. • **TIME FRAME:** UP TO 4WKS. • **TIME OF YEAR:** SPR./SUM./FALL/WINT.

This is not a popular idea but it does make money – if your office is in a multi-story building. Introduce a 25-cent elevator fee for all staff arriving at work each Monday. This practice encourages staff fitness and fills charity collection boxes which should be highly visible, and, with the agreement of staff and management, placed in the central lobby from 8:00 a.m. to 10:00 a.m. each day. Staff unwilling to pay the 25 cents can use the stairs. You may even be able to extend this idea to other appropriate office buildings in the area.

Entry Fees in Kind

If your organization plans to hold an auction in the future, obtain suitable salable items by asking people attending other events to donate an auctionable item in lieu of entry fee. You will find that many people donate items worth much more than the cost of a ticket. Sometimes you can even ask people to donate an item at the door instead of paying the entry fee. Many charity organizations ask their supporters to donate a food item in addition to an entry fee at their events, particularly as food banks become more and more common. If your organization adopts this policy, it is likely to receive great support from the public.

Entry Passports

• **CATEGORY:** GENERAL • **GROUP SIZE:** SM./MED. • **TIME FRAME:** UP TO 4WKS. • **TIME OF YEAR:** SPR./SUM./FALL/WINT.

Small towns or communities often raise money by setting up road blocks (with local police cooperation) and asking residents to purchase passports before they are allowed in or out. Some people may be offended, but this fundraiser has been around for a long and successful time.

Environmental Fines

• **CATEGORY:** ENVIRONMENTAL/GENERAL • **GROUP SIZE:** SM./MED. • **TIME FRAME:** UP TO 4WKS. • **TIME OF YEAR:** SPR./SUM./FALL/WINT.

Environmental fines are very effective in offices and industrial buildings because management has a vested interest in their success. Fines are levied against people responsible for waste or environmental vandalism. Employees can be fined by their fellow workers for leaving doors and windows open; for failing to turn off lights, computers and equipment; for throwing recyclables into the garbage; for using equipment for personal use (especially phones, fax's, and photocopiers); for using new paper as scratch pads; and for shoddy work causing wasted materials or time. Fines for smoking or drinking alcohol should be mandatory. Add some humorous misdemeanours as well.

Compile a list of infractions, with the suggested fines for each and assemble a series of suitable collection boxes. Place a list prominently over each collection box. There should be no shortage of volunteers to be office "Environmental Cop."

Exclusive Clubs

Membership of an exclusive club sometimes bestows a certain aura to those on the inside which makes those outside want to join, whatever the cost. The creation of such a club is not difficult, because it usually is more of a mental division than anything else, although members should be granted certain privileges.

The club name must reflect the prestigious nature of membership, or it can also be graduated to reflect hierarchy. For example:

The Million Dollar Club	*Donations of $1 Million or more*
Diamond Club	*Annual contributions of $10,000 or more*
Gold Club	*Annual Contributions of $5,000 or more*
Silver Club	*Annual Contributions in excess of $1,000*
Lifetime Supporter	*Ten years or more of support at any level*

Include corporate donations and donations in kind, along with deferred donations. A business owner who arranges a $500,000 loan, organizes a $100,000 fundraising campaign and has a $400,000 life insurance policy in the name of the organization has, in effect, donated a million dollars, although he/she has taken nothing from pocket. This person is just as much a million-dollar club member as the guy who writes out a cheque for $1,000,000.

Club members at each tier should receive benefits not available to general members: special seats at events; positions on the Board of Directors; invitations to dine with guest celebrities and politicians; names published in prominent places; real wine glasses at functions, not disposable ones; real wine! The privileges should increase in correlation to the status of membership.

Food Banks:

Obtaining Food

• **CATEGORY:** GENERAL • **GROUP SIZE:** SM./MED. • **TIME FRAME:** UP TO 4WKS. • **TIME OF YEAR:** SPR./SUM./FALL/WINT.

Food banks are a growing North American phenomenon. The philanthropic concept of the rich giving food to the poor is both time-honoured and laudable, however, there are ramifications from a charitable point of view which render such schemes less effective than they otherwise might be. Food banks generally rely on two sources of supply: surplus food donated by manufacturers, wholesalers and retailers who cannot find a market for their products, and donations of food by the public. A good deal of food comes from public donation, and consists of products purchased at full retail price from regular stores. Such donations are far less effective than a financial donation of the same value from both a charitable and personal perspective.

Compare these two examples:

Person "A" fills a bag with $20 worth of food at regular retail price and donates it to the food bank. Some of the products may be less than nutritious, and some may be products that no one will actually want.

Person "B" gives the food bank a $20 cash donation, receives a tax receipt and can recover approximately seven dollars of his/her donation from the government. The food bank is able to purchase nutritious and usable food, in bulk, direct from a manufacturer or wholesaler, and will receive at least twice as much food for the $20 as it did through the retail purchase by the donor.

With person "B", a food bank can provide $40 worth of food, at retail price, for every $13 donated in cash (after tax relief). The food bank thus becomes 300% more effective by encouraging financial donations rather than food.

Many store owners will actually allow food bank collections in-store, once customers have passed the checkout. By holding food bank collections within stores, retailers give the impression of being philanthropic, but pay nothing because the food was sold at full price.

If you have established an advertised food bank collection point within a larger store, ask the store owner to make a financial donation to your cause in thanks for the good publicity you are giving him/her, and for all the extra food sales.

When holding a food drive in a food store, ask the owner to match whatever has been donated by giving you the same amount of food again.

Many people donate food which is either unnecessarily expensive or of little nutritional value. When collecting at a store, ask the owner to exchange unwanted items for more suitable ones of the same value.

Food "Swap"

• **CATEGORY:** GENERAL • **GROUP SIZE:** SM./MED. • **TIME FRAME:** UP TO 4WKS. • **TIME OF YEAR:** SPR./SUM./FALL/WINT.

A food "swap" can be operated with the assistance of your local supermarket and can be based on the Pakistani ritual of LenaDena (taking and giving), which stipulates whenever a present is given, a more expensive one must be given in return.

Ask your supermarket owner to donate ten small bags of rice and permission to set up a display near the store exit. Assemble a group of volunteers, all wearing identification from your charity. Give each one a bag of rice and tell them to persuade customers to swap more valuable food items for that bag. The idea is to swap two items for each bag of rice. Put aside one item and swap the other for another two items with the next customer, and so on. Members of the public will soon catch on and should enjoy helping you in this way.

Profit Sharing

• **CATEGORY:** GENERAL • **GROUP SIZE:** SM./MED. • **TIME FRAME:** UP TO 4WKS. • **TIME OF YEAR:** SPR./SUM./FALL/WINT.

Whenever food is purchased at full retail price to be given as a donation to a food bank, the store owner has made profit. Ask him/her to share this profit with your group on a 50/50 basis. If he/she doesn't agree, you can always set up your collection point at some other store.

Gift Vouchers for Food Banks

• **CATEGORY:** GENERAL • **GROUP SIZE:** SM./MED./LARGE • **TIME FRAME:** UP TO 6 MTHS. • **TIME OF YEAR:** SPR./SUM./FALL/WINT.

Rather than soliciting donations of food for a food bank, why not ask people to buy gift vouchers in fixed amounts, say $5, $10 or $20. Supermarkets and food stores would sell the vouchers to the public, who would donate them to your organization, which would redeem them in participating stores for food that is actually needed. The store should be asked to help you redeem your vouchers by selling the food at wholesale prices.

"Free" Donations

• **CATEGORY:** GENERAL • **GROUP SIZE:** SM. • **TIME FRAME:** UP TO 4WKS. • **TIME OF YEAR:** SPR./SUM./FALL/WINT.

Does your local retailer give "free" cups of coffee to customers? Perhaps your hairdresser, doctor or lawyer's office has a "free" coffee machine, or the gas station provides "free" air. Wherever you see business giving away something for nothing, you have an opportunity to raise money for your cause. Ask if you can place a collection box, together with a neatly printed sign, next to the "free" product.

Suggested wording:

This (coffee) is provided free of charge by . . .

You may if you wish make a donation to . . .

an organization which we support.

Signed. Management

Gift Cards

• **CATEGORY:** GENERAL • **GROUP SIZE:** MED./LARGE • **TIME FRAME:** UP TO 1 YR. • **TIME OF YEAR:** SPR./SUM./FALL/WINT.

Give a gift to charity in someone else's name. Sell celebration cards, especially those for birthdays and anniversaries, in return for a donation. The cards should be beautiful and should contain suitable messages such as:

Dear

I was going to buy you a really expensive gift to celebrate...(our anniversary)...and then I heard about the plight of ...(These people) (This person)(This thing) who is/are desperately in need of help because.... Knowing what a warm and caring person you are, I knew you wouldn't mind if I gave a donation in your name instead of buying the gift. I gave $____ as a way of saying how much I love you and how much we both care about others.

P.S. You can claim the tax relief.

Include a charitable tax receipt with the card, made in the name of the person for whom the card is being purchased.

Setting A Goal As An Event

People work toward goals throughout their lives, from baby's repeated struggles to walk, to passing exams at school, to reaching a sales target or productivity level at work. Give people a target and most will attempt to achieve it purely for the satisfaction of saying, "I did it." If the target is both concrete and realistic, most people will attempt to help.

If, for example, your organization needs $50,000 to purchase a special bus, paint an outline of a bus onto a large plywood panel, and price each item on the picture: Front wheels – $1,000 each. Seats – $250 each. Engine – $5,000. Mirror – $50 each. Doors – $3,000 each. And so on. Place the picture in the most visible place available, accompanied by a sign asking for donations to buy the bus and, as the money is raised to pay for each item, paint that item in bright colours.

The same procedure can be used to raise money for any physical object, or to pay for restoration work on a building.

Grants & Loans

Government Grants

• CATEGORY: GENERAL • GROUP SIZE: SM./MED./LARGE • TIME FRAME: 1 YR.+ • TIME OF YEAR: SPR./SUM./FALL/WINT.

Many government bodies offer grants and low interest loans to charities and N.F.P. groups, although this practice has been diminishing and is likely to diminish further in the future. Grants have been available, in certain circumstances, from all government levels; in most cases, however, the money must be used for specific items like the purchase of premises or equipment, the creation of a new position, building improvements or staff training. Research is the key to finding the granting government body that best meets your group's needs. Write to the various governmental agencies involved in the same areas as your group. Ask for the details. Talk to members of groups similar to your own to discover if they have been successful in obtaining grants. Contact your M.P.'s office.

Information about government grants and subsidies may be obtained from *The Handbook of Assistance Programs* published by The Canadian Research and Publication Centre. Their telephone number is: (800) 363-1400. This publication is available in sections and is updated bi-monthly. Sections are sold separately and are available for British Columbia, Alberta, Manitoba, Ontario and Quebec in addition to one section relating to federal assistance. Each section costs $130 per year which includes updates. A discount of $35 is given if the Federal publication and one province are purchased together. The handbook is available in many public libraries and it may be wise to consult a copy prior to purchase.

Note: This publication was formerly called *The Handbook of Grants and Subsidies*.

Foundation Grants

• **CATEGORY:** GENERAL • **GROUP SIZE:** SM./MED./LARGE • **TIME FRAME:** UP TO 1 YR. • **TIME OF YEAR:** SPR./SUM./FALL/WINT.

There are numerous foundations, trusts, agencies and organizations which provide grants to charity and N.F.P. groups and there are a number of books which give details of such funding, especially *The Canadian Directory to Foundations* published by the Canadian Centre for Philanthropy. Your organization may well qualify for one or more such grants. Start researching today. Many grants are available for special projects. Even if you have previously been refused funding by a particular institution, there is no reason why you should not try again.

Private Grants

• **CATEGORY:** GENERAL • **GROUP SIZE:** SM./MED./LARGE • **TIME FRAME:** UP TO 1 YR. • **TIME OF YEAR:** SPR./SUM./FALL/WINT.

The private sector also offers grants to various groups and individuals. Many of these grants are offered by civic minded companies or individuals who want to see that certain organizations are given the necessary funds to succeed. There are many books available detailing specific information about such grants, including eligibility criteria and the application process.

For more information about grants available in Canada you can visit: *The Canadian Centre for Philanthropy*, Internet website *www.ccp.ca* or *Prospect Research On-line*, at *www.rpbooks.com* which offers information about sources of Canadian funding including the top 100 private foundations, personal information regarding the top 200 key executives of major corporations, corporate profiles of most major corporations, and information regarding employee charitable trusts. The annual fee for accessing this information depends on the size of an organization, but starts at $995.

Note: The information now available from *Prospect Research On-line* was previously available in book form as the *Private Foundations Directory* and the *Directory of Employee Charitable Trusts*, both published by Rainforest Publications of Vancouver. These publications are no longer in print.

House-to-House Canvassing

• **CATEGORY:** GENERAL • **GROUP SIZE:** MED./LARGE • **TIME FRAME:** UP TO 1 YR. • **TIME OF YEAR:** SPR./SUM./FALL/WINT.

House-to-house collection is probably the most effective means of soliciting donations in some areas, and the process is used by many national organizations. House-to-house canvassing satisfies the two basic rules of all fundraising: getting someone's attention and asking for money. Most of the ideas in this book are nothing more than elaborate schemes to attract someone's attention so that you can ask for the donation. Knocking on the front door is the simplest method, and should often be considered before any other forms of fundraising. The disadvantage is that you need a large number of reliable volunteers, and/or paid staff, to campaign at a specific time not already being utilized by other charities.

Work with teams of collectors rather than individuals. People working together tend to encourage each other, while an individual working alone can easily become disheartened and give up. Teamwork also reduces the chance of any collector being assaulted or robbed.

Set goals and stick to them. Knocking on doors for donations can quickly become demoralizing, particularly if people are reluctant to give, or don't even answer the door. To be successful, you need to set a realistic target for the number of donations required and continue until that target is reached.

Children are much better at door-to-door collections than many adults, and the presence of a child may deter certain types of people from making suggestions as to what you should do with your collection tin. Never, never send a child to collect on his/her own, or with another child.

Planning is essential. A few collectors randomly choosing streets that they consider suitable will always net some returns, but a properly orchestrated campaign will bring much greater rewards. Neighbours make much better collectors than total strangers; find one local volunteer for every street in the town, or area. (Several volunteers might be needed for long or heavily populated streets.) Make each volunteer responsible for collecting from a relatively small number of houses in his/her immediate area, from people known or at least recognized. Potential donors are more likely to trust someone who lives only a few doors away. It is always much more difficult to refuse a solicitation from someone you know, rather than a total stranger.

Finding volunteers is time consuming. Find the number of residents for any given street using a CD-ROM telephone directory, and call until you find a volunteer. Allocate 30 or 40 houses to each person. Divide the solicitation area into designated sections and your neighbours will trudge the streets instead of you and your staff.

A note regarding the employment of professional canvassers vis-à-vis volunteers: Many organizations employ professional canvassers for door-to-door campaigns. Professional canvassers will almost certainly raise more money per household than volunteers, especially if they are being paid a commission on the amount collected. Your members and volunteers, however, will be much more likely to recruit new members and make important contacts.

Household Collection Envelopes

Discreet little envelopes delivered to homes in a neighbourhood and collected a few days later when the householder has had an opportunity to fill them with money is a time honoured and effective fundraising device. This solicitation relies on the power of the message printed on the envelope, and the reputation of the organization to elicit large donations. Most people will give a few coins rather than suffer the embarrassment of returning an empty envelope. Show residents you mean business and, at the same time, make it difficult for anyone to ignore your appeal by using LARGE envelopes for household collections. Large envelopes cost more, but they offer a much greater area on which to print details of your appeal. Large envelopes also provide an opportunity to give publicity to commercial sponsors, who in turn, can be asked to pay for the envelope costs.

When collecting for a community cause, a new youth centre perhaps, you may have more success with a household appeal if you can put a funny message on your envelope. Here is one suggestion, to be printed in very small writing on one side:

Hey! If you think that you've got a lousy job maybe you should try mine. I spend four hours a day pushing silly envelopes into people's mailboxes and half of 'em don't even bother to read them. I get chased by dogs, cats and old men with white sticks. Why no young ones I ask?

I don't mind people pretending to be out, saying they can't find any money, or telling me they don't agree with my views, but I hate the ones who give me a dime and ask for change.

Heck, I'm only a volunteer.

Thank you very much for supporting . . . .

It is possible to increase the amounts that people place in household collection envelopes (and increase the likelihood of collecting them) by introducing a third stage in the process.

Normally, a collector drops envelopes into mail boxes and collects them two or three days later – a two stage process. A third stage can be introduced on the 1st or 2nd day after initial delivery. It involves telephoning the occupant with the following suggested message:

"Mrs Jones, I delivered an envelope on behalf of the (Disorganized Dentists Association) yesterday afternoon. Did you find it in your mailbox?"

" (Reply)"

"Will 7:00 p.m. tomorrow evening be a good time for me to come and collect it?"

By introducing the third stage, you simultaneously personalize and reinforce the request. You are gaining a commitment for the donor to be at home at a given time. The telephone call also provides an opportunity to answer any questions the householder may have regarding your organization.

House Meetings

• **CATEGORY:** GENERAL • **GROUP SIZE:** SM./MED./LARGE • **TIME FRAME:** UP TO 4WKS. • **TIME OF YEAR:** SPR./SUM./FALL/WINT.

House meetings gather a group of like-minded people together so that they can be informed of an organization's work, while being asked to provide support in various ways. Although it is counter-productive to encourage people to attend such a meeting under false pretences, the wording of your invitation can be sufficiently vague so as not to alarm anyone who may be put off by a request for money.

"An opportunity to meet your (political party) candidate in person," may be suitable for a political fundraiser, whereas, "An opportunity to discuss the (whatever cause)," may be appropriate in other cases. Careful wording of the invitation will ensure maximum attendance, but no one will be terribly surprised when donations are solicited. Pandering to people's self-interest can be particularly effective in ensuring a good response to a house meeting. A campaign which benefits the local community, or addresses a local concern, is more likely to galvanize support at a house meeting than a national appeal. Provide guests with a few light refreshments, and keep the meeting as informal as possible.

Long Distance Telephone Calls

• **CATEGORY:** GENERAL • **GROUP SIZE:** SM. • **TIME FRAME:** UP TO 6 MTHS. • **TIME OF YEAR:** WINT.

Some major corporations allow members of the public to make

free long distance telephone calls from their offices just before the December holidays, thereby giving people the opportunity to keep in touch with friends and family abroad. Make sure all of your members and clients are informed of any such offers. If you have clients you know would benefit from such a service, but none is available, contact local corporations to solicit assistance in setting up such an offer. Remember, too, whenever such a service is being offered, ask if you can place collection boxes next to the telephones. People unable to afford the full cost of the call may be happy to donate a few dollars to charity.

Name That ... ?

• **CATEGORY:** GENERAL • **GROUP SIZE:** SM./MED./LARGE • **TIME FRAME:** UP TO 6 MTHS. • **TIME OF YEAR:** SPR./SUM./FALL/WINT.

Fundraising for something new can be facilitated with a naming competition. The name of a newly born animal at a zoo, for example, can be suggested by any number of people, each of whom makes a small donation with each name suggested. A building, park or even an organization can be named by holding a public, or restricted, competition.

Office Christmas Gifts

• **CATEGORY:** GENERAL • **GROUP SIZE:** SM./MED./LARGE • **TIME FRAME:** UP TO 6 MTHS. • **TIME OF YEAR:** WINT.

Most offices and groups of workers operate some kind of holiday gift exchange, and almost everyone ends up with something that he/she doesn't want, would never use, or would not want to be seen dead wearing. Instead of giving gifts to one another, wouldn't it be nicer if the entire office gave a donation to your organization. Of course it would. All that is required is for someone to suggest that fact. So go on, suggest. You cannot lose.

Old Boy's or Girl's Network

• **CATEGORY:** GENERAL • **GROUP SIZE:** SM./MED./LARGE • **TIME FRAME:** UP TO 6 MTHS. • **TIME OF YEAR:** SPR./SUM./FALL/WINT.

Most effective fundraising is accomplished through an old boy's/girl's network. University alumni, in particular, can raise millions of dollars for their institutions with a few well-placed phone calls, because the people contacted have a commitment to the establishment, and to the person making the call. Challenge all of your members, whether part of the fundraising team or not, to personally contact at least ten old friends, asking directly for a substantial donation. Friends should be chosen on perceived ability to pay large sums, not just because the friendship is a very good one. Ask your members to name people with whom they attended school or university, specifically those who have since become famous or rich. Target these persons directly. Politicians at all levels of government can be particularly useful, and should be wooed at every opportunity, even if they donate little in the way of cash.

Apologies

• **CATEGORY:** GENERAL • **GROUP SIZE:** MED./LARGE • **TIME FRAME:** UP TO 6 MTHS. • **TIME OF YEAR:** SPR./SUM./FALL/WINT.

What better way of saying "Sorry" when a mistake has been made than to give a donation to charity. Restaurants are ideal establishments for the implementation of this scheme. Ask restaurateurs to add the following message to their menus: "If we got your order mixed up or fail to give you the service you expect, please let the manager know. In addition to making things right with you, we will make a donation of five dollars to charity."

Banks might also be encouraged to adopt a similar policy. One bank already offers customers five dollars if they are kept waiting in line for service longer than five minutes. Other banks should be asked to follow suit, with a donation to charity instead of to the customer.

Payroll Deductions

• **CATEGORY:** GENERAL • **GROUP SIZE:** LARGE • **TIME FRAME:** UP TO 1 YR. • **TIME OF YEAR:** SPR./SUM./FALL/WINT.

One time honoured and very successful way of raising money is to request that all employees of a company make a regular donation to charity directly from their wages. Any employer with a close affiliation to your organization may be willing to put such a scheme into operation, and may even be prepared to match employee contributions. This particular avenue of fundraising is used extensively by the United Way. Payroll donations do not come quickly or easily but, once arranged, they can provide a charity with guaranteed ongoing support.

Petitions

• **CATEGORY:** GENERAL • **GROUP SIZE:** SM./MED./LARGE • **TIME FRAME:** UP TO 4WKS. • **TIME OF YEAR:** SPR./SUM./FALL/WINT.

Whatever an organization stands for, or against, every time people are asked to sign a petition they should be invited to make a small donation. Everyone signing the petition is presumably a supporter, so why shouldn't they be asked for financial support as well.

Pledges

• **CATEGORY:** GENERAL • **GROUP SIZE:** SM./MED./LARGE • **TIME FRAME:** UP TO 6 MTHS. • **TIME OF YEAR:** SPR./SUM./FALL/WINT.

Asking people to give money is expensive, both in terms of time and finances. It is much more efficient from an organization's point of view to concentrate on getting people to make regular donations monthly, semi-annually, or just once a year. The ideal situation is for the donor to issue written instructions to his/her bank, or fill out a credit card authorization which allows the donation to be paid on certain dates during the year. Tax receipts can be issued automatically, and your organization will be able to make plans knowing that a certain amount of money is forthcoming.

Some donors are reluctant to make commitments of this type because they feel that they have lost control of their finances. Others fear that they may not be able to cancel such an arrangement, while still others worry that they may forget to cancel such an order and carry on payments forever. One way to counter such fears is to restrict all such pledges to a fixed term, one year perhaps. Although renewing pledges annually is more labour intensive, the renewal does provide an opportunity to make personal contact with the donor and, perhaps, increase the size of the donation.

Snafu Boxes

• **CATEGORY:** GENERAL • **GROUP SIZE:** SM. • **TIME FRAME:** UP TO 4WKS. • **TIME OF YEAR:** SPR./SUM./FALL/WINT.

Distribute printed boxes around offices suggesting that all employees be fined by colleagues when they screw up. A list of SNAFU penalties could be printed on the box or employees can make their own rules. Poor time keeping, misplaced equipment, incorrect orders and missed deadlines could all result in stiff penalties. There is no reason why this should not become a permanent part of the office scene.

Note – SNAFU is an acronym of: "Situation normal; All fouled up."

Swear Boxes

• **CATEGORY:** GENERAL • **GROUP SIZE:** SM. • **TIME FRAME:** UP TO 4WKS. • **TIME OF YEAR:** SPR./SUM./FALL/WINT.

Find those offices where swear boxes already exist, and ask if the contents can be given to your charity. Should the staff be reluctant to agree, ask them to consider a 50/50 split, or some sort of division – as long as some of the proceeds go to your organization.

If no swear box exists, then introduce one. Make your own printed swear boxes, and have them distributed around offices, factories, clubs, and bars. For every cuss and curse an employee utters, he/she should pay a set fine. It's all in good fun.

Stocks and Shares

• **CATEGORY:** GENERAL • **GROUP SIZE:** LARGE • **TIME FRAME:** 1 YR+ • **TIME OF YEAR:** SPR./SUM./FALL/WINT.

Playing the stock market with charity funds, and any other form of gambling, may be an anathema to many small charity and N.F.P. organizations. This is somewhat surprising considering so many charities raise much of their revenues through the operation of gambling schemes, be they Sunday afternoon bingos, charity lotteries, raffles or draws. The fact is that we consider it perfectly all right for members of the public to risk losing money to charity but not vice-versa. On the other hand, many major charities have considerable investments in the stock market and fund managers will be delighted to assist you in investing your charity's money, if you wish to do so. Many large investment houses operate departments dealing solely with the investment of charity funds.

Stock Donations

• **CATEGORY:** GENERAL • **GROUP SIZE:** SM./MED./LARGE • **TIME FRAME:** UP TO 1 YR. • **TIME OF YEAR:** SPR./SUM./FALL/WINT.

Due to changes in the 1997 Federal Budget, it is now possible for a donor to receive income tax relief on stocks donated to charity. Consult with your organization's accountant to discuss how this change may be of benefit to your group.

Dividend Donations

• **CATEGORY:** GENERAL • **GROUP SIZE:** SM./MED./LARGE • **TIME FRAME:** UP TO 1 YR. • **TIME OF YEAR:** SPR./SUM./FALL/WINT.

This scheme does not hold any risk of loss to the charity and, although it involves stocks and shares, no gambling as such is involved.

A group of individual investors each hold stock shares in the name of your charity (effectively, they donate the shares to charity for an indeterminate period of time) and the charity becomes the beneficiary of the annual dividends. Share purchasers can retrieve their original shares at any time. Both parties involved in the transaction win, assuming that the shares are chosen wisely, and rise in value over time.

Creative accounting may permit tax relief to the shareholder at the time the share is donated to charity, but may require tax to be paid when the share is recovered at a later date. Consult an imaginative accountant and an honest stock broker. You may be able to operate a very lucrative fundraising scheme without risk. Should you choose to try this idea, a suitable advertising slogan might be: *BUY A SHARE IN SOMEONE'S HAPPINESS!*

Street Give-Away

• **CATEGORY:** GENERAL • **GROUP SIZE:** SM./MED. • **TIME FRAME:** UP TO 1 YR. • **TIME OF YEAR:** SPR./SUM./FALL/WINT.

The next time you think of holding a street collection or house-to-house collection, have a "give-away" instead. A crazy idea? Of course it is. No one in their right mind would stand on the street offering to give money to passers-by, unless, that is, they have studied enough psychology to know that although most people will give money to strangers, very few people will accept money from strangers. Children are warned constantly never to take anything from strangers. This creates fears that remain throughout life.

Choose your collection area very carefully and tell your "collectors" to say, *"I'm giving away money on behalf of . . . to anyone who really needs it. Do you need some?"* On most occasions the answer will be "No thank you" in which case the response should be, "In that case, can I please ask you to make a donation." Usually the answer is positive, and your response should be to request a specific amount. Warning: Do not offer money to street people, groups of teenagers or young children. The street people and teenagers will take the money, while children's parents will phone the police.

This idea is a practical application of the journalist's dictum: "Man Bites Dog is news." It is almost certain to gain the attention of the press.

Telemarketing

• **CATEGORY:** GENERAL • **GROUP SIZE:** LARGE • **TIME FRAME:** UP TO 1 YR. • **TIME OF YEAR:** SPR./SUM./FALL/WINT.

Telephone fundraising campaigns and telemarketing of events can be very effective in certain circumstances, although it is increasingly apparent that large numbers of people are really annoyed by unsolicited phone calls, especially at supper time. Consequently, more and more households are resorting to the use of call-displays and answering machines as ways of screening unwanted calls. Few executives will accept calls from unknown callers. Many really busy executives now schedule telephone calls as they would personal meetings.

Tele-fundraising and telemarketing campaigns are most effective for organizations with well maintained, up-to-date membership and supporter lists. A person who made a donation last year, or attended an event or performance within the past six months is much more likely to be amenable to a telephone solicitation than someone chosen at random from a telephone book.

Professional telemarketing companies have the equipment and personnel available to contact the vast numbers of people necessary to establish a successful campaign, and it may be wise, even though certainly much more expensive, to employ their services. Most volunteers hate making face-to-face requests, and will find any number of excuses not to do so, or will do so only half-heartedly.

• **CATEGORY:** GENERAL • **GROUP SIZE:** SM./MED./LARGE • **TIME FRAME:** UP TO 4WKS. • **TIME OF YEAR:** SPR./SUM./FALL/WINT

Every staff member and volunteer within an organization can assist with fundraising if they are encouraged to request a donation from each person with whom they communicate by telephone. It is very easy for people to make a donation using a credit card, so take advantage. Every person who telephones your office, for whatever reason, should be reminded that you need funds to provide the service that you do. Most callers are phoning because they want something from you, so why shouldn't they pay something in return? If you and your staff are embarrassed about asking for a donation from someone on the phone, then have a machine do it for you. Instead of playing background music when you put someone on hold, play a recorded message briefly outlining your work and ending with a polite request for a donation. Make the message fairly short and say something like, "When your call is answered, please offer a donation if you can. We really do need your help."

When personally asking for a donation, or when using an automated request, increase the overall donation by asking support for a specific cause, and changing the cause every few weeks. For example: "This month we are holding a special collection for . . . . We would very much like your support and help."

Television Telethons

• **CATEGORY:** HEALTH RELATED/CHILDREN & YOUTH • **GROUP SIZE:** LARGE • **TIME FRAME:** 1 YR+ • **TIME OF YEAR:** SPR./SUM./FALL/WINT.

Successful telethons raise huge sums for charities. Whether there is room for a new one is difficult to judge. If you are fortunate enough to have the ear of a television executive, discuss the possibility. Watch other telethons, and consider how you might do it differently or more effectively.

Tip Top Day

• **CATEGORY:** GENERAL • **GROUP SIZE:** SM./MED. • **TIME FRAME:** UP TO 6 MTHS. • **TIME OF YEAR:** SPR./SUM./FALL/WINT.

Wherever tips are given, restaurants, hotels, salons and barbershops in particular, ask all willing recipients and participants to have a "Special Day" and donate a proportion of all tips to charity. Provide participating businesses with special collection boxes. Announce the day publicly. You may wish to try this event in conjunction with other charities so that everyone in the community is involved.

Water

• **CATEGORY:** GENERAL • **GROUP SIZE:** LARGE • **TIME FRAME:** UP TO 6 MTHS. • **TIME OF YEAR:** SPR./SUM./FALL/WINT.

People want to throw money in water. Do not disappoint. If your local shopping mall has an enclosed pool, or a running stream, or the foyer of a large building has a particularly lovely fountain, ask management if you can put up a sign requesting donations. You may have to wade in from time to time to collect, but money is money. And these coins are clean. Make sure the location is secure so the donations will not be stolen.

If you do not have access to a suitable fountain, consider having one installed by a benefactor in memoriam. What nicer way could there be to honour someone's memory.

Wishing Well

• **CATEGORY:** GENERAL • **GROUP SIZE:** SM./MED. • **TIME FRAME:** UP TO 6 MTHS. • **TIME OF YEAR:** SPR./SUM./FALL/WINT.

Wishing wells have been around as long as people have had change in their pockets and if you have access to a real one, you are fortunate indeed. Place a metal grid just below the water line to collect the money thrown in. Erect a suitable sign. If you do not have a real wishing well, build a wellhead, complete with a roof and bucket, in the centre of a shopping mall or other suitable location. Create the illusion of depth with mirrors, water, and lighting. Invite people to make wishes as they throw in money for charity. Wishing well projects generate a modest income. Ensure that the construction is sturdy. Don't forget to scoop out the coins regularly, and always remember to leave a small scattering to act as magnets for others.

SPORTS, FITNESS & RECREATION

Aerobics

• **CATEGORY:** WOMEN'S GROUPS/FITNESS, SPORTS & SOCIAL • **GROUP SIZE:** SM./MED. • **TIME FRAME:** 1 YR+ • **TIME OF YEAR:** SPR./FALL

Large numbers of people spending time together, doing something they like, always create a positive environment for raising money. Aerobic enthusiasts, and/or experts, can coax hundreds, even thousands, of people to participate in Aerobi-thons, which make excellent, invigorating and healthy fundraisers. Aerobi-thons can also become successful business ventures for health clubs who may use them to attract new members. Check for health clubs in your neighbourhood. Ask to meet with the manager, or the membership director, explain the purpose and goals of your organization, and suggest that an Aerobi-thon might be a beneficial activity for both institutions. You will need detailed plans, skilled instructors, insurance, prizes and refreshments.

Assault Course Orientation

• **CATEGORY:** FITNESS, SPORTS & SOCIAL/GENERAL • **GROUP SIZE:** SM. • **TIME FRAME:** UP TO 1 YR. • **TIME OF YEAR:** SPR./SUM./FALL

Is there a military, police, or firefighters' training facility in your vicinity? If so, you may be able to gain access to an assault course which has been designed to test the physical strength, agility, concentration and stamina of young recruits for these disciplines. There are many persons who would never normally have the opportunity of testing themselves on a challenging course of this nature, and who would be prepared to pay handsomely for the experience. If you feel that a large percentage of adults in your community would welcome such a challenge, contact the officer in charge of the assault course. Describe your organization and its goals, and suggest that it might be to everyone's mutual advantage to hold an "Open House, Try It Yourself" day at the facility, to acquaint the public with the aims of the installation, and to benefit your charitable organization. You could offer to undertake publicity and administration for such an event, including ticketing, transportation, refreshments, signage, crowd organization and insurance as needed. The facility would, in turn, offer its course for public tours, and carefully monitored tests, together with expert spotters/leaders to guide adult participants safely through the basic requirements of each exercise.

An assault course sponsored challenge consists of a carefully devised time competition on a local military assault course between specifically chosen military personnel and specially trained opposing teams of civilians. Each team should be sponsored by friends, relatives and colleagues with 50% of the sponsorship money going to your charity, and 50% of the money going to the charity of choice for the winning team. Like the assault course orientation above, the assault course challenge should be held on a weekend with friends, guests and relatives of the participants invited to cheer on their teams, for a small entry fee, naturally. Many different organizations could be invited to enter teams, especially those with members who may already have some experience of this type of challenge. Police, fire and rescue organizations would be obvious choices together with fitness and athletic associations. However, there is no reason why any group of physically fit individuals should not enter a team.

Ballooning

Ballooning is now a very popular sport with many thousands of exponents throughout the world. It is understandable that people would like the opportunity of taking a flight, and there are a growing number of commercial operators who cater to this desire. Obviously, there are risks involved with ballooning and injuries occur, although fatalities are rare. Anyone taking a ride for charity must be made fully aware of all the risks and should be prepared to absolve the organization of all liability.

Tethered Rides

• **CATEGORY:** GENERAL • **GROUP SIZE:** SM./MED./LARGE • **TIME FRAME:** UP TO 6 MTHS. • **TIME OF YEAR:** SPR./SUM./FALL

One way to make money at any outdoor event is to offer balloon rides as one of the attractions. A tethered balloon simply takes people up a few hundred feet so that they may get a great view for a few minutes. You take a percentage of the day's takings.

Other ways in which you can utilize the novelty aspect of ballooning while making money for your organization, and providing a commercial balloon operator with a steady flow of customers are:

Flights

• **CATEGORY:** GENERAL • **GROUP SIZE:** MED./LARGE • **TIME FRAME:** UP TO 6 MTHS. • **TIME OF YEAR:** SPR./SUM./FALL

The Flight of Fancy In-House Lottery works when you have good relations and/or contacts with a large number of employee groups: schoolteachers, police officers, factory workers, hospital staff, office staff etc. You will also need an employee in each workplace willing to operate the lottery for you by promoting an annual or monthly event, wherein a free balloon flight is given to the lucky winner (to be taken by the winner, or any designate named by the winner, within a specified time). Tickets are sold at five dollars each and the draw takes place after the sale of 100 tickets. The flight costs $200 and you collect a $300 profit. Multiply these figures by the number of schools and/or factories in your area to obtain an idea of how much revenue it might be possible to collect per annum. Large factories or offices might be receptive to weekly draws or, alternatively, you could merely increase the number of flights/tickets sold per draw.

A "Balloon Charity Flight" promotion is a straight sale of balloon flights based on your organization's ability to negotiate a favourable price break on volume. Arrange a special charity weekend with a commercial balloonist, where members and supporters of your organization have the chance to enjoy a balloon flight in return for a donation equivalent to the normal price for a flight. Part of the money is paid to the balloonist to cover his/her fee, and the remainder is held as a charitable donation. With the co-operation of commercial balloonists across the country, charities with branches nation-wide could promote a national, "Fly for . . . (Whatever) Weekend," involving as many balloonists as possible, each of whom donate a percentage of the receipts to the charity.

Balloon flights are relatively risk free from your organization's financial point of view. You pay only for flights actually taken and make a profit on each one. Balloonists will participate as long as they believe they can make money from the event, and your supporters will participate because balloon flights are novel entertainment where anyone can enjoy themselves while helping others.

Fly for Charity

• **CATEGORY:** GENERAL • **GROUP SIZE:** SM./MED./LARGE • **TIME FRAME:** UP TO 1 YR. • **TIME OF YEAR:** SPR./SUM./FALL/WINT.

Flying clubs and flight training centres are constantly seeking new members willing to pay for flying lessons. The fly for charity fundraiser idea gives such centres considerable advertising as well as providing them with a constant flow of potential customers.

Approach those flying clubs in your area which offer flying lessons. Suggest that each offer FREE orientation flights (15 minutes duration) to anyone who donates a specified amount to your charity. This amount should be less than the going rate for an initial lesson. The flying instructor could use this initial flight as an opportunity to persuade novices to take the next step – flying lessons. The donor can claim tax relief for his/her donation.

Advertise your "Fly for Charity" through the media, through your membership, on all of your publicity material, and on posters at suitable locations. This can be a year-round fundraiser. Encourage people to purchase orientation flights as gifts with the wording "Give someone special a flight to remember," on your ads.

All of the administration, including the collection of donations, can be handled by the flight centre. Alternatively, you may wish to process applicants and collect money directly, before referring each to the flying school.

If a flying school is reluctant to give free flights, perhaps it would consider participating in your "Fly for Charity" promotion for a small percentage of the donation.

Parachute Jumping

• **CATEGORY:** GENERAL • **GROUP SIZE:** LARGE • **TIME FRAME:** UP TO 1 YR. • **TIME OF YEAR:** SPR./SUM./FALL

How much would you pledge to charity to see your husband, wife, or boss jump out of a plane at 10,000 feet? Perhaps you would like to give someone an unusual birthday or holiday gift. Parachute jumping for charity can be a rewarding experience for all.

Suitable for any major charity or N.F.P. organization, the success of this idea depends on a charity's ability to negotiate a price/volume reduction. Approach a number of parachute clubs in the area, and finalize an arrangement whereby each will charge an agreed sum for taking a novice up on his/her first parachute jump.

Your intention is to encourage large numbers of people to jump for charity, each person being sponsored to do so by family, friends and colleagues. If, for example, the parachute clubs agree to offer the first jump for $75, your charity should require each participant to raise $125 in sponsored pledges.

Distribute sponsorship forms at local businesses, service clubs, government agencies, universities, and public places such as libraries. Each form should offer a basic training course, and an initial jump, in return for a $125 minimum pledge to the charitable organization. All of the paperwork and collection of pledges should be carried out by each parachute club, which deducts its fee, passing on the pledge form together with a minimum of $50 for each participant.

Each parachute club should receive a steady stream of potential new members as a result of this project which can be an ongoing one. Once the scheme is in motion, it's relatively easy to operate; all that is required is the constant circulation of information posters and sponsorship forms.

Bungee for Charity

Jumping from a tall structure while attached to the end of an elastic band is not everyone's cup of tea, but you may be surprised at how many people are really willing to try. Any organization member or supporter intending to take a bungee jump should be encouraged to raise sponsorship money from friends and family.

There are now many commercial "bungee" operators who charge considerable sums for a jump, and there are several ways in which you can take advantage of this new sport to raise funds.

Before you begin, however, take warning. Bungee jumping is dangerous. Make sure your organization is not liable should someone be injured or killed during a jump.

Bungee Day

• **CATEGORY:** FITNESS, SPORTS & SOCIAL/SERVICE CLUBS • **GROUP SIZE:** SM. • **TIME FRAME:** UP TO 6 MTHS. • **TIME OF YEAR:** SPR./SUM./FALL

"Bungee for Charity" days succeed because a percentage of each jumper's fees are donated to the charity/not-for-profit group of his/her choice. Invite ALL charitable organizations in your area to participate in an event of this nature on the basis that each group will receive donations from anyone jumping on its behalf. Ensure that your group receives the donations from any person who has not specified a charity of choice.

Participation of all of the charity and N.F.P. groups in the area ensures maximum publicity, in addition to making it worthwhile for the bungee operator to give you a substantial percentage of the take. Make additional money by holding ancillary events, and by selling refreshments.

Don't forget sponsored bungee jumping which can be arranged with a commercial operator. Devise a sponsorship form which requires a person to raise a minimum amount of money to earn the right to a "jump." Distribute your forms and explanatory posters to offices, factories, police stations and other local areas. You want to encourage groups of workers to sponsor one of their number, or perhaps the manager, to jump for a good cause. The person so sponsored submits a completed sponsorship form to your organization, receiving in turn a pass entitling him/her to a "free" jump. Once the jump is over, the jumper collects his/her sponsorship money, which is paid to your group and from which you pay a fixed amount to the bungee operator.

One British Columbia organization raises considerable sums, and a great deal of international publicity, by holding an annual naked bungee jump event.

Bar Games

Darts, pool, snooker and other bar games can all be used as fundraisers on a community level. Players of these games are always open to challenges, and charity matches can be easily arranged.

Tournaments

• **CATEGORY:** FITNESS, SPORTS & SOCIAL/SERVICE CLUBS • **GROUP SIZE:** SM./MED./LARGE • **TIME FRAME:** UP TO 1 YR.
• **TIME OF YEAR:** SPR./FALL/WINT.

Inter-bar, regional, or even national tournaments can all be arranged for charity. Sponsorship by a major brewing company should be assured once you are able to convince it that people playing games for charity are likely to drink large quantities of beer. All that is required is a catalyst, a worthy cause and a request for help. Organize a tournament between teams from two local rival bars or pubs. To raise a more substantial sum you will need to involve hundreds of bars, and persuade the marketing division of a major brewery to offer both trophy and prize money sufficient to attract a large number of entrants. (The "Carlson Lager" trophy, together with cash prizes totalling $10,000 perhaps.) The competition, in aid of your organization, should be publicized by the brewery, and leaflets explaining rules and entry requirements circulated to all bars and beer stores. The brewery should bear all the organization expense, including that of the Grand Finale, where the regional champions battle for the trophy and money in front of an enthusiastic crowd. Charity revenue can be generated through sales of finale tickets and entrance fees from each team (channelled to the chosen charity through the event sponsor). Not every charitable group wants to be involved in a bar game tournament, but this event does have potential to produce considerable revenue.

Bar games are also ideal events for sponsored marathons, wherein a team of dart, pool, or video game specialists will attempt to play non-stop for 24 hours, or even seven days, playing in relays. These people are sponsored by friends, relatives, and bar patrons, and they have the potential to raise substantial sums for a small local group.

Bowling Tournaments

• **CATEGORY:** FITNESS, SPORTS & SOCIAL/SERVICE CLUBS • **GROUP SIZE:** SM./MED. • **TIME FRAME:** UP TO 1 YR.
• **TIME OF YEAR:** SPR./SUM./FALL/WINT.

Ten-pin, five-pin or lawn bowling aficionados can all be persuaded to take part in charity tournaments. You need a reasonable prize, trophies and a good cause. Approach your local bowling club to arrange a tournament. If you are lucky, the club should do nearly all of the work for you. Some organizations have raised substantial sums from bowling tournaments by soliciting corporate sponsorship for each contestant, in addition to paying substantial fees to attend the event and its celebratory dinner.

Club Trial Memberships

• **CATEGORY:** HEALTH RELATED/GENERAL • **GROUP SIZE:** SM./MED./LARGE • **TIME FRAME:** UP TO 1 YR. • **TIME OF YEAR:** SPR./SUM./FALL/WINT.

Many fitness, golf, tennis, martial arts and amateur sports clubs of all types offer a period of free trial memberships to potential patrons. Why not ask if they would offer something similar – a day, a week, or a month's free trial to anyone making a donation to your organization. You would promote the deal, persuading as many members and supporters as possible to take advantage of it. If, at the end of the day, the club attracts some new members, perhaps it will welcome a repeat offering at a future date. This idea is especially suitable to any organization raising money for health related issues where personal fitness is a factor.

Do It for Charity

• **CATEGORY:** GENERAL • **GROUP SIZE:** SM./MED./LARGE • **TIME FRAME:** UP TO 6 MTHS. • **TIME OF YEAR:** SPR./SUM./FALL/WINT.

Dance for Muscular Dystrophy, Sing for Lungs, Play for Arthritis – these are all examples of events in which people can be encouraged to do something they enjoy once a year for charity.

Entertainment professionals in almost any discipline can be asked to perform in such charitable performances. Whether such an event is a carefully choreographed performance or a free for all will depend on the artists, performers and organizers. Athletes at all skill levels can participate in "Do It" events. Any game or sport can be undertaken just for the fun of it, and in the name of charity. "Shoot for Cystitis" or "Score for the Scouts" may be suitable titles for such events.

Sled Racing

Dog

• **CATEGORY:** FITNESS, SPORTS & SOCIAL/SERVICE CLUBS • **GROUP SIZE:** SM. • **TIME FRAME:** UP TO 6 MTHS. • **TIME OF YEAR:** WINT.

If there is plenty of snow, a charity dog sled race can be organized anywhere. This is the type of event which attracts tourists en masse to a winter resort area. It should be sponsored and supported by resort operators and municipalities.

Human

• **CATEGORY:** FITNESS, SPORTS & SOCIAL/SERVICE CLUBS • **GROUP SIZE:** SM. • **TIME FRAME:** UP TO 6 MTHS. • **TIME OF YEAR:** SPR./SUM./FALL

For a fun event without the snow and cold, why not run races with human sleds. These feature wheeled sleds pulled by teams of two, four or even six persons.

Fishing Competitions

Several authorities claim sport fishing is the world's premiere participation sport. We do know that it also provides ample opportunity for serious fundraising. Fishing derbies are held in lakes all over Canada. Why not offer a charity trophy to the organizers of any fishing derby in your area, in return for the right to solicit donations from entrants, or for the right to charge an entry fee to any aspiring trophy seekers.

Major Competitions

• **CATEGORY:** HEALTH RELATED/GENERAL • **GROUP SIZE:** LARGE • **TIME FRAME:** UP TO 1 YR. • **TIME OF YEAR:** SPR./SUM./FALL/WINT.

Fishing competitions in all areas of the world are sponsored by fishing equipment manufacturers and suppliers. It is unlikely these firms would be willing to sponsor a tournament on behalf of a charity not directly connected with fishing, but there is no harm in asking.

Don't forget local competitions. Many people enjoy fishing who do not have the time, expertise or resources to enter major fishing competitions. Your organization can organize an annual charity fishing competition in conjunction with the local fishing club. Make it enjoyable. In addition to a prize for the biggest catch of the day, offer awards for the most fish caught, regardless of size: the smallest fish; the most species caught; the ugliest fish; the fish caught on the most unusual bait; and the weirdest object found in the river or lake. How about a fly-tying exhibition, or a casting contest.

Golf Events

Golfers have been targeted by charity fundraisers more than any other sporting group. Possibly this is because anybody who pays a substantial sum of money to use his/her own clubs to knock his/her own ball into a hole in the ground is likely to be an *easy* touch. Golfing events are major moneymakers for a significant number of charity and N.F.P. groups.

Golf Ball Collection

• **CATEGORY:** FITNESS, SPORTS & SOCIAL/SERVICE CLUBS • **GROUP SIZE:** SM. • **TIME FRAME:** UP TO 4WKS. • **TIME OF YEAR:** FALL

Involve the non-playing family members of your golf fanatics by organizing this annual end-of-season event. All entrants line-up at the 1st tee and, at an appointed time, set out to find as many golf balls as possible, arriving at the 18th hole within a specified time, say two hours later. The winner is he/she who retrieves the most balls. Offer a suitable prize, charge a small entrance fee and resell all usable balls collected.

Golf Cart Grand Prix

• **CATEGORY:** FITNESS, SPORTS & SOCIAL/SERVICE CLUBS • **GROUP SIZE:** SM. • **TIME FRAME:** UP TO 6 MTHS. • **TIME OF YEAR:** SPR./SUM./FALL

Organize a golf cart grand prix around a circuit laid out in the parking lot as an adjunct to any golf tournament, and you will have a way to keep golfers amused while waiting for their tee-off time. Arrange races to suit the circumstances and the course.

Golf Cart Passport

• **CATEGORY:** FITNESS, SPORTS & SOCIAL/SERVICE CLUBS • **GROUP SIZE:** MED. • **TIME FRAME:** UP TO 1 YR. • **TIME OF YEAR:** SPR./SUM./FALL

Hiring a golf cart is a major expense at most golf courses. Ask courses in your area to offer a substantial discount to golfers who purchase a book of cart-hire vouchers from your organization. Sell these passports to all regular golf players.

Golf Tournaments

• **CATEGORY:** GENERAL • **GROUP SIZE:** MED./LARGE • **TIME FRAME:** UP TO 1 YR. • **TIME OF YEAR:** SPR./SUM./FALL

A charity tournament provides any golfer with the satisfaction of knowing that his/her endeavour has benefited a worthwhile cause. A tournament with its attendant publicity, especially for a "popular" charity, can be a moneymaker for the course and would attract new members. Many courses are only too pleased to do most of the organizational work for such an event. You will need to find prizes and sell tickets. Theoretically, you cannot lose when holding a golf tournament. The golf course provides the facilities, the prizes should all be donated by local businesses, and each entrant pays a fee plus donation.

Additional revenue can be raised from a range of ancillary events – golf personality lunches or dinners; a golf memorabilia auction; raffles; lease of selling space to retailers and manufacturers of equipment; car trunk sales; early bird breakfasts. Don't forget to include other events to entertain non-playing members and spectators. As a charity or N.F.P. group, you will certainly not be alone if you organize a golf tournament, however, the number of charity golf tournaments has increased to the point where you may find yourself alone on the golf course if you do. The following ideas may be helpful in organizing an uncommon tournament:

New Course Competition

• **CATEGORY:** GENERAL • **GROUP SIZE:** SM./MED./LARGE • **TIME FRAME:** 1 YR.+ • **TIME OF YEAR:** SPR./SUM./FALL

Watch your local media, and at the merest hint of a new golf course opening, contact the developer immediately to put in your bid for its first tournament. The owner should be delighted with the attention his/her course attracts before it is even born. He/she will appreciate the publicity value of holding such a prestigious event as soon as the new course is open and will want as many golfers as possible to try out the new facilities. You must be prepared to wait a year or so, but work with the owner and you may find yourself with a major fundraiser.

Safari Golf Tournament

• **CATEGORY:** GENERAL • **GROUP SIZE:** MED./LARGE • **TIME FRAME:** UP TO 1 YR. • **TIME OF YEAR:** SPR.

A round of golf involves eighteen holes. Who says that all eighteen holes have to be on the same course. Choose nine different golf courses over as wide an area as possible. Issue each golfer a passbook which entitles him/her to play any two holes at each course. All entrants start at the same course where each is allocated two holes from 1–18. At a given time, each player tees off and as soon as he/she has completed their first two holes, the remaining are played at each of the other courses (2 per course). Transport to the alternate courses, the order of play, and holes selected are all up to each individual entrant. The rules specification is for play of 16 different holes at 8 different courses.

One course is designated the final course, and at the 17th and 18th holes their scrutineers can verify that each entrant has played 16 different holes at 8 different courses prior to play of the last two holes. Prizes should be awarded to the lowest score; the first person to complete the "course;" a combination of score and time; and any other factor that makes the competition more fun (innovative means of transport, fancy dress, furthest travelled etc.)

This event should take place over a two or three day period. A good time to organize it is at the very start of the golfing season, when each golf course owner has an opportunity to target potential new members.

Major Prize Tournament

• **CATEGORY:** GENERAL • **GROUP SIZE:** SM./MED./LARGE • **TIME FRAME:** UP TO 1 YR. • **TIME OF YEAR:** SPR./SUM./FALL

A general rule applicable to most events is, "The bigger the prize, the greater the turnout." Golf lends itself to this principle well, because while any golf tournament always has a winner, it is rare for someone to get a hole-in-one. Offer a really substantial hole-in-one prize by arranging insurance to cover against the risk of a winner (or more). Any insurance company can calculate the odds against a hole-in-one during your tournament, dependent upon the number of participants and the difficulty of the course. A prize valued at $100,000 may attract an insurance premium of $1,000 based on odds of winning at 100–1. You pay the insurance company $1,000, plus a fee to cover the cost of an independent scrutineer, and you offer the major prize.

Contact any Canadian insurance broker to obtain details of insurance companies offering this type of policy.

Golf Passports

• **CATEGORY:** GENERAL • **GROUP SIZE:** MED./LARGE • **TIME FRAME:** 1 YR+ • **TIME OF YEAR:** SUM.

Ask all of the golf courses in your local area to participate in a two-for-one deal which you can sell to the public. Each golf course receives a page in a "passport," printed as an advertisement for the course, used as a coupon entitling two people to play for the price of one. Each page can only be used once and is cancelled when used. Participating golf courses benefit from attracting new clientele, the golfers benefit from playing at half-price, and your organization collects the fee from selling the passports.

Putting Competitions

These are always popular fundraisers either as contests within themselves or as adjuncts to large golf-related events.

Lake Golf

• **CATEGORY:** GENERAL • **GROUP SIZE:** SM./MED.• **TIME FRAME:** UP TO 4 WKS. • **TIME OF YEAR:** WINTER.

Canadian winters provide excellent opportunities for lake golf tournaments, and the popularity of the sport would ensure good turnouts. Any safe stretch of ice can be suitable for the golf course, and the equipment used need be no different than that used on a grass course. The balls should be red. Participants can either walk the course or travel by snowmobile.

Horses

Horse Racing: Charity Cup

• **CATEGORY:** HEALTH RELATED • **GROUP SIZE:** MED./LARGE• **TIME FRAME:** UP TO 1 YR. • **TIME OF YEAR:** SPR./.SUM./FALL

An effective way of raising money, and public awareness, is to invite a major beneficiary of your organization to provide an annual prize for an established horse race. The size of the purse depends entirely on the type of track and the quality of the entrants likely to be attracted. A major national charity, for example, would obviously aim for a race at a national course. Once someone is willing to put up a prize, you can negotiate with the racetrack as to how your organization will raise money from the event. Here are some ideas:

- A percentage, or all, of the entrance fees for the charity cup race
- A percentage of spectators' entrance fees
- The right to hold a collection on race day
- Peripheral events pre-arranged with the racecourse

Race sponsors could use the event to reward customers, staff, and suppliers by inviting them to attend the racecourse on that day, and holding a special luncheon or reception. All guests could be invited to make a charitable donation to your cause, or to place a bet in the name of charity. Your organization should encourage all of your members and supporters to attend the race, and its other ancillary fundraising events.

Horse Shows & Gymkhanas

• **CATEGORY:** HEALTH RELATED/CHILDREN & YOUTH • **GROUP SIZE:** SM./MED. • **TIME FRAME:** UP TO 1 YR. • **TIME OF YEAR:** SUM./FALL

Horse and pony riding is very popular. While many riders belong to clubs which hold their own fundraising events, there is no reason why a contra deal beneficial to your organization and to the riding club cannot be arranged. If, for example, your charity or N.F.P. group is for disabled or disadvantaged children, approach a local riding club with a proposal that you should jointly organize a gymkhana.

Think of a catchy title, "Jump for Joy" perhaps, and invite riders to enter a wide range of sponsored events, for prizes donated by local businesses and celebrities. Arrange special events to be enjoyed by your members and feature side-shows, refreshments, and exhibits. The riding club will benefit from the publicity. It also has good reason to hold a competition, and will benefit financially from a profit-sharing agreement.

Horse Trekking

• **CATEGORY:** HEALTH RELATED/CHILDREN & YOUTH • **GROUP SIZE:** SM./MED./LARGE • **TIME FRAME:** UP TO 6 MTHS. • **TIME OF YEAR:** SPR./SUM./FALL

A sponsored horse or pony trek can involve a few riders raising money for a private club or several hundred, even thousands, of riders riding to raise money for a major charity. Horse lovers enjoy riding together.

Contact riding clubs in your area and suggest an annual "Ride for Rickenbacker Disease" or whatever. Hint that a few corporate sponsors may be willing to offer prizes of tack for best groomed animals, smartest turn out etc. The clubs may do most of the organizing for you.

Pedal Powered

There are many pedal powered machines which either float, fly, or run on wheels. All of them can be used to make great events with a little imagination, organization, and publicity. Here are some suggestions for bicycles:

Bicycles

Rally

• **CATEGORY:** GENERAL • **GROUP SIZE:** SM./MED./LARGE • **TIME FRAME:** UP TO 6 MTHS. • **TIME OF YEAR:** SPR./SUM./FALL

Required: a sunny Sunday afternoon, a carefully selected route away from traffic, and a group of friendly people with bikes. Add a picnic or barbecue, and a few children's games for a great time.

For an adults only rally, substitute a bar lunch for the picnic, and add some serious games like poker or bridge at each stop.

A mammoth rally can involve hundreds or even thousands of cyclists, particularly if access could be gained to a new stretch of highway before it is opened to traffic, or if permission were granted to close a regular automotive route for the duration of the event. A two-day sponsored event can be as challenging or as easy as the organizer wishes to make it. Serious cyclists could be given an arduous mountain route while families could meander along on the flats.

Racing

• **CATEGORY:** GENERAL • **GROUP SIZE:** SM./MED. • **TIME FRAME:** UP TO 1 YR. • **TIME OF YEAR:** SPR./SUM./FALL

There are many organizations and clubs for the serious bicycle racer. Contact any in your area and ask them to consider holding a race, or an entire race meeting, for the benefit of your organization. If you, or a committee member, has connections within a cycling club, so much the better.

Riding Endurance

• **CATEGORY:** GENERAL • **GROUP SIZE:** LARGE • **TIME FRAME:** 1 YR+ • **TIME OF YEAR:** SPR./SUM./FALL/WINT.

Several people have already ridden around the world on bicycles, and if someone else is willing to try this to raise money for your organization, don't stop them. Give them all the encouragement you can as long as they are raising money and awareness for your group. People who have already determined to attempt such a ride for charity will raise money for someone else if you turn them down.

If you don't want to compete with existing events for cyclists, consider the following:

Bicycle Made for Fifty

• **CATEGORY:** FITNESS, SPORTS & SOCIAL/SERVICE CLUBS • **GROUP SIZE:** MED./LARGE • **TIME FRAME:** UP TO 1 YR. • **TIME OF YEAR:** SPR./SUM./FALL

Build a huge bicycle to carry an enormous number of people. Claim the world's record, then take your fantastic transport to fairs, carnivals and similar events and charge people to ride it.

Ride of Friendship

• **CATEGORY:** SERVICE CLUBS/GENERAL • **GROUP SIZE:** LARGE • **TIME FRAME:** 1 YR.+ • **TIME OF YEAR:** SPR./SUM./FALL

Invite a well-known manufacturer to design and build a machine to carry ten people. Then begin riding the bicycle from coast to coast using teams of ten from each community along the way. Involve national service club members or charity group teams in every town and community on the route, riding the machine to the next town where a new team would take over. Each team would be sponsored by friends and supporters, and would make a donation to your organization. Public collections would be held all along the route. Hundreds of teams and thousands of people would be required to transport the bicycle through every province. Long distances between some communities might require a relay of riders. The route could be as straightforward or circuitous as desired. The more communities involved, the greater the fundraising potential. Each team of riders should be invited to sign a friendship card, and all of the cards would be accumulated then carried with the bicycle across the country so that an exhibition can be mounted at its final destination. A good Big Brothers event.

Cycling on Water

• **CATEGORY:** FITNESS, SPORTS & SOCIAL/SERVICE CLUBS • **GROUP SIZE:** SM./MED. • **TIME FRAME:** UP TO 1 YR. • **TIME OF YEAR:** SPR./SUM./FALL

Offer a substantial prize for anyone who can ride their bicycle across a lake or river. Encourage youth and service clubs to enter teams. Lay down rules regarding floatation devices and permitted modifications. Engineering students should be able to come up with some wacky designs.

Paddle Boat Racing

• **CATEGORY:** FITNESS, SPORTS & SOCIAL/SERVICE CLUBS • **GROUP SIZE:** SM./MED. • **TIME FRAME:** UP TO 6 MTHS. • **TIME OF YEAR:** SUM./FALL

Paddle boats may be designed for entertainment but there is no reason why they shouldn't be used for some serious racing. Organize an annual event in conjunction with a paddle boat operator at the start or end of the season. Invite local dignitaries and celebrities to participate in invitation races, and hold serious races for substantial prizes and trophies. Solicit teams from sports and athletic clubs and from service clubs, in addition to police, fire and military establishments. Raise money from entry fees or sponsorship.

Set a long distance record, say 160 km, for paddle boat racing and bill your event as "the world's longest paddle boat race." Aim to attract entrants from around the world by offering a substantial prize. You should attract considerable media attention with an event of this nature. Set a suitable course and borrow sufficient paddle boats.

Pedal Car Racing

• **CATEGORY:** FITNESS, SPORTS & SOCIAL/SERVICE CLUBS • **GROUP SIZE:** SM./MED. • **TIME FRAME:** UP TO 6 MTHS. • **TIME OF YEAR:** SPR./SUM./FALL

Pedal Car Racing is an environmentally sound event producing no pollution and providing exercise and fun. A pedal car race can be incorporated into many different events as a way of raising additional funds. Racing a child's pedal car requires considerable effort, but specially designed pedal cars are able to travel at considerable speed over long distances. If your organization is concerned with environmental matters, maybe you should consider starting a national grand prix series of pedal car races. Such an event has enormous potential and could become a classic.

Pedal Plane Flying

• **CATEGORY:** FITNESS, SPORTS & SOCIAL/GENERAL • **GROUP SIZE:** LARGE • **TIME FRAME:** 1 YR.+ • **TIME OF YEAR:** SUM.

Now that a pedal powered aircraft has flown the English Channel, it is time to start an annual pedal powered plane race. Initially, there will be few entrants, but a great deal of spectator interest. Contact universities and plane manufacturers to generate support. Encourage entries from youth groups, who probably have little chance of winning, but might enjoy participating. This event needs at least two years advance planning to be successful.

Roller Blades

• **CATEGORY:** FITNESS, SPORTS & SOCIAL/GENERAL • **GROUP SIZE:** SM./MED. • **TIME FRAME:** UP TO 6 MTHS. • **TIME OF YEAR:** SPR./SUM./FALL

Roller blades, or in-line skates, were around in the 1930s, and have seen a remarkable recent revival. Entrepreneurs have yet to catch onto all of the possibilities that this equipment offers. Roller blade marathons over a full marathon distance could become as well attended and established as the traditional marathon. Who will organize the first in Canada?

Roller blade events like speed skating competitions and roller-thons in roller rinks can all be used as fundraising vehicles for a youth or fitness club. How about roller hockey? This sport has yet to achieve the notoriety of the ice variety, and it may still be possible to start a charity league where all the matches are played in support of various organizations.

Who will be the first person to skate across Canada? Will he/she be raising money for your group? Publicity and sponsorship will be the key to making this effort a financial success. A nation-wide relay event can also attract a great deal of support. Skaters from each community could convey a token from one side of the country to the other. Each skater, or team of skaters, would be sponsored as skaters take the token from their community to the next.

Skiing

• **CATEGORY:** SERVICE CLUBS/GENERAL • **GROUP SIZE:** SM./MED./LARGE • **TIME FRAME:** UP TO 1 YR. • **TIME OF YEAR:** SPR./WINT.

Consider organizing a charity ski marathon or a ski-a-thon. Your organization sets the rules and entry requirements. You need a group of committed skiers who are prepared to ask sponsors to back them. Contact ski resorts and ski clubs at the end of the season to discuss the possibility of organizing a charity event for the following year. What if someone skied across Canada from coast to coast to raise money? The publicity could be considerable.

Snowmobile Competitions

• **CATEGORY:** FITNESS, SPORTS & SOCIAL/SERVICE CLUBS • **GROUP SIZE:** SM./MED./LARGE • **TIME FRAME:** UP TO 6 MTHS. • **TIME OF YEAR:** WINT.

Snowmobile owners are often involved in many lucrative fundraising events. Rallies and races are held annually for many charities. Snowmobilers themselves can select the event, rules, and location. Your mission is to give them a reason to support your cause, and to offer suitable inducement in the form of prizes.

Tennis Tournaments

• **CATEGORY:** SERVICE CLUBS/GENERAL • **GROUP SIZE:** MED./LARGE • **TIME FRAME:** UP TO 1 YR. • **TIME OF YEAR:** SUM./FALL

Charities often hold tennis tournaments to raise money. Contact one of the professional tennis associations, or your local tennis club, to discuss the possibility of holding a tournament. All that is required is a venue, some serious prize money and a prestigious trophy.

Walks

Walking is one activity requiring almost no preparation, no special skill, and no expensive equipment. Depending on the distance and the terrain, almost anyone can participate in a charity walk if he/she chooses to do so, and many people do.

Sponsored Walks

• **CATEGORY:** FITNESS, SPORTS & SOCIAL/GENERAL • **GROUP SIZE:** SM./MED./LARGE • **TIME FRAME:** UP TO 1 YR. • **TIME OF YEAR:** SPR./SUM./FALL

Sponsored walks of all types can raise money: "Walk for

Whales", "Hike for Heart" and "Perambulate for Pandas" are just a few of the catchy titles that can be adopted to publicize a sponsored walk.

Participants in walks of any distance should be asked to pay an entry fee or be required to raise a minimum amount of sponsorship pledges. Fixed distances of 5, 10 and 20 kilometres appear most popular, but there is no reason why a sponsored walk should not be of any length. It might even be held as a timed event with entrants obtaining sponsorship based on the number of kilometres walked within a specified time. A good walker covers 25 kilometres in four hours.

Here are some ideas:

Speed Walking

• **CATEGORY:** FITNESS, SPORTS & SOCIAL • **GROUP SIZE:** SM./MED. • **TIME FRAME:** UP TO 1 YR. • **TIME OF YEAR:** SPR./SUM./FALL

Warm everyone up with a walking race and offer a prize for the fastest.

Endurance Walk

• **CATEGORY:** GENERAL • **GROUP SIZE:** LARGE • **TIME FRAME:** 1 YR+ • **TIME OF YEAR:** SPR./SUM./FALL

How far would someone walk for your organization? What about a walk round the world? All that is required is determination and planning.

Marathon

• **CATEGORY:** GENERAL • **GROUP SIZE:** LARGE • **TIME FRAME:** – • **TIME OF YEAR:** SPR./SUM./FALL

Perhaps it is time that someone started a series of walking marathons.

Marches

• **CATEGORY:** FITNESS, SPORTS & SOCIAL/GENERAL • **GROUP SIZE:** MED./LARGE • **TIME FRAME:** UP TO 1 YR. • **TIME OF YEAR:** SPR./SUM./FALL

Marching is a popular European pastime and contestants march 160 kilometres or more per day. Groups of marchers vie for team and individual awards. Everyone seems to enjoy the pain and suffering of marching non-stop. Everyone also pays substantial entry fees.

A well-known shoe manufacturer could provide a prestigious trophy and a few dozen pairs of suitable shoes in order to start an event of this kind.

Fancy Dress Walk

• **CATEGORY:** GENERAL/CHILDREN & YOUTH • **GROUP SIZE:** SM. • **TIME FRAME:** UP TO 6 MTHS. • **TIME OF YEAR:** SPR./SUM./FALL

Why not hold a fancy dress walk in a park or public place. The distance can be chosen to suit all ages and/or capabilities.

Walking the Boundaries

• **CATEGORY:** GENERAL/CHILDREN & YOUTH • **GROUP SIZE:** SM./MED. • **TIME FRAME:** UP TO 6 MTHS. • **TIME OF YEAR:** SPR./SUM./FALL

This is an ancient annual ritual commonly used to mark out town boundaries so as to be sure that the neighbouring village has not encroached. Mark out the boundaries of your town or city on maps and select a route to keep people off busy roads. How many people actually know the boundaries of their own town?

Walking the Houses of Worship

• **CATEGORY:** RELIGIOUS • **GROUP SIZE:** SM./MED./LARGE • **TIME FRAME:** UP TO 1 YR. • **TIME OF YEAR:** SPR./SUM./FALL

This sponsored walk takes place in a small town or a large city, and should appeal to all houses of worship in need of funds. Walk to every house of worship in your town or city. Each should have a small ceremony of welcome for the walkers, with refreshments available for both walkers and spectators. Raise money from sponsorship and from collections at each stop en route.

Weekly Walk for Wellness

• **CATEGORY:** HEALTH RELATED/GENERAL • **GROUP SIZE:** SM./MED./LARGE • **TIME FRAME:** UP TO 6 MTHS. • **TIME OF YEAR:** SPR./SUM./FALL/WINT.

Weekly walking sessions, especially for seniors, encourage a healthy lifestyle. Charge a small administration fee. Hold the walk in a public park, or shopping mall, and encourage large numbers to participate.

Tiny Tots Toddle

• **CATEGORY:** GENERAL • **GROUP SIZE:** SM. • **TIME FRAME:** UP TO 4WKS. • **TIME OF YEAR:** SPR./SUM./FALL

An ideal fundraiser for a day-care centre or junior kindergarten. Tiny tots need only toddle a few hundred yards to win the admiration, and sponsorship money, of adoring relatives. Fancy dress and teddy bears will liven up the event considerably.

Pets Parade

• **CATEGORY:** GENERAL • **GROUP SIZE:** SM. • **TIME FRAME:** UP TO 6 MTHS. • **TIME OF YEAR:** SPR./SUM./FALL

Encourage pets and owners to participate in a sponsored parade in a public park. Offer prizes for costumes, obedience, unusual pets etc.

Walking Tours

• **CATEGORY:** GENERAL • **GROUP SIZE:** MED./LARGE • **TIME FRAME:** UP TO 1 YR. • **TIME OF YEAR:** SPR./SUM./FALL/WINT.

Walking tours take in any number of interesting locations or sights depending on the type of organization involved, and potential public interest. Historical routes, historical places, and even cemeteries will appeal. Nature walks on a sunny afternoon make a pleasant outing, especially when led by a knowledgeable botanist. Architectural walks are popular as well. Charity walks can be arranged to suit any taste. Some organizations could even benefit from organizing a bar or pub crawl.

Zoo Walk

• **CATEGORY:** HEALTH RELATED/GENERAL • **GROUP SIZE:** MED./LARGE • **TIME FRAME:** UP TO 1 YR. • **TIME OF YEAR:** SPR./SUM./FALL

Many people, adults and children alike, enjoy a walk through the zoo. Why not arrange for a special day at the zoo for members and supporters. Include a special admission price for everyone supporting your cause.

War Games

• **CATEGORY:** FITNESS, SPORTS & SOCIAL/SERVICE CLUBS • **GROUP SIZE:** SM./MED. • **TIME FRAME:** UP TO 6 MTHS.
• **TIME OF YEAR:** SPR./SUM./FALL/WINT.

An increasingly popular sport imported from Europe involves groups of people making mock guerrilla warfare, and shooting at each other with pellets of paint. Operators of war game venues need to attract large numbers of people and they usually offer considerable discounts to group purchasers. Consider playing for an entire day. Invite your members and the public to "fight" for your cause. Make money by selling tickets at regular rates.

Wheelchair Sports

• **CATEGORY:** HEALTH RELATED/FITNESS, SPORTS & SOCIAL • **GROUP SIZE:** SM./MED. • **TIME FRAME:** UP TO 6 MTHS.
• **TIME OF YEAR:** SPR./SUM./FALL/WINT.

Organize a series of competitions pitching able-bodied athletes against those in wheelchairs. Obviously all participants must be in wheelchairs. Wheelchair athletes are particularly good at archery, basketball, volleyball, handball, and wheelchair racing. You can schedule many different events.

The competitions should be in aid of a charity not directly connected with the participant's disabilities. Disabled athletes raising money for disadvantaged people makes good publicity. Money would be raised from sponsorship, entry fees and spectator collections.

Water Sports

Inflatable Dinghy Racing

• **CATEGORY:** FITNESS, SPORTS & SOCIAL/SERVICE CLUBS • **GROUP SIZE:** SM./MED. • **TIME FRAME:** 1 YR+ • **TIME OF YEAR:** SUM./FALL

Each year, a small town in southern England attracts thousands of people to take part in an annual dinghy race which raises more than $100,000 for charity. The concept is simple and can be utilized almost anywhere where there is a small river or lake, and inflatable dinghys or canoes. The event requires teams of four people to race the boats over a short course including obstacles like embankments, moored logs, and other natural or artificial barriers.

The British event takes place over a two-day period and uses a series of small canal ponds each separated by an embankment over which each team must carry its own dinghy. There are qualifying rounds and several final rounds. Anyone can enter and, although there are prizes in different categories for the winners, the main idea is to have fun. Each team is sponsored to participate by friends, relatives etc. Additional funds are raised through the sale of refreshments, car parking, raffles, craft sales etc.

Swimming

So many people are leisure swimmers that many charitable events can be organized around the sport. The following are just a few examples:

• **CATEGORY:** SERVICE CLUBS • **GROUP SIZE:** SM./MED. • **TIME FRAME:** UP TO 6 MTHS. • **TIME OF YEAR:** SPR./SUM./FALL/WINT.

Sponsored events for individuals swimming lengths of pools and teams swimming for long periods are always healthy fundraisers. Swim-a-thons are arranged for a variety of age groups, depending on ability. You could organize a 24-hour endurance race using teams of four or six, or even a stamina event for single swimmers.

• **CATEGORY:** SERVICE CLUBS/GENERAL • **GROUP SIZE:** SM./MED./LARGE • **TIME FRAME:** UP TO 1 YR. • **TIME OF YEAR:** SUM./FALL

Lake Ontario, the English Channel, the St. Lawrence River or Juan de Fuca Strait – swims of any length can be used as sponsored fundraising events. In 1995, a Frenchman swam the Atlantic Ocean. Once a particular stretch of water has been conquered, further attempts can be made to swim it faster or repetitively. Any such attempts can be major fundraisers.

Polar Bear Swims

• **CATEGORY:** SERVICE CLUBS/GENERAL • **GROUP SIZE:** SM./MED. • **TIME FRAME:** UP TO 1 YR. • **TIME OF YEAR:** WINT.

Jumping into an icy lake or sea in the middle of winter to raise money for charity is crazy. Canadians do it all the time. Organize a polar bear swim and see who the brave or foolish are. December and January seem to be the popular times.

Warning: Many people have died of heart attacks while participating in polar bear swims.

Windsurfing

• **CATEGORY:** FITNESS, SPORTS & SOCIAL/GENERAL • **GROUP SIZE:** SM./MED. • **TIME FRAME:** UP TO 1 YR./1 YR+ • **TIME OF YEAR:** SUM./FALL

Some day someone will attempt to windsurf across the Atlantic or Pacific Ocean. Charity involvement in such an event can generate considerable funds, but the possibility of a tragedy is very real and few organizations could withstand the resultant publicity. Sponsorship and organization of less demanding windsurfing journeys might in various ways be lucrative. Talk with windsurfers, or with the executive members of windsurfer organizations; ask them if they would hold an event in aid of your group.

Yachting

Yachts have been described as "depressions in water into which the owner constantly throws money;" and yacht owners are good fundraising targets. The secret is to catch them on shore, in the clubhouse.

• **CATEGORY:** GENERAL • **GROUP SIZE:** MED./LARGE • **TIME FRAME:** UP TO 1 YR. • **TIME OF YEAR:** SPR./SUM./FALL

Yacht clubs regularly hold races for trophies awarded by past commodores or other dignitaries. There is no reason why a charity yachting trophy can not be offered by one of your sponsors, accompanied by a cash prize. Arrange the trophy and prize first, then approach a yacht club requesting that it hold a charity cup to be sponsored by your organization.

• **CATEGORY:** GENERAL • **GROUP SIZE:** MED./LARGE • **TIME FRAME:** UP TO 1 YR./1 YR+ • **TIME OF YEAR:** SPR./SUM./FALL

Mobilize a flotilla of yachts to sail from point A to point B starting at the same time. Ask any number of yachting clubs to solicit their membership for participation, with each owner paying a sponsorship fee. Encourage the public to watch the spectacle and hold collections along the waterfront as the flotilla sails by.

• **CATEGORY:** GENERAL • **GROUP SIZE:** MED./LARGE • **TIME FRAME:** UP TO 1 YR. • **TIME OF YEAR:** SPR./SUM./FALL

Invite rival yacht clubs and owners to issue charity challenges. Suggest that one club offer to race against another in an unusual manner. Ten yachts from each club might set out from their home harbour simultaneously en route to the challenger's clubhouse, whereupon arriving, all sailors would be asked to complete a series of challenges before setting sail to return back to home harbour. The first club with all yachts back at anchor would be declared the winner, and would hold and display your charity trophy until the next challenge match.

A FEW FINAL THOUGHTS AND IDEAS:

In a World of Copycats – Be an Individual

Always organize your event in ways that others have not. Separate yourself from the pack and show people that you are making an effort and deserve to be supported. Individualism attracts attention and this fact is very important in the fundraising arena.

And last but by no means least:

ALWAYS give people more than they expect.

ALWAYS go the extra mile.

Whatever the event, whatever the campaign, when everything has been arranged and finalized, ask yourself and your group: "Is there one little extra thing that we can do which will make people say, 'WOW,' and dig a little deeper into their pockets?" You want to make sure supporters return for your next event with friends, and the event after that with more friends. Fundraising is rather like an art form and you've got to give it everything you've got. And then some.

Good Luck!

RESOURCES FOR FUNDRAISING IN CANADA, AND AROUND THE WORLD

Web Resources for Not-for-Profit and Charity Fundraising

1. Important Sites for Canadians

Canadian Centre for Philanthropy (CCP)

1329 Bay Street, Suite 200, Toronto ON M5R 2C4, Email ccp@ccp.ca URL http:/www.ccp.ca

A national charitable organization dedicated to advancing the role and interests of the charitable sector for the benefit of Canadian communities. The Centre invites membership. Major publication is *The Canadian Directory to Foundations and Grants 1996/7, 12th edition*, which will be available on-line, September 1997.

Membership includes membership in Imagine. A research program provides statistics on the not-for-profit sector, via *Affiliated Research Bulletins* six times a year. *Front & Centre* newspaper covers the fundraising scene in Canada and worldwide. There is a Bi-Monthly fax newsletter, plus Imagine's *Inter-Sector* newsletter.

Publications which can be ordered from the CCP include:

Creating Effective Partnerships with Business: A Guide for Charities and Nonprofits in Canada, 1996

Floyd, Gordon, *Foundation Forum '95*

Hall, Michael, 1996. *Charitable Fundraising in Canada*. Includes fundraising methods and revenues attained by charities, costs associated with these methods, use of fundraising consultants, Board policies in fundraising.

Rostami, Janet, and Michael Hall, *Employee Volunteers: Business Support in the Community*, 1996

Rotterdam, Ingrid van, 1995. *Building Foundation Partnerships: The Basics of Foundation Fundraising and Proposal Writing*

Wyman, Ken. *Planning Successful Fundraising Programs*, 1991

Charitable Fundraising in Canada, 1996

Portrait of Canada's Charities, 1994

The Effects of Health Care Reform on Philanthropy in Canada, 1996

Imagine community partner program is run by the Centre, seeking to build partnerships between the charitable sector and businesses which have committed to donate at least one percent of pre-tax profits to charitable voluntary organizations. Over 800 Canadian charitable and voluntary organizations belong, helping create a favourable climate for charitable causes. On its website, Imagine carries a list of corporations which are members for researching prospective business partners. URL http://www.ccp.ca/#Imagine

Community Partnership Program, Canadian Identity Directorate, Heritage Canada

Tel: (819) 994-2255, Fax: (819) 997-8777. Free publications in English and French.

Ken Wyman, 1993. *Face to Face: how to get better donations from very generous people*

– 1995 *Fundraising Ideas that Work!*

David Ross, 1994. *How to Estimate the Economic Contribution of Volunteer Work*

Douglas McKercher, 1994. *Low-Cost Small-Scale Publishing*

Volunteer Canada, The Canadian Association of Volunteer Bureau

URL http://www.volunteer.ca, library, links, CentrePoint Newsletter, annual conference on volunteerism. Volunteerism Resource Kit.

Volunteer Ontario

2 Dunbloor Road, Suite 203, Etobicoke ON M9A 2E4, Tel: (416) 236-0588, Fax: (416) 236-0590. URL http://www.volontario.org Email webmaster@voluntario.org

Free Resource Catalogue available by fax 1-800-300-3270 or online. The trade name of the Ontario Association of Volunteer Bureau/Centres, a not-for-profit incorporated in Ontario and registered with Revenue Canada, promoting volunteerism through information, resource development and distribution, consultation and support to individuals and organizations. Many services for members including Monthly Faxletter, library, discounts. It is developing customizable products, available online. Well-maintained site has links to Charity Village and Volunteer Canada. An arrangement allows links to amazon.com for a selection of "most useful books" for Canadian N.F.P.s. An excellent source for hard-to-find books.

Charity Village

URL http://www.charityvillage.com

A thousand pages of news, jobs, information and resources for staffers, donors, and volunteers in Canada's not-for-profit sector. Newsweek section has news, fundraising events, conferences, seminars, gossip. The Library and Downtown have research materials, book reviews and the link to amazon.com.

Canadian Conference on the Arts

189 Laurier Avenue E., Ottawa ON K1N 6P1

URL http://www.culturenet.ca/cca/index/html Email cca@mail.cu

Canada's oldest and largest arts advocacy group, impressing upon governments and the public the importance of the cultural industries. It is a non-partisan registered charity. Bulletins, news briefs, publications, membership invited, small fee, links to arts, music, publishing, film theatre etc. groups.

In Kind Canada

Suite 583, 420 Main St. E. Unit C. Milton, Ontario, L9T 5G3, Tel: 905-821-6309, Fax: 905-821-6312. Email inkind@informamp.net

A national association that provides a clearinghouse service to charities and not-for-profit helping them access donations from businesses of furniture, equipment and other resources. They are currently working with more than 340 not-for-profit agencies and in 1996 saw more than $1 million in value returned to their members. They have more than 80 corporations that they have worked with and are working on increasing this number.

Gifts in Kind International

333 North Fairfax Street, Alexandria VA 22314. London, Toronto, Washington, DC. Tel: (703) 836-2121 Association Service Team. Fax: (202) 274-4690 for The Agency Partner (TAP) registration form.

URL http://www.GiftsInKind.org Email ProductDonations@GiftsInKind.org

Has distributed more than $1 billion in newly-manufactured products to the needy in neighborhoods around the world. Organizes donation programs for corporations on issues and geographic areas of special concern. Canadian recipient organizations must be registered with Revenue Canada.

The Council for Business and the Arts in Canada (CBAC)

165 University Ave, Suite 705, Toronto ON M5H 3B8, Tel: (416) 869-3016, Fax: 869-0435.

An association of corporations that support the arts through strategic community investments. CBAC provides annual surveys of performing arts organizations, museums and galleries across Canada, and advice on corporate practices on sponsorship and campaign participation to arts groups. It publishes books, encourages business to participate on arts boards, and runs award programs and forums. Arts organizations participate in surveys and programs and are welcome to subscribe to the newsletter and purchase publications. Newsletter Ripple covers business support for arts in Canada. Publications include: *Business Support of the Arts 1997* ($10), *Approaching Corporations for Support* ($7.50), *Business Sponsorship of the Arts* ($7.50), *Forging a Strong Business/Arts Partnership* ($7.50).

Association of Canadian Orchestras, Orchestras Ontario

56 The Esplanade, Suite 311, Toronto ON M5E 1A7, Tel: (416) 366-8834, Fax: (416) 366-1780. URL http://home.ican.net/assoc Email assoc@ican.net

This association does an excellent job assisting Canadian orchestras in fundraising, and has links with the American Association of Symphony Orchestras. Their *Fundraising Handbook 1993*, now out of print is worth looking for. They sell a number of publications particularly aimed at symphony orchestras.

The Canadian Centre for Business in the Community, a division of the Conference Board of Canada.

255 Smyth Rd, Ottawa Tel: (613) 526-3280, 1-888-801-8818. URL http://www.conferenceboard.ca Email pubsales@conferenceboard.ca

Research Centres, forums and special projects, for community economic development and business-community partnerships and alliances. Membership is aimed at corporations but there may be help for your organizations. Publications include *Voluntary Environmental Initiatives in Canada* and *Corporate Community Investment in Canada 1995-96*.

Resources in Canada

URL http://www.contact.org/canada.htm. Canada Council, regional arts councils and many more.

Internet Non-profit Center

URL http://www.nonprofits.org

CultureNet

URL http://www.culturenet.ca

CultureNet is working with a wide variety of cultural organizations and individuals across Canada who are providing information about their seasons, their programs and themselves. Many Links to Canadian cultural organizations and associations. En Francais as well.

Phillip A. Walker's Non-Profit Groups on the Internet

URL http://www.clark.net

Best maintained, most links.

2. Some Important International Sites

The Foundation Center

79 Fifth Avenue, New York NY 10003-3076, Tel: 1-800-424-9836, (212) 260-4230, Fax: (212) 691-1828. Email many, see site. URL http://fdncenter.org/

Links to Foundation Center Services, including publications and CD-ROMs, libraries, including an online library and databases, prospect worksheet, a proposal-writing short course, common grant application forms, news, career opportunities, training and seminars. Links to private foundations and grantmakers on the Internet, and research highlights. Newsletter is *Philanthropy News Digest*.

Publications include *Grantmaker Directories* (e.g. Guide to US Foundations, their Trustees and Donors); *Grant Directories*, and *Regional/International Directories*.

U.S. National Center for Nonprofit Boards

URL gopher://ncnb.org:7002/1 Email ncnb@ncnb.org.

Information to improve the effectiveness of nonprofit organizations by strengthening their boards of directors.

Join Together Online

Join Together: 441 Stuart Street, 6th Floor; Boston, MA 02116; Tel: (617) 437-1500, Fax: (617) 437-9394.

URL http://www.jointogether.org

Funding News (http://www.jointogether.org/jto/funding/funding.html), its online newsletter with an archive of over 1,000 documents, foundation profiles, a grantsmanship centre and a feature: *Follow the Money: Links to foundations* (funding sites), US federal agencies online.

CharitiesDirect, CaritasData Ltd.

Kemp House 152-160 City Road, London EC1V 2NP Tel: +44(0) 171 1777. URL http://caritasdata.co.uk Email info@caritasdata.co.uk

An information service covering 5,000 of UK's leading charities with information from CaritasData's charity Database. Lists and links to top 1,500 charities by income and expenditures.

America's Charities Homepage

Tel: 1-800-458-9505. URL http://www.charities.org Email charities@interramp.com

Database maintained by National/United Service Agencies. Coalition of prestigious national charitable organizations, partnering employers and employees to meet needs in human service, health and education, civil and human rights, and the environment.

Action without Borders, Idealist

350 Fifth Avenue, Suite 6614, New York, NY 10118. Tel: (212)-843-3973. http://www.idealist.org Email idealist@idealist.org

A global network of individuals and organizations sharing ideas, information and resources to help build a world where all people can live free, dignified and productive lives. It works through the Internet and through local chapters to facilitate collaboration, volunteerism and investment in support of these goals. It has a newsletter.

Idealist is an online resource for not-for-profit and community organizations, allowing organizations to enter and update information about their services, volunteer opportunities, job openings, internships, upcoming events, materials and publications. 3,000 organizations in 80 countries use Idealist. Add your organization profile. Links to many valuable resources. Many Canadian organizations participate.

Global Partnership, Box 1001, London SE24 9NL. Tel: +44 (0) 171 924 0974. URL http://www.proteusweb.com/gp/ Email gp@aris.demon.co.uk.

Supports events promoting its philosophy of celebrating the diversity of the world's cultures and giving a voice to people who are disempowered. Sponsors a world fair annually, concerned with global issues, including fairly-traded arts and crafts, exhibiting work of NGOs, and anyone working in areas of development, environment and human rights.

UK Fundraising

URL http://www.fundraising.co.uk

The Altford Group sells fundraising, strategic planning and leadership development services. Site includes links to organizations and sources, private and government in the UK for the not-for-profit sector.

European Union Grants Directory

7 Bladons Walk, Kirk Ella, Hull, England, HU10 7AX, Telephone +44(0) 1482 651695, Fax: +44(0) 1482 659281. URL http:// www.gpg.co.uk/sample/index.htm Email 100551.760@compuserve.com

An invaluable electronic tool for organizations worldwide looking for European grants, from European Consultancy Services, "Your Guide to European Grants."

European Foundation Centre

(http://www.poptel.org.uk/aries/efc/)

3. Online Newsletters

Philanthropy Journal Online

URL http://philanthropy-journal.org

Includes fundraising ideas, news and resources on volunteers, fundraising, foundations etc. Published once a week. Includes not-for-profit Web Talk. Information research service at URL.

New Media Philanthropy Journal

URL http://www.pj.org Email seanbaily@mindspring.com

Flash News, European Consultancy Services URL http://www.gpg.co.uk

Fund$Raiser Cyberzine.

See also Canadian Centre for Philanthrophy, Charity Village, Volunteer Canada, JTO.

4. Discussion Groups, Listservs

Amphilrev discussion group, send Email to Majordomo@tab.com with subscribe talk-amphilrev (your Email address).

Gift-PL list, supported by the National Council on Planned Giving, send Email to listserv@indycms.iupui.edu with *subscribe gift-pl (your name)*.

PND-L, Email version of *Philanthropy News Digest* of The Foundation Centre, every Tuesday. Send Email to listserv@lists.fdncenter.org with *SUBSCRIBE PND-L <<I>your name>* in the body of the message.

Philanthropy Journal Alert! Send Email to pjalert@mail-list.com, leaving subject field blank and putting subscribe in the body.

For Internet Resources, look up the latest editions of *The Grantseeker's Handbook of Essential Internet Sites* or *Where the Information Is: A Guide to Electronic Research for Nonprofit Organizations*, see below.

5. Researching Canadian Corporations

Many of these books, diskettes, and CD-ROMs, are expensive references with new editions every year. Look for them in your local library.

Canadian Centre for Philanthropy

The Canadian Directory to Foundations and Grants 1996/7, 12th edition, available on-line, September 1997, pp. 850. Granting policies, how and when to apply, application information, personnel, U.S. foundations which give in Canada, list of recent grants over $5,000.

Copp Clark Professional,

Tel: 1-800-815-9417, (416) 597-1616. URL http://www.CanadaInfo.com Email orders: copp@mail.CanadaInfo.com

Canadian Almanac & Directory, 1997. Organizations, federal, provincial and municipal, government directory, business and finance, health, education, legal directories. Book and/or CD-ROM.

Financial Services, Canada 1997. Banks, credit unions, trust, insurance, CA firms, mutual funds, government agencies, key contacts. Book and/or CD-ROM.

Canadian Environmental Directory 1997/1998. Fully indexed, environmental companies, trade and industry associations and NGO's. Government, organizations, law, conferences, markets, products and services. Book and/or CD-ROM.

Associations Canada 1997/98. Canadian and foreign associations active in Canada, headquarters, branches, contacts, budgets, conferences, publications, mailing lists. Book and/or CD-ROM.

PanCaribbean Business Directory & Handbook, 97-98. Contacts in the business sectors of 39 Caribbean companies. Book.

Canadian Business Media Ltd

Tel: (416) 596-5100, 596-5156.

Who's Who in Canadian Business, 1998, CD-ROM, including addresses, Email, websites, of 6,000 powerful Canadians. Also, *Canadian Business Magazine,* Performance 500, Profit 100, Entrepreneur of the year. Prints out contact sheets and mailing labels.

Canadian Research and Publications Centre (CRPC), a division of CCH Canadian Limited.

1-800-363-1400, Montreal (514) 293-2644. 33 Racine Street, Farnham PQ J2N 3A3.

Handbook of Grants and Subsidies: Government Aid to Nonprofit Organizations, Bi-monthly updates of a looseleaf handbook, federal and provincial agencies, health and social services, employment and development, cultural affairs, education and research. Similar service for business.

DB Dunn & Bradstreet Canada

Tel: 1-800-668-1168, 905-568-6176.

The Canadian Key Business Directory, 1997. 20,000 listings of Canada's largest companies, over 60,000 key contact names. Book and/or CD-ROM.

The National Services Directory, 1997. 17,000 listings of top service companies. Book.

The Guide to Canadian Manufacturers, 1997. 50,000 Canadian manufacturers in 3-volume set by region. 3 Books.

The Regional Business Directory. Vancouver, Toronto, Montreal. 55,000 businesses, 200,000 names. Books.

The Financial Post Datagroup

Tel: 1-800-661-7678. URL http://www/canoe.ca/fp

1998 Directory of Directors, lists 15,500 individuals from 1,800 companies

1997 Survey of Industrials, 2,700 manufacturing and services companies

1997 Survey of Mines & Energy Resources, 3,000 mining and energy resource companies

1996 Canadian Markets, 700 markets, based on 1991 Census statistics, 1996 estimates and 1998/2002 projections, abridged version on disk

Canadian Company Histories, Toronto Gale Canada 1996

Globe Information Services

Tel: 1-800-268-9128, ext 5345. Local (416) 585-5249 URL http://www.TheGlobeAndMail.com

The 1997 Report on Business Canada Company Handbook and Diskette, includes Corporate rankings, websites, Email addresses, TSE 300 companies, Top 1,000 rankings on Diskette.

The Guide to the Canadian Financial Services Industry, 1997, timely information on 1,000 financial service organizations, key contacts, biographies, positions and titles of 15,000 senior executives.

InfoGlobe Online, includes top 2500 companies, Corporate Canada Online, ROB Corporate Database, Canadian Books in Print, Canadian Federal Government Online, Canadian Financial Services Online, Canadian Parliamentary Guide, Canadian Who's Who, entry to Dow Jones News, Nielsen Marketing Research. Flat Fee Pricing.

Micromedia Ltd.

Tel: 1-800-387-2689, (416) 369-2589. Email info@micromedia.on.ca URL http://www.micromedia.on.ca

Canadian Associations Database, 1997/1998. Find an association to partner your next event. 17,000 business, professional, trade and consumer organizations. In print format, on CD-ROM, diskette, magnetic tape, or pressure sensitive labels. Includes executive names, titles, addresses, telephone, email and URL addresses.

Canadian Libraries Database, 1998. 6,500 Canadian libraries, resource centres, business information centres, professional associations. In print format, diskette, CD-ROM, via the internet.

ProFile Canada, a database of marketing intelligence on 25,000 Canadian companies and organizations.

International Self-Counsel Press Ltd.

1481 Charlotte Road, North Vancouver B.C. V7J 1H1, Tel: Ontario and East: (905) 450-0336, West of Ontario (604) 986-3366. U.S. (360) 676-4530. Email sales@self-counsel.com

MacLeod, Flora, 3rd edn., 1995. *Forming and Managing a Non-Profit Organization in Canada*.

Young, Joyce, and Ken Wyman, 4th edn., 1995. *Fundraising for Non-profit Groups: How to get money from corporations, foundations, and government*.

Yahoo! – Business and Economy,

URL http://pacbell.yahoo.com/Business_and_Economy/tree.html

Also, contact trade associations, chambers of commerce, service clubs etc. for particular industries.

6. Other Resources

Gale Research Inc.

Braun, Gary, ed. 1997. *Gale Directory of Publications and Broadcast Media, 129th edition*, Newspapers, magazines, journals, radio shows, TV shows, cable systems. Many updates. 1-800-877-GALE.

Zahalik, Joanna, ed. 1996. *Gale Guide to Internet Databases*.

Matthews Media Directories, a division of Canadian Corporate News

Suite 500, 25 Adelaide St. E., Toronto ON M5C 3A1. Tel: 1-800-363-9296, (416) 362-5739, Fax: (416) 955-0705. URL http://www.matthews.ca, http://www.cdn-news.com.

On diskette, CD-ROM, labels.

Matthews Media Directory (original Red Book) updated twice yearly, over 25,000 names of editorial/journalistic and management staff of 1,650 Canadian media organizations including newspapers, TV, radio, business and trade, newswires, networks, press galleries.

Matthews CCE Directory (the Green Book) updated twice yearly with 16,000 names, 2,650 organizations including community papers, consumer magazines, ethnic and aboriginal media, university press and radio.

Matthews CATV Director (the Blue Book) updated twice annually, over 5,000 names and operations details for 900 Canadian cable TV systems including specialty and pay channels, suppliers, microwave, satellite services.

Prospect Research Page

URL http://wever.u.washington.edu/~dlamb/research.html

Includes links to information on companies, foundations, news sources.

Securities and Exchange Commission

URL http://www.sec.gov/

Online database of corporate information for research.

Switchboard

URL http://www.switchboard.com

Internet NonProfit Center

URL http://www.nonprofits.org

7. National and Provincial Arts Councils

One directory lists 312 local arts councils in Canada. There is probably one in your area.

Alberta Community Development, 10158, 103 Street, 3rd Floor, Edmonton AB T5J 0X6. Tel: (403) 427-6315, Fax: (403) 422-9132. Email jbisbee@mcd.gov.ab.ca

Alberta Foundation for the Arts, 10158, 103 Street, 5th Floor, Edmonton AB T5J 0X6. Tel: (403) 427-9968, Fax: (403) 422-1162.

British Columbia Ministry of Small Business, Tourism and Culture, 800 Johnson Street, 5th Floor, Victoria BC V8V 1X4. Tel: (250) 356-1718, Fax: (604) 387-4099.

The Canada Council, Box 1097, 350 Albert St. Ottawa ON K1P 5V8. Tel: 1-800-263-5588. URL http://www.canadacouncil.ca/ccintro.htm

The Outreach Program will supply travel assistance and presenters' program will help you bring Canadian artists to your community to be part of your event.

Manitoba Arts Council, 93 Lombard Ave., Suite 525, Winnipeg, Manitoba R3B 3B1. Tel: (204) 945-2237, Fax: (204) 945-5925. URL infobahn.mb.ca/mac Email manarti@mts.net

Manitoba Culture, Heritage and Citizenship, 213 Notre Dame Ave., 6th Floor, Winnipeg MB R3B 1N3. Tel: (204) 945-3847, Fax: (204) 945-1684.

New Brunswick Department of Municipalities, Culture and Housing. Box 6000, Fredericton NB E3B 5H1. Tel: (506) 453-2555, Fax: (506) 453-2416.

Newfoundland and Labrador Arts Council. Box 98, Station C. St. John's NF A1B 4J6. Tel: (709) 726-2212, Fax: (709) 726-0619.

Northwest Territories Dept. of Education, Culture and Employment, Box 1320, Yellowknife NT X1A 2L9. Tel: (403) 920-3103, Fax: (403) 873-0205.

Nova Scotia Department of Education and Culture, Box 578, Halifax NS B3J 2S9. Tel: (902) 424-6389, Fax: (902) 424-0710. Email hlfxtrad.educ.wattpa@gov.no.ca.

Ontario Arts Council, 151 Bloor Street West, Suite. 500, Toronto ON M5S 1T6. Tel: (416) 969-7438, 1-800-387-0058, Ontario only. Fax: (416) 961-7796.

PEI Council for the Arts, 115 Richmond Street, Charlottetown PE C1A 1H7. Tel: (902) 368-4410, Fax: (902) 368-4418.

Quebec Ministere de la Culture et des Communications, 225, Grande-Allee Est, Quebec QC G1R 5G5. Tel: (418) 643-4211, Fax: (418) 643-4457.

Saskatchewan Arts Board, 3475 Albert Street, 3rd Floor, Regina SK S4S 6X6. Tel: (306) 787-4056, Fax: (306) 787-4199.

8. Book Resources

Allen, Nick, ed., 1997. *Fundraising on the Internet: Recruiting and Renewing Donors Online.* Strathmoor Press.

American Symphony Orchestra League Staff. *The gold book 1994-95: a sourcebook of successful and creative orchestra fundraising, education, ticket sales and service projects.* American Symphony Orchestras League, 777 14th St. NW, Suite 500, Washington DC 20005.

Amos, J. S., 1995. *Fundraising ideas.* McFarland & Co, Inc. (910) 246-4460, 1-800-253-2187, Email McFarland2@AOL.COM.

Arledge, Rick and David Friedman, 1992. *Dynamic fund-raising projects.* Precept Press.

Bauer, David G., 1995. *The "how to" grants manual: successful grantseeking techniques for obtaining public and private grants, 3rd ed.* Phoenix AR, Oryx Press.

Bauer, David G., 1995. *The Fundraising Primer.* Scholastic.

Bergan, Helen J., 1996. *Where the information is: A guide to electronic research for nonprofit organizations.* BioGuide Press.

Bergan, Helen J.,1992. *Where the money is: a fund raiser's guide to the rich, 2nd ed.* BioGuide Press.

Blum, Laurie, 1996. *The complete guide to getting a grant: How to turn your ideas into dollars.* New York, Wiley.

Brentlinger, Marilyn and Judith M. Weiss, 1987. *The ultimate benefit book: How to raise $50,000 plus for your favorite organizations.* Octavia, Ohio.

Brody, Ralph and Marcie Goodman, 1987. *Fund raising events: Strategies and programs for success.* Human Sciences Press.

Brown, Peter C., 1986. *The complete guide to money-making ventures for nonprofit organizations.* Taft Group.

Burke, Mary A. and Carl Liljenstolpe, 1993. *Creative fund raising.* Crisp Publications Inc. (415) 323-6100, 1-800-442-7477.

Burlingame, Dwight F. ed., 1997. *Critical issues in fundraising*. New York, Wiley.

Burnet, Ken, 1996. *Friends for Life: Relationship Fundraising in Practice*. White Lion Press Ltd., in association with International Fund Raising Group.

Burnett, Ken, 1995. *Relationship fundraising*. Bonus Books.

Burton, Cynthia, M. Jemiolo, and Richard T. Burton. *The Directory of corporate giving in Canada, 1990*. Rainforest Publications. Also, *Directory of Employee Charitable Trusts*. Publisher seems to be out of business.

Canadian Centre for Philanthropy, 1989. *The major corporate gift: a fundraiser's guide*.

Chase's Calendar of Events, 1998: A Day-to-Day Directory to Special Days, Weeks and Months. Contemporary Books.

DeAngelis, James, ed., 1997 *The Grantseeker's Handbook of Essential Internet Sites*. Capitol Publications.

Doyle, William L., 1995. *Fund raising ideas: For all nonprofits: charities, churches, clubs, etc*. American Fund Raising.

Edles, L. Peter, 1992. *Fundraising: Hands-on tactics for nonprofit groups*. McGraw.

Financial Post, 1986. *Corporate sponsorship of sports and arts: earning the best return*. Toronto.

Flanagan, Joan, 1993. *Successful fundraising: A complete handbook for volunteers and professionals*. Chicago, Contemporary Books.

Flanagan, Joan, rev. 1992. *The grass roots fundraising book: How to raise money in your community*. Chicago, Contemporary Books.

Foundation Centre, 1988. *The non-profit entrepreneur: creating ventures to earn income*. New York.

Gordon, Micki, 1996. *The fundraising manual: A step-by-step guide to creating the perfect event*. Fig Press, from Q Corp, 49 Sheridan Ave., Albany NY 12210.

Greenfield, James M., 1991. Fundraising: evaluating and managing the fund development process. New York, Wiley.

Grensheimer, Cynthia F.,1993. *Raising funds for your child's school: Over sixty great ideas for parents & teachers*, Walker & Co. 1-800-AT-WALKER, Tel. (212) 727-8300.

Hopkins, Karen Brooks and Carolyn Stolper Friedman, 1997. *Successful fundraising for arts and cultural organizations, 2nd ed*. Phoenix AR, Oryx Press.

Innes, Eva, 1990. *The Financial Post 100 best companies to work for in Canada*. Toronto, Harper Collins.

Janowski, Katherine, ed. 1995. *The directory of corporate and foundation givers, 1995: A national listing of the 8,000 major funding sources for nonprofits*. Taft Group.

Kaitcer, Cindy R., 1996. *Raising big bucks through pledge-based special events*. Bonus Books.

Keegan, P. B., 1994. *Fundraising for non-profits: How to build a community partnership.* Harper-Perennial.

Klein, Kim, 1995. *Fundraising for social change, 3rd ed.* Chardon Press.

Kraatz, Katie and Julie Haynes, 1987. *The Fundraising Formula: 50 Creative Events Proven Successful Nationwide.* OP. amazon.com offers to help find a used one.

Lindahl, Wesley E., 1992. *Strategic planning for fundraising: how to bring in more money using strategic resource allocation.* San Francisco, Jossey-Bass Publishers.

Lynn, David and Kathy Lynn, 1996. *Great Fundraising Ideas for Youth Groups: over 150 easy-to-use money-makers that really work.* Zondervan. check

Meiners, Phyllis A. and Hilary H. Tun-Arz, 1996. *Corporate and foundation fundraising manual for Native Americans.* Corporate Reserve Consultants.

Panas, Jerold, 1989. *Official Fundraising Almanac.* Precept Press.

Ross, Dorothy M., 1990. *Fundraising for Youth: Hundreds of Wonderful Ways of Raising Funds for Youth Organizations.* Meriwether Publications.

Smith, Craig. *Giving by Industry: A Reference Guide to the New Corporate Philanthropy, 1996-1997 edn.* Capitol Publications Inc.

Trenbeth, Richard P., 1986. *The membership mystique. How to create income and influence with membership programs.* Ambler PA, Fundraising Institute, try Taft Group.

Warwick, Mal, 1995. *Raising money by mail: Strategies for growth and financial stability.* Strathmoor Press. Also, *How to write successful fundraising letters; Technology and the future of fundraising; 999 tips, trends and guidelines for successful direct mail and telephone fundraising.*

Many of these excellent books on fundraising are published by smaller or specialty publishers. The following addresses will be helpful. Call or write them and ask for their most recent catalogues.

BioGuide Press, Box 16072, Alexandria VA 22302, Tel: (703) 820-9045.

Capitol Publications Inc. 1101 King Street, Suite 444, Alexandria VA 22314. Tel: 1800-655-5597.

Gale Research Inc. Box 33477, Detroit MI 48232, 835 Penobscot Bldg, Detroit MI 48226-4094. Tel: (313) 961-2242, 1-800-877-GALE, Email gale.com

The Foundation Centre, 79 Fifth Avenue, New York NY 10003.

Jossey-Bass Publishers, Inc., 350 Sansome St., San Francisco CA 94104, distributed by American Society for Training and Development. URL http://www.josseybass.com

The Oryx Press, 4041 N. Central Ave., Suite 700, Phoenix AZ 85012-3397, Tel: (602) 265-2651, Fax: (602) 265-6250, Email info@oryxpress.com

Precept Press, a division of Bonus Books Inc., 160 East Illinois Street, Chicago IL 60611. Tel: 1-800-225-3775.

Strathmoor Press, a division of Gale Research Inc., 2550 Ninth St., Suite 1040, Berkeley CA 94710-2516. Tel: (510) 843-8888, Fax: (312) 467-9272.

The Taft Group, a division of Fund Raising Institute, 12300 Winbrook Pkwy, Suite 520, Detroit MI 48226, Tel: 1-800-8238, (301) 816-0210.

Don't forget amazon.com. If you link from Volunteer Ontario you will go directly to their selection of best books on not-for-profit and perhaps save a lot of time. Other online bookstores may also be of help.

INDEX